Chile in the Nitrate Era

Chile in the Nitrate Era

The Evolution of Economic
Dependence, 1880–1930

Michael Monteón

The University of Wisconsin Press

Published 1982

The University of Wisconsin Press
114 North Murray Street
Madison, Wisconsin 53715

The University of Wisconsin Press, Ltd.
1 Gower Street
London WC1E 6HA, England

First printing

Printed in the United States of America

For LC CIP information see the colophon

ISBN 0-299-08820-0

Photographs in photo essay courtesy Chile House
and the Nitrate Corporation of Chile, Ltd., London;
obtained with the assistance of Mr. D. G. Hunter.

Contents

v

Illustrations

Tables

Introduction

When I began to study Chile in 1971, it was a constitutional
republic with universal suffrage and an unfettered press. A newly
elected administration had embarked on the "peaceful road to socialism." As his first steps in that direction, President Salvador Allende intended to nationalize all mineral resources, carry
out a sweeping agrarian reform, and sharply improve the living
standards of the working class. While opposition parties controlled Congress and the government of the United States was obviously hostile to his electoral success, Allende accomplished
many of his promises. When I arrived, the country seemed open to
a general change in its political economy. I wanted to analyze
Chile's past in order to find some clues as to how such a change
could come about.

The present sometimes alters what is important in the past.
Dr. Allende was overthrown on September 11, 1973, in a carefully
planned and violent military coup. He was killed in La Moneda,
the executive building; his chief administrators and most vocal
supporters were executed, imprisoned in concentration camps, or
sent into exile. The military declared a state of internal war
and murdered as many as 10,000 leftists over the next three years
in order to destroy the popular bases of Allende's administration.[1]
Today, a junta composed of the senior officers of the armed forces
and the national police, and headed by General Augusto Pinochet,
prohibits any political activity, censors the press, and is determined to "cleanse" the nation of communist and socialist ideas.[2]
Chile is no longer a model of political civility. An examination
of the past must now help us understand whether the breakdown of
constitutional norms is an historic aberration or is rooted in
the nation's development.

This is not a book about the Allende government, yet the
questions it poses about Chile's past have been shaped by that
government's disastrous end. I cannot demonstrate that what happened to Allende was either avoidable or inevitable. Events never
repeat themselves in such detail that the lessons of one period
can be strictly applied to the problems of another. But the study
of an earlier period, particularly within the same country, can

reveal a pattern of evolution, a way in which the elements of a
society change in relation to one another. This is not the first
time that the collapse of civilian rule ended in a military dictatorship; and this is not the first time that the military, having gained power, used the existence of a left-wing labor movement
to suppress all political opposition. The creation of a native
Left, the crisis of civilian government, the rise of the military
also occurred in the nitrate era. My study of that period led me
to conclude that Chile's modern history consists of the relation
of her export-based economy to the political organization of
power. It is a history best understood within the framework of
the country's overall dependence on more advanced capitalist nations.

Chile's economic growth has always been tied to her foreign
trade. Since the Second World War, her basic export has been
copper. But in the five decades covered by this study, it was
sodium nitrate or *salitre*, a mineral compound found in the Atacama
Desert. Its chief value is as a fertilizer, although it has also
been used in munitions. The nitrate era begins during the War of
the Pacific (1879-83), when Chile seized portions of the desert
that belonged to Peru and Bolivia. It lasts until the Great Depression when low prices and increased competition ruined most of
the nitrate producers. The historic importance of the period is
that the trade in *salitre* exceeded, in quantity and value, that
of all previous exports. It altered the possibilities for development. A tax on nitrate exports became the government's chief
source of revenues. Buoyed by the new wealth, the government
spent on an unprecedented scale. The nitrate trade and government
expenditures reshaped the domestic economy: they created a larger
and richer upper class; they financed urban construction and
generated greater demand for domestic production; and they drew
laborers to the nitrate provinces and expanding cities.

Economic growth increased the power of the central government but it did not insure political stability. Rivalries within
the national government increased as it began to overwhelm the
power and authority of provincial centers and nongovernmental institutions. In 1891, only a decade after the nitrate boom began,
a quarrel between President José Manuel Balmaceda and his opposition in Congress led to civil war. The Congressional rebels won
the war and changed the political rules in order to reduce the
power of the executive, but they proved unable to create either
honest or consistent administration. By 1924, another dispute
between the executive and legislative branches ended in a military
coup. Civilians regained the government long enough to establish
a new constitution in 1925 before surrendering to the establishment of a military dictatorship in 1927.

Changes in the political economy generated class conflict.
In 1890, workers in the nitrate province of Tarapacá rebelled
against declining real wages and dangerous working conditions.
Theirs was the first in a series of labor uprisings. Each met
with violent repression. Repression alone could not stop the development of a nascent Left, which grew in response to inflation,

widespread social resentment, and electoral politics. After the First World War, the government refined its labor policies combining social reforms with such administrative changes as the creation of a national police; but force remained its final and usual response to demands for social justice. The nitrate era is, therefore, the precursor of the modern Chilean state and contemporary forms of repression.

The most important consequence of the period was that Chile remained dependent on foreign capital. Foreign entrepreneurs ran much of the nitrate trade; foreign bankers sustained the government's solvency; and foreign enterprises started many of her most important new sectors, as well as redeveloping her languishing copper mines. Why was this so? Why was the country unable to use its nitrate fortune to create a more autonomous pattern of growth?

The existing literature on Chile generally sidesteps this question. Only a few works examine the period, and they usually avoid a discussion of the nitrate sector. Such standard histories as those by Frederick Pike and Arnold Bauer have little to say about *salitre*.[3] The epic survey by Francisco Encina stops with the civil war of 1891; and Encina jumps from one topic to another without presenting a rigorous analysis of the political economy.[4] Those that do discuss nitrates and politics have a narrower focus than this work, or a different one. Markos Mamalakis, in an essay well known to Chilean specialists, blamed the nation's failure to capitalize from the nitrate boom on the government's devotion to free trade. However, he gives no real explanation of the government's motives.[5] His views are derived from Aníbal Pinto Santa Cruz and Albert Hirschman; in chapter 1, I explain why such views are an inadequate explanation for the pattern of Chile's development. Other studies concentrate on the early nitrate period, and particularly on the controversies surrounding the civil war of 1891; this subject is discussed in chapter 2.

A younger generation of scholars is gradually formulating new generalizations about Chile in the nitrate era. Three of them deserve mention because this study draws upon their discoveries. Thomas O'Brien is apparently writing a definitive account of the nitrate industry from the 1860s until the civil war of 1891. Henry Kirsh has completed an excellent monograph on the early industrialization of the country. The dissertation of Peter De Shazo provides a wealth of new data on the Chilean working class between 1902 and 1927, and an almost blow-by-blow account of the strikes in Valparaiso and Santiago.[6] However, no one has looked at the era as a whole, or explained how the major changes in politics and economics are related to the pattern of export-oriented development.

A second body of literature, consulted for the purpose of finding theoretical explanations for what happened in Chile, is devoted to the process of development in any country. Much of it proved irrelevant to my topic. Theorists often talk past each other or substitute jargon for analysis.[7] Much of their evidence is derived from the period after the Second World War or from the experiences of western Europe and the United States. Consequently, very little of the literature treats the pattern of dependence in Third World countries before 1945. Contemporary capitalist theory tends to ignore dependence altogether, preferring to explain the poverty of some nations and the wealth of others in purely economic terms. Such theory sounds increasingly preposterous as it assumes that somehow dependent nations can imitate the success of more developed capitalist countries. What is technically true is often politically untrue: a poor country can improve its productivity and position in world markets; but such an improvement does not assure an increased leverage in the world economy. A nation's economy may grow, it may even industrialize, and that nation may still fail to gain greater control over its economic fortune. In many respects, rapid growth can even increase a nation's dependence as outsiders increase the role they play in sustaining growth. This, in fact, was the experience of Chile in the nitrate era.

Contemporary Marxists perceive the social and political pitfalls of capitalist theory, and my work owes much to the thoughts of Paul Baran, Samir Amin, and Theotonio Dos Santos.[8] Like them, I think that the persistence of dependence is a central cause of underdevelopment and that both dependence and underdevelopment are related to the role poor nations play as suppliers of raw materials, food, and fiber to rich, capitalist countries. Amin, in his introduction to *Accumulation on a World Scale*, nicely summarizes the leftist interpretation of underdevelopment. It consists, he says, of an enormous disparity within a national economy between economic sectors; some enterprises are technically advanced, others extremely primitive. He does not add, but might have, that the disparity is often cultural as well, with some segments of the population achieving high levels of education and "modernity," and others remaining illiterate and backward. An underdeveloped economy is also "disarticulated," meaning that growth of the more advanced sectors does not lead to the rapid spread of modern technology and improved production in the more primitive ones. Often, growth has little internal effect on much of the country. Finally, the economy is dominated from outside. Amin links this domination to the fact that underdeveloped countries are the "periphery" in the world capitalist system. They exist as suppliers of material and cheap labor and importers of manufactures but they never initiate major changes in the system. They progress from one dependent economic state to another in a direction Amin and others call "the development of underdevelopment."[9]

As Marxists use the concept, dependence is as much a political as an economic phenomenon. One nation may rely on another for several reasons. It may need raw materials, new technology, infusions of capital, or managerial and marketing abilities that only a more "advanced" economy can provide. But dependence as they and I use it here implies much more than the reliance of one nation upon another. Foreign investors and their governments dramatically influenced Chile's history. They affected patterns

of investment, altered the course of domestic conflicts, caused
labor riots, and exacerbated financial panics. In short, they
exercised power. Understanding how they acquired power, what kind
of power they had, and how they used it is essential to understanding the course of Chile's development.

Despite my broad agreement with contemporary Marxists, they
are unlikely to agree with my conclusions. Marxist studies of
Chile before 1945 are poorly researched. In correcting their errors, I have also corrected some of their interpretations. For
example, in the second chapter I explain why neither the Marxist
nor the anti-Marxist views on the civil war quite describe its
origins and consequences. A more fundamental difference is that
I do not use Marxist terminology nor a Marxist frame of interpretation. Marxists argue that modes of production, the social relations of production, and class struggle determine the development of any country. In general, this is true; but in the specific sense of overcoming dependence, it is obviously untrue. Some
capitalist countries develop greater initiative and autonomy than
others. How can we explain the difference? The classic Marxist
answer is that capitalists in the most advanced industrial nations
control the international exchange of goods and intervene in underdeveloped areas in order to increase their profits and extend
their control. As a result, the rate of economic growth in the
underdeveloped areas is slowed and the pattern of development is
distorted. An economy develops that serves the foreign capitalists rather than the native population. Such an answer, unfortunately, raises more questions than it resolves. In the case of
Chile, it raises the issue of why a politically independent people
would accept such a situation. Marxist literature on economic
history before 1945 tells us very little about how capitalists
created "neocolonial" nations, nations which are politically independent but economically subservient. In searching for the
details to that process, I found that many dependence theorists
have refused to face some hard facts about the domestic factors
that maintain a dependent economy.

I had reached that conclusion before reading Tony Smith's
attack on dependence literature. Smith attempts to discredit
dependence theorists by arguing that they overgeneralize the experience of the Third World and ignore the importance of native
elements—"feudal and bureaucratic estates, castes and clans, as
well as tribes"—to each nation's development. He believes that
dependence writers have not adequately explained why those in
political power behave in a manner that complements the ambitions of foreign interests. The literature, he charges, is especially weak in its analysis of the role of the state, that is,
the role of those who control the government, in promoting economic growth. Political leaders are, in his view, something
more than servants of a "ruling class." They initiate economic
decisions and often impose decrees in defiance of some elite interests. Smith demonstrates the weaknesses of some of the
literature, but his comments should not discourage us from con-
tinuing to develop interpretations of dependent development.[10]

We lack a coherent theory of dependence, but we do have a
collection of insights into the fallacies of capitalist theories
of development. Even Smith admits that many of these insights
are true. We also lack a sociology of the state, an explanation
of how modern governments develop their various functions, how
the motives of government leaders differ significantly from those
of a nation's dominant class, and how to account for apparent
differences between political leaders and dominant economic interests. But this shortcoming is not specific to dependence
literature. It is a characteristic of the social sciences as a
whole and one which scholars from a variety of disciplines and
ideologies are only now beginning to correct.[11] Given the difficulties of combining economic analysis and an explanation of
political motives, no theory of dependence may fit the history
of every underdeveloped nation.[12] My purpose is not theoretical;
I instead try to extend established insights to new situations and
to demonstrate the limits of existing generalizations. The emphasis throughout this work is on identifying the conditions of
Chile's evolution and not on proving or disproving any specific
model of dependence. I stress, however, the relation between the
behavior of foreign capitalists and the organization of political
power. This seems to me the heart of any dependence analysis.
Tony Smith notwithstanding, the two are related. At the same time,
I avoid Marxist questions that seem fruitless. I found little evidence that Chile's politicians see themselvs as *compradores,* mere
functionaries in a neocolonial regime; I, therefore, do not paint
them as such. I also abandon the issue of whether or not foreign
capitalists retarded Chile's economic growth. It is impossible
to answer such a broad issue definitively, nor, as I have already
stressed, are economic growth and dependence mutually exclusive
phenomena.
     The nexus of Chile's evolution was the relation between the
growth of a centralized government in Santiago and the expansion
of foreign control of her key exports. This relation grew, on the
one hand, as the result of the government's need for a tax base
with which to finance its growth, and, on the other, from the attempts of foreign and domestic capitalists to profit from export-
ing the nation's raw materials and financing government expansion.
The motivations of the capitalists were simple enough. Those of
the Chilean political leaders require extensive explanation. I
argue that their driving ambition was the organization of political power—specifically, the creation of a more powerful state.
This goal, for reasons I explain in the first chapter, was central to their ideas about economic development, and it precluded
a more nationalistic form of economic expansion.
     With one exception, each chapter after the first carries
this theme through the stages of Chile's history from 1880 until
1930. Each stage is defined in terms of the relation of political
issues to the evolution of the nitrate trade; the issues involve
not only the growth of a private economy but the problems of government financing. At each stage, some of Chile's political
leaders confronted key questions about dependence; and at each,

they failed to resolve them. The dilemmas of dependence permeated the entire economy as Chile increasingly relied on imported technology and raw materials as well as foreign capital. Her problems in the 1920s resemble to a remarkable degree those of the 1970s; the conclusion elaborates on this resemblance.

I depart from chronological sequence in chapter 4 in order to explain the impact of the nitrate economy on the labor force. I do not believe we can understand the pattern of dependence by looking only at government and capitalists. Labor is not only a basic element of production; laborers are capable of becoming a political entity. I treat the subject of labor in every chapter after the first; but in chapter 4, I go further and explain the origins of Chile's Left. At first glance, the labor movement does not seem to exist as a political actor. There are instead a series of violent strikes and the proliferation of new political factions. However, these two aspects of the social struggle are related to one another, and both affected the government and were affected by the nitrate trade. No one who tries to comprehend Chile's Left should forget that it emerged as a movement within a dependent economy; the politics and conduct of the labor force have always been conditioned by that fact.

This is not a general history. It does not discuss the world capitalist system. There is nothing on the arts and little on culture. Its contribution to contemporary scholarship is to explain the course of dependent development in far greater detail than is available in any other study of Latin America for the same period. It is also intended to provide historical perspective on such contemporary issues as the centralization of government, the development of social inequalities, the persistence of inflation, the history of labor, and the diplomacy of trade in underdeveloped nations. I end my narrative with the capitalist disaster of 1930-31 because it ruined the nitrate producers and reduced *salitre*'s importance to the world nitrogen market. The many changes within Chile after 1930 also make the Depression a useful dividing point between one era and another.

Like any scholarly work, mine owes as much to the institutions that have supported me and to the encouragement of people around me as to any theory. A desire to be brief is my only excuse for this inadequate acknowledgment. Harvard University through its graduate fellowship program, paid for my first stay in Chile; the University of California, San Diego, financed research trips to Santiago and to several cities in the United States. John Womack, Jr., supervised my dissertation at Harvard; John Parry and Tulip Halperín Donghi read that early effort and encouraged me to do more. Ramón Eduardo Ruiz, James Scobie, Earl Pomeroy, David Ringrose, and Michael Parrish read all or portions of the manuscript and helped me improve it. Readers for the University of Wisconsin Press, through their critical comments, greatly influenced the final draft. My debts extend to many who are not academics. Karen Lindvall and Fran Rudman spent countless hours helping me locate research materials. Students at U.C.S.D. pressed me to refine my explanations of dependence. Jacqueline Garreaud, in addition to her friendship, provided valuable observations on her country's past and present. Her family helped me live in Santiago and taught me a good deal about the courage and generosity of the Chilean people.

Finally, I offer my appreciation to Natalie. I dedicate this book to her because I would not have completed it without her love and support. I hope one day Elena and Diana will take an interest in it, and I can tell them of Chile and a time their parents spent there when so many things seemed possible.

Chile in the Nitrate Era

1. The Origins of Economic Dependence

> Not so many years ago the inhabitants of the
> central region spoke of those in the South as dis-
> tant and unknown, without the beneficial influence
> of civilization or the protection of the Govern-
> ment. Those in the upper altitudes considered
> those of the valleys as residents of another hemi-
> sphere, to which one could not travel except at
> great risk and financial sacrifice. Anyone who
> claimed that he had gone to Santiago or come from
> the South was treated as a dreamer or a liar; if
> he could prove with documents and irrefutable
> witnesses that he had made the journey, he was
> celebrated as if he had gone to China. This was
> because, to go to or leave Santiago, one had to
> arm and equip himself as though on an expedition.
>
> Pedro Ruíz Aldea
> *La Tarántula* (Concepción)
> August 9, 1862

From the colonial period until the late nineteenth century, Chile
remained a traditional Hispanic society. The elite were a caste
apart from the general population of mestizos and Indians and
jealously defended its position through its control of rural resources and political power. It controlled the government and
the Church, and exercised its authority from the principal towns.
A few dozen aristocratic families owned the richest estates, ran
the state administration, and held the high offices in the Church.
Those families that dominated the capital, Santiago, were the
most powerful. In the eighteenth century, Basques who had established new merchant fortunes entered the elite, and in the last
decades of the nineteenth century, successful British and European
merchants married in as well. But these adjustments did not alter
the social attitudes of those who ruled. The Nicaraguan poet
Rubén Darío lived in Santiago in the 1880s and described its society as "aristocratic." "It tries to appear dressed in democracy, but the closet preserves its pompous, heraldic suit."[1]

⎡The Hispanic conquerors established government as an
instrument of personal aggrandizement; those who had political
power were entitled to use it to extort income or labor from
others.⎦ Pedro de Valdivia and his enterprising soldiers surveyed
Chile's central valley in the 1640s for its mineral resources.
They established settlements from Coquimbo to Concepción, divided
the lands about these towns into latifundia, and forced the in-
digenous inhabitants into servitude. The natives "entrusted" to
the conquerors worked on the land and in the mines under conditions dictated by their overlords. From the very beginning,
political leaders were mineral exporters, and sent gold to Spain
in exchange for manufactured products.[2] The elite relied on its
control of the government and of the land to maintain control of
the people, but it invested its assets in its families and preserved the interconnections between landed wealth and political
power through intermarriage.

The early government was small, more of a city-state in
After achieving independence from Spain, the rebels who controlled Santiago confronted the formidable task of transforming a
colony into a nation-state. This involved constructing a government and finding the means to sustain it. Chilean historians describe the nineteenth-century rulers as an "oligarchy" or an
"aristocracy." They mean to imply a basic continuity of the social structure from colony to nation. Claudio Véliz argues that a
list of the most powerful families in 1850 and even in 1963 would
include "a very high proportion" of the 500 clans that dominated
the colony in 1800. Recent research indicates the importance of
extended families in the early republic; in a study of the Larraín
clan, Mary Lowenthal Felstiner demonstrates that the family was
the unit of landholding, of commerce, and of politics—the unit
of identity and allegiance. The principal families were Basque
and Castilian in origin and proud of the lineage that set them
apart from the rest of the population. This social homogeneity
was important to the development of political order, yet not
every rich family held power in Santiago or decided issues that
influenced the course of economic development. More studies like
those of Felstiner are needed before generalizations about the
elite can be very exact, but, in the early nineteenth century,
the ruling clique in Santiago could not have included more than
fifty or sixty families. No more than two dozen families could
have dominated the cities of Coquimbo and Concepción—the provincial centers of the north and south. The rulers owed their position to the colonial accumulation of land and to their control of
the military, the national treasury, and commercial monopolies.[3]

The early government was small, more of a city-state in
Santiago than a national administration. In order to extend
their authority, its leaders had to increase its income. Taxing
domestic commerce proved inadequate. The population of a million
inhabitants was generally poor and scattered throughout a large
number of hamlets. Foreign trade, and the customs revenues it
generated, offered better prospects. Strong domestic interests,
including the great clans, favored an export-oriented economy,
and foreign demand for Chile's raw materials was rising. By

promoting exports, the government might improve its political base
or, at the very least, neutralize possible opposition. Government
officials could regulate international trade more easily than domestic commerce, a fact that facilitated taxing such trade and
using political power to favor friends over enemies. Increased
exports also generated domestic improvements in a manner that
furthered the centralization of credit and transportation. In
brief, influence over foreign trade gave Santiago's leaders broad
leverage within the political economy.

But a reliance on exports created Chile's dependence on
British entrepreneurs. British smugglers began trading on the
Chilean coast during the War of the Spanish Succession. This il-
licit commerce became a significant part of the colonial economy
by the end of the eighteenth century.[4] At the time of independence, the new government opened its ports to ships from all nations. The British took advantage of the new order because only
they had the ships and capital to do so. The penetration of the
country was capped in 1826 when the London firm of Antony Gibbs
opened its first office in Valparaiso. The port became the center
of British trade in Chile and that made it the center of all foreign trade.[5]

The government encouraged the arrival of foreigners not only
as commercial middlemen but as settlers. As Gideon Sjoberg re-
minds us, preindustrial elites often rely on "outsiders" to conduct trade because they do not seem to threaten the political
order and because their alien status limits the subversive impact
of ideas they bring from abroad.[6] The British gained trade supremacy in Chile because they dominated the Atlantic economy.
But Chilean leaders were determined to develop the country into a
"European" nation. To this end the government recruited several
thousand Germans in the 1840s and settled them on the southern
frontier.[7] The President, Manuel Bulnes, boasted to one foreign
visitor that "Chile alone of all the ancient Spanish Colonies has
flourished under the Republican system of government" because it
had corrected "the two most mischievous errors in the character
of the Spanish race, pride and contempt of foreigners." He added
that his administration "received with willingness, and enter-
tained with respect, every foreigner who landed on her shores,
impressed with the assurance that whatever might be his objects
or pursuits, they would be either directly or indirectly benefi-
cial to the commonwealth."[8] This desire for European labor skills
was part of a larger concern of the elite which the President did
not mention, the fact that the ruling criollos were a minority
amidst a mestizo nation.

In several respects, Chile's pattern of development worked
to her advantage. Although the population remained small, it increased in size to two and a half million by 1875. Export earnings rose steadily so that in that year they were three times
greater than they had been in 1830.[9] A larger minority enjoyed
the amenities of urban life, and a small number of the *gente bien,*
the shopkeepers, small merchants, and functionaries, acquired a
university education and even entered politics. Proud of their

achievements, the ruling class began to call itself "the English of South America," a phrase that indicated not only their "model" of development but their cultural aspirations.

As the nation prospered, the political leaders acquired the ambivalent attitudes of any modernizing clique. They attacked tradition but tried to retain the social privileges tradition bestowed. By 1871, the Liberal Party controlled both the presidency and the legislature. It enacted political reforms that increased the number of voters and reduced the authority of the Church, and it embarked on an ambitious series of public works. But these reforms did not alter the social composition of the government or the rulers' elitist attitudes. The British commercial representative in Santiago reported in 1876 that, despite the nation's obvious progress, the capital, "with its well-dressed, refined-looking women gliding along the well-swept pavement, the absence of hustle, the concentration of all trade and shopping in a few central thoroughfares," reminded him of "the residence of some dreamily-quiet, orthodox, luxurious Court."[10]

Two years after this assessment, Chile plunged into financial crisis. The government had come to depend on rising exports to sustain its own expansion, but the concentration of wealth and power in the capital and in the hands of a few oligarchs and plutocrats had limited the benefits of progress and the strength of the economy. When Chile's major export, copper, fell on the London market at a time of bad harvests and a poor balance of payments, its decline placed the government and the financial structure of the country in jeopardy. The crisis is important for two reasons. It led to the War of the Pacific, the conflict in which Chile won her nitrate fortune. It also illustrates the pattern of development and of government behavior that became characteristic of the nitrate era. In other words, the problems of Chile's dependence preceded the nitrate boom.

Chile's dependence began because of the government's reliance on the British for foreign trade, but its persistence can only be explained by the social and economic expectations of her rulers. They capitalized on the benefits of export development in order to pursue their own narrow interests. They increased the size of the central government and extended its control of national resources and the population; then they used this control to entice more foreign investors and secure foreign loans. As long as the national income rose, the rulers did not worry about the consequences of dependence. When income fell, they fought one another for shares of the power and wealth that remained, or they borrowed from abroad in an effort to refinance the government. Not everyone, of course, agreed with this use of political power, but those who did not had little effective say in government. When a crisis became truly serious, the ruling elite was capable of anything that might assure its hegemony, even war.

EXPLANATIONS OF UNDERDEVELOPMENT

Contemporary historians offer alternative explanations for Chile's dependence on British trade and capital in the nineteenth century.

Those who approach the society from the view of contemporary
capitalist analysis, particularly Aníbal Pinto Santa Cruz and
Albert Hirschman, stress the influence of free trade ideas on
Chilean government policies.[11] In their view, political leaders
in the late 1850s adopted the principles of laissez faire capitalism and abandoned earlier attempts to protect native industry.
They blame the change in economic strategy on a change in the
political coloring of the elite, and say that the older, more
conservative group which had established effective rule after Independence gave way to a newer, more liberal generation. This
generation aped British and European ideas without regard for the
practical consequences of applying them in an as yet backward
society. The result left native manufacturers and the national
merchant marine helpless before cheaper British imports and the
more efficient British merchant fleet. It also led in 1860 to
new legislation that fostered wildcat banking. The government
thereafter lacked effective control over the money supply and internal credit and this further weakened its ability to respond to
foreign trade crises.

The Marxists, while agreeing that free trade policies began
in the late 1850s, place the blame on the British. Hernán Ramírez
Necochea and André Gunder Frank, who popularized Ramírez's arguments in the United States, claim that British capitalists supported a retrograde elite within Chile and encouraged it to adopt
policies that would retard the development of native industries.
"One must remember," Ramírez writes, "Lenin's remark that imperialism does not diminish but 'rather that it intensified the differences in the rhythm of growth in various parts of the economic
work.' This remark is proven in the case of Chile: imperialism
prevented the rhythm of growth within the Chilean economy from
becoming sufficiently rapid and intense so that it might come to
have a capitalist mode of production similar to that already
existing in more developed nations."[12]

Frank adds that the structure of trade followed the
"metropolis-satellite structure of world capitalism," which led
to underdevelopment in Chile. For Frank, "underdeveloped" is not
to be confused with "undeveloped." It is not a primitive state
but a dynamic process which colonial "satellites" undergo, and
represents the opposite side of the capitalist coin of progress.
In his view, the Chilean rulers served foreign imperialists because "the rulers were thereby able to continue their exploitation
of the people of the Chilean periphery." Imperialists convinced
the elite that free trade policies were in its best interests,
and, in effect, such policies "reintegrated the Chilean metropolis
and its most powerful interest groups into the world capitalist
system, this time as a satellite of Great Britain."[13] The British
fed on the meat of Chile's resources, and the elite in Santiago
was content to take what crumbs came from exploiting its provinces.

Differences aside, all four historians agree that government
policies changed in the late 1850s. Pinto Santa Cruz and Hirschman claim that the French economist Jean Gustave Courcelle-Seneuil
altered the thinking of Chilean leaders after his arrival in
Santiago in 1855. An enthusiast of laissez faire doctrines, he

taught economics at the national university and served briefly as
Minister of Hacienda (Finance) before leaving in 1863. He trained
individuals who later became Chile's ministers during the nitrate
era and he advised Presidents on economic legislation. His advice, say Pinto and Hirschman, led to Chile's disastrous policies
on tariffs, banking, and the merchant marine.[14] Ramírez and Frank
place greater emphasis on the actions of British investors and the
British government. They note that in the 1850s the British invested heavily in Chilean mining and thereby acquired greater influence over Chile's foreign trade; the Foreign Office then used
its influence to protect their new enterprises.[15]

These established explanations are unspecific where they
should be precise. Pinto Santa Cruz and Hirschman are surprisingly vague about the class interests within Chile that supported
the change in politics. Why would the native elite seek advice
from a laissez faire economist unless it was already disposed to
accept his theories? In this regard, the Marxist argument is
more plausible—policy changes followed economic influence. Unfortunately, Ramírez and Frank provide little evidence of how
"imperialism" changed the government in the 1850s. The imperialists of the period and their connections to the elite are
not identified. In several sections, both historians seem to
equate foreign trade with imperialism, and they draw few distinctions between British capitalists and the British government.
Worse, neither author specifies how Chile's wealth was apportioned
between Santiago and the "metropolis" abroad and how the imperialists persuaded the Chileans to accept a "colonial" situation.

In fact, Chile's leaders encouraged dependent development because they equated it with "progress." They proved unable, however, to create a sound fiscal policy or generate a pattern of
domestic investment that would gradually reduce the nation's reliance on foreign capital. This short-sightedness was not the
result of British capitalists, who, on the contrary, forced the
elite to think with greater precision about its interests. It
was the result of the social attitudes within the ruling class,
attitudes that colored its selective acceptance of foreign practices. The elite proved capable of creating greater political
participation but not of developing a political culture which
supported economic efficiency and social improvement. Government
was more a matter of the distribution of export-derived benefits
than it was a means to create a dynamic economy. Politics was
more a means of social mobility and the protection of already
established interests than of arbitrating conflicts among entrepreneurs. The elite believed that by controlling the political
apparatus they controlled the economy as well. In any economic
crisis, it used the government to protect itself at the expense
of those below.

The elite view of government politicized the society without
strengthening the economy. Each group, as it acquired some economic means, aspired to political power not only because this was
an attribute of high status but also because it was necessary for
continued economic survival. At first, conflicts were limited to

the oligarchy, when its factions developed different interests
within the export economy. These weakened the elite's ability to
act as a class vis-à-vis foreign entrepreneurs. Lacking internal
cohesion and unable to survive without foreign trade, contending
factions mobilized against each other by recruiting support from
other social strata. Power remained in the hands of one elite
group or another but the elite required an ever-expanding export
economy with which to buy support from those below. The more the
elite extended the government and its importance throughout the
country, the more dependent the entire state apparatus became on
foreign trade. But the extension of political power was an essential prerequisite to the acquisition of economic authority,
which, in turn, permitted the elite to offer foreign investors
favorable opportunities. Those who acquired power looked upon it
as a means by which to "rent" Chile's resources to foreign interests, and live from this "rent."

Clearly, the origin of this dilemma lay in two and a half
centuries of Spanish colonialism. Alexander Caldcleugh observed
in the early 1820s that maps of the nation distorted the real extent of settlement. Towns existed where maps indicated, but "what
is here called a town could scarcely rank with a European vil-
lage." The country engaged in mining and agriculture, yet "no
great wealth has been accumulated by the creoles."[16] Other
sources indicate that many of the mines and estates created during an expansionary phase of the late colonial era had been
looted and destroyed during the war for independence.[17] Chile
suffered from the limitations of her primitive technology, the
absence of good transportation, and an unequal distribution of
income. Labor-intensive techniques dominated mining and agriculture: when the richest veins were exhausted, mining enterprises,
rather than invest in more efficient equipment, abandoned operations; on the large estates, in order to separate the grain from
the chaff, laborers piled the wheat into a circular corral and
ran horses over it. Goods were expensive to produce but cost
even more to transport. Even short journeys were hazardous and
expensive: in the 1840s, to travel between Santiago and its
major port, Valparaiso, took several days. Ships carried most
intraregional trade, and until the 1850s the government prohibited
foreigners from engaging in it. Chilean vessels, built in Maule
and Chiloé, were crude and small, most of them less than 200 tons.
Merchants in 1849 complained that shipping charges and the shortage of credit prevented them from sending greater quantities of
flour to the copper mines in the north.[18]

Domestic production was of poor quality, the output of artisans and owners of small sweatshops. The market consisted of the
unsteady consumption of the working poor, or the expensive tastes
of an upper class that preferred its goods imported. According
to Caldcleugh, manufactures consisted "of the commonest utensils
of copper, some coarse woolens and ponchos, which are worked by
hand, hats and some articles of earthenware." Another English
visitor in the 1820s, Maria Graham, wondered at the endless
Congressional debates over protective tariffs; she saw no

industries worth protecting. In his memoirs, Vicente Pérez Rosales reflects on his experiences and those of other ambitious but unsystematic industrialists and reveals that they often overcapitalized production and lacked the technical knowledge and marketing skills to succeed.[19]

In the 1820s the country was governed by liberal leaders, each of them aware of the limitations of domestic production. Only one, Bernardo O'Higgins, tried to protect native manufactures with high tariffs, and the attempt was a disaster. O'Higgins, the nation's "liberator," ruled as Supreme Director from 1818 until 1823. In 1822, his government imposed a Commercial Regulation, with import duties as high as 80 percent on over 200 items. His ministers hoped the regulation would shield domestic producers while not interfering with exports. It did the opposite. Exports fell as merchants stopped trading; and smugglers undermined the regulation's protective purpose. Despite a loan from London, the government became insolvent—and in April, 1823, O'Higgins was overthrown in a coup led by the commander of the garrison in Concepción, Ramón Freire.[20] The new Supreme Director abolished the high tariffs and, in order to reduce the foreign debt, established government monopolies on importing and selling tobacco, snuff, playing cards, wines, liquors, and teas. His administration granted individual merchants control of these monopolies, and they agreed in return to repay the government's English creditors. Since the monopolies earned profits as high as 400 percent, competition for the state concessions and public resentment against monopoly prices were intense. Monopoly merchants or *estanqueros* organized to defend their interests; their association became the economic nucleus of a conservative revolt.[21]

Their leader, Diego Portales, formed an alliance with General Joaquín Prieto, who then commanded the garrison in Concepción. In 1830, Prieto attacked and defeated the liberal forces, and the victors, who were called Pelucones or "big-wigs," installed him as President. The general expectation, as reported by the United States Consul in Valparaiso, was that the new regime would be short-lived. The Pelucones were small in number and consisted of extremely disparate elements: Santiago merchants, hacendados, the clergy, and military officers. But Portales and Prieto were more successful in their improvisations than their predecessors had been. They restored clerical courts and primogeniture and gained allies among those offended by the liberal regimes of the 1820s. They also encouraged foreign trade. Modern historians have misunderstood the Pelucones in labeling them protectionists and economic nationalists. The Prieto administration protected its supporters and nothing more; its vested interests consisted of state monopolies, agriculture, and coastal shipping. In every other respect, the regime was open to foreign and, particularly, to British investment. One of the reasons the Pelucones went to war, in 1836, against the Peruvian Confederation was that its tariffs and shipping policies threatened Valparaiso's supremacy on the west coast. The British merchants in Valparaiso flourished in the 1830s, and by the end of the decade, the former hamlet had become a small city.[22]

The Pelucones relied on British entrepreneurs because the latter were willing to develop new foreign markets for Chile's exports and because of the importance of Valparaiso to government finances. In general, the Pelucones and the British worked well together. Foreign investors organized an important trade in silver in the 1830s, and the export of copper and wheat in the 1840s. As the economy grew, so did the government's income. Between 1831 and 1850, the government's ordinary income—that is, excluding loans and special levies—rose from 1.5 to 4.3 million pesos. Tariffs, in those years, provided half the income and became the fastest-growing portion of the revenues. By comparison, income from the state monopoly of coining specie and from tithes, the second and third major sources of revenue, rose only two and a half times during the period in which customs revenues tripled. By the early 1850s, import duties alone raised more than half of all ordinary income; and Valparaiso collected 98 percent of all import duties.[23] Chile's economic dependence did not, therefore, begin with the arrival of Courcelle-Seneuil or the resurgence of a liberal political movement in the late 1850s.

But the historians who cite the 1850s as a decisive decade are correct. Wheat exports rose dramatically from 1848 until 1856; the result of the demand created first by the California gold rush and then by the gold rush in Australia. At the same time, the British increased their use of Chilean copper. The value of total exports between 1848 and 1857 rose from 8.3 to 19.7 million pesos per year. This extraordinary rise in earnings quickened economic growth throughout the central valley. President Manuel Montt used the higher state revenues from import duties to build a railway linking Santiago to the agrarian south and began another line from the capital to Valparaiso. Private capital, much of it British, extended the mining railroad in Copiapó, turned the small Pacific Steam Navigation Company into a major enterprise, and established telegraph lines that connected the nation's major cities. Hacendados borrowed heavily and cleared new lands on the southern frontier in order to take advantage of the exceptional wheat market. The value of land near Talcahuano and Concepción doubled in a few years.[24]

The boom ended in the late 1850s. It did not last long enough to reach many rural areas, and it did not alter the general social structure or create a sustained demand for native manufactures. Wages in the mines and haciendas remained extremely low; the newly rich preferred imported commodities to native goods; therefore, the domestic market remained too small to provide an alternative to exports. During the boom, however, many hacendados and mine-owners became overextended and vulnerable to any decline in the foreign market. The slump that followed the decline of trade with Australia caught them unprepared, heavily in debt and unable to sell a large part of their output.

Historians, Marxist or not, have generally misperceived the decade and the changes it caused. It was the cycle of boom and bust and not British imperialism or the rise of liberalism that altered government policies. The Chilean government tried to help its supporters and itself to as much of the export income as

possible. The policies it created to that end deepened Chile's
dependence on the British and changed the laws on shipping, banking, and tariffs. During the boom years, export interests pressed
the Montt administration—Montt is known in Chilean history as the
last Pelucon—to reduce the costs of transportation, imports, and
credit. Montt responded by beginning the construction of railways, opening the coastal trade to foreign ships, and permitting
foreign investment in the merchant marine. He was not abandoning
a protectionist policy for Chilean ships but favoring one vested
interest over another. Claudio Véliz, in his analysis of the
merchant marine, demonstrates that in the late 1850s it was
Chilean in flag only: British merchants financed its operations
and foreign crews manned its vessels.[25] Montt, in effect, replaced the monopoly privilege of Chilean shipping interests, a
privilege many had rented to British and other foreign investors,
with a policy that lowered the overhead of merchants and primary
producers.

The importance of Great Britain as a consumer of Chilean
minerals and the centrality of British merchants and shipping to
Chile's foreign trade made Montt anxious to cement trade relations
with London. This does not mean, as the Marxists argue, that Santiago became a colonial outpost of London. Montt never ceded the
British Foreign Office any influence over trade policy. Ramírez
and Frank, in their effort to prove the imperialist thesis, cite
a Foreign Office complaint in 1853 against a new Chilean export
duty on copper. The complaint was made, but they fail to mention
that Chile retained the duty in spite of it, and the export tax
on copper became a principal source of government revenue in the
late 1850s.[26] Montt wanted some guarantee of Chilean access to
British markets, and was willing to accept the principles of free
trade in order to get it. On October 4, 1854, his administration
signed a "Treaty of Friendship, Commerce, and Navigation" with
Great Britain that guaranteed "freedom of commerce" between the
two nations. It prohibited discriminatory tariffs—any impost
levied on British trade was to be levied against all foreign
trade—and declared that citizens and subjects of each nation
would "be at liberty to buy from and to sell to whom they like
and absolute freedom shall be allowed in all cases to the buyer
and seller, to bargain and to fix the price of any goods, wares,
or merchandise or licit traffic, imported into or exported from
the territories of either the High Contracting Parties respectively."[27]

The Treaty raises another issue, this one stressed by Pinto
Santa Cruz and Hirschman, about the rise of liberal, that is,
free trade, ideas within Chile. According to their thesis, the
government adopted the free trade theory of an international division of labor without regard for the consequences of that theory
on an underdeveloped country. They mention the arrival of the
French economist Courcelle-Seneuil as the event that changed
tariff and banking policy. The evidence indicates the economic
historians have reversed cause and effect: material interests
preceded a change in intellectual outlook; the government began

to espouse free trade because of the tangible benefits the boom of the 1850s brought to it and its supporters. The change in tariffs caused by the reform of 1861 was not as great as many have believed. Throughout the 1850s the Montt administration had permitted a council of Valparaiso merchants, including representatives of British firms, to alter import charges. The merchants met each fall, reviewed the demand for specific goods, and advised the government on revisions in tariffs on popular commodities. Their advice was usually followed, and the effective duty was an ad valorem rate of 4 to 30 percent. The reform of 1861, which Courcelle-Seneuil had a hand in designing, simplified the tariff structure and reduced the range of imposts: the new duties varied from 15 to 25 percent. The new tariff did not give the British any new leverage over trade.[28]

These same historians blame Courcelle-Seneuil and liberal ideas for the banking law of 1860. The more immediate cause, however, was the export slump of the 1850s. In 1855, landowners had pushed the government into creating a *Caja de Crédito Hipotecario* or Mortgage Credit Bank. Landowners paid 12 percent to the new bank instead of the 18 to 70 percent available through short-term loans from merchants. But the export decline of 1857-59 created a tight money situation at a time when many of the exporters were having to repay their loans.[29] The government's remedy was the 1860 law that (in Frank Fetter's words) "fixed no minimum capital requirement, no limitation on the nature or maturity of loans to directors, and no provision for inspection [of banks] by government."[30] It also failed to regulate commercial checks. But it rescued the indebted landowners and miners.[31] It is also unlikely that the government, still small and without trained personnel, would have been able to enforce a more complicated statute.

The pattern of Chile's evolution thus had little to do with the British government or with Courcelle-Seneuil. It is best explained as the result of government policy improvisations, which in turn were a consequence of trade fluctuations. The outcome of these improvisations was greater dependence on British merchants and shipping; and British capitalists exploited the opportunity which their knowledge of the international trade and Chilean law had given them. In 1861, the United States Consul in Valparaiso, with more than a touch of envy, described them as "all powerful." "They have from twelve to fifteen millions [of pounds] in mines and steam coasting and they stand commercially at this, the principal port, as first, the French are second, and we third."[32] British merchants and shipping firms virtually ran the entire coast. The Pacific Steam Navigation Company, that began operations with a government concession in the 1840s and survived with a mail contract from the British government, became the major line on the coast in the 1860s.[33] A British vice-consul reported in 1867 that British investors owned half the railroad in Copiapó, from which they received 11 percent dividends, and that the total return on British capital in the Atacama Province alone amounted to more than five million pesos a year—more than half the total value of Britain's imports from Chile that year.[34]

Santiago did not try to counter increasing British influence
over the economy because it did not see any reason to do so. Of-
ficially, Chile in the 1850s had a favorable balance of trade with
Great Britain. Unfortunately, the true balance of payments cannot
be known because available data does not include remittances on
British investments. But the value of exports exceeded imports
by twenty-six million pesos. In this respect, the evolution of
political rhetoric followed apparent fact; freer trade policies
did seem to favor Chile with a comparative advantage. But what
the new rich gained from Great Britain, they spent on French
finery. Purchases from France exceeded exports to that country
by 21.5 million pesos. Although investment in production increased during the boom of the 1850s, Chileans spent more to import silks than to buy railway equipment; they spent three times
as much on imported jewelry as on machinery, and consumed huge
quantities of sweets—refined sugar made up 11 percent of all
imports.[35]

The economic ideal of the nineteenth century remained that
of a rentier—someone who makes his fortune in one quick speculation and thereafter lives on land rents or some other long-term
yield. Domingo Sarmiento in 1842 referred to the effect of this
ideal on native entrepreneurs: southern hacendados and northern
mine-owners left their affairs in the hands of supervisors and
moved to Santiago where they "tried to imitate or rather parody
the European Aristocracy."[36] Those who made fortunes in real
estate or in merchant and mining ventures then acquired luxurious
estates and urban villas, where they could live as country squires.
New money married mortgaged tradition and quickly developed the
pretensions of the established upper class. A provincial essayist
in 1845 complained that rich provincials who moved to the capital
became "more pelucon than a liberal who has gained a cabinet post."
Aristocratic attitudes persisted and were refinanced by the export
economy.[37]

Government policies reflected and advanced a political culture that was emerging within a dependent economic order. Economic growth increased the number of exporters and merchants who
demanded a say over policies that influenced their prosperity.
It also increased the number of educated young men who wanted
political power. Placating foreign trade interests and coopting
political opponents required a larger and more expensive government. As the cost of government increased, so did its dependence
on the revenues derived from foreign trade. The specific characteristics of this political culture and its relation to the rising
cost of government and the dependence of the government on foreign
trade are best illustrated by examining the factors that led to a
crisis of the political economy in the 1870s.

THE HIGH COST OF GOVERNMENT

Diego Portales, in the Constitution of 1833, revived the enlightened despotism of Spanish rule in the eighteenth century but

presented it in a republican form. The President had the power
to appoint all judges and national officials, including the chief
administrators—the intendants and their subordinates, the governors—of the provinces. Congress met only a few weeks a year; in
its absence, a small council, dominated by the President, acted
on its behalf. In addition, the President could declare states
of siege; and Congress could confer "extraordinary powers" upon
him. These powers included the suspension of all civil rights,
called "individual guarantees." In the 1830s, the Pelucones left
the provinces alone and relied on a national militia of 50,000
reservists to protect their control of Santiago. Militia officers
held Congressional seats and cabinet posts; in the presidential
election of 1841, they dominated the list of voters in Santiago
Province, who cast 2,000 of the total 4,100 ballots.[38]

The growth of the export economy complicated national politics because it increased the number of persons qualified by income or property to vote. As that occurred, Presidents Bulnes
and Montt had provincial subordinates falsify voting registers,
stuff ballot boxes, and even seize the polls by force. The
Presidents also declared states of seige in 1840, 1846, and 1858,
and acted with extraordinary powers in 1833, 1836, 1837, 1851-53,
and 1859-61.[39] In 1851 and 1859, those unhappy with despotic
government resorted to civil war; but in both conflicts, President Montt and his supporters prevailed.

Political rivalry stemmed not only from opposition to the
Pelucon monopoly of office but also from the increasing importance of the national government in financing and allocating concessions for state railways, recognizing mining claims, and selling public lands. Most of the resources it was opening for
development lay outside of Santiago. A new generation of liberals
combined a desire for honest elections, the separation of church
and state, and an end to primogeniture with a demand for a larger
provincial role in national decisions. The attempts of such men
as Benjamín Vicuña MacKenna, Frederico Errázuriz, and Domingo
Santa Maria to overthrow the Pelucones failed, but the Montt administration was forced to make some changes in its policies. In
a famous dispute with the Church, President Montt established the
primacy of the civil courts over clerical courts. He also signed
legislation in 1852 and 1857 that gradually abolished primogeniture. His successor, Joaquín Pérez Mascayano, admitted some
Liberals—those that favored the growth of centralized power—
into his cabinet; those who supported greater authority for the
provinces remained an outgroup.[40] The Pelucones thus set a pattern of weakening the opposition by coopting some of its members.

The rise of the Liberals, therefore, began within a cen-
tralizing regime run by the Pelucones and dependent on foreign
trade. The chief innovations of the Liberals, as they expanded
their political base and won election to the Congress, were intended to reduce the Pelucon bases of authority: the Church and
the militia. The Liberals did very little about the economic
base of the government and their economic policies were an elabora-
tion of those set by President Montt. The cost of developing

Liberal rule was a massive expansion of state expenditures, much of it devoted to state railways and the rest to creating more offices. Costs soon outran income, and the government continuously resorted to domestic and foreign bond markets to cover the difference.

President Pérez was the first to confront the problem of government debt. Through the 1860s, when he was in office, Chile sold wheat to Europe during its winter and continued to increase her copper exports to Great Britain. But Montt had left the new President saddled with the cost of the railroad construction program. Railroads reduced transportation charges and helped exporters but they cost more to run than they earned. Pérez also increased the size of the bureaucracy in order to accommodate the Liberals, but he had to do so at a time when government income was low because of the export slump and the tariff reform of 1861. Later administrations would borrow heavily in London, but Pérez became embroiled in a war involving Spain and Peru; London would not handle his bonds. By 1865, his administration owed 1.5 million pesos on the previous year's budget and expected another 1.5 million deficit in the coming year. The bankers in Valparaiso, several of them descendants of English settlers, lent the government the three million pesos at 8 percent interest, and imposed harsh conditions for repayment.[41]

The financial problems of the Presidents in the 1870s were more complex than those of Pérez and stemmed not only from the increasing complexity of the export economy but the changing organization of political life. The most important political changes involved the growth of parties and the diffusion of power from the executive to the legislature. In the early republic, parties had been little more than gatherings of a few elite families. But in the 1870s they represented a larger number of the rich and an increasing population of professionals, small tradesmen, and successful artisans. Politics remained an elite sport, but the number of players had grown and that meant an increase in the number of office-seekers. The dominant figures in the parties gathered in clubs—the most prominent was the Union Club—where they could discuss investments and patronage.[42] Power remained concentrated in the capital but became dispersed among a number of factions. The Presidents confronting this enlargement of political participation tried to maintain their authority through their ability to provide offices and contracts for public works.

But they also faced a movement for political reform that aimed at diminishing executive control of the government. The reformers included those who favored Santiago's primacy over the political order but wanted a broader distribution of power between the legislature and the executive and those provincial liberals, such as the Radicals, who wanted a geographic decentralization of authority over taxes and patronage. The former group pushed for legislative oversight of government revenues; the latter emphasized local control of the polls. Together, the reform interests managed to diminish executive initiative. In

1869, a new law banned the police and military from voting and
placed voter registers in the hands of local committees. In 1871,
another reform prohibited an official in the executive branch from
simultaneously holding a seat in the legislature. In 1873, Congress limited the President's use of extraordinary powers; and in
the following year it extended suffrage to all literate, adult
males, and banned a sitting President from seeking reelection.
Throughout the 1860s and 1870s the government created new provinces and their subunits, departments, and increased legislative
review of the treasury and government expenditures.[43]

This gradual liberalization of the government did not, however, lead to a consistent view of the role of the state in the
economy. Liberals argued over specific government programs and
projects and disagreed about the state's role in promoting economic growth. Some worried about the social consequences of increased spending; others held a firm belief in laissez faire and
resented the increasing cost—even though it was largely indirect
—of government. Still others pushed for more public spending.
José Victorino Lastárria, for example, a university don and the
foremost essayist of the era, wanted the government to develop more
schools. But Marcial González, a prominent economist, rejected
any need for them. Knowledge, González argued, is good in itself,
but the expansion of agricultural exports, because it increases
demand for rural labor, was more important to the "agricultural
classes" than schools. "Far from being, as [rural workers] once
were, mere slaves or laborers in *encomienda,* now they are truly
free men, who live with a certain pride and who, in order to be
happy, only need acquire an increased understanding—that is, to
cultivate a better attitude and greater frugality and morality
in their conduct."[44] González did not elaborate on how the laborers would acquire greater self-discipline. As another example,
Benjamín Vicuña MacKenna, one of the major political figures of
the period, insisted the national government should create long-
term economic plans. Appointed intendant for Santiago Province
in 1871, he established the capital's first comprehensive scheme
for future public construction. However, another economist,
Miguel Cruchaga, objected to "pointless" public works and to the
rapid growth of public employment.[45] These differences reflected
a fundamental dilemma of the elitist liberals: a regime devoted
to progress and private property needed to be large enough to
enforce its economic objectives and protect property holders—
it needed to instill public respect for itself and its goals—but
such a regime would also be sufficiently powerful to appropriate
elite income. How was the elite to protect itself against state
encroachment on the prerogatives of local authority and social
status?

The reformers never faced this problem. They instead confused state power with executive authority, an understandable
error given the presidential system created by the Pelucones.
They proposed to limit the President and assumed a more powerful
legislature and a change in election laws would resolve the issue.
In response, Presidents Frederico Errázuriz and Aníbal Pinto

tried to undercut the reforms through the use of force,
intervention in elections, and patronage to sway local election
committees. The conflict between the executive and legislative
branches influenced Chile's dependence because it increased the
cost of government in a manner that reflected elite quarrels
rather than any coherent strategy for development.

Government debt continued to rise: in 1860, it amounted to
16.7 million pesos; in 1878, it was 70.9 million. Debt service
in 1860 was only 1.3 million pesos or 17 percent of the budget;
in 1878, it was 7.3 million—44 percent of the budget. An increasing portion of this debt was owed to British bondholders.
Between 1865 and 1875, the government floated five loans in London
worth 7.9 million pounds, about 39.9 million pesos. This debt
completed the structure of Chile's economic dependence. A government in debt and deriving a major part of its income from customs
revenues was not going to disagree with its creditors or those who
controlled the flow of foreign trade. In addition to supplying
the government credit for its public projects, Great Britain in
1875 purchased 59 percent of Chile's exports and provided 41 percent of her imports. [46]

Government expenditures followed the elite pattern of consumption. The capital acquired new roads, buildings, and schools,
while the provinces lacked basic public services and relied on
traditional resources or new, inadequate improvisations.
Linares, for example, had fifty men in its constabulary in 1875;
the government paid only thirty of them a salary. The rest sub-
sisted on fines and graft. The region of Maullin was without a
police force. Authorities there recruited posses which, the governor admitted, "in most cases, either refuse to help or serve so
incompetently that criminals enjoy complete immunity from arrest."
Intendants and governors throughout the southern provinces reported that they needed schools and jails, paved streets in the
provincial capitals—in short, more money. Their resources remained poor despite the importance of the south to the growth of
agricultural exports. [47]

The new rich of the provinces came to Santiago and accelerated the concentration of political and economic power. The
wealthy continued their conspicuous consumption; as late as 1875,
the country spent as much to import jewelry as to import machinery.
Ambitious youths went into law—the most popular field of university study. Export income and the pattern of its public and private expenditure intensified the cultural disparities between
rich and poor. [48] A North American geographer commented in 1880,
"The upper strata of society through wealth, education, and foreign travel, are refined and liberal minded, but elevating influ-
ences have not reached the mining and agricultural populations,
who are ignorant and superstitious." [49] The concentration of income in one region and within the growing elite also created an
extremely weak and vulnerable economy, a fact that became evident
in the collapse of the 1870s.

The export crisis of that decade was far worse than that at
the end of the 1850s. It began with a poor balance of trade and

declining export revenues and was accentuated by a series of poor
harvests in the last half of the decade. Chile imported more
than she exported in 1870, 1874, 1875, and 1877. She lost most
of her European wheat market to new international competition;
and the London price of copper in 1878 was 60 percent of its value
in 1872. The export crisis, a product of a contraction of credit
throughout Europe, reduced the nation's ability to import and
caused a flight of capital. Gold and silver specie virtually disappeared in Santiago. The value of the peso in London, which had
hovered between forty-four and forty-eight pence from the 1840s
through the early 1870s, fell in 1878 to thirty-seven pence.[50]

The crucial moment came on June 30, 1878, when the directors
of the Bank of Chile, the nation's largest financial institution,
told the government that the bank's paid-up capital amounted to
only 24.6 percent of its liabilities. Throughout the 1870s,
Chilean investors had supported a feverish speculation in mining
and banking stocks and ignored a worsening export situation.
Speculators took the plunge on a number of dubious projects; one
of the hottest issues of the decade was a mining company, organized by a French confidence artist, devoted to the production
of gold from copper. To attract investors in this market, banks
paid high dividends. The Bank of Chile paid 20 percent on its
shares each year between 1872 and 1878. It paid its last dividend shortly before advising the Pinto administration of its insolvency.[51] The government then faced a dual crisis: the collapse of the bank meant the failure of the entire banking system;
it also meant that the government would be unable to borrow, as
it had intended, from the Bank of Chile. Once informed of the
situation, the administration immediately suspended trading on
the bank's stock, called the legislature into secret session, and
on July 22 succeeded in getting the representatives to approve
the inconvertibility of the peso. The new law took effect the
following day. The law authorized the six largest banks to issue
up to 9.1 million pesos after depositing their bonds as collateral
for the currency.[52] This legal novelty, like the banking law of
1860, successfully reduced the cost of the credit crisis to exporters and passed the consequences to other groups. Exporters
now also had the advantage of lower exchange rates, which reduced
the real cost of their labor and made their commodities cheaper
in London.

At the height of the crisis, President Pinto despaired of
resolving it. He faced, in nascent form, the "parliamentarianism"
that flourished in the nitrate era. As he put it, he was opposed
by "five or six little circles" in the Chamber of Deputies, each
"with a considerable contingent of egotists and charlatans."[53]
The legislative opposition viewed him as corrupt and incompetent,
and interrogated his officials as a means of harassing the administration. Pinto knew that he could no longer increase patronage, and tried placating factions by rotating his ministers:
in his five-year term, he created six cabinets.

The crisis had not yet lifted late in 1878 when the Chileans
became involved in a border dispute with Bolivia that saved the

Liberal regime. A thriving trade had developed, in the Atacama
Desert, in sodium nitrate or *salitre;* in the 1860s the product
began to displace Peruvian guano as a fertilizer in Europe. The
major mines were in the Peruvian province of Tarapacá and the
Bolivian territory of Antofagasta. Chilean-British interests,
based in Valparaiso, supplied the nitrate factories or *oficinas*
in Tarapacá and handled exports from the region. In the Bolivian
territory, they owned the Antofagasta Nitrate and Railway Company,
the region's major enterprise; and they controlled the area's silver mines. To many of the Valparaiso merchants, *salitre* seemed
the solution to Chile's problems. But the governments of Peru
and Bolivia were also deeply in debt and desperate for export
revenues. In 1875, Peru imposed a state monopoly in its nitrate
zone and removed Tarapacá as a field of investment. Then in 1878,
the military government in Bolivia tried to collect higher taxes
on silver and nitrate. In an earlier border dispute, Chile and
Bolivia had signed a treaty in which Bolivia promised not to impose new taxes on Chileans in Antofagasta. Valparaiso merchants
cited this clause in asking Santiago for help against the Bolivian
tax increase. The Bolivians argued that they were not taxing
Chileans. The mining enterprises were controlled by British
capital and therefore excluded from the treaty's provisions.
When the Bolivian authorities tried to collect the higher taxes
from the Antofagasta Nitrate and Railway Company, its English
manager fled. The Bolivians appropriated the company for non-
payment.[54]

The Pinto administration cited the takeover and the mis-
treatment of Chilean laborers in Antofagasta as grounds for declaring war on Bolivia in January, 1879. Bolivia then appealed
to Peru. The two countries, at Peru's instigation, had entered
into a secret, mutual defense pact against Chile. When the
Chileans learned of the pact, hawks in Congress immediately demanded war on Peru as well. Pinto resisted broadening the conflict, but jingoist sentiment forced his hand. In April, Chile
declared war on Peru. During the War of the Pacific, she seized
the nitrate zones of both enemies; and with this new wealth, she
refinanced her government and entered a period of unparalleled
prosperity. The nitrate era had begun.[55]

An analysis of the evolution of dependence must begin with
the requirements of state power, with the financial as well as
political tasks involved in building a national government.
Those who seized power in the early Chilean republic saw that
they lacked the means to govern effectively and, in order to
broaden their financial base, opened the country to foreign investment. Foreign investors, most of them British, settled into
Valparaiso and a few other ports and used their economic freedom
to expand Chile's international trade. Customs duties generated
by this trade supplied the government in Santiago with new revenues and a basis on which to borrow additional funds at home and
abroad. Once the government perceived the importance of foreign
commerce to its own solvency, and once native interests began to

profit from the expansion of the export economy, laws governing
credit, transportation, and tariffs were altered to expand trade
even faster.

In addition to supplying the state with money, foreign trade
increased the importance of Santiago over the provincial centers
of political power. The role of the national government was central to the legal structure of the export economy: it monopolized
the sale of public lands, controlled tariffs and laws governing
the merchant marine, provided credit to landowners, and awarded
contracts for major public works such as the construction of railroads. Provincial leaders resented the concentration of power in
Santiago and rebelled against it, but their rebellions failed.
After the civil war of 1859, the Pelucones made the decision to
open participation in the government to some Liberals. This
change, however, entailed the distribution of power among the
political factions of the capital. But the reforms that accompanied this change and signaled the growing strength of the
Liberal Party did not redistribute power from the capital to the
provinces. They instead fragmented authority within a geographi-
cally centralized regime.

The problem of Chile's economic dependence is closely tied
to the large role the state continued to assign to foreign entrepreneurs. Given their capital, their understanding of trade, and
their control of shipping, the British found it relatively easy to
dominate the early export economy. Unfortunately, political leaders never mastered the economic side of political power. They
did not learn to organize trade in new exports or to use the government to gain leverage over the terms of trade in established
exports. They lacked any strong incentive to learn these skills.
The return on exports was apparently higher than that of any domestic sector, leading domestic capitalists to support the prevailing economic direction. The government found that customs
revenues, while they excited the envy and resentment of those out
of power, were easy to collect and certainly caused less turmoil
than more direct forms of taxation. It also discovered that reliance on exports decreased its dependence on powerful native interests such as the Church, merchant monopolists, and provincial
landowners. In short, the advantages of promoting an export
economy outweighed any apparent disadvantage. Historians have
tended to minimize the extent of political strife after 1830; but
it is true, as President Bulnes pointed out, that Chile avoided
the series of coups, dictators, and countercoups that plagued
other Latin American republics. The price of this relative success was the integration of Chile's economy into international
markets over which she had no control.

The export economy and the state grew together; each reinforced the success of the other, and their interaction created a
pattern of dependent development. The state expected foreign
trade to sustain its growth; exporters expected help from the
state. By the 1870s, the political economy had become extremely
vulnerable to any reverse in exports. The political leaders of
the decade no longer questioned the prevailing importance of the

British within Chile.   They were much more concerned with the
distribution of export income between the state and the private
sector and the distribution of public patronage and contracts.
The presidential system was being undermined by the very interests it had strengthened.   The War of the Pacific rescued the
existing order by providing it with a new source of export income,
but the political dilemmas of the dependent economy persisted and,
in 1891, led to civil war.

2. The Nitrate Economy and the Civil War of 1891

> Balmaceda, who lacked many of the qualities
> of a true statesman (although his patriotism was
> sufficient to remedy this fault), was not able to
> judge the depths of the trouble or the causes
> that were producing it. More a man of theory
> than an observer, he could not comprehend that a
> machine that, according to his principles, should
> work well was breaking down, and he fell into the
> easy error of considering as an effect of cabals
> and the perversity of men, what was in fact the
> sad but inevitable result of the decomposition of
> the country's old political traditions, of the
> loss of direction in the Liberal Party, of the
> unsettling actions of theological disputes, and,
> more than anything else, of the nation's poor
> preparation for a regime implanted by means of
> the triumph of liberalism.
>
> Alberto Edwards, *Bosquejo histórico
> de los partidos politícos chilenos,* 1903

The elite's crisis in 1889-91 was, on the one hand, a repetition
of earlier conflicts over political authority and, on the other,
the result of specific difficulties stemming from the nitrate
economy. In the traditional sense, the problems of the government revolved about the allocation of patronage, the role of
the Church, and the centralization of power in the presidency.
Beneath these controversies lay the strains of rapid, uneven economic expansion: the shift in population from rural areas to
cities and the new nitrate zones, a high rate of inflation, and
the beginnings of class conflict. In order to deal with the
multiplicity of difficulties, the government needed a new set of
rules to guide public spending and the distribution of export income. More than that, it needed a new social consensus, one that
incorporated a larger proportion of the population, as the base
of its legitimacy. The elite, however, fell to quarreling over

which branch of the government would be supreme; the result of
the quarrel was civil war.

The war began over a budget dispute. On January 1, 1891,
President José Manuel Balmaceda announced a budget which had not
been approved by Congress. His opponents controlled both houses
of the legislature and had refused to pass new appropriations until he agreed to their demand for political reforms. Rather than
accept his budgetary decree, on January 6 they boarded six naval
vessels in Valparaiso Harbor and declared a revolt against his
"dictatorship." Admiral Jorge Montt, head of the navy, became
their leader. Balmaceda retained the support of most of the army.
In the first weeks of the war, the President lacked the ships with
which to attack the rebels, while they could not attack effectively on land. This stalemate lasted until early March, when the
rebels captured Iquique, the major nitrate port. By collecting
the export duty on nitrates, they gained the means to create an
army, drafting workers from the port and the nitrate factories.
In late August, their army invaded Valparaiso and won two decisive
battles. On September 3, it established a provisional government
with Admiral Montt as President. Balmaceda received asylum at the
Argentine embassy, where he awaited the end of his term. Two
weeks later, on September 19, he composed a final testament and
shot himself.[1]

In justifying their actions, both sides invoked liberal purposes and constitutional rights. Balmaceda believed his opponents
were a selfish and short-sighted group within the oligarchy, in
league with British nitrate interests, who intended to undo his
progressive programs.[2] The Congressional rebels interpreted the
struggle as one between democratic forces and an authoritarian
executive; they saw Balmaceda as the last of the autocrats that
had ruled since 1833. The President cited the Constitution and
its passage in which the executive was called the "supreme authority," entrusted with the preservation of public order. The
rebels often called themselves "Constitutionalists," dedicated to
executive accountability and the separation of powers.[3] For
Balmaceda, Chile's progress required a centralized authority, an
executive directly accountable to the people and one above regional interests and petty issues. For the rebels, only the
creation of a "parliamentary" government and the decentralization
of authority could assure the evolution of popular sovereignty.[4]

These views, expressed at the war's onset, have remained its
opposed interpretations. Defenders of the President's position
include the Marxist, Hernán Ramírez Necochea, who argues that the
rebellion was a "counterrevolution," undertaken to reverse Balmaceda's ambitious development projects and to prevent him from reducing British control of the nitrate-based economy.[5] Others,
particularly the English historian Harold Blakemore, believe the
war began with a falling out among Chile's political leaders and
had little to do with British predominance in the nitrate sector.[6]

The controversy raises basic issues about Chile's development. Why was she unable to use her nitrate riches to become
less dependent on Great Britain? Would she have developed

differently had Balmaceda won? Chile's economic nationalists
blame the persistence of poverty and technological backwardness
on the victors of the civil war. Had Balmaceda won, they believe,
Chile would have gained a greater share of the nitrate income,
protected her nascent industries, and developed more rapidly.
Others, such as Blakemore, do not find the answer to Chile's economic problems in the outcome of the war; Balmaceda's supporters
and opponents do not fall into opposing economic camps.[7]

Was Balmaceda an economic nationalist? A nationalist leader
of a dependent country must simultaneously perform several difficult tasks. At a minimum, he must intervene in key export sectors
in order to gain leverage over his nation's terms of trade and to
try to turn export income into capital investment. Usually, these
objectives require restraining the flow of imports into the country and of capital from it. They also require a mobilization of
public support in opposition to capitalists, foreign and domestic,
who stand to gain from "free trade" policies. Balmaceda embarked
on Chile's most ambitious development program in the nineteenth
century. He wanted to do everything at once, build schools,
roads, railroads, harbors, and expand the armed forces. It seemed
he had the means. The government's income, measured in pesos, was
in 1890 three times what it had been in 1879. But that income depended on the nitrate industry, for the export duty on nitrates
provided a quarter to half of it in any given year. Nitrate sales
also sustained the volume of imports, and import duties were the
second major source of government revenues.[8] When British nitrate
producers began planning in 1889 to reduce output in order to
raise the price, the President attacked their plans and began
urging government intervention to assure increased production and
a larger share of nitrate income to native capitalists.

An evaluation of the significance of the 1891 conflict must,
however, go beyond the nitrate sector. Elements within the elite,
and many liberal intellectuals, believed that the President's
basic intention was not so much to develop the country as it was
to preserve autocratic rule. Like the President, they were not
democrats. But they did believe that Chile was becoming more
democratic; she had extended the suffrage to a larger proportion
of the adult population than could then vote in England. They
argued that a more decentralized political system, organized
about political parties, was the prerequisite to greater government accountability and a broader distribution of the national income. In their view, British entrepreneurs were allies who provided the economic basis and the political model for an emerging
"parliamentary" order.

The crisis should sound familiar to any student of "underdevelopment." An imperious President, intent on building his
country while defending the prerogatives of his office, is confronted by ambitious domestic opponents and foreign capitalists.
The details of the struggle reveal that each side contained progressive and traditional elements, and that each had a different
conception of how state power should subsidize a capitalist
economy. Balmaceda was the first executive to confront the

dilemmas of "modernization." He had to enact reforms to placate new interest groups while preserving the stability required for capital accumulation; he had to spend the export income in order to maintain his power and yet avoid antagonizing the old guard with rapid social change; and he wanted Chile to become a great nation but remained dependent on foreign investors to sustain his projects. In the end, he failed. He was, for the reasons that will be examined in this chapter, unable to mobilize suffi- cient support for his programs or to reconcile the economic re- quirements of his programs with the demands of foreign trade in- terests.

BALMACEDA AND THE BRITISH NITRATE INTERESTS

Balmaceda's attempt to intervene in the nitrate sector oc- curred late in his administration and surprised both the British entrepreneurs in Chile and a large proportion of the native elite. Before 1889, neither he nor any other executive had questioned British predominance in either that industry or in Chile's for- eign trade. It seems unlikely that the President would have raised the issue of state intervention had the British producers not begun planning a second nitrate combination that would reduce exports. Balmaceda had served in the administrations of Aníbal Pinto and Domingo Santa Maria, the first as diplomat, the second as Minister of the Interior, and it was during their administra- tions that the British nitrate "circle" had formed. He had not objected then or during his campaign for the presidency to its economic and political influence. The explanation of the Presi- dent's conduct in 1889 is the conflict that developed between his desire to carry out rapid economic development while preserving executive authority and the British producers' intention of in- creasing their margin of profit.

The British gained control of the nitrate sector because of policies instituted by the Chilean government during the War of the Pacific. Pinto and Santa Maria wanted to defeat Bolivia and Peru, seize the nitrate zones of both countries as reparations, and use the income from *salitre* to refinance an economy in crisis. Pinto told Congress in July, 1881, that the nation's renewed growth would in large part be based on the exploitation of the nitrate lands and an increase in government spending. The govern- ment's central concern in developing its conquests was to revive the nitrate trade as soon as possible. It pursued that goal not only because it needed new revenues but also because Great Britain, the United States, Germany, and France were pressuring Chile to give up its conquests.[9] Santa Maria succeeded in divid- ing the major powers and pitting foreign interests against each other, but until 1883 he did not know if Chile would succeed in its diplomatic defense of the war.[10] Establishing economic supremacy over the area and encouraging new vested, even if for- eign, interests in the conquered lands helped strengthen Chile's claim to them. In their haste to resume production, the Chilean

authorities turned to British immigrants in the nitrate areas and
at Valparaiso for help. Temporary arrangements became permanent
as the British used their opportunities to purchase the most valuable nitrate properties and to tie the nitrate trade to networks
of shipping and credit that they controlled.

They first succeeded in Tarapacá where they purchased the nitrate plants or *oficinas* for a fraction of their real value. The
Pinto administration appointed a commission to study the disposition of the captured factories; and the commission, after a perfunctory review of the legal and economic issues, decided that
possession of Peruvian bonds should become the basis of property
claims. Peru had issued the bonds in 1875 when she established a
state monopoly of *salitre*. Before then, Peruvians owned 60 percent of the nitrate plants and the region's only railroad. But
Lima replaced her native entrepreneurs with state managers, some
of whom were British immigrants.[11] When Chile captured the area,
she also turned to British technicians and appointed one of them,
John Harvey, inspector of the captured *oficinas*. Harvey, an
engineer, learned through his official contacts of the Pinto commission's recommendation before it became public. He teamed with
John T. North, a mechanic turned merchant, to take advantage of
this inside information. They approached John Dawson, the branch
manager of the Bank of Valparaiso in Iquique, the principal port
of Tarapacá, for the capital they needed. North and Harvey then
purchased bonds on the open market in Lima—bonds that had depreciated because the Peruvian monopoly was a failure and because of
Peru's military reverses—which entitled them to ownership of
several valuable factories. In 1883, North returned to his native
Liverpool, where he acquired operating capital from the Lockett
merchant firm.[12] From there he went to London and became head of
the "nitrate circle," a speculative combine in nitrate stocks.
He watered the stock in his companies and used his profits to gain
sole ownership of the water supply of Tarapacá, a controlling interest in the regional railroad, and possession of Iquique's
largest machine shop and new nitrate lands. Harvey remained in
Iquique for several years in order to run the *oficinas* he owned
with North; Dawson eventually became the Iquique manager of
North's Bank of London and Tarapacá.[13]

British influence in the trade extended beyond North's holdings and his position among the nitrate stockholders. Although
Iquique was the export center, merchants in Valparaiso handled
the commercial end of the trade. They supplied credit to producers, arranging shipping, and maintained their control over Chile's
imports. German farmers were *salitre*'s major consumers; they used
it to raise sugar beets. But London banks issued the ninety-day
drafts that were the principal currency of the trade; British
ships carried the nitrate to Europe, and its price was set on the
London exchange.[14]

Until 1884, the Chilean Liberals and British entrepreneurs
shared the same goal, to expand sales. Then, the rise in nitrate
production began to depress its price. Before the war, *salitre*
averaged twenty-two shillings a hundredweight; in 1884, its value

fell below ten shillings.[15] In August that year, producers formed
a "combination" or trust to raise the price by reducing production
and exports. Each factory was assigned a quota based on its "productive capacity." While the combination, based in London, succeeded in its immediate objective and the price rose to more than
10 shillings in 1885, it hurt the Chilean economy: in a single
year, the volume of nitrate exports fell 22 percent, the government lost five million pesos (10 percent of its income), and 3,000
miners became unemployed.[16]

José Manuel Balmaceda took office in late 1886 as the combination began to collapse. The price increase attracted new producers while those within the trust began to cheat on their quotas.
In 1887, the producers dissolved their agreement. Total exports
then rose steadily. By 1888, their volume was 44 percent greater
than it had been in 1884. Government revenues increased accordingly; from a low of 11.7 million pesos in 1886, income from the nitrate duty reached thirty-five million pesos by 1890. In the
latter year, the duty contributed 48.1 percent, a new high, of
all ordinary revenues.[17] Supported by this income, the President
embarked on the most expansive program of public projects in
Chile's history. Government spending, which rose from 35.5 million to fifty-eight million pesos between 1881 and 1886, climbed
under Balmaceda to seventy-five million by 1890. His administration spent heavily on the armed forces, especially the navy, and
on public education, but his favorite item was public works. In
1887, he created a new ministry to handle the many projects, and
by 1890 it was the government's most expensive department. In
that year, it spent twenty-six million pesos, a third of the total budget.[18] In designing his program, the President assumed nitrate exports would continue to increase. However, in 1889, the
producers, led by North, began considering another combination.
Given the increased importance of the nitrate duty to the state
and the larger expenditures of the government, a second combination posed a far greater threat to Balmaceda than the first had
to Santa Maria.

Imports had also increased dramatically and had to be maintained from nitrate income because Chile's traditional exports
could not replace any decline in nitrate sales. After 1881, competition from the United States and Spain reduced Chile's copper
exports. Her ore deposits were superior but her industry was
inefficient, able to exploit only the highest grades, and hurt by
high costs in shipping and fuel. Between 1876, a peak year, and
1890, total production fell 60 percent. Chile's share of the
transatlantic market dropped from 44 to 5 percent.[19] Production
revived briefly in 1887, the result of a copper trust formed in
France, then collapsed when the trust failed in its attempt to
corner the market.[20] Chile's wheat producers were in a better
situation. She exported a quarter of her wheat, most of it to or
through Great Britain, but the volume of the trade was no longer
sufficient to sustain the government. Even in a banner year,
such as 1883, total sales abroad amounted to only 123,000 tons,
worth 5.2 million pesos. The export of flour to Brazil, Peru,

and Ecuador declined between 1881 and 1883 from 18,000 to 6,600 tons.[21] By 1890, the hacendados were beginning to feel the effect of the stiff competition from other countries that ruined their wheat trade in the following decade.

Despite these difficulties, Balmaceda was not in a desperate economic position in 1889 and 1890. He had revived the Liberals' earlier policies and increased the government's foreign debt; it rose 36 percent between 1886 and 1890. But he avoided the squeeze on credit to the state that had trapped President Pinto. His administration negotiated a massive debt conversion in 1887 for 6.7 million pounds, then worth 17.1 million pesos, through the Rothschilds in London. It reduced government debt service to less than a tenth of what it had been under Santa Maria. Had he reorganized his policies around a temporary decline in state revenues or pushed for higher tariffs on imports, he might have avoided the deficit spending and poor trade balance of 1889 and 1890. Surprisingly, despite the nitrate combination and the civil war, total nitrate sales remained steady in 1891.[22] Of course, the President could not foresee this, and in 1889 he felt he had to fight against any reduction in exports. The nitrate duty had become the chief instrument of presidential authority; any threat to income from that source seemed to him a threat to the nation itself.

In a famous address, delivered on a visit to Iquique in March, 1889, the President attacked the formation of another combination and outlined the policies he thought would protect state interests. He rejected any attempt by the government to go into nitrate production and specifically denied any ambition to form a state monopoly in the industry. His central concern was to protect the nitrate duty revenues, and toward that end, "The state will always have to conserve enough nitrate lands to protect production and sales, and with its influence, frustrate, in every instance, an industrial dictatorship in Tarapacá." The state, in other words, would sell new lands to owners outside the combination. The increased production from the new factories would then defeat the combination's purpose. The President also proposed to take over North's nitrate railroad and have the state run it. This would bring "low freights to help develop *oficinas*, and at the same time add to the value of the [nitrate] lands."[23] He was promising a reduction in transportation costs as an alternative to the combination's proposal to increase prices.

Ramírez Necochea cites the address of proof of Balmaceda's nationalism. In fact, the President did not intend to alienate foreign investors. In his opening remarks, he praised Tarapacá for having "given life to hundreds of undertakings, all of which spring with complete freedom, and without fear as to the rights of natives and foreigners because here as elsewhere we are all of us equal before our institutions." He blamed Chilean capitalists for the fact that the British owned most of the nitrate factories. "It would be preferable for Chileans to own that property as well, but if Chilean capital is indolent or timorous, we should not be surprised if foreign capital fills with foresight and intelligence

the void that, in the progress of this territory, is caused by
the negligence of our countrymen." By quoting only the first
phrase of this passage, Ramírez Necochea seriously distorts Balmaceda's views on foreign investment in the nitrate region.[24]

In order to prevent the combination's formation, the President began to pit foreign interests against one another. He
gradually began an attempt to gain influence over Chile's terms
of trade and credit. A North American firm received a major
railroad contract. Chile took out its first loan with Germany;
part of the bargain included buying guns and steel rail—commodities the British had dominated before—from Germany's largest
foundry, the Firma Friedrich Krupp. Such sharp changes in policy
naturally infuriated the British. Their minister in Santiago,
J. G. Kennedy, complained that Balmaceda favored French firms
whenever possible and seemed openly hostile to British interests.[25] In commenting on the President's speech at Iquique, *The
Chilian Times* thought it "emanated from a very natural and laud-
able desire to stimulate Chilian capitalists to invest in nitrate
undertakings," but rejected his proposals for the nitrate railway.
It noted that his comments on foreign capital "are looked upon in
some quarters as exhibiting a large amount of narrowness of spirit
coupled with a certain degree of national antipathy." British
comments in more provincial centers were more direct; Balmaceda
in the opinion of many merchants had become an enemy.[26]

It was impossible, given the role they played within Chile,
for the British to avoid being drawn into the country's politics.
For example, in June, 1890, Balmaceda gave the American Cable Company permission to lay a new telegraph cable along the northern
coast to Valparaiso. The concession endangered the monopoly on
the coast then held by the English Submarine Telegraph Company.
Kennedy objected on the company's behalf. Balmaceda, while not
commenting on the new concession, demanded that the English company
stop supplying *El Heraldo*, an opposition paper in Santiago, with
foreign news. He told the company that unless it complied with his
demand he would withdraw all government business from it and send
official messages over the Andean wire. When the English company
refused, he carried out his threat.[27] The deteriorating relation
between British enterpreneurs and the administration led Kennedy to
hope in August, 1890, that the formation of a new cabinet that included members of the President's opposition would "prove of considerable advantage to British interests in Chile." He described
the President as "a clever but featherheaded man."[28]

The President's tactics were well-timed in terms of foreign
competition. Germany and the United States were seeking markets
for their manufactures. But the British had acquired too strong a
position in the economy; and they used it to renew their predominance over imports as well. Between 1881 and 1886, their share of
imports had declined, but with the end of the first combination and
the rise in nitrate sales between 1887 and 1891, it rose from 20.4
to 29.5 percent.[29] Moreover, the pattern of Chile's development
and diversification was intensifying her dependence on the British-
controlled nitrate sector. Industrialization was just beginning,

and many of the new industries relied on imported raw materials or assembled foreign products. Farmers in even remote provinces now counted on the growing markets of Santiago and Valparaiso; the prosperity of both cities was tied to income from the north.[30] Chile was developing an integrated national economy, but its chief stimulus was the nitrate trade; little wonder that her merchants, bankers, industrialists, and hacendados refused to support any attack on the British.

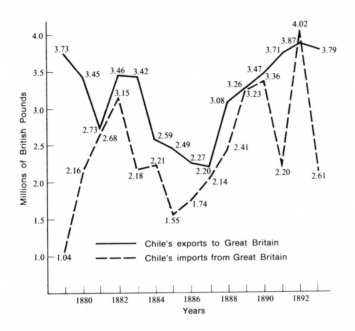

Figure 2.1 Chile's Trade with Great Britain, 1879–93.
Source: Great Britain, *Statistical Abstract for the United Kingdom, 1879-1893*, pp. 50-51.

What seemed a narrow but important problem could not be solved in its own terms. Balmaceda could not find an economic alternative, in so short a time, to dependence on Great Britain, and his search for one antagonized both the British and powerful domestic interests. The President did not try to negotiate a change in government participation in the nitrate sector with North, whom he met in late 1889, because he knew North's primary objective was not merely a combination but the formation of a single monopoly which he would dominate. The President, as Thomas O'Brien demonstrates, devised an intelligent strategy against North by

dangling a valuable railroad concession before the firm of Antony
Gibbs and Sons. Gibbs, through 1889 and 1890, refused to side
with North in his conflict with the government.[31] The tactic
thwarted the formation of a monopoly, but falling prices forced
the nitrate companies to form the second combination in January,
1891.

The development of strong domestic opposition to the President was an underlying reason for his weakness vis-à-vis the
British. The native elite turned against him, not only because
he had attacked the British in control of the nitrate sector, but
even more because it began to fear the internal consequences of
his programs. A Congressional majority formed against him, determined to reduce his personal control of public spending. Balmaceda tried to appease his opponents, but he ultimately refused to
surrender what he considered the essential prerogatives of his
office. He also tried to recruit public support for his positions, in regard to the British and to the structure of authority
in the government; but he did not break out of established political circles to create a popular movement. In the civil war, only
a minority of the "political class" supported him.

THE PRESIDENT'S PROGRAMS AND THE POLITICAL ECONOMY

Balmaceda believed that the secret of Chile's progress, of
her orderly development was the centralization of power in the
hands of the President. He admired the Pelucon state in every
respect but one, its support of state religion. He was educated
at a seminary and early in his career defended Church-state ties,
but he began in the early 1870s to demand an end to them because
he felt the Church had become an obstacle to attracting European
immigrants and was therefore blocking Chile's advance. As Minister of the Interior under Santa Maria, he supported reforms that
established civil marriage and public cemeteries, and reduced the
Church's role in education.[32] In the expansive and optimistic
mood of his early administration, he declared, "The modern state,
in accomplishing its earthly mission, carries within it the seeds
and expansive power of limitless action which sustains science,
labor, [and] intellectual freedom in their most varied and bene-
ficent forms."[33] Liberalism was his secular faith, one that
rested not on democracy or a community of values but on the
"limitless" possibilities of enlightened rule.

For the President, the modern state was synonymous with his
office. He possessed an aristocratic confidence in his abilities
and understanding and little insight into the plight and attitudes of the common people. In his introduction to the census of
1885, he noted that in many villages the people had run away at
the sight of the census taker, and he expressed dismay at their
ignorance. They had nothing to fear from a poll.[34] Nor did he
understand the evolution of political parties, although he had
been an active member of the Liberal Reform Club. To him, liberalism was a doctrine but not a movement. Parties represented selfish

interests, and he felt Chile would need greater direction than the
sum of such interests could provide. He rejected the creation of
a "parliamentary" government because it would lead to the fragmentation of state authority and create a "congressional dictatorship."[35] The attitude was not as contradictory as it sounds. He
was afraid reform would eviscerate his office, leaving the President unable to initiate policy and subject to the whims of legislative lobbies.

At the beginning of his administration, he intended to combine political reforms with a stronger executive. In January,
1886, in accepting the Liberal Party's nomination, he outlined a
program that included additional religious reforms, more schools
and better teaching methods, a larger military force, more public
works, and better housing for laborers. But who would administer
these changes? Congressional leaders, stung by Santa Maria's
abuses—including his intervention in the Congressional elections
of 1882 and 1885—wanted to reduce presidential authority. They
wanted local townships or "municipalities" to gain complete control of elections, and they wanted to increase their own role in
the distribution of patronage. In 1884, they had forced Santa
Maria to accept substantial changes in election procedures and
legislative initiative. Balmaceda, in his acceptance address,
said he favored fiscal independence for local government but
thought it "imprudent suddenly to substitute the most advanced
municipal regime in place of an old and effete system." The reforms passed under Santa Maria would, in his opinion, "protect individuals from any abuse of authority, limit the prerogatives of
the government's officials, provide easy means for fixing the responsibility of authorities who commit abuses and . . . surround
voters and liberty with protections they never before enjoyed."[36]

Unfortunately, these reforms were ineffectual. Local government lacked the means to carry out basic projects and provide adequate services, let alone protect civil liberties. Most localities were financed by a combination of fees collected for running
the local meat market, fines, and subsidies from the national government. The majority were deeply in debt. For example, Valparaiso in 1885 had an income of 718,000 and expenses of 930,000
pesos; of those expenses, 240,000 pesos was for debt service.
Concepción spent all the income it received from the national
government at the beginning of each fiscal year to cover the debts
from the previous one.[37] Small towns such as Cochapel and Maipó
had budgets of only 1,000 to 2,000 pesos. Short of resources,
towns constantly petitioned Congress for bills to permit them to
increase their debts, consolidate loans, or begin new projects
with national subsidies.[38]

Measures that had extended suffrage and placed elections
under the scrutiny of municipal committees had no effect on political morality. Local government was still an appendage of
national administration. The President appointed the intendants
and their subordinates, the regional governors; they could usually
dominate locally chosen *alcades* or councilmen. The governor in
Taltal falsified the census of 1885 in order to boost the number

of voters in his district, and then used the election register to promote or defeat candidates for local offices. Another at Freirina arrested and flogged citizens without bothering with trials. A third at Tocopilla raided the municipal treasury; when an *alcalde* objected, the governor had him arrested.[39]

In their determination to win elections, parties armed themselves and fought for control of the polls. One battle during Santiago's municipal race in 1886 left fifty dead. During the Congressional election of 1888, parties purchased votes by competitively bidding for the support of local police officials and the members of the election committees created by the reform in 1869.[40] Although the President did not participate in this corruption, the fact that the officials could be bought increased Congressional insistence that the President alone should not control the government's patronage.

Balmaceda responded to the political demands and to scandals in the administration of customs and government mining offices by enacting further reforms. Factions in Congress created and dissolved coalitions, and the President had to change his ministers as the composition of the Congressional majority changed. But before 1889, he and Congress seemed to work well together. A new law in 1887 freed *alcades* from overt interference by the national government in the operation of municipalities. Governors, the President, and his Council of State were prohibited from trying to "approve, modify, or obstruct the resolutions of Municipalities or to reverse them."[41] The following year, the government lowered the voting age from twenty-five to twenty-one. Other laws created a *Tribunal de Cuentas* (Fiscal Judiciary) to oversee government spending and prevent graft, established requirements of age and competence for judges, prevented legislators from holding executive positions, and reformed the mining code. None of these changes, however, altered the President's control of spending priorities or affected his use of administrative orders and executive decrees. With these powers intact, in fact enhanced by the nitrate income, he remained predominant within the political system.[42]

Legislators who favored political decentralization began to insist, as the presidential election approached, on reductions in government spending. In 1889 and 1890, dissident Liberals and the Conservatives attacked Enrique Sanfuentes, the Minister of the Interior and Balmaceda's favorite as his successor; they used their control of appropriations to exact further concessions from the President, including Sanfuentes' withdrawal as candidate.[43] They also wanted to control appointments to the cabinet and to give municipalities complete power over elections. The delay of one appropriations bill in July, 1890, forced the President to compromise. He agreed in August to a new cabinet that included members of the opposition. He approved the extension of the *voto acumulativo* to Senate and municipal races. First applied to the Chamber of Deputies in 1874, the measure parceled out posts according to the percentage of votes each party received for all of its candidates. It was intended to strengthen the party system

and enhance the ability of minor parties to win office. On October
14, the compromise collapsed because of the inflexibility of the
opposition leadership. The President dissolved Congress before it
had enacted the budget for the following year. He then created
another cabinet composed only of his supporters.[44]

By November, the public understood that civil war was imminent. In the capital, the opposition clashed with police as its
leaders tried to hold demonstrations and public meetings in their
clubs. In one incident, the Conservatives acquired a student
martyr. On December 20, Balmaceda decreed that all political re-
unions would require official approval. On the other side, seventy deputies and nineteen senators signed "an act to depose the
President," in which they declared that if he did not reconvene
Congress by January 1, they would no longer recognize the legality
of his administration.[45]

Although Balmaceda had only a short time remaining in his
term, he decided to fight to defend presidential government and
his program of state capitalism. He intended to save Chile from
the "disintegration of the Liberal Party, the disorganization of
the traditional, historic parties," and the "deplorable anarchy"
the party system had produced in Congress. Congress had become
corrupt, working for "foreign gold," and its members "fluctuated
between vices and ambitions." He contrasted the behavior of the
"oligarchy," which had "corrupted everything," with that of the
"common people," who "remained peaceful and happy."[46] The President interpreted his task as that of serving the higher interests
of the republic rather than the specific ones of the ruling class.

The President's program tried to accomplish too much too
fast. It was poorly coordinated, wasteful, and plagued by graft.
Although 16,000 workers were employed on various projects, in
1889 and 1890 most of these were not very far along. Cities were
dotted with half-finished schools and administrative buildings.[47]
In one instance, the government was the victim of a major fraud.
It accepted a bid to build a railroad from the Railroad Construction Company of North and South America, a company put together
by Chicago speculators. It existed only on paper, but gained a
hefty advance from the administration because it promised to
build the line in three years instead of the expected eight.
Discovery of the fraud helped destroy the President's claim to
progressive leadership.[48]

Many of the President's proposals, such as that on immigration, were not well considered. The President wanted to attract
25,000 European laborers in a single year as part of his plan to
settle isolated areas, especially the Araucanian frontier, and
remedy what he considered a "labor shortage."[49] The success of
Argentina in attracting an even larger number of immigrants made
the plan seem plausible. But Chile's nitrate economy did not require the army of laborers used in producing Argentina's agricultural exports. At a time when Chile was losing her small share
of the Atlantic wheat market, the government did not ask how the
immigrants in the new territory would succeed as farmers. Nor
did it raise the issue of what skilled laborers would do while

they waited for Chile to industrialize. Instead, proponents of
immigration argued that somehow a more skilled labor force would
stimulate agricultural efficiency and new industries.[50] They
also naively expected that, once settled, immigrants would stay
in one place. Those newcomers who did succeed, by clearing land
or establishing a retail outlet, often sold their farms or businesses for speculative gain and went home. Although it drew a
record 10,000 laborers in 1890, the program failed to fulfill
anyone's expectations. Hundreds of new arrivals, whom private
immigration agents had recruited for the government, arrived in
Valparaiso only to go to their consulates and beg for return
passage.[51]

While the shortcomings of the President's administration
provided his opponents with specific illustrations of incompe-
tence and graft, inflation and the maldistribution of income
created social tensions, strikes, and labor riots. Income remained concentrated along traditional lines. The rich held political office, or were involved in merchant speculation, agriculture, and mining. The largest fortunes were made in financing
the export economy.[52] A handsome income, however, was available
to anyone in the upper echelons of the bureaucracy. In 1885, a
postal administrator in Pisagua received 3,566 pesos a year; the
governor of the region was given 7,474 pesos a year. In 1887,
the commander of the municipal guard in Tarapacá was paid 4,200
pesos.[53] These salaries were five, six, or more times what the
best paid laborers could earn.

New fortunes migrated to the capital, which underwent another construction boom in the 1880s. Most of the new mansions
mimicked the famous architecture of other cultures. A journalist
reported the incongruous results: "One man has built himself a
Pompeian house, magnifying the proportions to a scale the original was never intended to support. Another citizen delights in a
gloomy pseudo-Tudor house. A third has thought that nothing
could be more original than a Turco-Siamese villa with gilt domes
and minarets on the roof."[54] Aside from conspicuous consumption,
the plutocrats invested in irrigation projects, mining stocks,
and real estate, and in the extension of agriculture in the
south.[55]

By contrast, real wages of the working class declined after
the War of the Pacific. While nominal wages remained constant,
from thirty to sixty centavos a day in the countryside to one to
three pesos in the cities and northern mines, the peso's value in
British pence fell from 39.5 in 1878 to 23.9 in 1890.[56] Its decline raised the price of essential imports; their increase
generated inflation. While the peso's fall helped, for a short
time, to sustain copper and wheat exports, it reduced the benefits the nitrate boom might have provided for the rest of the
economy. Workers lacked enough purchasing power to generate a
surge in domestic manufactures.[57]

Balmaceda tried to improve the peso's value and reduce inflation by removing government notes from circulation. During the
War of the Pacific, the government increased the volume of its

notes from 19.8 to 27.2 million pesos; by 1888, they amounted to only 23.2 million.[58] In June, 1890, the President vetoed a Congressional attempt to re-expand the money supply. But he could not stop private banks from increasing the volume of their notes, and these rose from 12.2 to 17.6 million pesos between 1881 and 1888. At the same time, state and private mortgage banks increased the volume of their loans from 31.4 million to 117.1 million pesos between 1881 and early 1892.[59] Chile was awash in currency. H. Pérez de Arce, Minister of Hacienda in 1886, summarized the weakness of the government's strategy:

> the efforts of the treasury gradually to remove its notes
> are cancelled by the issues from new banks, which, with-
> out special guarantees and without metallic reserves, are
> free to launch notes into circulation amounting to 150
> percent of their effective capital—in circumstances in
> which the market cannot absorb any more money without the
> risk of depreciation.[60]

So long as the working class was unable to defend itself against inflation, it bore the consequences of the peso's decline. Then an outbreak of cholera changed the availability of labor. The epidemic began in Italy in 1884 and arrived in Argentina via Spain in late 1886. The government usually did nothing about epidemics, leaving municipalities to fend for themselves. Although the mortality in Argentina was unusually high, the Balmaceda administration failed to close the border before the disease crossed over from Mendoza. It struck Chile's central valley from Santiago to Concepción in two waves: the first attack lasted until April, 1888, and, according to official figures, killed 10,000—3,481 in Santiago alone; the second broke out in October and this time settled into the shanty towns of the cities, killing 26,878.[61] Medical eyewitnesses claimed that official figures understated the fatalities by at least 25 percent.[62] It was Chile's worst disaster since Independence and killed more citizens than perished in both the War of the Pacific and the civil war of 1891. Wages rose immediately after the first outbreak. The United States consul in Valparaiso reported, "It has been very difficult to obtain workmen for harvest, mining, and the railway extensions and improvements." Railroad workers, who once received sixty to ninety centavos a day in paper currency, now earned 1.40 pesos in gold.[63] The rise in wages hurt wheat and copper exports; the harvest near Talcahuano was delayed. By mid-1888, the chief advantages of paper currency were at an end. Before, the British consul in Valparaiso reported, loans could be paid in paper and wages were not rising "in proportion to the depreciation of the dollar." Now, "the great mortality from cholera, and the fear of this epidemic, has caused many of the labourers in the south to migrate to the nitrate districts and to the Argentine Republic."[64]

The rise in the cost of labor created a clear choice for Balmaceda, but he failed to perceive its importance. On the one

side, capitalists tried to offset higher wages through price
increases and the manipulation of credit to employees. On the
other, workers fought to protect their real income through strikes
and riots. Both sides turned to the President expecting help.
Chilean Marxists have argued that laborers failed to understand
the issues involved in the civil war and, therefore, remained neutral or fought for the Constitutionalists.[65] They are mistaken:
the failure was not that of organized labor but of the President.
In the social conflicts that began in 1888, he sided with capitalists, foreign and domestic, against labor and destroyed any
possibility of rallying the politicized segment of the workforce
to his side.

Balmaceda's antilabor record begins in the aftermath of the
epidemic. Capitalist attempts to increase prices led almost immediately to labor violence. The most famous incident took place
in Santiago when the new Democratic Party attempted to attract
popular support by organizing a rally against a half-cent increase
in tramway fares. The rally ended with demonstrators turning over
tramway cars and setting them afire; the President called out the
army, forcibly ended the demonstration, suppressed the party, and
put the Democratic leaders in jail.[66]

Capitalists retained the offensive because labor organizations were weak and politically isolated. There were guilds in
several crafts and among day laborers in the ports, but they were
not linked to one another. Workers had mutual aid societies,
some of them dating from the 1850s, but none of them were organized to engage in strikes. The societies maintained reading
clubs and social centers and provided cheap burial insurance.[67]
The success of labor in these circumstances was unlikely unless
its organizations received recognition and encouragement from the
government. But the labor situation from 1888 through 1890—high
wages and the determination of capitalists to lower them—forced
workers in the capital and the ports to carry out numerous strikes.

Striking laborers had many complaints, but, in general, they
focused on two: inflation and *fichas*. The two were related because employers used the *ficha* system to reduce the real cost of
labor even as nominal wages increased. By paying workers only
once a month, they forced workers to live on credit.[68] *Fichas*
were tokens or chits issued as an "advance" on wages and could be
cashed only at a company store. Although a law of 1854 prohibited
the private issue of coins, the government regularly exempted
hacendados, merchants, mine-owners, and railroad companies from
its provisions.[69] The conflict over the *ficha* system in the nitrate province of Tarapacá led to Chile's first labor rebellion.
Balmaceda's conduct in that rebellion and the strikes that followed in other areas cost him the support of militant laborers
during the civil war.

The rebellion began at Iquique. It was a mining boomtown
of 23,000, a largely male society housed in wooden tenements.
Most of the population worked handling *salitre*; foreign merchants
and British nitrate companies were the principal employers. In
January, 1890, the prices of meat and bread rose sharply, but

aside from the outcry in labor newspapers, workers took the blow
quietly.[70] Then in June, Balmaceda withdrew the army from the
province. He wanted a show of force in Santiago to pressure Congress into passing an appropriations bill. The conflict in the
capital had two consequences for the north. Employers were left
without military force, and the absence of an appropriations bill
meant the customs house in Iquique would have to close. Once it
closed, the handling of nitrate would stop. On June 28, the
boatmen and handlers in the customs house petitioned their superintendent for permission to go on working despite the legislative
impasse. The Day-Laborers Guild recommended that he establish a
special fund into which customs duties could be paid until the
bill passed. The superintendent, a Balmaceda appointee, refused;
he apparently hoped closing the port would pressure Congress to
hurry the appropriations bill. On July 1, hundreds of customs
workers and boatmen were locked out. The following day, the
Day-Laborers Guild declared a strike and told officials they
would not return until its members were paid in silver rather
than *fichas*.[71]

The strike spread quickly to cart drivers, artisans, and the
nitrate miners, who drifted in from nearby *oficinas*. The first
massive demonstration, on July 3, drew 5,000 who demanded that
everyone now be paid in hard currency. The crowd marched through
the main street, carrying a Chilean flag and a pennant proclaim-
ing "in union there is strength," and shouting *vivas* for Balmaceda. At one point, they rallied in front of *El Nacional,* a
Balmacedist newspaper; its editor, Enrique Vergara, told them to
remain calm and have faith that the President would support them.
The provincial intendant, however, had sided with Congress against
Balmaceda. He had the police shoot blanks at the demonstrators;
when they did not break the crowd, he ordered a saber charge.
The workers scattered, Vergara was arrested, and *El Nacional* was
closed.[72]

A cycle of official violence and labor retaliation had begun.
Balmaceda tried to mediate the situation by telegrams from Santiago, but the men who carried out his orders, especially the intendant, were much more intent on repression than on a peaceful
settlement. Workers hit back on July 4, by burning a Conservative
newspaper and attacking the fire station; they also forced retailers and foundries to close. The President sent troops by
naval cruiser, but also asked businessmen, in a telegram on July
4, what they were doing to reach an agreement with the strikers.
His question infuriated the merchants and nitrate company managers. John Dawson was their leader and was advising the intendant
on whom to arrest; Dawson told Balmaceda that acceding to the
strikers' demands would ruin the province because it would
double wages.[73] After that initial question, Balmaceda did little to stop the escalation of the conflict. By July 7, the port
and its surrounding nitrate plants were closed. Workers tore up
the railroad leading into Iquique in order to prevent the arrival
of more troops. On July 8, they sacked the *oficina* "Tres Marias,"
and set the San Donato Nitrate Works and one other plant on fire.

The intendant told employers they must give in for he could not
assure public safety. Day laborers and nitrate miners won their
demand for pay in silver and an end to the use of *fichas;* artisans
in the city won wage increases as high as 50 percent; the companies also promised to stop physical harassment of the strikers.
But the concessions were only temporary. On the 10th, the government amassed enough troops to suffocate the movement. Merchants
and mining companies then dismissed the strike leaders and rein-
stituted the *ficha* system.[74]

The example of Iquique led in the following weeks to strikes
in Antofagasta and Valparaiso. In each instance, Balmaceda sided
with employers against the workers. The walkout at Antofagasta
began on July 11. This time the authorities reacted quickly; the
next day, soldiers shot two dozen strikers during a labor rally.[75]
At Valparaiso, the administration helped smash one of the most
powerful labor guilds in the country. In March, 1889, it had decreed a 50 percent reduction in wages paid for handling government
supplies in the port. It also helped merchants renege on debts
they owed to the Day-Laborers Guild. Finally, it raised the fees
laborers had to pay in order to work at the customs house.[76] On
the morning of July 21, 1890, the day laborers and boatmen walked
out. About 800 marched to the intendant's office; they wanted
the government to abolish all fees and they wanted to be paid in
silver. The intendant refused their demands, saying he lacked
authority. The laborers left his office, then regrouped in the
retail center where they began to loot the stores. By four in
the afternoon, the looting had drawn 10,000 into the area.
Groups of strikers went from one shop to another shouting support
for Balmaceda and forcing businesses to close. Strikers fought
the police and soldiers into the evening; their uprising was not
repressed until midnight when troops arrived from Santiago. In
all, seventy workers died; 360, including thirty women, were arrested.[77]

The central reason Balmaceda lacked labor support during the
civil war is that he worked with Congress to destroy organized
labor before the war began. The labor uprisings became an important political issue, and Balmaceda sacrificed labor interests as
a concession to his opponents. The opposition accused the President of having failed to protect private property. Some Congressmen thought that he deliberately provoked the strikes in
order to declare martial law.[78] He answered that Congressional
failure to pass the appropriations bill had thrown thousands out
of work and set the stage for the strikes. His administration
also said Congress interfered in the government attempts to control the strikes by holding hearings at which opponents harassed
the Minister of the Interior.[79] On August 25, 1890, Senators
Agustín Edwards and David MacIver introduced a bill to abolish
all guilds, saying the measure would reduce the cost of living.
The bill passed the Senate and the Chamber of Deputies by nearly
unanimous votes. Balmaceda signed it and it went into effect on
September 4. In addition to ending all guilds, it permitted
authorities in any city to forcibly dissolve any labor association,

take over its pension fund, and if recipients for the fund were not found, turn the money over to the state treasury.[80] Balmaceda's co-operation on this bill failed to win him any friends in Congress or in the business community, but it meant that on the eve of the war, workers no longer shouted *vivas* for his administration.

Balmaceda never understood the possible importance of labor to his administration just as he, like his aristocratic opponents, failed to comprehend the social consequences of rapid development. He supported public education and social reforms, and before 1890 he even courted labor support, but his view of workers was paternalistic. Social reforms were not as important to him as presidential rule; he never placed labor interests on the same level as the interests of foreign and domestic capital. In an illustrative incident of September, 1890, the United States consul in Talcahuano telegrammed the U.S. minister in Santiago complaining that a strike was imminent and the minister should wire Washington for a battleship. The minister, Patrick Egan, instead sent a message to Balmaceda, who assured him that "foreign interests" would be protected against any labor turmoil.[81]

Without labor, the President lacked any new social base for his administration, while his conduct had offended the traditional supporters of centralized government. In the last months of 1890, some of his opponents began to doubt his sanity.[82] He had become secretive and acted erratically—the classic manifestations of political weakness. His objectives required exactly what his opposition would not concede, an increase in the President's role in the export economy.

THE ROLE OF THE BRITISH GOVERNMENT

The final aspect of the conflict involves the role of the British government. Unfortunately, historiographic controversies about imperialism have distorted the issue. Marxists are mistaken when they argue that British officials worked with capitalists in Chile to cause the civil war. Non-Marxists such as Harold Blakemore, however, downplay the importance of the government's behavior to the outcome of the war. The Foreign Office records reveal that British officials, in Chile and in London, helped defeat the President.

Traditionally, the minister in Santiago tried to remain above commercial details. In fact, London politicians, who had a commercial interest in Chile, complained that he paid too little attention.[83] Hugh Fraser, who occupied the post in the 1880s, answered such complaints with the view that he could do little to shape economic activities. In 1886, he explained the recent decline of British exports to Chile as part of a Darwinian order. The English merchant had abandoned the market to "men contented with harder conditions and lower profits than himself":

This is the constant story of declining British trade. It becomes supplanted by the efforts of a hungrier, more

tenacious, perhaps even less scrupulous competition. . . .
The evil is one beyond the reach of official processes,
and only to be remedied by individual effort and stronger
self denial.

Government action might make matters worse. While demands
for assistance were understandable, "it is easy to do infinite
harm and difficult to do even a little good in the matter":

Every country in the world is full of British houses
of commerce, long established and directed by men per-
fectly familiar with everything belonging to the country
they live in, its men, ways, means and habits, and equally
well known themselves. What can a diplomatist or a consul, here today and gone tomorrow, as soon as he has begun to collect a little information, have to teach men of
this kind, or to tell to the trade at home which they
could not tell far better? With a little mutual help and
organization, British merchants themselves could do far
more to advance British commerce in general than any official could hope to do.[84]

Fraser's successor, J. G. Kennedy, had the same attitude. He
reported in May, 1890, "Since my arrival my time has been fully
occupied with the important questions of the Peruvian bondholders,
[the] Nitrate Railways Company, and Emigration, leaving me little
time for commercial questions."[85] His words reveal, however, that
a lack of interest in the details of local trade did not mean in-
difference to Balmaceda's policies or broad trade interests. The
bondholders wanted a slice of Chile's export pie. The railways
issue involved a complex lawsuit in which private interests were
trying to break North's Tarapacá railway monopoly; its outcome
held ramifications for the cost of transportation in the nitrate
zone and the flow of exports abroad. Finally, Kennedy openly opposed the President's project for attracting skilled British
laborers to Chile.[86]

After the Congressional revolt, Kennedy maintained an official attitude of neutrality. This seemed the wiser course, although he thought the President was in the legal right. In his
report on January 24, 1890, he wrote, "Each party accuses the
other of being outside the Constitution, but according to the Constitution the President cannot be accused or deposed until after
the termination of his period of office, whilst no right can be
claimed under the Constitution of armed revolt—against the Executive branch." He added on January 29 that Her Majesty's Government should not take sides because:

It is important to bear constantly in mind, that all
conflicts and disputes in Chile can be classed as family
quarrels in which it is proverbially dangerous to interfere; an unexpected event such as the death of the President, the capture or destruction of two or three vessels

of the fleet, the desertion to the opposition of two or
three regiments of soldiers, might bring the actual civil
war to a sudden end, whereupon the enemies of yesterday
would combine in a fierce attack against the persons and
property of any foreigners who had manifested strong sym-
pathies for the other side.[87]

Kennedy's intentions notwithstanding, British shipping dominated the Chilean coast. If the British cooperated with one side
against the other, even informally, their conduct could decide
the winner. This was clearly understood by everyone. As early
as January 16, Domingo Godoy, the Foreign Minister (and later
Balmaceda's draconian Minister of the Interior), called the representatives of the United States, Germany, and Great Britain to a
meeting at the presidential palace. All three ministers agreed
to avoid recognizing the revolutionaries and to instruct all consuls to protest any attempt by the revolutionary navy to blockage
Chilean ports. The Congressional leaders could not expect official British support for rebellion. But they did request the
Foreign Office to maintain a neutral policy.[88] Without formally
replying to the request, the British government adopted a neutral
stance. It wanted cheap *salitre* and to preserve the property
rights of its subjects in Chile. In pursuit of these objectives,
the Foreign Office eventually aided the Congressional forces.

Both sides initially assured Kennedy that they would try not
to destroy British property. But then the Congressional forces
attacked Iquique on February 16. Balmaceda ordered his officials
there to destroy the nitrate factories rather than permit them to
fall into enemy hands. Kennedy cabled the Foreign Office and
recommended sending the battleship H.M.S. Warspite to protect the
oficinas from the President's forces.[89] London rejected the suggestion in favor of a protest against "the intention of destroying the nitrate factories," on the grounds that "it can scarcely
be said to be a measure dictated by military necessities." Kennedy was instructed to tell the President, "H.M. Government will
hold Chile responsible for losses to British subjects arising out
of acts of wanton destruction."[90]

When the Congressional forces captured Iquique on March 7,
they turned the port into their headquarters. They began to collect the nitrate duty there—before the conflict, it had been paid
in Valparaiso. When the British government permitted them to tax
British ships, it in effect provided them with the means to raise
and equip an army. Balmaceda tried to cut off their revenues on
April 3, when he decreed the ports of Chañaral, Tocopilla, Antofagasta, Iquique, Caleta Buena, Junin, and Pisagua closed. Vessels landing in these sites would be confiscated if they later arrived at a port controlled by his army. At the same time, his
administration demanded that nitrate firms continue paying their
export duties in Valparaiso. Germany and Great Britain refused
to recognize the government's right either to collect the duties
or to close the ports. When Balmacedist officials seized ships
that had landed in the north, the German minister in Santiago

requested that his government send a squadron of four cruisers and an ironclad from China.[91]   Kennedy, following instructions from London, warned the President:

> H.S. Government cannot admit the right of the Chilean government to close by Municipal Decree ports which are in the effective possession of the insurgents or endorse infiltration of penalties on vessels which have visited such ports in the regular course of trade, or under the Decree generally.
>
> I am further instructed to state that Her Majesty's Government must hold the Chilean Government responsible for loss or damage caused to British subjects by any action of the Chilean Government on these respects, and that Her Majesty's Ships in Chilean waters are instructed to protect British vessels from molestation.[92]

A rebellion that Kennedy considered illegal now had London's permission to collect taxes from British subjects. But if the President attempted to impose sanctions against those trading with the enemy or to collect taxes under already established laws, Her Majesty's Government demanded that his administration pay for any damage inflicted on her subjects. It was clear that if British warships became involved, it would be to attack the President's forces. In pursuing their own commercial interests, foreign governments, and especially the British, now limited Balmaceda's authority over his own country.

The British attitude was all the more galling to the President because he knew British subjects were assisting the revolutionary cause. During the battle for Iquique, his military commander had reported that English managers of the nitrate factories had ordered their Chilean laborers to fight for the rebellion. They paid each worker who enlisted two pesos a day and threatened to blacklist anyone who refused service. The revolutionaries openly bragged of contributions from merchant firms, and cited North's gift of 100,000 pounds. In late July, the Balmacedists also discovered that British warships had been carrying revolutionary correspondence between Iquique and Valparaiso.[93] But the President could do little to change the situation. He needed British cooperation to continue supplying the central valley with imports. He was reduced to periodically harassing British shipping.[94]

During the conflict, the Foreign Office asked the Crown's law officers for guidance in dealing with the President. The war was almost over when the officers sent their definitive reply. Their conclusion is valuable not because it influenced the outcome but as an illustration of London's official attitude toward economically subordinate nations in South America. The law officers considered the question of Balmaceda's rights in international trade; specifically, did he have the right to restrict trade with belligerents when Her Majesty's Government did not recognize the belligerents or recognize that a state of war

existed? They decided that, despite the novelty of the situation,
he did not. Balmaceda's actions violated British statutes, for
the "powers given by Section 147 of the Queenslaw Customs Act of
1873 must be exercised without discrimination as to the persons
or localities to which the goods are exported."[95] Queenslaw, in
this interpretation, applied to a foreign head of state in his
own nation.

Legal questions aside, the President could not attack the
enemy. He instead resorted to a passive and expensive strategy.
His 30,000 troops tried to maintain control of the cities while
preparing to repel any invasion. To meet the soaring cost of his
policy, Balmaceda forced loans from banks, raised sales taxes,
minted three million silver pesos, and issued thirty-five million
pesos in notes.[96] But his army was destroyed by a foreign military leader he had invited to Chile. Emil Körner, a German colonel, began teaching at the Santiago military academy in 1887; his
task was to create a more "professional" army. In January, 1891,
he sided with the insurgents. By August, he and his subordinates
had turned the miners and port laborers of Iquique into an expe-
ditionary unit, armed with new Mannlicher magazine rifles. The
insurgents' training and superior weapons won the war: At
Concón, the Congressional forces lost 800, the Balmacedists
5,000; at Placilla, they lost 400 to the government's 3,000.[97]

After the Congressional government was installed at Santiago,
Kennedy revealed the extent of cooperation during the war between
British subjects and the insurgents. On September 15, he reported:

> President Montt tells me that he can't do enough to
> show his gratitude to Her Majesty's Naval Officers for
> their steady sympathy and service toward the Chilean
> Fleet since the beginning of the revolution. We British-
> ers are in tremendous favor with all classes. There is
> no doubt our Naval Officers and the British community of
> Valparaiso and all along the coast rendered material as-
> sistance to the opposition and committed many breaches of
> neutrality. . . . I was obliged in self-defence and in de-
> fence of British interests to be strictly neutral with an
> apparent leaning towards Balmaceda. Moreover, I really
> believed that Balmaceda would complete his term of
> office.[98]

Kennedy, however, was sorry the war had taken place. In a
report, written after his return to London, he expressed misgiv-
ings about the outcome and Chile's future. The insurgents, in
his view, had not established a "parliamentary" order, since the
President was still popularly elected and could not dissolve the
legislature. Nor did he expect the victors to govern effectively.
The Liberals would divide again, because "in Chile political
hatred is perhaps more intense than in any other community." He
dismissed the rhetoric of the war and thought, "The Chilean revolution may be described as an interested movement of political
parties for obtaining power. The question of principle found but

little place in the struggle." Although he disliked the President,
the new government might be worse:

> Balmaceda was an able and honest man, but he was de-
> ficient in firmness, sincerity and elevation of character
> and he was devoured by extraordinary vanity. His election
> to the Presidency was a mistake but a far greater mistake
> was involved in effecting a disastrous and possibly a
> fruitless revolution when only a few months remained of
> Balmaceda's term of office.[99]

His remarks reveal more than a diplomat's abhorrence of rebellion. Kennedy was lamenting the end of the Pelucon state. The
war was "fruitless" because it was neither a political nor an
economic advance. This was a curious attitude to take at a time
when both the Chilean elite and British merchants in Chile were
celebrating Balmaceda's defeat. But Kennedy feared that a more
fragmented political system might not be in the interest of either
the elite or the British. In the best of worlds, he would have
preserved the presidential regime but without Balmaceda. In one
sense, he was right. Chilean politics became more disorderly and
disorder was not conducive to foreign investment. It is interest-
ing that, across opposed positions, he and the President shared
the illusion that rapid economic growth and political conflict
were unrelated, that such conflict when it occurred was the result
of weak "character" or political foolishness.

British trade interests benefited from the President's downfall. They established another nitrate combination; and they regained their position as the principal suppliers of Chilean railway equipment. But North's empire collapsed before he died in
1896. He relied too long on the monopoly position of his nitrate
railroad and was unable to reenact the speculative coups of his
early career.[100] While disappointed in some aspects of the new
regime, the British nitrate producers and merchants were content
with Balmaceda's defeat. For the next two decades, Chile remained dependent on their decisions.

Balmaceda was ambitious for his country and his place in its
history. He thought that Chile would become a great and progressive nation. And he was right to believe that the state would be
crucial to modernization. But he never intended to wage a struggle for nationalist economic policies. He anticipated some of
the characteristics of contemporary state capitalism, but his administration is best understood within the traditions of an enlightened aristocratic order. He was a Pelucon espousing the new
secular faith of economic growth.

His dream of progress led him to fight against British control of the nitrate economy. Had he succeeded, he would have
thwarted the creation of a second combination; but this achievement would not have changed the predominance of British financial
institutions, merchant houses, and shipping in Chile's foreign
trade. His attempts to attract capital from Germany and the

United States might have diversified Chile's dependence and given the state a better negotiating position vis-à-vis foreign investors. But he pursued it too late in his administration.

Had Balmaceda embarked on a program to redistribute income to a larger portion of the population and give labor a political stake in his survival, the civil war would have involved more significant issues. But he was even less of a social democrat than a nationalist. He undercut real wages by promoting immigration and suppressing labor militance. His view of presidential rule did not include the political mobilization of labor. The key issues that Chile faced in the nitrate era—economic dependence and social justice—remained unresolved by the conflict. But the President had noble impulses and in comparison with his successors he seems a giant.

3. The Era of Easy Money

> It seems we are not happy; one notes a
> malaise, not in a particular class or region but
> throughout the country and among most of its in-
> habitants. Traditional pleasures have been re-
> placed by stinginess; enthusiasm for life's
> struggles, by laxity; confidence, by fear; expec-
> tations, by disillusionment. The present is un-
> satisfying, and a startling future seems imminent
> and surrounded by specters that produce uneasiness.
> Enrique MacIver, address to the
> Atheneum Club, August 1, 1900.

Those who had cheered Balmaceda's defeat were soon disappointed
in the conduct of the victors. The "Parliamentary Regime" became synonymous with political corruption, administrative in-
competence, and missed economic opportunities. The President's
opponents had spent more time preparing his downfall than they
had considering how they would govern in his place. They quickly
enacted changes in the political system that decentralized control of elections and distributed power among a greater number of
players. The players, however, soon disagreed over the distribution of the spoils.

The new regime did not represent the rise of a new social
class or the triumph of reaction. In the 1890s, its leaders declared three goals: they wanted to give municipalities effective
political power, to put Chile's currency on the gold standard,
and to continue the development of public administration, transportation, and social services. The civil war did not change the
composition of the elite. The Presidents from 1891 until 1915
came from the same powerful families that had ruled since the
1850s. Their advisors were drawn from the same circle or from
the English and French merchant families that had acquired land
and married into the oligarchy.[1] None of the Presidents or their
administrations can be described as reactionary, and opposed to

nineteenth-century liberalism; none tried to extend the power of
the Church, and each continued the pose of enlightened rule. All
believed that the state should promote progress. The Liberal
Party and progressive splinter parties which were committed to
that policy dominated both houses of Congress throughout the
period. While it is true that the national budget of the early
1890s was smaller than it had been under Balmaceda, the victors
felt they had to economize to pay for the costs of the civil war.
By the late 1890s, the government was spending as much as Balmaceda had spent and, by 1910, government expenditures were more
than double those of 1889 (figure 3.1).

The regime lost public esteem because it failed to achieve
its liberal objectives. Nitrate prosperity increased the size of
the electorate; and the spread of literacy increased a general
interest in national politics. The new electoral rules respected
these changes, even encouraged them, and opened politics to new
groups and to political entrepreneurs, men able to develop local
movements, court favor with established interests, or do both.
The Balmacedists, pardoned soon after the war, re-entered politics in 1894 and quickly gained influence in Congress. Radicals
and Democrats drew new adherents, mobilizing professionals, small
businessmen, artisans, and urban laborers. In 1912, leftist
Democrats formed a Socialist Workers Party.[2] These developments
did not alter the elite's control of the system, because changes
in political rules were not accompanied by any attempt to redistribute economic power. Bankers, hacendados, and mining interests
financed political candidates and could, through their economic influence, isolate anyone who opposed them. The system became more
responsive to special interests but was still unrepresentative.

In terms of its promises, the regime's decisive failure was
the collapse of the gold standard in 1898. President Jorge Montt
believed that his government's prestige was tied to the creation
of a hard currency, and spent his authority and a major portion
of the nation's income in achieving the Monetary Conversion Law
of 1895. Neither Montt nor his advisors had considered all the
consequences of the law. Given the poorly supervised banking
system, the act only led to currency speculation, the flight of
capital, and the return of inconvertible money.

The regime continued to extend Santiago's reach into the
provinces; but state administration evolved within an extremely
unstable framework. The multiparty system in Congress made it
difficult for any President to form a legislative majority. After
the civil war, Congress gave itself the power to depose unpopular
cabinets, and as legislative coalitions formed and collapsed, so
did ministries. One historian has counted 120 ministerial "crises"
from 1891 to 1930.[3] The system did not reward political loyalty,
and its leaders often seemed without principles or self-discipline.
In 1895, *The Chilian Times* provided this description of the Liberal Party, that led the rebellion against Balmaceda:

> Impotent to govern by itself, it has been compelled
> to negotiate alliances by which on more than one occasion

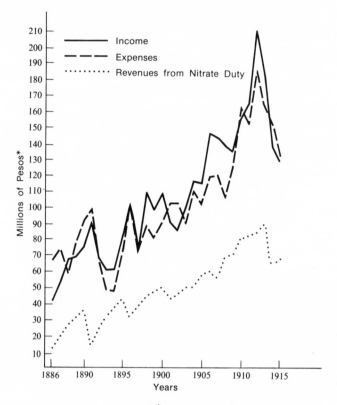

*At 18 British pence per peso.

Figure 3.1 Government Income and Expenses,
1886-1915. Sources: *Sinopsis*, 1916,
p. 66. Hacienda, *Antecedentes*, p. 21.

it has completely stultified itself. Even now, it is in
power by the merest suffrance, and it may be kicked out
of office at any moment. But notwithstanding all this,
the members of the party in Congress are so many free
lances [sic] who acknowledge no leaders, and who fight
when they please and how they please.[4]

Poorly designed and with an economic base dependent on foreign markets and entrepreneurs, the Parliamentary Regime survived
because, with all its shortcomings, the elite saw no reason to
risk replacing it. The victors felt a moral obligation to make
"parliamentarianism" work or at least appear to work. How else
could they justify the rebellion against Balmaceda? More important, it served the interests of the upper class, if not perfect-
ly, at least well enough not to bother trying to imagine an alternative system. Finally, its leaders could argue that the
regime's failures could be corrected by further reforms; in this,
they were seconded by a growing and ambitious corps of political
reformers and administrative technicians.

As long as the nitrate boom continued, the *politiquería*
could continue at apparently little cost to the public. Nitrate
duties made the establishment of a sounder fiscal system, based
on other, more unpopular taxes, unnecessary. But the strains between domestic and foreign interests and between capital and labor, that had appeared by 1890, remained. Chile's leaders created
an explosive mix of foreign investment, stock market speculation,
and influence peddling. The economic result was a dispiriting
cycle of boom and bust, punctuated by an international recession
in 1907 and a depression in 1914. The social result was an increasingly militant labor movement that threatened the regime
with strikes, riots, and support for new political leaders. To
make sense of this crucial period, it is necessary to separate
the nonsocial from the social issues of the political economy.
The first involves an examination of the political system, public
administration, and the government's fiscal policies and their
relation to the nitrate sector; it is the subject of this chapter.
The second, dealing with the rising anger and frustration of labor, is covered in chapter 4.

LIBERAL DESIGN AND POLITICAL REALITY

The victors in the civil war proposed to create a state with
the best features of the governments of the United States, England, and Switzerland. From the United States, they retained the
separation of powers already declared in the Constitution of 1833;
from England, they introduced legislative control of the cabinet;
and from Switzerland, they borrowed the idea of giving local government control of elections. This mixture appealed to an elite
that was uncertain of the modern value of its traditions and
anxious to have the best from more advanced cultures. The supporters of the Parliamentary Regime did not adjust their innovations to the existing structure of political power, nor did

they carefully project the results of their reforms. The result,
of course, did not operate in practice as it was intended to in
theory, and the effects of one reform often contradicted those of
another. Party strife and mutual distrust spilled into administration, dissipating funds and destroying initiative, dismaying
honest officials, and rewarding scoundrels. This was Chile's
gilded age, and the ambitious made the most of it.

The new system was neither parliamentary nor presidential.
Congress could force the cabinet to resign, but the President
could not dissolve Congress and call for popular elections to resolve a dispute between the two branches. This meant that the
cabinet had to win and maintain support from a majority within a
badly fragmented legislature, and the President had to change the
cabinet's composition as often as alignments changed among the
parties and factions in Congress. The frequent change of ministers that had occurred under Balmaceda resumed as soon as the
civil war was over.

President Jorge Montt tried briefly to head a government of
national unity in which all the victorious parties would participate. But the Liberals did not take him very seriously. He was
an unimposing figure: short, stout, a man who had spent his
adulthood in the hierarchy and social isolation of the navy.
Government insiders told the British Minister that Chile now had
her Queen Victoria.[5] The President appointed two Conservatives
and four Liberals to his first cabinet. It lasted only two
months. Liberals insisted that all judicial appointments be from
their party, and the Conservatives, when the President failed to
oppose this view, resigned.[6] The next cabinet, composed only of
Liberals, endured only a few more months. On June 1, 1892, the
new Congress met, and Liberal deputies fell out over who would be
their chamber's vice-president. On June 2, the controversy divided the cabinet, and its members resigned.[7]

The new political rules favored small groups seeking favors.
In Congress, every majority depended on the support of minor parties or maverick factions, and the absence of businesslike procedures was an advantage to special interests. Every item in the
budget was voted on individually, members of Congress could refuse to assemble in sufficient numbers to make a quorum, and once
they were assembled, it took only one member's objection to call
a recess if the usual hour of adjournment had passed.[8] Factions
acquired the power to extort concessions from the majority by con-
tinually delaying bills, and especially by delaying the passage of
appropriations and the budget. Their success encouraged the formation of other factions and the development of further delays.
In short, the same tactics the legislators had used so successfully against Balmaceda they now used on one another. Commenting
on one cabinet "crisis" in September, 1903, the U.S. minister,
Henry Wilson, concluded that the new ministry would also be brief:

> All the political parties are rent by internal dis-
> sensions, and such government, as the various parties are
> able to give the country, is the result of intrigues,

having for their object, the furtherance of the selfish
interests of various little cliques which dominate their
councils. There is no such thing as a distinct political
program, nor do any of these later Chilean ministries
rise or fall on questions of principle. The power and
opportunity to control public patronage, or secure individual profit, seems to be the decisive factor.[9]

The system was supposedly based on local government. In
fact, legislative factions tried to use the national administration as Presidents once had, to secure election for themselves or
for favorites. The elections were run by local committees, but
these were frequently corrupted by factions in Santiago. Government became, in the words of one observer, "merely a compromise
delicately balanced in patronage." "With one or two insignificant exceptions all the Senators of the Republic and by far the
greater number of Deputies live in Santiago and have never re-
sided in the districts which they represent, and visit them only
at election time. The elections are notoriously fraudulent.
Bribery is practiced openly."[10]

The reform of December, 1891, did not define a municipality
or set any administrative requirements on its operation. Citizens
petitioned Congress for recognition as a community without demon-
strating either that the area they wished to incorporate would be
able to sustain a government or that their petition represented a
majority sentiment within the region.[11] Partisan considerations
decided whether or not a petition was approved; each party tried
to use the law to create captive districts. The first result was
a zoning disaster. Initially, the deputies and the Senate granted
approval to separate petitions so the boundaries of localities
incorporated by one body did not always coincide with those
created by the other.[12] A more common problem was the tendency
toward balkanization. In 1897, for example, the small township
of Yumbel, with 3,000 inhabitants, lost almost half of its income
when a group of 900 residents created "Las Perlas." The creation
of so many localities, however, suited the interests of more af-
fluent provincials. It gave them political offices and control
of local tax rolls and election registers.[13]

The law required each municipality to have nine corporate
members, that is, three *alcaldes* (councilmen) and six *regidores*
(magistrates). One of the alcades served as chief officer. If a
city contained more than 20,000 residents, it could add one corporate member for every 10,000 additional inhabitants. The largest cities were divided into subunits; in 1892, Santiago had ten,
Valparaiso five, and each subunit had three members. In these
cities, the subunit officials, taken together, formed the corporate body.[14] The struggle for power among local officials was
often petty and vindictive and sometimes violent. The alcades in
Valparaiso spent months in 1895 choosing their chief officer. A
municipal meeting in Chillan in 1897 led to a rock-fight in which
the police refused to intervene and which ended with one group
seizing the city books.[15] Describing the situation in Bio-Bio,

the intendant there admitted in 1910 that, despite numerous
reforms, municipalities were not providing adequate social services. Officials were too busy seeking political favors to accomplish anything.

The law also conferred new tax powers on the municipality.
Specifically, incorporated areas could collect from one to three
pesos per resident to be used for schools, a property tax of up
to 3 percent of evaluation, a sales tax on tobacco and alcohol,
license fees on industries and professions, rents from municipal
property, and fines for civil offenses.[16] In addition, Congress
voted sums each year to subsidize municipal services. In practice, localities were perennially short of funds, not only because they had been poorly organized in terms of their tax base
but also because local officials persistently undervalued property.[17] At times, powerful landowners created municipalities
that coincided with the extent of their estates. In 1897, the
Larraíns and the Leteliers, two prominent families within the
oligarchy, petitioned to have two of their haciendas, which bor-
dered on one another, recognized as an incorporated area.[18] The
more common practice was that one or two large estates, surrounded by numerous small farms, made up a rural municipality.
It was in this situation that local politics became dominated by
what one intendant called "political godfathers."[19]

These godfathers were frequently absentee landlords who re-
sided in Santiago. The key to their influence was their control
of election boards. The board of a municipality consisted of the
twenty-five largest taxpayers. The board could have more than
twenty-five if more than one person had paid the same amount in
taxes; if it were short of the required number, individuals who
had professional degrees or owned real estate could serve.[20] Although local "caudillos" ran the show, as the governor of Cauquenes remarked, local issues were rarely at stake. "One could
say that in these cases, money is the great elector, which forms
temporary majorities without exactly reflecting the aspirations
of the society's members."[21] The rich did not always agree. The
U.S. minister reported of the Congressional contest of 1903, "In
probably half the election districts, the canvas of votes has
been attended by scenes of violence, acts of usurpation and fla-
grant frauds." Election boards had sometimes issued certificates
of victory to the loser; some of the board presidents had exercised their office under military protection.[22]

Money controlled the outcome because it bought the votes.
Candidates would approach the party bosses in Santiago, and as
one observer explained, assure them of a "willingness to pay the
required sum to carry the election." In rural areas, the laborers
would choose a spokesman to represent them and offer their votes
as a lot for bids from party representatives. "When convinced
that they cannot secure more the peons close with the highest
bidder, and march in single file to the voting place. One by one
their names are called, and as their right to vote is admitted,
the agent of the candidate making the purchase deposits the vote.
After the voting is completed according to agreement, the peons

receive the money in the presence of the [election] inspectors, politicians and other voters."[23] The number of votes involved was not very lage. A senator in Valparaiso province was elected in 1908 with 6,500 of the 17,000 votes cast; some deputies won with as few as 1,000 votes. By 1906, *El Ferrocarril* complained that not only had bribery gotten out of hand but the price of votes had risen. The average cost of a seat in the Senate was 100,000 pesos and that of one in the Chamber, 10,000. At their convention in 1907, Liberals proposed legally to limit election expenses to 10,000 pesos for a candidate to the Senate and 5,000 for a candidate to the Chamber of Deputies.[24]

The *voto acumulativo* complicated political life even more. It was now applied at every level of government; parties were entitled to representation according to the percentage of votes they received. It encouraged fragmentation of parties, since each grouping could hope to gain at least some offices. In order to assure themselves of Congressional seats, parties pooled their support and assigned seats to each party within their coalition.[25] This meant that a representative held his seat not by popular vote but according to the coalition to which he belonged in Congress, and to whether or not it still assigned his seat to his party. The voting system also affected presidential contests. Chile had an electoral college, but unlike that of the United States where each citizen votes only once, in Chile a voter cast as many ballots as his province had electors. In Santiago province, he could cast twenty-four ballots for a single candidate to the college. Each party then received a number of positions to the college based on its percentage of votes in each province.[26] A candidate to the presidency had to run at the head of a coalition in order to assure that he would not be destroyed by minor party candidates. Even then, the system was so complex that in several cases no one knew who had won the contest until the college met and voted; this first occurred in 1896, when Frederico Errázuriz Echaurren was chosen.[27]

Victory in the popular vote frequently did not decide the outcome. Widespread fraud and bribery and the confusion of the *voto acumulativo* justified losers in appealing many contests. Their appeals, to municipalities or to Congress, consumed a major part of the time of alcades and legislators. In 1903, the Chamber of Deputies, with ninety-four seats at stake, was asked to review twenty contests; between June 1 and July 18, it resolved only five appeals. Observers commented that, at that rate, not enough time remained in the three-month session to decide the remaining cases.[28] By reviewing the validity of returns, the majority in a municipality or Congress could reverse the popular result and thus reinforce the importance of party connections and inter-party coalitions. Every candidate needed a political sponsor. He often had a financial one as well, for only a powerful party figure could guide him through the shoals of both the election and its subsequent review.[29]

Three groups, the Liberal Alliance, the Conservative Coalition, and the Balmaceda Liberals, shared power in Congress. Each

had a broad program: the Liberal Alliance and the Balmacedists
spoke in favor of electoral reforms and public education; the Conservatives defended the role of the Church in public life.[30] But
the elite never let ideology interfere with its immediate objectives; the distinctions between Conservatives and Liberals gradually lost significance. In 1901, Pedro Montt lost when he ran
for the presidency with Church support; in 1906, he campaigned as
a Liberal, the "regenerator" of public life and a strong anti-
clerical, and he won.[31]

A better example of opportunism is the Balmacedists, who
were also called the Democratic Liberals and were considered one
of the most progressive elements in Congress in the mid-1890s.
They stunned the Conservatives in 1894 when they won six of the
thirty-two Senate seats (sixteen seats were at stake in the election) and twenty-two of the ninety-four deputy positions. Aside
from extolling Balmaceda's memory, they wanted a return to presidential government and, a contradictory demand, further decentralization of administration. They also campaigned in favor of protective tariffs for industry.[32] Soon after returning to public
life, they began participating in coalitions that included the
leaders of the 1891 rebellion. The party split into two factions,
led by Juan Luis Sanfuentes, brother of Balmaceda's Minister of
the Interior, and Claudio Vicuña. The faction led by Sanfuentes
was particularly unprincipled. It joined with Conservatives at
one point and, at other times, with doctrinaire Liberals, Radicals, and Democrats. President Errázuriz Echaurren began his administration with the support of Liberals and Conservatives who
had rebelled in 1891. Within a year, his cabinet was composed of
Liberals, Balmacedists, Radicals, and Democrats. When the budget
of 1897 was proposed, the Radicals and the doctrinaire Liberals
split from the Balmacedists and those Liberals who supported the
President. By 1900, the President's legislative base consisted
of Sanfuentes' Balmacedists, Conservatives, and one Liberal
faction.[33]

Although no dramatic shifts occurred in the distribution of
power in Congress, persistent infighting reduced administration
to petty questions of patronage. Government was wasteful and disorganized. But administrations were forced to expand the bureaucracy in order to placate their supporters. As the export economy
expanded, government also grew to meet the demands of merchants,
exporters, and foreign investors for public safety, improved
transportation, and social services. The Minister of Hacienda remarked in 1904, "Expenses of Public Administration have almost in-
variably increased in these last years . . . and leave the impression of a fiscal policy that dispenses too much and is even
spendthrift."[34] In general, the government concentrated its expenditures on the capital and neglected the provinces. It did,
however, gradually expand the ability of state administrators to
manipulate local officials. By 1897, governors began to reverse
municipal decisions whenever these threatened "public order."[35]
That year, intendants and governors also took control of the provincial police from municipalities.[36]

TABLE 3.1   COMPOSITION OF CONGRESS IN 1897, 1900, AND 1913

	Chamber of Deputies			Senate		
	1897	1900	1913	1897	1900	1913
Conservatives	26	21	19	13	8	9
Liberals	22	29	22	4	8	12
Balmacedists	21	25	28	7	8	9
Radicals	17	16	22	3	3	3
Democrats	2	3	5	0	0	1
Independents	6	0	0	5	5	1
Nationalists	0	0	0	0	0	2
Total	94	94	106	32	32	37

SOURCES: Henry Wilson no. 137, Mar. 24, 1900, U.S. *Despatches,*
reel 47; and Roland B. Harvey no. 421, Nov. 11, 1913,
U.S. *Internal Affairs,* reel 11.

The spending priorities of administrations differed from one
another, but the most important changes in the pattern of expenditures before and after the civil war were sharp increases in financing the military and the fiscal administration (Hacienda).
Leaders of the Parliamentary Regime clearly preferred guns over
butter and railroads over schools. (See table 3.2.) This does
not mean that the government spent less on social services but
that even though the amount spent on them increased they took up
a smaller percentage of the budget. Spending on schools, for
example, increased from 9.0 million to 27.3 million pesos between
1900 and 1910.[37] The government also developed new programs in
public sanitation and the police.

The elite's military motivations were the same as Balmaceda's;
the ruling cliques believed until the First World War that Chile
could become one of the two military powers on the continent. The
government maintained the national militias, but a permanent army
of 6,000 men and a large and well-equipped navy were now the core
of its defense.[38] From 1896 until 1902, Chile and Argentina argued over their southern boundary, and it seemed in 1898 that the
two might go to war. After they settled their differences—Chile
relinquished its claim to a major part of the southern pampa—the
elite continued to spend on the military because it was an instrument of social discipline and a source of national prestige. In
1900, the government began to draft men between the ages of twenty
and twenty-one; the burden of service fell exclusively on the
poor.[39] Military spending offered the upper class the additional
advantage that, since heavy armaments and all ships were imported,
it did not intensify competition for labor as Balmaceda's public
projects had done.

A related development was the organization of a national

TABLE 3.2 PATTERN OF GOVERNMENT EXPENDITURES, 1886-1915

	Interior	Foreign Affairs	Justice	Education	Hacienda (Finance)	War	Navy	Industry & Public Works	Size of Average Budget[a]
M. Balmaceda 1886-90	12.5%	3.6%	4.6%	8.8%	37.1%	10.8%	8.6%	13.6%[b]	73.8 m.p.
J. Montt 1891-96	8.8	2.9	4.1	6.3	22.5	23.9	16.2	15.2	73.5
F. Errázuriz 1897-1901	13.0	3.5	4.4	6.9	32.0	18.2	12.6	9.3	87.6
G. Riesco 1902-6	13.1	3.9	4.2	9.7	28.7	11.9	16.6	11.9	105.2
P. Montt 1907-10	16.3	3.8	3.8	10.1	24.2	11.8	12.5	17.3	129.3
1911-15	15.2	2.9	3.5	12.5	27.9	14.2	11.3	12.3	131.6

SOURCE: Data in *Sinópsis*, 1916, p. 71.

[a]In millions of pesos; one peso worth eighteen British pence.

[b]Balmaceda's expenditures on public works were higher than this figure indicates. The Ministry of Public Works was not begun until 1887, and so public works spending in his first two years is scattered through other ministries.

police. Banditry, endemic in the southern countryside and northern
mining camps, remained a problem until the eve of the First World
War. Immediately after the civil war the number of bandits increased because of unemployment among veterans. In 1892, the
country had 2,200 homicides, a rate close to seven per 1,000, but
local officials lacked the police to deal with the problem.[40]
The national government tried to reduce crime by sending the army
into some provinces and creating a special investigative unit in
Santiago; but these efforts were inadequate. Seasonal banditry
in rural areas continued.[41] Then in 1903 the government created
an elite army cavalry unit of 202 troops, called the *Cuerpo de
Jendarmes*, to attack the most notorious bandit gangs. The unit
worked in small groups under the direct orders of the Minister of
the Interior. In 1906, the government changed its name to the
Cuerpo de Carabineros; the following year, President Pedro Montt
incorporated its activities into a master police plan. By 1911,
there were 8,000 regular police and 1,500 *carabineros*; the latter
had come to replace the former in the countryside. By 1915, the
2,000 *carabineros* who patrolled the smaller mining towns as well
as rural areas finally succeeded in containing banditry.[42]

The extension of state police powers was part of a slow rationalization of the nation, the integration of the country into
a single market organized about the needs of the rulers in Santiago. Toward that end, the government reduced the control of
landowners and merchants over regional markets and the local police; but regional interests were often glad to have the help of
the national government, which reduced their risks by providing
railroads, some tariff protection, and the *carabineros*. Even so,
poor administration and the prevalence of inefficient methods of
production limited the geographic and social extent of the government's actions. State railroads and programs in sanitation and
education illustrate the point.

The railroad program during this period had two phases; in
the first, the government concentrated on the purchase of existing
lines; in the second, beginning with President Pedro Montt, it
emphasized the construction of new ones. The government bought
unprofitable private companies in order to subsidize exports, especially copper. In 1888, the Balmaceda administration took over
the Chañaral Railway; the Parliamentary Regime took over the
Coquimbo Railway in 1895, the Tongoy Railway in 1901, and the
Copiapó Railway in 1911. President Pedro Montt (1906-10), the
most far-sighted of the chief executives after 1891, completed
the Transandine line in 1910. In 1906, his administration granted
a concession to Belgian contractors to build a longitudinal line
from Valparaiso to Copiapó. Construction began in 1909. His
projects continued under President Barros Luco when Chile built
2,500 kilometers of track, the largest expansion in the system's
history.[43]

State lines operated at a profit before 1900, although during the 1890s the margin of profit was negligible. Between 1900
and 1915, they were in the red more often than not, and the government had to cover a total loss of seventy million pesos.[44]

The cost was not, as some believed, causing the government to exceed its income, but it did cut deeply into the fiscal surplus of those years.[45] Politics caused mismanagement and inefficiency. The government maintained fixed rates, giving shippers the full benefit of inflation, and it favored new projects over repairing old lines because of the importance of construction contracts to patronage. By 1907, the deterioration of the trunk line between Valparaiso and Santiago was causing numerous accidents; by 1912, whole sections of track on other lines were abandoned.[46] Building the longitudinal line to the nitrate provinces was obviously uneconomical (little freight moved on the return route from the north to Valparaiso), but it facilitated the movement of troops in the event of war or a labor uprising.[47]

In a similar fashion, in developing social services the government placed established interests and political cliques above the needs of the nation as a whole. It built sewer and water supply systems to prevent epidemics, but by 1910 these systems existed only in Santiago and a few provincial centers. Within those cities, they connected the business districts with the homes of the rich on main avenues.[48] Beyond these improvements, even large cities remained unsanitary. A newspaper candidly described Valparaiso as a "filthy, stinking hole."[49] Critics of life in the nitrate towns complained of animals left to rot in the dusty streets, the proximity of garbage dumps to residential areas, and the putrid taste of the drinking water.[50] The government built model hospitals, an orphanage, and a mental asylum in Santiago, but these were more symbols of progress than effective means to combat disease, abandonment of children, and mental illness. The poor diet and generally poor health of the population kept the mortality rate high.[51] Efforts in education were more successful but reflected the same disparity between the capital and the provinces. By 1915, most children received some schooling: 322,000 attended primary schools, 41,700 were in secondary schools. The country had no provincial universities; the national university in Santiago graduated 970 that year. Most of them preferred the traditional studies of the humanities and law—only nineteen completed work in engineering.[52]

In all, the basic concerns of the government were the same after as before the civil war: creation of a national administration, expansion of the national income, and maintenance of class rule. The complex political system was the adjustment made by an oligarchy to an age of new money; it reflected the problem that had plagued government leaders since the beginning of the republic —how to accommodate new interest groups created by the export economy. It had little to do with ideology. Leaders gave lip service to democracy, but the unequal distribution of income kept the majority out of politics. The government did not pay its legislators; instead, it required senators to have a minimum income of 2,000 pesos a year, and deputies 500 a year.[53] The concentration of landholding continued to be an important prop of formal power: in 1902 73 percent of the senators and 52 percent of the deputies owned large estates; as late as 1918, 67 percent

of the senators and 40 percent of the deputies were hacendados.[54]
Despite this predominance, established opinion worried as early
as the 1890s about the new social elements that were gaining office; the system, said critics, favored political enthusiasts
rather than "the most capable citizens."[55]

The regime's leaders decentralized elections and then used
bribery, patronage, and deals struck in the Santiago political
clubs to recentralize decision-making. The process invited dishonesty and disorder at every level. It deprived local communi-
ties of effective government while it generated insecurity among
national administrators. It created a larger bureaucracy, which
lacked coherent direction. The governor of Caupolican noted in
1912 that the number of intermediate officials—General Inspectors of Primary Education and of the Civil Register, General Directors of Posts, of the Treasury, of Telegraphs, or Prisons, of
Industries and Public Works, of Statistics, of Alcohol, of the
Inspectors of Police—had grown without any clear definition of
responsibilities. "All of these offices have direct contact with
provincial subordinates; they dispatch certificates, promote and
dismiss employees. Since matters are carried out outside of
proper channels, they produce confusion and undermine the authority of Executive ministers."[56] Nonetheless, the elite settled
for this system because it could still use government to transfer
the costs of development to consumers of Chile's exports and, in
the form of inflation, to the Chilean working class.

NITRATE PROSPERITY AND THE REINFORCEMENT OF DEPENDENCE

In the twenty-three years between the civil war and the First
World War, the Chilean upper class enjoyed an unprecedented prosperity. Total exports, led by world demand for nitrates, almost
tripled. The central economic idea of the regime, the one which
every administration repeated, was that private entrepreneurs
would reinvest the nitrate profits and increase the nation's productive capacity. The intended result required that investments
be protected by a sound currency. At the end of the period, however, the most noticeable consequence of government policy was
the continued depreciation of the peso.

Chilean intellectuals proposed a number of explanations for
the low rate of domestic savings and the slow pace of industrialization. As early as 1894, Francisco Valdés Vergara put the
blame on the nitrate boom, claiming that far from developing
Chile it was corrupting the nation, turning it from a society of
enterprising hacendados into one of dandies, fortune hunters, and
parasites.[57] Others argued that the government was the culprit,
that it had deliberately followed an inflationary monetary policy
in order to reduce the cost to hacendados of their mortgages.[58]
In 1911, Francisco Encina blamed the government's policy of free
trade and the nation's slavish imitation of Europe for the lack
of development. "From 1870 onward, Chile stopped its spontaneous
evolution, progress no longer was a result of the organism's own

efforts. The changes in ideas, feelings, institutions, customs,
etc., are determined by the influence of Europe's example."[59]
    Critics recognized that Chile relied on foreign capital, mar-
kets, and technology. Encina called her a "satellite" of more
advanced powers.[60] They also recognized that this dependence was
tied to the nation's values and brooded that the Chilean people
might be unfit for the modern era. Tancredo Pinochet Le-Brun believed Chile was already conquered by foreigners. He granted
that Chileans were inferior to Europeans, but pleadingly asked,
"Don't we have minds in this country that can go to Europe to
learn what professors, whom we have imported and continue importing, have studied? Are we truly incapable of steering our own
ship?"[61] Encina was convinced the answer was yes. The native
element in the Chilean population would retard her intellectual
advance. "The blood of the Araucanian aborigene circulates abun-
dantly in the veins of our people; and although it is noble blood,
it cannot cross in three centuries the distance Europeans have
traversed in close to two thousand years."[62]
    Nícolas Palacios, who wrote *Raza chilena,* one of the most
famous works of the period, used racist premises to prove that
the Chilean laborer was not an inferior being. Palacios believed
Chileans were descended from "Gothic" Basques and from Araucanians,
who possessed a physiology and social organization similar to
those of the Goths. The Chilean *roto* was therefore unlike the
mestizos of the rest of Latin America; he was not an offspring of
"Latins," but a superior hybrid. The answer to Chile's problems
lay in the better use of the people's talents, in better education, including the creation of more technical schools, and in an
improvement of the workers' standard of living and their treatment by the government:

> The high mortality rate and the low marriage rate in
> our country indicate a profound social malaise in our
> race. In order to comprehend the immense importance of
> these facts, to understand their causes, and to apply
> remedies, the country needs the leadership of superior
> men, or at least of administrators who love the people,
> who feel in their own hearts the anxious clamors which
> respond painfully from one end of the country to the
> other in the form of petitions, tears, and strikes. We
> are far from having such men.[63]

Like Palacios, other critics emphasized the need for better
political leadership and more nationalistic policies. None examined the possible consequences of higher tariffs on inflation or
the effect of tighter monetary policies on the availability of
credit. Only a few (to be discussed later) examined the government's export strategy. Palacios, a physician, and Alejandro
Venegas, a teacher who wrote under the pseudonym Julio Valdés
Canje, tried to relate Chile's problems to the uneven distribution
of income.[64] They perceived but inadequately analyzed the relation of the concentration of wealth to the pattern of Chile's use

of her resources. Until another social class became capable of
challenging the elite's control of power, the elite would not see
a need to build schools or develop industries at a faster rate.
Palacios and Venegas, however, were interested in preventing the
spread of socialism in the Chilean working class. Palacios at
one point expressed gratitude that neither Jews nor Socialists,
whom he saw as one and the same, had yet gained influence among
the *rotos*.[65]

The reigning opinion within the elite was that the export
economy would assure Chile's development and that the nation
should exploit its comparative advantage in international trade.
Agustín Ross Edwards typifies the views of many in the upper
class. Descended from two powerful merchant clans in Valparaiso,
he served as the rebels' emissary to London during the civil war,
and as a Conservative senator in the mid-1890s.[66] He helped de-
sign the Monetary Conversion Bill, sometimes called the Ross Act,
and enthusiastically supported Chile's ties to Great Britain. He
believed the country's difficulties stemmed from economic inefficiency, monetary instability, and the actions of nitrate speculators. The remedy to these problems was free trade. Chile's workers lived in "miserable huts" because they were an "improvident
lot" and because they had to pay for the high cost of domestic
manufactures.[67] Lower tariffs would bring "civilization" and
satisfy the demands of the "masses." The country should also return to a gold standard because fluctuating currency values
created uncertainty. And the government should do all in its
power to prevent another nitrate combination; Ross hated North
and his associates and believed the combination of 1891 had robbed
the government of essential revenues.[68]

In practice, the administration of Jorge Montt did not go as
far as Ross and other free-trade militants would have liked. It
raised tariffs to increase revenues and to accommodate some protectionist demands. During the panic of 1894, artisans and small
industrialists demanded higher tariffs, and in 1897, despite
Ross's opposition, the government increased duties on clothing,
furniture, lumber, and other finished goods by 36 to 60 percent.[69]
The strongest demand for protection came from cattlemen, and they
benefited from the new law; duties on imported meat rose 60 percent.[70] The drift toward protection did not mean that the elite
was abandoning its traditional orientation but that it was making
politically necessary exceptions to the general rule of cheap imports and production of raw materials for export. The bulk of
imports continued to consist of coal, textiles, and consumer goods;
machinery made up only 16.8 percent of imports in 1906 and 9.6
percent in 1910.[71]

The new tariffs did not alter the pattern of Chile's trade,
and as a result, the British continued their predominance. Each
year from 1895 to 1912, they sold Chile from 35 to 46 percent of
her imports; by comparison, Germany supplied 24 to 27 percent,
and the United States 6 to 10 percent. Their share of nitrate
exports declined as a result of a shift in the industry from
Tarapacá to the development of deposits in Antofagasta. This

change was a result of technical improvements in the Shanks system
of refining—a system that originated in England and used steam to
liquify the ore and large vats to begin the crystallization of the
salitre—that permitted exploiting the lower-grade ore in the
more southern province. Chileans, because of earlier investment
in the Antofagasta Nitrate and Railway Company and the purchase
of new companies in the Antofagasta boom, became the major exporters in the industry. Their position in the trade, however, does
not mean that they ran the industry. The British managed several
Chilean-owned companies; and they usually managed those like the
Antofagasta Nitrate and Railway Company (the province's largest
enterprise), which included both Chilean and British capital.[72]

TABLE 3.3 NITRATE EXPORTS BY NATIONALITY

(Percentage of Total Exports in Each Year)

	1895	1897	1907	1911
British	59.6%	42.4%	40.6%	25.0%
Chilean	12.7	15.6	21.0	31.0
German	8.1	13.1	19.8	23.7
Spanish	5.2	9.6	7.5	4.5
Italian	4.0	4.3	3.0	4.1
Peruvian	0	5.7	5.1	4.1
French	2.0	8.3	0.7	3.3
Austrian	0	0.7	2.0	3.9
Other	8.4	0.3	0.3	0.4

SOURCE: Fernando López Loayzo, *La Provincia de Tarapacá, 1912-
1913* (Iquique: Edward W. Muecke, 1913), pp. 70-72.

Although Chilean ships had a strong position in the national
coasting trade, Great Britain supplied the major part of Chile's
international shipping. For example, Valparaiso in 1900 handled
540,000 tons in coasting trade; of that, Chilean vessels carried
60.6 percent and British vessels 30.2 percent. But of the
845,000 tons handled as international trade at the port, Chilean
ships carried only 10.9 percent; German ships carried 27.3 percent; and British vessels carried 53.8 percent.[73] When asked to
explain the poor position of the United States in Chile, the director of Wessel, Duval and Company, a North American merchant
firm, blamed the preponderance of British shipping, and the fact
that it cost more to transport goods to Valparaiso from New York
than from London. He explained that the problem was not "a lack
of an American merchant marine" but the fact that Chilean exports
were shipped to Europe in far greater quantities than to the
eastern United States.[74]

The force of custom, and ties between purchasing companies

and English suppliers, reinforced the British position. In 1900,
the British consul in Valparaiso noted that British and German
merchant houses there were "almost equal" in importance, but consumer preference for British goods was so strong that the Germans
frequently imported them. He considered the future of British
trade secure.[75] The United States consul in Iquique complained
that the British supplied most of the coal to the nitrate factories although "American oil interests have been trying for over
three years to introduce oil as a fuel for the railway and the
oficinas." All the firms in the port were "closely connected
with London houses, and between these connections and relatives
there, they are very much compromised. This does not sound like
a business but it is the truth."[76]

If the government was not going to promote development by increasing its share of the nitrate income or reducing the nation's
dependence on foreign shipping and on imports, then it would have
to rely on private investment to do so. Jorge Montt's administration accepted the argument of fiscal conservatives that it
must create a gold peso in order to encourage domestic savings
and foreign investment. Despite the effects of the civil war,
Montt tried to accumulate the metallic reserves needed to establish a hard currency as soon as possible. In December, 1892, the
government passed new taxes to go into effect on January 1. It
raised fees on professions and licenses, property taxes, charges
for storing goods in government warehouses, import duties, and
even a tax paid on railroad tickets. It did not raise the nitrate duty, but it did sell new nitrate lands and deposited the
revenues in the reserve fund.[77]

The new imposts hurt working people, for, as one newspaper
observed, they fell "on the immense majority of people that have
to live on their salaries or incomes which it is not in their
power to augment."[78] Montt stood firm against public complaints.
In his address to Congress in 1893, he declared the "economic
situation is not unfavorable." He was determined "to end the regime of paper money . . . and in that way serve the interests of
the Republic."[79] The following year, he admitted times were bad:
the price of silver had fallen and so export earnings on that commodity were down, the wheat harvest had been poor, the value of
the peso was depressed, and businessmen had lost confidence in
the future; it did not seem "propitious to abolish the forced
currency." These difficulties, however, were "accidental and
transitory, and could be overcome or reduced by the action of the
law and the power of the State which is the financial power of
the entire nation." He insisted that he would not "abandon directly or indirectly the proposal to abolish the forced currency
and remove paper money [from circulation]."[80] He expected the
gold peso to help industrialize the country. In 1895, he told
Congress, "The security that the use of metallic money offers to
capital, protecting it from speculation and unexpected contingen-
cies, is a powerful factor in the development of new enterprises
and the expansion of those already established."[81]

The Congressional majority agreed to create a gold peso but

could not agree on its exact value, on whether it should be worth
the gold equivalent of sixteen, eighteen, or twenty-four British
pence. It finally decided on eighteen, a windfall for speculators.[82]* In 1894, before the conversion, the paper peso was
worth only eleven pence in London. From June, 1892 until December, 1893, landowners had increased the volume of their mortgages
by twenty-seven million pesos; it was clear they were borrowing
in order to buy pesos and then redeem them after conversion at
the higher rate. British merchants also supported conversion.
The higher value of the peso would make their imports more com-
petitive, and they stood to collect in gold debts that had been
contracted in paper.[83]

The period of conversion coincided with a time of economic
difficulty. The civil war, the nitrate combinations of 1891 and
1896, and a drop in copper and wheat exports all played a part in
depressing the economy. The export situation steadily improved
because of rising nitrate sales, and during the three years of
conversion, Chile's formal balance of trade was 11.6 million
pesos in her favor.[84] The production of copper and wheat employed
many more people than the nitrate industry; and they were in
trouble. Copper had steadied at half the level of exports obtained during the booming 1870s; then exports dropped from six
million pesos a year in the early 1890s to two million in 1895.[85]
A succession of poor harvests and international competition almost eliminated wheat from Chile's trade. Talcahuano shipped 1.1
million hectolitres of wheat in 1895, 414,000 hectolitres in
1899, and only 69,000 in 1900.[86]

Worse, the favorable trade balance did not reflect the flow
of profits from Chile to England. The outflow of capital from
company dividends and merchant houses, according to one estimate,
amounted to 138 million pesos in the three years of conversion.
In the same period, the government paid out over forty-six million pesos on its foreign debt.[87] Chilean records do show that
between 1895 and 1898, 849,000 pesos worth of gold went out of
the country and 20,504 pesos came in. British statistics on
trade in gold bullion and specie in these years give a balance of
834,844 pounds or 11,123,000 pesos in Great Britain's favor.[88]
By whatever estimate, Chile was sending out more than she took
in, and the government had to maintain the gold peso in the face
of this outflow.

The government removed paper notes from circulation and replaced them with gold and silver coins. During the conversion, it
issued 42.6 million pesos in gold and reduced government notes in
circulation from 29.4 million to 1.1 million. However, it did
not pressure banks to reduce their notes at the same pace; their
volume fell from 19.9 million to 17.1 million pesos. Banks apparently used their own notes to fulfill the government's reserve
requirements.[89] As investors began to export specie, the public
withdrew their gold from banks, expecting by 1897 that the gold

---

*All references to the peso, unless stated to the contrary,
are to the official value of eighteen British pence or 18d.

TABLE 3.4   BANK DEPOSITS AND BANK NOTES, 1895-98

(In millions of pesos)[a]

		Deposits	Notes in Circulation	Combined Deposits and Notes
May 31,	1895	128.4	19.8	148.2
June 30,	1895	130.5	19.5	150.0
Nov. 30,	1895	111.0	19.5	130.5
Jan. 31,	1896	113.3	19.1	132.4
June 30,	1897	96.5	17.1	113.6
July 31,	1897	40.1	17.4	57.5
Jan. 31,	1898	89.5	12.2	101.7
June 30,	1898	91.0	10.9	101.9

SOURCE: Robert Espinosa, *La reforma bancaria i monetaria en Chile* (Santiago: Imprenta Barcelona, 1913), p. 292.

[a]The peso was worth eighteen British pence.

standard would end.   From the very beginning of conversion, the government had sustained its scheme by borrowing in London through the Rothschilds: in 1895, it issued 26.6 million pesos (2 million pounds), and in 1896, another 56.8 million pesos, in bonds. The gold standard collapsed when President Errázuriz discovered the Rothschilds would not float another loan.[90]

Confidence in conversion was never very high.   Rumors circulated as early as 1896 that paper money would be reintroduced in a few months.[91]   The nitrate combination and the unemployment it caused in the north, the problems of Chile's other exports, and the decline of Chilean bonds on the London market—they fell from 94.5 in May, 1896, to eighty-five in July—contributed to the uneasiness.[92]   Foreign investors lost confidence in the bonds when, within six months after the Minister of Hacienda announced the economy of the nation was sound, four banks had liquidated.[93]   By mid-1897, hoarding of gold had so restricted financial life that the staid *Chilian Times* called the situation a depression.[94]   *El Ferrocarril* urged the government to reinstall faith in the peso by making the gold standard a part of the Constitution.[95]   The most striking aspect of the course of conversion is not that it ended but that Errázuriz held on until 1898.

On July 8, 1898, a run on the Bank of Chile forced the government to close all the banks.   A few days before, it had publicly discussed the possibility of returning to a paper currency, and this set off a panic.   On July 11, Congress declared a moratorium on the collection of debts.   The banks then reopened but rationed amounts they paid out.   According to the U.S. minister in Santiago, Henry Wilson, "The immediate effect of this unprecedented policy was the closing of all factories and establishments with large payrolls, and thousands of working men were thrown out of employment."[96]   On July 13, President Errázuriz asked Congress for "measures of a transitory nature" that would permit the issue of fifty million paper pesos. His proposal, Wilson reported, caused demonstrations in Santiago. "Among the small tradesmen, artisans and people of the working classes generally, who appear to universally favor the gold standard, and oppose with extreme bitterness an issue of paper money by the government, feeling ran very high, and, in several instances, had found expression in tumultuous and threatening gatherings." In one instance, on July 20, Wilson reported that 6,000 had marched on the President's residence, La Moneda, and demanded that the gold peso be maintained. The President blamed Congress for the situation. When the crowd turned to march on the Congressional building, it was scattered by the police. On July 30, 1898, the legislature finally agreed on a "moratorium" on the gold peso and the issue of fifty million in paper.[97]   Thereafter, Congress repeatedly extended the expiration date, so that the moratorium lasted for the next twenty-eight years.

Years later, when Chileans tired of inflation, opponents of paper currency blamed Errázuriz and the Liberal Party for abandoning the gold standard. Agustín Ross believed that "It was the triumph of the conspiracy of the friends of paper money to inundate the country again with forced currency."[98]   Others have argued that conversion failed because of a decline in public confidence, itself the result of mounting economic difficulties at home and the possibility of war with Argentina.[99]   Such explanations ignore the real reason for the failure: the government lacked the power to protect the gold peso.

The 1895 law did not give the government the authority over banks and trade required to maintain the gold standard. Gold, of course, was never the money of final redemption. Most business, throughout the period of conversion, was conducted in checks and bank note transfers. Banks used this fact and their influence in Congress to delay the incineration of their notes.[100]   Bankers and those in foreign trade treated the conversion plan as a speculative opportunity. Specie was steadily withdrawn from the economy; and in 1898, the government could no longer borrow abroad to keep the system going. Just before the moratorium was enacted, the government admitted in secret session in Congress that it had only 30,000 pesos with which to meet its obligations.[101]   Opponents of the gold standard then argued that if business failures continued at the current rate, the government's revenues would decline to the point of unbalancing the budget. Having made their profit from conversion, the upper class—and not only the Liberal Party—wanted to return to inconvertibility in order to reduce the cost of credit. Had it stood by the gold peso, the government would have risked fiscal disaster and ruined a major part of the elite.

The end of conversion was not the tragedy it seemed to so many at the time. Rising nitrate sales provided Chile with the possibility of maintaining a strong currency based on sterling

income. The banks did not regain the right to issue notes, so
now the government exercised exclusive control over the expansion
of currency. An export policy aimed at controlled growth and a
tax policy favoring the diversification of domestic production
would have maximized the benefits of the nitrate sector. But the
elite lacked the economic insight or patience to pursue such policies, and it lacked the political coherence to carry them out
even had it recognized their desirability. Government policies
instead increased inflation and the foreign debt and left Chile
as dependent on nitrates in 1915 as she was in 1891.

The duty on *salitre* exports remained the most important tie
between the government and foreign trade. The level of taxation
was unchanged; the government continued to raise exports by selling new nitrate lands; and the producers tried to raise prices by
forming combinations to restrict exports. The government sold
lands in 1894 and 1895 to back the gold peso, and in 1896 the
producers agreed to a combination that limited output to 35 percent of each factory's "productive capacity."[102] In 1900, the
pattern was reversed: a combination formed to control prices was
soon undone by another land auction. Forming combinations ceased
to be an effective tactic for producers after 1906, because new
technology rapidly increased the output from even old deposits.[103]

Throughout the early 1890s the British nitrate circle retained its predominance, but its leadership gradually divided.
Newer, more efficient companies tried to avoid entering combinations, since they could hope to profit while older companies collapsed. An influx of German capital, led by Gildemeister and Company, complicated attempts at cooperation among producers.[104] There
was also, as the directors of the Nitrate Association complained
to its members in 1898, a pronounced preference among producers
to speculate with their stocks or sell them immediately rather
than undertake the risks involved in trusting their colleagues to
hold down exports.[105] The problems of combinations increased as
producers became more ingenious at manipulating the terms of any
agreement. They would boost production just before a combination
formed in order to establish as high a "productive capacity" as
possible; they also swapped production quotas.[106] Nonetheless,
the Nitrate Association, which served as the producers' lobby in
Congress and advertised the virtues of *salitre* abroad, never
abandoned the hope of monopoly. In 1910, a government official,
in league with the Association, approached J. P. Morgan's representatives in London, hoping the New York financier would help
build a nitrate trust. Morgan expressed some interest in the
project then backed out, claiming he knew too little about the
business.[107]

In the 1890s, the British circle exercised considerable influence within Chile. Member companies jumped claims of smaller
producers, bribed officials, and filed fraudulent land titles.
John E. Franz was a typical victim of their tactics. In 1891, he
owned a small claim near Tocopilla that he tried to sell to the
Anglo Chilian Nitrate and Railway Company. Anglo Chilian refused
to buy; then, without authority, it built two factories on the

TABLE 3.5   NITRATE PRODUCTION AND EXPORTS, 1894-1915

	Factories in Operation	London Price (£/ton)	Production (1,000 metric tons)	Exports (1,000 metric tons)	Related Policy
1894	51	9.31	1,093	1,094	Government land sale
1895	53	8.14	1,307	1,237	Government land sale
1896	53	7.86	1,138	1,104	Combination forms
1897	42	7.68	1,186	1,176	Government land sale
1898	46	7.46	1,314	1,291	
1899	58	7.60	1,440	1,395	
1900	51	8.19	1,507	1,452	Combination forms
1901	66	8.50	1,328	1,258	Government land sale
1902	80	9.29	1,349	1,382	
1903	72	9.25	1,485	1,456	Government land sale
1904	76	9.76	1,559	1,498	
1905	90	10.58	1,854	1,649	
1906	96	10.91	1,822	1,727	Combination forms
1907	110	11.03	1,846	1,653	
1908	113	9.98	1,970	2,050	
1909	102	9.54	2,110	2,133	
1910	102	9.18	2,465	2,333	
1911	107	9.25	2,421	2,445	
1912	118	10.32	2,585	2,490	Government land sale
1913	127	10.58	2,772	2,735	
1914	137	10.01	3,403	1,845	
1915	116	11.39	1,755	2,020	

SOURCES: Chile, Ministerio de Hacienda, *Antecedentes sobre la industria salitrera*, pp. 13, 21, 57; Chile, Ministerio de
Hacienda, *La industria de salitre en Chile*, pp. 6-8;
and Great Britain, *Statistical Abstract for the United
Kingdom, 1892-1906*, pp. 236-37, and *1906-1920*, pp. 108-9.

land.   When Franz tried to protect his claim, Anglo Chilian tied
his case in legal knots.   It introduced witnesses to prove the
validity of its false title, and the case was heard before a
judge related to one of the company's submanagers.   He ruled in
its favor.   Franz was not even permitted to cross-examine the company's witnesses.   He then took a new legal tack and asked to
have the entire area resurveyed, but the courts refused on the
grounds that "it would be a hardship unnecessarily imposed" on
the company and would jeopardize the volume of exports.[108]   In
1895, his case was still pending appeal.   Franz, a U.S. citizen,
wrote his minister in Santiago, pleading for help, and explained,
"A friend of mine some time ago speaking to Mr. Sterling, the
Manager of the Company, asked him why the Company did not buy my
property when I offered to sell it to them and he is supposed to

have said that the company at the time was in a critical condition
and had not the wherewithal to buy and that now they are going to
keep fighting until I am worn out and leave them alone." "It is
a question of a giant against a child. The Company has a capital
of about a million sterling and I have nothing but my right."[109]

The most famous instance of British influence involved John T.
North's relation to Julio Zegers. Zegers was an important figure
in the Liberal Party, a staunch ally of Balmaceda before turning
on the President in 1888; he was an important leader of the rebellion in 1891. A London inquiry into North's affairs after his
death revealed that North and Robert Harvey had paid Zegers 100,000
pounds in the late 1880s to protect North's railway monopoly in
Tarapacá. Some of the correspondence between Zegers and North indicated that the Chilean, in protecting his client, had bribed
judges and legislators. Harvey, who became the Nitrate Railroad's
president in 1897, when asked about the evidence, replied that
Chilean standards of justice were not as high as those in England.[110] Balmacedists quickly linked the case to the origins of
the civil war and claimed that John T. North had used Zegers to
help instigate the conflict.[111]

The truth was that the law had become, as it usually does,
an instrument of monied interests. Given the frequent conflicts
over concessions and land titles, companies used Chilean lawyers
to delay the enforcement of any claim against them. They did
this both before and after the civil war. In 1896, 1905, 1911,
and 1914, there were scandals involving extensive bribery of
treasury officials, who registered claims and deeds. In one instance, the English Lomax and Company was exploiting a deposit
750 kilometers from the site of its claim.[112] A government attorney dealing in claims admitted in 1914 that Chile's laws had
little effect on the major companies; fraudulent land titles and
the false registration of factory locations were commonplace.[113]

A constant tug of war took place between government and industry over a share of the profits, which varied not only with
the market price but also with transportation costs and the technology and richness of ore deposits of each factory. Mining company statements in 1903 indicate that less-efficient companies
that year earned only 1.4 to 3.5 percent over their share capital
while the more efficient ones gained 19 to 21 percent.[114] A
long-term account of the London Nitrate Company reveals that between 1887 and 1905 it paid its shareholders in dividends and
capital returns about 420,000 pounds on an original investment of
160,000 pounds, or an average of 14.5 percent per year.[115] A
list of the dividends paid out by eleven large London-based companies between 1908 and 1910 gives a range of return from nothing
at all to 100 percent in one year; the average dividend among
them was 23.5 percent.[116]

Whenever political leaders complained of company profits,
the producers replied that their major cost was the nitrate duty.
One Chilean estimate in 1904 was that the duty represented 32
percent of the total cost of production; English producers in
1911 argued it was equal to all their other costs put together.[117]

A Chilean government study in 1925 found it was then equal to 51 percent of the production costs.[118] Although the weight of the tax was bound to vary with each company's circumstances, in general it increased over time because, while it never varied, the quality of ore being worked declined. According to Roberto Hernández, when the duty was first levied, the average content of *salitre* in the ore was 50 percent; by 1919, it was 17 percent.[119] A comparison of the nitrate duty revenues to the total value of nitrate exports reveals that the Chilean government was taking 22 to 34 percent of the total value of the nitrates as priced in London. (See table 3.6.)

The government's strategy toward the nitrate sector not only helped the elite but shielded its revenues from price fluctuations. Private capital assumed all the risks. When prices

TABLE 3.6   THE CHILEAN GOVERNMENT'S SHARE OF
NITRATE EXPORTS, 1894-1915

	Nitrate Exports (£1,000)	Nitrate Duty Revenues (£1,000)	Government Share of Total Value (%)
1894	10,185	2,802	27.5
1895	10,069	3,297	32.7
1896	8,677	2,355	27.1
1897	9,031	1,735	30.2
1898	9,630	3,334	34.6
1899	10,602	3,554	33.5
1900	11,891	3,761	31.6
1901	10,693	3,312	30.9
1902	12,838	3,400	26.4
1903	13,468	3,717	27.5
1904	14,620	3,817	26.1
1905	17,446	4,301	24.6
1906	18,841	4,513	23.9
1907	18,232	4,211	23.0
1908	20,459	5,185	25.3
1909	20,348	5,392	26.5
1910	21,416	6,030	28.1
1911	22,616	6,265	27.7
1912	25,696	6,379	24.8
1913	28,936	6,802	23.5
1914	18,468	4,928	26.6
1915	23,012	5,116	22.2

SOURCES: Chile, Ministerio de Hacienda, *Antecedentes sobre la industria salitrera*, pp. 13, 21, 57; Chile, Ministerio de Hacienda, *La industria de salitre en Chile*, pp. 6-8; and Great Britain, *Statistical Abstract for the United Kingdom, 1892-1906*, pp. 236-37, and *1906-1920*, pp. 108-9.

increased, so would production and exports; when they fell, the inability of a combination to hold exports down for more than a year or two meant exports would remain high and eventually increase. From 1901 to 1905, the London price rose 34 percent, exports 31 percent, and duty revenues 29 percent. From 1906 to 1910, the price fell 16 percent; exports, however, rose 35 percent and revenues 33 percent. (Derived from tables 3.5 and 3.6.)

The strategy had two major shortcomings: it left the structure of the industry in the hands of foreign entrepreneurs, and it encouraged the quickest possible utilization of the nation's basic resource. British entrepreneurs not only controlled a sizable proportion of the industry, they also ran its railroads and ships, and supplied its coal. Railroad charges were exorbitant, and the lines were so poorly managed that at peak periods they often ran out of cars. One of the smaller northern lines grossed an average profit of 22 percent between 1897 and 1913, and during the boom years of 1909-13 one of the larger lines, from Pisagua to Pintados, grossed 50 percent.[120] Shipping costs added 10 to 20 percent to the price.[121] Shippers, however, kept down the cost of transporting coal from England and Australia in order to have a cargo going into the northern provinces. The result was that the nitrate industry did not use Chilean coal. Chilean nationalists and domestic coal producers tried in 1903 to impose a protective coal tariff, but they failed. The nitrate companies argued that foreign coal was harder and therefore burned more efficiently while domestic coal was too expensive and its use would drive up nitrate prices and reduce exports.[122] This was true; but the "efficiency" of foreign coal was a result of lower transportation costs and the use of British equipment that had been designed to burn hard coal. Chilean coal, mined in the south near Concepción, supplied the northern copper sector with its fuel in the nineteenth century. The fact that it did not do so for the nitrate sector is an indication of the degree to which the British now monopolized the "linkages" within the nitrate trade.

Critics of the government policy focused on the foreign control of the industry and argued that the government should directly intervene in the sector to increase the internal benefits of its development. But they did not discuss the increased risks a more nationalistic policy would entail. Their general advice was to reduce speculation and create economies of scale. Alejandro Bertrand, a government expert with extensive diplomatic experience in Europe, argued against the producers' view that the industry was in a crisis in 1910. He claimed that speculators were using a temporary drop in the price as an excuse to form another combination and boost nitrate company shares. The government should prevent another combination, encourage industrial concentration, and change its tax policy to levying a percentage of company profits rather than a flat rate on exports.[123] Carlos Besa, a government attorney, went further and that same year urged the government to use its land sales to accelerate the industry's rationalization. He wanted it to limit its sales to

large companies capable of exploiting the land they purchased and
to cut out small buyers who speculated with their holdings. He
also wanted the government to construct a model factory where research could be conducted, and to improve housing and working conditions on the pampa.[124] In 1913, he suggested the state develop
a "nitrate policy" (*política salitrera*) that would include the development of new technology, more advertising, the reduction of
transportation costs, and help for the industry in meeting increased competition from "synthetic" nitrates such as ammonium
sulphate.[125]

Supporters of a more nationalistic nitrate policy proposed
in 1912 that the government help domestic capital run a larger
share of the industry. Senator Gonzalo Bulnes introduced a bill
to establish a National Nitrate Company, "the shares of which
shall be held exclusively by Chileans or foreigners resident in
Chile."[126] A similar bill was reported in the Chamber of Deputies. Under the measure, three of the seven directors would be
chosen by the President, the others by the shareholders. Bulnes
wanted the public lands at Peña Grande, which the government was
about to sell, to provide the new company's ore. The company's
stock would be divided into 1.2 million shares, worth a British
pound each. Carlos Gregorio Alvarez, Ramón Balmaceda, Carlos
Besa, Luis Barros Borgoño, Manuel Bunster, Alberto Edwards,
Javier A. Figueroa, Manuel A. Prieto, Joaquin A. Prieto, Ramón
Subercaseaux, and Luis A. Vergara, all members of the Santiago
elite or high government officials, were among its backers. But
the government, pleading that it had already promised to sell the
land, auctioned it off. It was able to sell only the southern
half of the area, and it accepted a very low bid, from Gildemeister and Company, for 5.4 million pesos (about 405,000 pounds).
The U.S. minister explained the failure of Bulnes' proposal despite the nationalistic sentiment that it aroused in the press:

> It is recognized that there are practical and constitu-
> tional difficulties in the way. Most of the successful
> nitrate oficinas are principally financed and managed by
> foreigners, and the Chilean investor prefers a foreign
> managed company. Abstractly, all agree that the great
> volume of wealth derived from these deposits should re-
> main in Chile and redound to the benefit of their coun-
> try instead of going abroad to foreign investors, but, in
> practice, the problem is not so simple. The past experi-
> ence of private Chilean companies, the miserable failure
> of Government control in the operation of the railways,
> the scarcity of capital in Chile, even if disposed to go
> into the scheme, and other considerations of a practical
> nature, irrespective of the grave question of the consti-
> tutionality of the law which would limit the right of
> ownership of shares, lead me to believe that the success
> of this project, even if it becomes a law, is doubtful.[127]

Chilean investors and the Chilean government did not believe
Chileans capable of developing the nation's major resource. Those

enterprises under Chilean management, public or private, were
inefficient by comparison with foreign industry. The harbors
were in a pitiful state, causing numerous delays in handling.
Domestic copper mining was scattered among 20,000 small mines.
Despite some experimentation with machinery and new stock, agriculture remained as primitive as ever.[128] The most startling developments in the economy consisted of the Guggenheims' development of large copper mines at "El Teniente" in Rancagua Province
and Chuquicamata in Antofagasta, the French construction of a
steel mill at "El Tofo" in Coquimbo, and experiments by foreign
capitalists in fishing.[129] The country now had 4,758 "industries," most of them small-scale and concentrated in food and
clothing. The largest were run by immigrants or their sons, and
Chilean manufacturing relied on imports to provide 34 percent of
its raw materials.[130]

The export prosperity created a boom in domestic investment,
which relied heavily on foreign capital and foreign banks and,
when it collapsed, confirmed investors' distrust of Chilean enterprises. Seven of Chile's twenty-five banks were foreign; their
capital during the boom rose 228 percent, their deposits, 175 percent. In 1906, at its height, their capital amounted to 45.6 percent of all that invested in banking.[131] New investment in enterprises (*sociedades anónimas*) jumped from twenty-seven million
pesos in 1900 to 342 million in 1905 before falling to sixty-six
million in 1907.[132] As it had been in the boom of the 1870s, the
money was concentrated in mining and agriculture, especially in
Antofagasta's nitrate factories and the development of sheep
ranching in Magallanes.[133] One of the sheep-raising companies,
the Ganadera de Magallanes, paid out a 400 percent dividend in
1903; within three years fifty new companies had formed in the
same business and with 118 million pesos in capital. After the
bust, only ten remained.[134]

The first speculative shock was a stock market slide in
March, 1905. Luis Orrego Luco has captured the illusions and
panic of that moment in his novel, *Casa Grande*.[135] But by August
the economy recovered, because, as one observer remarked, "Money
has always been plentiful." Despite anxieties over the market's
earlier downturn, "an extraordinary fever of speculation" resumed
in November.[136] By May, 1906, it was obvious that banks had
overextended themselves. Two events then finished the boom: on
August 16, 1906, an earthquake leveled most of Valparaiso, destroying the merchant houses on which Chile's trade relied, and
early in 1907, a recession began with a stock market slump in the
United States, rippled through the Atlantic economy, and drove
down the price of *salitre*.[137]

The government tried to rescue the domestic credit structure
by increasing the money supply. Three bills passed in 1904, 1906,
and 1907, authorized the creation of a 200 million pesos—they
tripled the volume of currency.[138] In order to cover this increase and rising expenditures, the government, in six years, borrowed 329.9 million pesos from foreign lenders, all but 49.3
million from the Rothschilds. The money was quickly re-lent to
landowners, who increased the value of their mortgages by 300

percent between 1904 and 1914. Heavy foreign borrowing and an increase in imports depressed the value of the peso in London to less than eight pence by December, 1907. When the Rothschilds refused to handle any more state bonds, the domestic market crashed.[139]

In those months, Chile underwent simultaneous inflation and recession. From 1906 to 1910, the cost of food in Valparaiso rose 126 percent, and all prices increased 211 percent.[140] Investors, frightened by the declining value of the peso, withdrew their capital: between 1907 and 1908, bank deposits fell from 367.6 million pesos to 94.0 million; the outflow of gold was almost twenty-two million pesos—83 percent greater than it had been in 1898.[141] The value of Chilean bonds fell, and credit remained tight until 1909. The government was unable to revive the economy until the Rothschilds opened the credit line again in 1910. (See table 3.7.)

The pattern of Chile's dependence continued to involve foreign technology and entrepreneurs, foreign transportation and raw materials, and government reliance on foreign credit. The Chilean minister in London reported in 1904 that he had gone to great pains to stay on the Rothschilds' right side.[142] In 1910, they told him that they could not take on the five million pound loan requested, explaining that "neither the political nor the financial horizon are [sic] as clear as we should like them to be." But, "If Y.E. placed the business in our hands, giving us a certain latitude, we could make a proposal which would ensure the success of the loan and at the same time not prove detrimental to Chilean Credit." Would Chile accept two or three million pounds instead?[143]

On the eve of the First World War, Chile was as firmly tied to its export economy and to foreign capital as she had been in the nineteenth century. The elite during the nitrate boom had had the choice of maintaining leverage over the size and distribution of the export income or taking the risks required to obtain leverage over the structure of the export economy. It chose to exploit short-term benefits over long-term possibilities. The charge that landowners were to blame for inflation, repeated by a United States historian of the era, was only partially true.[144] A more accurate summation is that the elite as a class—one that included hacendados—was the culprit. Anyone who controlled resources or credit stood to enhance the value of his property and position, and reduce the cost of labor, through inflation. Bankers played a major role in the process, so much so that one Conservative deputy argued, "The truth is, the banks in Chile direct our politics."[145] They repeatedly pressured Congress, first to permit them to profit from conversion, then, after conversion failed, to expand the money supply and keep them solvent. Government leaders represented inflationary interests and used inflation to satisfy the complex demands of the system they had created. The one attempt to create a stable currency had threatened the elite with bankruptcy. Thereafter, when tariff

TABLE 3.7   CHILEAN CURRENCY, FOREIGN DEBT, AND
THE PESO'S VALUE, 1894-1915

	Paper Pesos in Circulation (Thousands)	Foreign Debt in Pesos[a] (Thousands)	Peso's Value on London Market (Pence)
1894	38,361	157,684	–
1895	21,439	183,150	–
1896	12,935	238,498	–
1897	10,811	236,530	–
1898	47,173	240,934	15.2
1899	50,797	234,289	14.5
1900	50,746	229,742	16.8
1901	50,769	227,234	16.0
1902	50,395	224,667	16.2
1903	50,467	241,991	16.6
1904	54,983	219,332	16.5
1905	80,611	241,124	15.6
1906	120,412	287,034	14.3
1907	150,536	282,826	12.0
1908	150,222	278,159	9.5
1909	150,251	313,366	10.7
1910	150,323	342,875	10.7
1911	150,848	469,058	10.6
1912	170,903	465,866	10.0
1913	186,041	457,987	–
1914	224,979	449,416	–
1915	177,911	439,701	–

SOURCES: *Sinopsis*, 1925, pp. 63, 71; and Espinosa, *La reforma
bancaria*, pp. 337-38.

[a]At eighteen British pence per peso.

revenues and export income were insufficient to sustain both government expansion and private speculation, the government printed
money and borrowed against future income—that is, it mortgaged
state resources—and passed the cost to wage earners.

Of all the executives in this period, only Pedro Montt
seemed to grasp the character of Chile's economic dilemmas. He
tried to increase government spending, not only in order to rebuild Valparaiso, but to revive the domestic economy and faith in
government after the slump in 1907. He tried as well to hold
down inflation by returning to the gold standard; in June, 1909,
he vetoed another bill to postpone conversion.[146] He was the
only chief executive who worried that Chile's economic dependence
might be used against her by one of the great powers. He awarded
the contract to build the longitudinal railway in secret, and
told the Belgians who won it:

Chile gives this contract to your syndicate because
Belgium is a small country and we have no fear that any
contingency will arise that will cause your government to
take possession of our territory. We will not give it to
the Americans, or the English, French or Germans because
we do not feel certain that our territo'ry would be held
inviolate by the governments of those countries in the
event of difficulties or complications with the contracting syndicate.[147]

But Montt could not change the structure of the political
economy. His veto was overridden in Congress. He was forced to
borrow from the Rothschilds to carry out his programs and back
the credit system. The endless quarrels over patronage wore him
down, and he died of a heart attack before his term was completed. The septuagenarian Barros Luco, a man known for his con-
ventionality and whose most famous remark was that there were
only two kinds of problems, those that solved themselves and
those that were without solution, became Chile's next elected
President.

Balmaceda's reputation rose as that of the Parliamentary Regime declined. The *politiquería* and inflation eroded respect for
the existing order; people became angry and convinced that they
had been cheated of a better future. Every one of the critics of
the regime attacked its "free trade" policies. Even Francisco
Valdés Vergara, who had denounced Balmaceda as a tyrant in 1891,
in 1913 called him an economic statesman who had attempted a
nationalistic nitrate policy.[148] But the decline of public respect involved more than nostalgia. Without meaning to do so,
Palacios, Venegas, Encina, and others were using the ideology of
capitalist progress to question the basis of class rule—the
elite's reliance on foreign trade and foreign capital to sustain
the political economy.

The civil war had not resolved any of the basic issues fac-
ing the nation's political leaders except the end of presidential
predominance. Even that achievement proved expensive. The Parliamentary Regime decentralized control of elections because its
leaders thought this the best means of ending presidential rule
and because they had to justify, in more idealistic terms, the
purpose of their rebellion. The regime had not intended to extend power to other social classes, but once it had changed the
rules it became a complex and expensive task to retain power.
Worse, the elite was required to mouth the ideals of democracy as
well as capitalist progress, a dangerous practice in any society
but particularly so in one with an oppressed rural population
that was becoming urban and literate.

The nation's economic problems paralleled its political ones
because the same actors controlled the government and private sectors. The system was dynamic. The size and number of Chile's
haciendas, mines, and industries increased. No one, of course,
was willing to pay the consequences of dependence and the periodic

failures of a market economy. Given the surge in export income
and the centralized pattern of development, the inflation of land
values was inevitable, and that alone would have increased most
prices. Given the tax structure, one virtually unrelated to increases in productivity, the government had little say in the pattern of investment decisions. But the basic problem remained
that the elite was unwilling to develop a different attitude
towards either government or the economy because it did not have
any compelling reason to do so.

4.   A Portrait of the Early Left

> We have been convinced for some time not to
> have anything to do with the anniversary of
> national independence . . . which only the bour-
> geoisie should celebrate because they, who revolted
> against the Spanish crown in 1810, conquered this
> country in order to enjoy it themselves and to
> appropriate for themselves all the advantages that
> independence could bring them; but the people, the
> working class, which has always lived in poverty,
> won nothing, absolutely nothing; nor have they
> gained anything from the independence of this
> country from Spanish domination.
>
> Luis Emilio Recabarren, *Ricos y*
> *pobres a través de un siglo,* 1910

The Left began in the years between 1901 and 1915. This decade
and a half represents a new direction for Chilean society and en-
compasses a series of events more significant than the civil war.
By 1915, enemies of the civil war had become political colleagues
and class allies. But the class warfare that erupted in this
period left permanent scars. Workers confronted the government
and capitalists, and fought for control of the streets. The
state and capital won the conflict, but the war persists;
Iquique, the site of the greatest labor uprising, remains part of
the class consciousness of the militant laborer.

The word "Left," in this context, is a shorthand term for a
variety of labor associations and political factions. Workers
never united behind one banner; and their leaders were often at
odds with one another. In several respects, the struggle after
1901 was a continuation of previous social conflicts. Laborers
maintained mutual aid societies despite the ban of 1890. Strikes
that led to riots were nothing new. It is the intensity and fre-
quency of the conflicts that set the period apart from any before.
Until 1901, a militant labor movement did not exist; by 1915, however divided into competing elements, it was an established fact.

The development of the Left involves many issues: the treatment of labor, the spread of political consciousness, the size of labor associations and labor-oriented political parties, the pattern of class conflict, and the victory or defeat of labor in terms of its objectives. All of these are subordinated here to three general questions: what did the workers want? how did they fight for what they wanted? and how was their struggle related to the dependent political economy? At the outset, it is important to remember that class confrontations involved only a minority of the workers and that most of those drawn into them were not organized into either labor associations or political parties. Workers engaged their opponents in a tentative manner and, in pursuing their goals, often created loose associations at the very moment of crisis.

Established labor organizations were small and isolated from one another, unable to create a national confederation with a common program. The first class-conscious units were *mancomunales* or militant associations that began in Iquique in 1901. Membership there reached 7,000 by 1904; in Antofagasta, it was only 500. A typical organization was much smaller: only 100 of the 400 boatmen in Iquique belonged to their association.[1] Most organizations kept a low political profile. In 1902, 400 delegates from 115 mutual aid societies gathered in Santiago and held a National Labor Convention. Their first act was a resolution declaring themselves apolitical. Other conventions followed on an annual basis but they did not establish an umbrella organization or a labor party.[2]

The politics of the Parliamentary Regime, however, helped spread labor dissidence. Only a small proportion of the workers voted, but their number was increasing with the diffusion of literacy and the growth of the export economy. Those who did not vote could contribute to party coffers. Political entrepreneurs, particularly the Radicals and Democrats who had little influence in Santiago's elite clubs, saw labor as a base of the future. Some of these party leaders were labor organizers. Malaquías Concha and Luis Emilio Recabarren, the two most important labor politicians of the period, tried to create party machines that included unions and guilds. During elections, mutual aid societies often approached political factions with offers of support in return for favors.

Initially, even the most militant labor leaders hoped for little more than government reform. Abdon Díaz, the head of the *mancomunal* in Iquique, wrote President Riesco in 1904 pleading for government labor regulations to help the nation's "ragged and starving sons." Their poverty, Díaz argued, was keeping Chile from occupying "the position she merits among the independent nations of the globe."[3] In 1906, the *mancomunal*'s executive committee urged members to vote for Pedro Montt for President; he had promised to increase government spending on public works. Labor support in the north helped him get elected; and workers expected his administration would help them. As late as August 31, 1907, less than two months before the government massacred workers in Iquique, the *mancomunal* eulogized Montt as a great man, "raised to the Throne of the Presidents of Chile, carrying as his crown, the radiant aureola of fame as an outstanding statesman and, in his hand, the great, enchanting program of public projects proposed during his candidacy."[4]

Most workers were not militant. Strikes became common after 1900, but were a last resort and undertaken, as workers well understood, at the risk of their lives. To avoid repression, labor leaders, whether heads of parties or of worker associations, generally avoided direct confrontation with authorities. For example, in 1906, the leaders of the Democratic Party in Iquique disavowed any desire "to incite people to strike much less to rebel, because the workers of Tarapacá, in making any complaint to their employers, will always do so with order and respect, in that way avoiding any bloodshed."[5] Government officials, touring the nitrate region in 1904, called the workforce servile and deferential.

Nonetheless, workers, particularly those in the nitrate provinces, the principal ports, and the capital, had a definite set of expectations. They wanted what everyone else wants from capitalist development, a higher standard of living. Their expectations were based, in part, on an awareness of what organized laborers earned in more advanced nations, and, in part, on the promises made by the elite. Members of labor organizations thought they knew what they needed. They wanted an end to inflation, which they believed the government could accomplish by reducing the amount of money it printed. They also wanted government programs that increased employment, and government policies which protected manufactures with high tariffs and reduced the cost of urban living through free trade in foodstuffs. In 1897, the artisans in La Union wrote their deputy, outlining a program of national recovery from the recession of that year; their program included the construction of more railroads, an increase in tariffs on manufactures, the distribution of public funds to help small industries, and the creation of provincial trade schools.[6]

When frustrated in their expectations, laborers blamed their plight on employers' "abuses." In 1903, an Antofagasta labor newspaper endorsed "Capital" as a "powerful and magnificent entity," but made a distinction between good capitalists and bad: "We do not attack Capital considered as a major element for progress; we fight against the unscrupulous capitalists who enrich themselves through scandalous abuses."[7] A nitrate miner, in 1909, asked President Pedro Montt, "the most beloved father . . . of the Chilean people," to reduce the cost of living, improve the schools, and "prevent the abuses" that employers inflicted on "these *rotos* of Tarapacá."[8]

Expectations are a product of public consciousness; and until 1900, there was very little discussion in Chile of social issues. In the 1890s, groups of artisans, inspired by the example of European immigrants in Argentina, formed socialist and anarchist cells in several cities; but they did little more than publish short-lived newspapers and a few pamphlets.[9] Those who advocated social reforms before 1900 usually referred to rural poverty. The Radical Party advocated subdividing haciendas into small farms and financing the *campesinos* with cheap loans from the *Caja de Crédito Hipotecario*.[10] Nothing came of their proposals. Instead, European immigrants were favored over Chileans in settling the frontier.[11] Philanthropists, bureaucrats, and politicians promoted the idea of elite social responsibility. The wine magnate Melchor Concha y Toro, influenced by the encyclical, "Rerum Novarum," of Pope Leo XIII, spent 100,000 pesos in 1898 on the construction of cheap housing for working-class families.[12] Invoking the same encyclical, Alejandro Huneeus, a government official, argued in 1903 that the government should study such issues as work accidents and death benefits, the use of *fichas*, and the creation of cheap housing and popular savings banks.[13] The government later established commissions to investigate these issues, and Congress passed new laws on housing and the *ficha-salario*. But the legislation proved inadequate to the scope of the problems.

When the elite spoke of the country's progress, it referred to its own prosperity. While enlightened rule required an occasional reference to the nobility of the worker, Conservatives and Liberals continued to believe in the traditional social hierarchy. Conservatives counted on religion to teach the worker his place. In 1887, Carlos Walker Martinez idealized the *roto* as "always resigned, always with a word of faith on his lips, and in his heart the hope of a more beautiful, higher destiny."[14] In 1901, he was still issuing platitudes as social policy. "[Let there be] liberty for all the oppressed, love between those above and those below, and devotion to everything moral and holy."[15] As late as 1904, Alejandro Fariña, a Conservative essayist, justified the existing order by combining an aristocratic view of power with a Darwinian view of wealth. Rulers, said Fariña, exercise a natural and not a divine right; but all authority comes from God and they should use it as His representatives. Wealth is the result of merit, which varies from one individual to another. The poor should seek consolation in their faith and in the knowledge that he who suffers in this life reenacts a "sublime mystery."[16] Liberals did not cloak their social sentiments in piety but rather in bewilderment. Why were workers complaining when they enjoyed the benefits of unprecedented economic growth? *El Ferrocarril*, for example, could not explain the labor uprising of Valparaiso in 1903; no reason existed for "hostilities between industrialists and workers, such as occur in older European societies or the enormous enterprises of the United States, where the conditions of life are extremely difficult and niggardly."[17] The liberal establishment, as one journalist later recalled, branded those who promoted social reform as "reds, vagabonds, and anarchists . . . dangerous revolutionaries," and called their proposals "mere fads."[18]

Many politicians simply used workers to advance their careers, and, once elected, abandoned labor issues. The Radical Party included a number of reformers of the 1870s, men such as

Enrique MacIver, who by 1900 wanted to freeze social and political change. MacIver, who was also a Mason, began as a member of the Reform Club of 1868, worked his way up the ladder of the Radical Party through service on a party newspaper, and became a deputy in 1876. At one point, he served as deputy for five different areas; he was also prominent in the rebellion against Balmaceda. After 1891, he became a senator and served in several cabinets.[19] Once he was included in the inner circles of government, he turned on the labor movement, even ridiculing one modest request from workers for Congressional support for a crafts exposition. At the party convention of 1904, obviously responding to events in Valparaiso the previous year, he warned his colleagues "of a real danger for the party in helping labor movements, which is that they will not believe us because we do not represent their basic tendencies, their own aspirations, and their specific interests." He recalled that thirty years before he had taught at a trade school and discussed politics with workers—"who were then more numerous in the party than they are now"—and learned that "workers were good people and well-intentioned, but one could say of them that they do not have ideas, only necessities, and they will only fight to satisfy those necessities."[20] MacIver, and the older generation of the party he represented, had come to fear the consequences of mobilizing labor.

In general, government officials were contemptuous of labor. In 1905, President Riesco visited Iquique and ignored labor associations that had asked to meet with him; he devoted his stay to a succession of banquets sponsored by nitrate companies and foreign merchants.[21] During the uprising in Valparaiso in 1903, the intendant told strikers that they had no reason to walk out on their jobs, they were well paid. The laborers complained that they could not feed their families. In that case, said the intendant, they should not have married. Striking sailors pointed out that seamen in England and the United States were paid four to six times the rate in Chile; the intendant replied, "In England and the United States, they earn it, but here you don't because you are all a bunch of drunks and degenerates who, when you get twenty pesos, spend twenty-five."[22]

Essayists and politicians who opposed labor militancy obscured the workers' motives by referring to class conflict as the "social question." Many of them genuinely believed that legal reforms would solve the problem. Others perceived that inflation was a direct cause of strikes and riots. But none tied the pattern of confrontations to the political economy and particularly to the cycles of the nitrate trade and the government's countercyclical monetary policy. The government could not solve the chief cause of labor dissatisfaction, because its expansion of the currency was an essential means of supporting domestic capitalists. Nor could it afford to pass reforms; it feared concessions would make workers more belligerent and legitimize labor-oriented politicians. Each side of the conflict, therefore, improvised its tactics. The government and capitalists discovered that by coopting some laborers with promises of higher

wages they could prevent the success of any labor uprising.
Workers discovered that it was only by striking often and occa-
sionally raising the specter of total war that they won anything
at all.

THE SETTING FOR A LABOR MOVEMENT

Students of revolutions since Karl Marx have recognized that op-
pression and poverty are not sufficient causes of social rebellion.
Soon after he and Engels argued that workers had nothing to lose
but their chains, Marx concluded that it was precisely those laborers who had gained from a capitalist economy who would most
resent their situation.[23] This was certainly the case in Chile.
Workers organized to protect their gains from the export economy,
and demanded that the government and capitalists live up to their
progressive promises. The course of labor protest is, therefore,
intimately tied to the structure of foreign trade and the politics of the Parliamentary Regime. Economic dependence created
the conditions for the major labor uprisings; it also set social
limits on the extent of the labor movement. But protests, strikes,
and riots soon became more than a reaction to the periodic con-
tractions of trade and rapid inflation. They were also an extension of party politics: the complaints that dissident politicians
made of the Parliamentary Regime became the laborers' complaints;
the labor rebellions and the government's response to them convinced many workers of the inadequacy of the regime and turned
them against elite rule.
     Chile did not have a revolution during the nitrate era. Un-
til the First World War, even the most militant laborers continued
to expect reform. The rhetoric of class warfare appeared in the
anarchist and socialist press, but in the early twentieth century,
left-wing essayists and journalists used radical language in order
to assault the deferential attitudes of workers toward their employers. None of the labor leaders, leftist politicians, or
journalists were distinguished theorists of any kind; there is
little evidence that any figure on the Left had mastered the
tenets of either Marx or the anarchists. Their best writing consists of reminding the workers of their daily experience, of mining the vein of social resentment within capitalist development.
     The absence of revolution is easily explained: the people
were too poor, the rich too powerful. Chilean society in 1900
resembled, in many respects, that of the late colony. Most of
the labor force was rural; a major part of it, nomadic. Three to
four hundred thousand tenant farmers (*inquilinos*) traded their
labor for their rent and lived in conditions that essayists compared to serfdom. An equal number of casual laborers formed an
underclass that followed the harvests, pursued employment in the
cities and mines, and supplemented their earnings by begging and
stealing.[24] The seasonal demand for labor in the countryside
created this tendency to drift. Peons worked the central wheat
harvest from January to March, the coastal crops in October and

November, and the irrigated southern zones in March and April.[25]
This effect was reinforced in the nitrate economy by the seasonal
rhythm of production in the north as producers keyed output to the
European spring and summer. The size of the *oficinas'* labor
force varied by as much as 36 percent a year.[26] Periodic gluts
of the market caused unemployment in the north and migrations
southward. A journalist, in 1909, believed that the nitrate workers were locked into a cycle of poverty, overwork, drunkenness,
and resignation: "the *pampino* is a permanently discontented man,
at every moment wanting to change his luck."[27] Aside from Santiago, the principal urban centers remained entrepôts of foreign
trade, and therefore urban laborers engaged in such traditional
occupations as dockworkers, boatmen, construction workers, ped-
dlers, cart drivers, and domestics. The perfunctory census of
1907 revealed that Chile had more domestic servants than factory
workers and more women taking in laundry than nitrate miners.[28]

The mechanisms of elite control remained, as in the colonial
era, the monopoly of resources, particularly of land, and the
control of government. Hacendados served as municipal judges,
bailiffs, and councilmen, and could use their offices to reinforce their social authority. They also controlled the regional
markets for capital. Most *inquilinos* were tied down with debt to
estate stores, which charged 25 to 50 percent annual interest.
They saw themselves as more fortunate than drifting peons, and
often repaid their hacendados with support during elections.[29]
Employers used the general misery in the countryside to depress
all wages. When urban workers would strike, rural laborers were
frequently recruited as strikebreakers.

In addition to these formal controls, the elite also exercised a cultural hegemony. The population professed a very superstitious form of Catholicism; and the Church, with a hierarchy
chosen from the oligarchy, was a strong supporter of the existing
social order and an unrelenting opponent of liberal innovations.
Employers reinforced the loyalty of their workers by becoming
godparents to the laborers' children.[30] Other, more informal in-
fluences over the population included the importance of dress to
social station and the sharp division that existed between elite
Spanish and the laborers' dialect, with its Araucanian terms and
grammatical constructions.[31] And finally, the elite established
what was patriotic, and through its control of the press, found
it easy to label labor organizers as enemies of the republic.

The situation of the nascent left, however, was not hopeless.
While the persistence of poverty and elite authority limited the
possibilities for mobilizing the workforce, dependent development
was undermining several elements of elite control. The creation
of a national transportation network, the growth of cities, and
the migrations of the labor force gradually disrupted the isolation of the rural poor. Beginning in the 1850s, Chileans left
the countryside of the central valley for other nations, the
cities, the nitrate zones, and the southern frontier.[32] The dis-
ruption of rural patterns of deference undoubtedly helped the
formation of the labor movement. In 1910, Chile's 433 mutual aid

Salitre Production and Shipment:
A Photographic Essay

Most of the photographs on these pages cannot be identified by
time or place. Photographs 1-9 are probably from Tarapacá province before the First World War. Photographs 10 and 11, originally printed in an album of the Nitrate Producers Association in
1930 to commemorate the silver anniversary of the industry's development in Chile, were taken in the 1920s; the steam shovel is
certainly from the Guggenheim "Oficina Maria Elena" near Tocopilla.
    The production of sodium nitrate (*salitre*) involved mixing
the ore (*caliche*) with a hot leaching solution, removing the im-
purities that settled in the solution, and collecting the nitrate
crystals that had formed. Once the solution cooled and the water
was removed, the crystals took nine to ten days to dry in the
open. Until the 1870s, primitive *paradas* produced *salitre* by
heating the solution in large copper pots, then ladling it into
cooling trays. This process was replaced in the 1870s by *oficinas*
employing four key improvements. They used steam to power the
machinery that ground the ore and to heat the solution indirectly
and more efficiently. They also employed a process developed in
England, the Shanks system, that reused the same leaching solution
several times. And they stacked the processing tanks and trays in
a series of descending steps so that gravity moved the solution
through its various stages. Figure 1, the Oficina "Agua Santa" in
Tarapacá, was one of the earliest new plants.

Figure 1

Figure 2

The ore deposits were located between the coast and the Andes.
In Tarapacá, they were on the eastern side of a coastal mountain
ridge that opened to the desert plain; in Antofagasta, they were
on the western side of the sloping rise to the Andes. Mining
consisted of digging a dry well under the ore (fig. 2), placing a
charge in the well, and blowing the *caliche* to the surface.
Miners worked the resulting pits individually or in small gangs,
separating the *caliche* from the desert crust and placing it on
mules or wagons to be taken to the plant. The largest companies
built narrow-gauge railroads between their plants and mining pits.

Figure 3

Figure 4

     Living and working conditions varied enormously. The largest *oficinas* became company towns (fig. 3), where most of the laborers worked in the processing plants or in making and repairing tools and machinery. Unfortunately, scenes of the processing plants are unavailable; figures 4-5 show men in a foundry and machine shop.

Figure 5

Figure 6

Once it dried, the nitrate was usually, although not always, bagged and loaded onto trains or wagons headed for a port (figs. 6-7). There, dockworkers and boatmen placed it on small boats that then loaded it onto ships in the harbors (figs. 8-9).

Figure 7

Figure 8

Figure 9

Figure 10

　　After the First World War, *oficinas* began to reduce their
labor costs by using power tools such as pneumatic drills and by
replacing the thousands of mules and wagons with trucks (fig. 10).
The Guggenheims took mechanization to the next step by introduc-
ing steam shovels for excavation (fig. 11), new chemical processes
that speeded crystallization, and refrigeration for cooling the
solution.

Figure 11

societies had 65,000 members: the provinces of Tarapacá and
Antofagasta contained 130 societies with 12,800 members; Valparaiso
had eighty-five with 10,800; Santiago, seventy-two with 12,000; and
Concepción, thirty-nine with 5,000.[33] These six of the twenty-
four provinces, all undergoing rapid urban growth, accounted for
62 percent of the total membership. The nitrate ports and Valparaiso were also the principal bases of the *mancomunales*.

Government encouragement of the export economy involved assisting British Protestants and reducing the power of the Church.
Contact with Protestants and travel to Europe reinforced a sentiment among liberal rulers that the Church represented all that
was "colonial" and backward in Chile.[34] But even as the Liberals
gained power and limited the Church's authority, they worried
about the growing irreverence of some workers. In 1871, the intendant of Valparaiso complained that the port's expansion was
leading to a social and moral breakdown. Crass materialism, the
success of Protestant merchants, and the anonymity of urban life
were generating public disregard for the government and traditional values.[35] His anxieties became common after 1900 when officials, not known for their piety, blamed labor militance on the
decline of religion. One of the first steps taken by the anti-
clerical administration of President Montt after the uprising in
Iquique was to appoint a new bishop there and encourage the revival of religion in the north.

The enactment of electoral reforms, the spread of literacy,
and the growth of political participation, in other words the development of the Parliamentary Regime, undermined the elite monopoly of political opinion. Political leaders, especially those in
the provinces, organized labor support by accusing the government
of denationalizing the economy. When laborers created their own
newspapers, they elaborated criticisms which unhappy members of
the elite were already directing against the government. They
portrayed the nation in the grip of an oligarchy that was failing
in its nationalist role: it was selling the country to foreign
capital, importing immigrants who reduced domestic wages, and
causing an inflation that undermined economic growth and the stability of institutions.

Laborers responded to two political developments. Politicians out of power tried to recruit them into parties; and the
established parties gradually lost public esteem. Dissident politicians needed to attract a labor following because the middle
class of professionals, bureaucrats, and small businessmen was
too small to provide an adequate political base; and most of it,
by 1900, was already organized into the more conservative factions of the Balmacedists and the Radicals.[36] Balmacedists in
Iquique, unhappy with their role in the party, began Chile's first
mancomunal. And the Democratic Party was originally little more
than a collection of disappointed Radicals. A Conservative
deputy, distressed by what he called the "accident of Valparaiso"
in 1903, blamed the labor uprising on "various parties devoting
their energies to presenting themselves as defenders of the workers."[37] Political upstarts did not lead the uprising, but they

did encourage labor resentment of the government. The second factor, the persistent squabbling among elite political factions and the apparent ineffectiveness of elite government, was almost as important as the first. *El Ferrocarril* in 1905 blamed the nation's social ills on "the bankruptcy of moral authority"; "we have constantly switched from a Ministry of the Alliance to one of the Coalition and then from that of the Coalition to one of the Alliance. This constant shuffling has ruined the prestige of our leaders, led to skepticism about all political figures, and destroyed the principle of authority, indispensable to all civilized society."[38]

Workers were reacting to something more than the spectacle of *politiquería*. They were increasingly offended by government policies and drawn into the debates about the course of development. Reformers, labor leaders, and left-wing politicians mounted a steady attack on the government once it left the gold standard. No other issue was as important to the origins of the Left as inflation. "The declining value of this filthy paper," complained *La Vanguardia* of Antofagasta, "radically increases the cost of consumer goods." Inflation, it argued, was ruining the armed forces, the schools, agriculture, and almost everything and everyone but "politicians and stock speculators."[39] The increases in the cost of living fall into two periods: before and after the crash in late 1907. Prices rose from 1902 through 1905 in response to the increase in national income and the government's protection of domestic beef. The cost of meat in Iquique rose 25 percent in 1902 alone.[40] By 1905, *El Ferrocarril*, commenting on the labor uprising in Santiago, admitted that the "exorbitant price of all food items" was assuming "proportions that are truly disturbing for most families of modest means and for our working class."[41] The worst was to come. In 1906 and 1907, the government's expansion of the money supply sent prices soaring; using 1905 as a base year, the cost of food throughout the country rose an average of 55 percent, the cost of meat 90 percent, by 1907.[42] *El Trabajo*, the newspaper of Iquique's *mancomunal*, blamed "this insupportable situation" on the "decline of exchange and the immorality of wholesalers."[43] The most intense period of labor activity, that included the organization of the *mancomunales* in the north and the uprisings in Valparaiso, Santiago, and Iquique, occurred between 1901 and 1908. In these few years, the "social question" became a permanent political issue. The rate of increase leveled after 1907. As exports increased, the peso's value in London also rose. Even so, food costs were higher in 1913 than they had been six years before. (See table 4.1.)

Other government policies, each of them tied to the success of the export economy, also provoked workers. Immigration, for example, was a major issue in the north, where British company managers imported thousands of Peruvians and Bolivians and played on animosities stemming from the War of the Pacific. Peruvians often became company foremen, Bolivians were used to undercut Chilean wages, and both were employed in the company police.[44] Chilean officials also encouraged the importation of Chinese,

TABLE 4.1 FOOD PRICES,[a] 1907 and 1913

	Iquique		Coquimbo		Valparaiso		Santiago		Concepción	
	1907	1913	1907	1913	1907	1913	1907	1913	1907	1913
Lard	0.97	1.94	1.50	1.90	1.89	1.76	1.36	–	1.54	2.00
Bread	0.29	0.80	0.30	0.43	0.40	0.55	0.36	0.43	0.60	0.40
Meat	1.04	1.80	1.50	1.50	1.17	1.66	1.26	1.58	1.40	1.35
Rice	0.55	0.80	0.75	0.51	0.81	0.76	0.58	0.73	0.52	0.62
Beans	0.26	0.52	0.35	0.34	0.34	0.35	0.27	0.36	0.17	0.45
Cheese	1.74	4.36	1.80	3.00	2.33	2.93	1.85	–	2.38	2.80
Flour	0.25	0.39	0.40	0.33	0.35	0.37	0.32	0.31	0.27	0.18
Potatoes	0.15	0.38	0.20	0.20	0.07	0.23	0.10	0.21	0.08	0.18
Lentils	0.34	0.76	0.65	0.76	0.52	0.70	0.46	–	0.39	0.78
Chick-peas	1.35	0.62	0.45	0.70	0.62	0.70	0.43	–	0.36	0.50
Total	6.94	12.37	7.90	9.67	8.50	10.01	6.99	–	7.71	9.26

SOURCES: *B.O.T.*, 1907, pp. 67–75, and 1915, no. 10, p. 134;
Chile, Cámara de Diputados, *Comisión parlamentaria encargada de estudiar las necesidades de las provincias de Tarapacá y Antofagasta* (Santiago: Zig-Zag, 1913), p. 213.

[a] In pesos per kilogram.

Japanese and Italians to the north. *El Trabajo*, during one of these immigration campaigns, editorialized, "This is the word of the day. We have gringo immigrants, we have Dutch, Austrians, Italians, Japanese and Chinese; now Congress wants to bring more immigrants, My God, in what have we sinned?"[45] In their protests against open immigration, Democrats and labor leaders used racist arguments and provoked antiforeign demonstrations. In March, 1907, several thousand *rotos* demonstrated in Iquique against Chinese immigration, making it politically impossible to bring more coolies into the area. In 1911, egged on by officials who were exploiting a war scare between Chile and Peru, Chileans demonstrated and finally rioted against Peruvians; they looted Peruvian businesses in Iquique, and fear of further violence drove thousands of Peruvians and Bolivians out of Tarapacá.

Dock hands and the nitrate miners, working under British and European company managers, also complained about the *ficha-salario*. Nitrate producers insisted that *fichas* and the company store were an "indispensable guarantee against laborers paralyzing operations by walking out." Their association claimed in 1902 that the use of *fichas* was "an irreplaceable element . . . of internal order." It denied that companies were using the tokens to create retail monopolies and reduce the workers' real wages.[46] But labor newspapers presented another view, and the

ficha-salario became a major point in their campaign against
foreign control of the nitrate sector. They noted that many of
the companies' tokens did not even state a cash value; they were
worth "a pound of meat" or "a cart of ore."[47]
    Housing was another important issue. Reformers stressed the
relation between housing and the spread of disease. Their campaign was important because it created the impression that government was neglecting the people and that poor health was hurting
national development. The bubonic plague epidemics that hit the
north and Valparaiso in 1903 and 1905 reminded the public that
little had been done about housing since the 1880s.[48] Government
statistics also demonstrated that infant mortality was increasing
and the rate of population growth declining.[49] Government officials admitted a calamitous situation. One in 1911 described the
nitrate encampments as "literally dung-heaps" without sewers or
running water, frequently located near mule stables.[50] Another
report on the pampa described bachelors living two or more to a
room, while families of seven lived in two-room structures, each
with a patio that served as kitchen, washroom, chicken coop, goat
and pig shed, and garbage dump.[51] Housing in the nitrate ports
consisted of shacks constructed from scraps of lumber and old nitrate bags. For many, the situation in Santiago, Valparaiso, and
in southern cities was as bad. In 1910, an official discovered
the capital had 1,574 tenements (*conventillos*) that contained
75,030 people in 26,872 rooms, "almost all of them terribly unsanitary."[52] A large number of the capital's residents rented
tiny plots on which they raised improvised dwellings. Smallpox,
tuberculosis, typhus, scarlet fever, measles, and diphtheria were
commonplace.[53] Describing the housing in Valparaiso, the Labor
Office reported that "in the majority of the cases dwellings con-
stitute a real danger for our people." In Valdivia, a government
labor official was moved to pity the "bastards whom necessity and
misery oblige to live in these obscure *conventillos*."[54]
    Whenever the government tried to respond to popular com-
plaints, the results confirmed the general belief that officialdom
was corrupt and incompetent, and cared little about the working
poor. Officials tried in 1903 and 1904 to reform the *ficha-
salario* by prohibiting discounts, establishing clear work rules,
and permitting workers to buy goods outside the company store.
In each instance, the government was unable to enforce its own
rules.[55] In July, 1905, the nitrate producers in Iquique, in a
show of open defiance, announced a uniform policy of discounting
fichas 10 percent.[56] The system continued into the next decade;
in 1913, workers at the Guggenheim copper mine of Chuquicamata
complained of 20 to 30 percent discounts.[57]
    The Housing Act of 1906 was also a failure. Under the law,
local officials were entitled to tear down tenements and shacks.
The government promised to appropriate money for model apartments.[58] In most of the country the law was never put into effect, since landlords quickly resorted to the courts to obtain
injunctions against the demolition of their buildings. Where it
was used, as in Santiago, it proved a boon to real estate

speculators, who with the government's assistance replaced labor tenants with families of bureaucrats and professionals who could afford the higher rents on new buildings.[59] Authorities in Valdivia tried to build labor housing and drew up plans to do so, but their first major project in 1911 required 200,000 pesos, and the central government had given them only 75,000 for the task.[60]

Most government regulations of working conditions and public morals turned into attacks against the working class. Laws enacted in 1901 and 1902 tried to reduce alcoholism by punishing drunks with jail and heavy fines and by preventing the sale of liquor near churches, schools, jails, military barracks, and hospitals. The punitive measures against drunks were enforced; those against distributors and retailers of liquor were delayed. When the regulations on selling liquor went into effect in 1905, one newspaper noted, "Nobody in authority remembered that such a law existed in the first place."[61] A measure to prohibit child labor in 1912 punished parents who put their children out to beg, permitted them to become vagrants, or had them work in amusement centers or prostitute themselves; but it said nothing about employers or labor contractors.[62] One law, the Sunday Rest Act, was directed against employers. Passed in August, 1907, by 1911 it led to so many infractions that the government declared it "futile" to try to enforce it. The intendant of Santiago admitted to two or three thousand denunciations of employers under the law, of which his office had prosecuted only twenty or thirty cases.[63]

Labor organizers began their efforts in the areas that were most important to the elite and to foreign entrepreneurs. Strikes in the nitrate provinces, Valparaiso, and Santiago threatened the lifelines of the economy. The government was particularly intimidated by railroad strikes because they disrupted the flow of goods to the capital and could not be broken by unskilled *peones*. Moreover, workers in these areas were open to new ideas and possibilities. They saw their strategic importance. They saw the wealth generated by the nitrate prosperity: the new mansions in Santiago and Valparaiso; the chalets of the British company managers in the north. They were exposed to foreign ideas. The nitrate provinces and Valparaiso contained the largest numbers of immigrants. And the literacy rates in these areas were higher than in other provinces.[64] It is likely that the dynamic economic centers attracted a high proportion of the ambitious, those who had a dream of owning their own farm or their own store.

Workers in these areas also drew on a long tradition of labor associations. Dockworkers in Valparaiso developed guilds as early as the 1830s; there were mining guilds in the northern provinces by the 1860s.[65] When the nitrate industry developed, Chileans transferred their guilds to Peruvian and Bolivian territories. These organizations played an important role in protecting them from hostile governments.[66] Even after the ban of 1890, informal organizations persisted among the dockworkers, and Chilean officials came to recognize them in practice if not in law.[67] The labor movement grew quickly in the north after 1900 because organizers built on this tradition and because dockworkers,

miners, and artisans had the means to support their own
associations.

In general, the best-paid workers—the nitrate miners and
artisans—were the ones who organized. Artisans remained the
most important group within the labor movement in Santiago and,
next to the dockworkers, the most important in Valparaiso as
well. Factory workers were not well organized. Although their
wages in the capital and Valparaiso were relatively high, the
higher cost of living reduced their purchasing power so that the
value of their wages was often no greater than in more isolated
cities. In Magallanes, a small but extremely militant movement
developed among dockworkers and ranch hands; wages were high and
prices low. The situation in that province, however, was complicated by the large number of Argentines there and the radical
labor tradition they brought with them. Unfortunately, the government did not collect unemployment statistics. Labor newspapers
surveyed employment prospects in various towns and found it was
easier to obtain a job in the major cities than in the countryside, and easier in Valparaiso and Santiago than in the outlying
centers.[68] Government statistics demonstrate that the wages of
miners and urban workers were uniformly higher than those of
inquilinos and *peones*. (See table 4.2.)

Data collected by the Labor Office provide some idea of how
labor families in different regions spent their income. The information in table 4.3 represents only seventy-three families;
and the questions asked and information collected varied from one
survey to another. Still, the results support a few broad but
important generalizations. Workers on the nitrate pampa and at
the copper mine "El Teniente" enjoyed the highest incomes in the
country and paid nothing for their housing. One government report indicated that in large cities and mining areas, workers increased their consumption of meat.[69] It is clear that they spent
more on food than those in the rural province of Chillan. Where
the reports indicate fuel expenditures, it seems that coal and
kerosene consumed 10 to 15 percent of a family's income. Workers
did not spend much on housing; perhaps after paying for their food
they had little left. Or perhaps they retained a rural attitude,
derived from the traditional provision of a shack by hacendados,
that it was unimportant. In any event, they often spent more on
clothing than on rent. Clothing, obviously, remained an important indicator of social station.

A large proportion of labor families, even of those in the
nitrate provinces, remained extremely vulnerable to any downturn
in the economy. Labor newspapers generalized that the average
wage was sufficient to support a bachelor but too small to sustain
a family. Information collected by the Labor Office on family
budgets (not included in table 4.3) indicates that larger families
were not making ends meet. Those families with four or more children, some 38 percent of the total sample, must have been frequently in debt; 61 percent of them spent more than they earned.
Only 30 percent of the families with fewer than four children could
not balance their budget. In all, 41 percent of the families

TABLE 4.2 NOMINAL AND REAL WAGES IN CHILE, 1907

Province[a]	Nominal Wages			Combined Price of 14 Items	Workdays Required to Buy 14 Items		
	Artisans	Miners and day laborers	Rural laborers		Artisans	Miners and day laborers	Rural laborers
Tarapacá	8.20	5.71	—	15.26	1.86	2.67	—
Antofagasta	8.03	4.80	—	19.35	2.40	4.03	—
Atacamá	4.96	2.27	1.75	15.09	3.04	6.64	8.62
Coquimbo	4.16	2.22	—	13.43	3.22	6.04	—
Aconcagua	4.72	2.43	1.39	12.86	2.72	5.28	9.24
Valparaiso	5.49	2.59	—	14.72	2.68	5.68	—
Santiago	4.87	2.45	—	14.12	2.89	5.76	—
O'Higgins	5.27	2.06	—	12.78	2.42	6.20	—
Colchagua	5.14	2.58	—	15.59	3.03	6.04	—
Curicó	4.71	2.21	—	11.33	2.40	5.12	—
Talca	4.38	2.14	1.10	12.65	2.88	5.91	11.50
Linares	3.80	1.73	1.18	8.63	2.27	4.98	7.31
Maule	2.97	1.29	1.47	11.05	2.84	5.58	7.51
Ñuble	2.72	1.55	0.63	9.13	3.35	5.89	14.49
Concepción	3.88	1.98	—	11.05	2.84	5.58	—
Arauco	3.62	1.65	—	9.15	2.52	5.54	—
Bío-Bío	4.54	2.37	—	9.44	2.07	3.98	—
Malleca	5.49	2.50	1.66	9.04	1.64	3.61	5.44
Cautín	3.89	2.19	—	9.80	2.51	4.47	—
Valdivia	4.41	2.33	—	7.62	1.72	3.27	—
Llanquihue	5.36	2.09	—	9.30	1.73	4.44	—
Chiloe	6.95	2.31	1.50	9.70	1.39	4.19	6.46
Magallanes	7.33	4.00	—	8.05	1.09	2.01	—

SOURCE: *B.O.T.*, 1907, pp. 43-46, 67-75, 79-82.

[a]No data for Tacna Province.

admitted their expenses exceeded their incomes. This is
significant because falling into debt was a calamity. Banks did
not lend to laborers. Pawnbrokers did; and before a change in
the law in 1898, they could charge anything they liked—some demanded 120 percent a year. Thereafter, the government limited
their interest to 48 percent a year.[70] In 1914, they gained
twenty-one million pesos on loans of forty-two million; by comparison, the *Caja de Crédito Hipotecario* earned only twenty-
eight million pesos on loans of 402 million.[71] One can only
imagine the anger of a laborer who migrated to a more dynamic
economic center in order to make his fortune and ended on a
treadmill of debt to a pawnbroker or the company store.

TABLE 4.3 WORKING FAMILIES' AVERAGE MONTHLY
INCOME AND EXPENSES, 1910-12

	Family Budgets		Distribution of Expenditures				
	Income[a]	Expenses	Food	Housing	Fuel	Clothing	Other
Oficinas-Tarapacá	272.6	264.3	62.1%	–	12.1%	15.8%	10.0%
Iquique	252.4	269.8	53.1	10.7%	–	21.1	15.1
Copiapó	164.3	171.7	61.5	10.2	–	13.7	14.6
Valparaiso	203.7	214.7	56.8	13.9	–	12.5	16.8
El Teniente-Rancagua	411.3	315.0	67.8	–	10.0	15.5	6.7
Chillán	133.1	113.7	40.8	8.5	–	16.7	34.0
Concepción	152.4	150.6	49.4	6.8	–	14.2	29.6

SOURCE: *B.O.T.*, 1911, no. 2, pp. 44, 54; 1911, no. 3, pp. 12, 33;
1912, no. 1, pp. 87, 235; and 1912, no. 4, p. 56.

[a]In pesos.

The nucleus of the Left began within three types of organizations: the *mancomunales* of the north, the anarchist resistance
societies of Valparaiso and Santiago, and the socialist faction
of the Democratic Party. All of them organized in the years
1901-4, in the wake of the first major wave of price increases
and the aftermath of the cutback in nitrate production caused by
the producers' combination. Activists were often involved in
two kinds of organization. Recabarren headed the left-wing Democrats and organized *mancomunales*. Anarchists joined the *mancomunales* when their own resistance societies began to weaken.
All organizations had similar concerns. In 1903, the Recabarren
Democrats proposed a new program for the party, and it illustrates the range of demands on the Left. It starts with the
usual list of Democratic reforms: laws to protect civil liberties, to establish the public initiative and referendum, to

increase the number and improve the quality of public schools, and to develop more trade schools. But the socialists also wanted statutes that would prohibit child labor, establish the eight-hour day, the six-day week, work accident insurance, safety and hygenic codes for factories and mines, and profit sharing—and that would end the *ficha-salario*. They insisted the government should stop inflation, provide credit to small businesses, reform the judiciary, and assist the generation of guilds, unions, mutual aid societies, and savings cooperatives.[72]

In brief, many leaders on the Left wanted to become partners in the development of the country. Explaining their goals, the organizers of Iquique's *mancomunal* declared:

> The workers' resistance societies are not, then revolutionary cells, created in order to bring anarchy to society and detain the industrial and commercial drive of the country. Their mission and purpose obey the highest ideals: they are inspired by the most just of sentiments, and their banner is none other than liberty and mutual respect.[73]

The government and capitalists were not about to recognize labor as a partner. As the early uprisings demonstrate, the establishment was genuinely offended at the suggestion. The history of the early Left, therefore, consisted of petitions that became strikes, strikes that became riots, and riots that produced martyrs.

THE LABOR UPRISINGS

The mass uprisings at Valparaiso in 1903, Santiago in 1905, and Iquique in 1907 crystallized class confrontation. They demonstrate the weaknesses of labor parties and organizations and the dilemmas of dependence which the workers, like the government and capitalists they opposed, only dimly perceived. Workers and their spokesmen saw that they were losing income because of inflation; many recognized the role foreign investors were playing in reducing real wages; but no one on the Left recognized how thoroughly the most prosperous sectors of the labor force were tied to the export economy. The movement's leaders resented foreign capital but offered no alternative export strategy as the basis of their activities. They disliked the political system but could only hope that the system would respond to their repeated pleas for reform.

Part of the movement's problem was that it lacked any figure capable of combining a sound strategy for political mobilization with a coherent analysis of the economy. It lacked intellectual orginality; in fact, it often lacked ideas. Peter De Shazo provides an account of the origins of anarchism and the early anarchist leaders and demonstrates that none of the major and only a few of the minor European anarchists and anarcho-syndicalists came to Chile. Native artisans headed anarchist associations and, although they were the most aggressive element of the Left, they derived their views as much from liberal free thinkers as from Proudhon or Bakunin. Their strategy was simple: they would form resistance societies, infiltrate the mutual aid societies with resistance members, threaten strikes or carry them out in order to improve wages and working conditions, win over new followers as a result of their victories, consolidate their support within the working class as a whole, and then overthrow the capitalist system. A general revolutionary strike would bring down the state and its supporters. In practice, the resistance societies were small (some with as few as twenty members), poorly financed, and short-lived; they began in 1901 but state repression and black lists destroyed them by 1904.[74]

The *mancomunales* and the socialist Democrats also advocated a more combative stance than was current among mutual aid societies. Some of the socialists, such as Recabarren, shared the anarchist view that the state would be vulnerable to a general strike. They differed from the anarchists in insisting that the movement should try to alter government policies rather than abolish the state. Instead of infiltrating organizations, they tried to group existing guilds and mutual aid societies into federations that would provide a collective leadership for the workers in each area.

Like the anarchists, the *mancomunales* and socialist Democrats lacked the money and members to change the political balance in any region. They also found it difficult to combine the development of associations that fought for wages and benefits with efforts to win elections. Recabarren was elected to the Chamber of Deputies in 1906, but he was an exception—usually leftist candidates lost. He became a celebrity on the Left in 1904 when the government in Tocopilla closed his newspaper, suppressed the *mancomunal* that supported him, and threw him into jail without trial. But his fame did not secure his position; his opponents in Congress called him a jailbird and expelled him when he refused to take a religious oath required to be seated. Recabarren's career is typical of the socialists in one respect: he spent more time creating and running newspapers than mobilizing laborers for strikes; his electoral campaigns removed him from the struggle in the workplace.[75]

Differences in ideology and party identity divided the Left into competing organizations. At one end of the political spectrum, the socialist Democrats vied with socially conscious Balmacedists and Radicals and with nonsocialist Democrats for the labor vote. The Radicals managed, in the first decade of the twentieth century, to consolidate a patronage machine in several northern cities and used their power to cut out competitors. A Radical judge issued the arrest warrant served on Recabarren in 1904. Recabarren also quarreled with Malaquías Concha, a lawyer and head of the Democratic Party, who believed that politics alone would solve labor issues. At the height of the Santiago uprising, Concha told laborers that "honorable suffrage" was the Democrats' principal weapon; that "a republican nation which enjoys suffrage has only to use its right to vote in order to change its institutions and laws."[76] The arguments between the two Democratic factions reached the break point in 1912, when Recabarren left to form the Socialist Workers Party (*Partido Obrero Socialista* or *POS*). On leaving, Recabarren denounced Concha as a "dictator," an "agent of the bourgeoisie," and a "political auctioneer who has sold the party to the highest bidder and has taught us servility, degradation, and civil, economic and social corruption." The Concha Democrats called Recabarren "the renegade of Iquique."[77]

At the other end of the spectrum, the socialists often fought with anarchists. Recabarren believed that anarchists were misleading the working class. He argued that only a socialist movement could defend labor: "I do not believe there is any camp other than the right organization for enrolling the army of the revolution, which, in possession of an exact understanding concerning our direction, must march to the conquest for future happiness."[78] Anarchists urged workers not to bother with politics and even to withdraw from the Democratic Party. But the differences within the Left were as much the result of personality, or perhaps more accurately of the political territoriality of the various leaders, as of ideology. The leaders built personalistic organizations and resented one another as competitors within a limited market. Abdon Díaz tried to control the *mancomunales* of Tarapacá; Recabarren to dominate the left in Antofagasta province; and Magno Espinoza, the hero of the early anarchists, to dominate the movement in Valparaiso.

Leftists, therefore, lacked a battle plan for any of the major confrontations. The uprisings at Santiago and Iquique seem to have completely surprised the movement's spokesmen. Recabarren was not present at any of them. In each instance, laborers rebelled in order to defend their real wages. In each instance, government repression was followed by a campaign of "white terror" against labor organizations and organizers. The elite became afraid of civil insurrection, but the victims were workers. At the end of this cycle of rebellion and repression, only the railroad workers had gained any appreciable leverage within the political economy. The dockworkers, miners, and day laborers, who led the most militant efforts, gained some concessions and a profound understanding that such uprisings would not change the distribution of income.

The government settled most conflicts by force. When workers in Iquique struck in December, 1902, the local judge confiscated the funds of the labor societies involved.[79] When dockworkers in Tocopilla walked out early in 1904 to protest the conduct of their foremen, General Silva Renard, military chief of the nitrate zone, arrived with a battleship full of marines and threatened to shoot anyone who did not return to work.[80] Government officials as well as employers maintained black lists. The government defended its conduct, whenever it felt the need to justify it, by invoking its duty to protect the rights of nonstrikers to work and to preserve public order.

Divisions within the labor force reduced the effectiveness

of strikes. The *mancomunal* of Tocopilla supported the aforementioned strike, but nitrate miners, although many were members, did not join it. Merchants and shippers used sailors to load their *salitre*, and after three weeks, the dockworkers gave up. Four weeks later, the miners at eight *oficinas* walked out, but their efforts lacked support from the dockworkers.[81] Workers were divided even within the same workplace. In April, 1905, the boatmen and cargo handlers in Iquique's harbor struck, but day laborers and stevedores there kept working, and as a result the strike failed.[82] In Tarapacá province, of course, the workers were also fragmented into competing nationalities.

In spite of these divisions, the laborers in the foreign trade sectors, especially those in the north, became increasingly militant after 1900. In December, 1900, dockworkers at Iquique walked out on the merchant firms and stayed out until the following February. Employers broke it by bringing shiploads of recruits from Valparaiso.[83] For the next two years dockworkers staged strikes each December, hoping to gain higher wages by disrupting trade during the peak period of exports.[84] So labor militance preceded the creation of *mancomunales;* the first *mancomunal* built its following among already resentful workers. Resentment rose with each price increase: there were three strikes in the nitrate provinces in 1901 and thirty-one in 1907; the same pattern occurred in the central cities—there were eight strikes in Santiago and Valparaiso in 1901 and thirty-one by 1906.[85]

All three of the major uprisings were preceded by sectoral strikes and campaigns by labor for government help against inflation. The strikes at Valparaiso and Iquique began among the dockworkers and followed a course reminiscent of events in 1890. The confrontation in Santiago began as a consumer protest over rising meat prices. But the obstinance of officials and employers left labor leaders without an alternative to mass action and to the desperate gamble that it would force the government and capitalists to make concessions.

A strike at Iquique a few months before the uprising at Valparaiso colored the official reaction to the latter event. On December 26, 1902, dockworkers in the nitrate port struck, demanding the British stop recruiting Peruvians and Bolivians, the merchants stop discounting *fichas*, and the railroad company roll back a recent fare increase.[86] In Santiago, Malaquías Concha, with his eye on the Congressional election, committed the Democrats to backing the workers. But government repression broke the strike after several weeks, and officials concluded that repression was sufficient to handle any outburst.[87]

On April 15, 1903, the boatmen, sailors, and day laborers of Valparaiso asked intendant José Alberto Bravo for help in their disputes with employers. They objected to the *ficha-salario*, to working conditions, and to the shipping lines withholding the back pay of sailors. They wanted the intendant to appoint a committee to review their grievances and to include two figures sympathetic to labor: Admiral Arturo Fernández, the maritime governor, and Anjel Guarello, a socialist Democrat. The merchants, shippers, and labor contractors rejected arbitration and forced the removal of Fernandez from his post. On April 17 the sailors struck the British-owned Pacific Steam Navigation Company, hoping to use the issue of foreign control to intimidate the company into granting higher wages, and then to use their victory as the new wage base in dealing with domestic lines.[88] The Democratic newspaper pledged full support for their "cry of rebellion."[89]

Bravo first tried to divide the strikers, then wear them down. On May 7, he succeeded in persuading the shippers to give sailors their back pay. The sailors returned to work but only after shippers promised not to use them to handle cargo. Bravo promised a commission would arbitrate the remaining disputes but he refused to appoint Fernandez or Guarello to it. The strikers rejected his offer. Then, three days after the sailors returned to work, the shippers began using them to unload cargo. This created the final confrontation. On May 10, Bravo met a labor crowd that insisted that their understanding with the shippers be enforced, and told it that labor associations lacked any legal standing and that "the seamen were making use of their right to work." On the 11th, the strike committee told Bravo that unless the sailors stopped unloading ships, the committee members would go home and cease to be responsible for what workers might do next. Bravo replied that they would be held responsible for any disturbance of the "public order . . . that this was a responsibility they could not escape."[90]

The intendant had kept the police on alert throughout the strike, and when it continued, he increased their presence on the docks. He also had 550 marines on reserve. Workers began their protest on the morning of May 12 in front of a domestic line, the South American Steamship Company. When some of them tried to prevent the unloading of a vessel, the chief of police fired into the crowd and killed a demonstrator. The crowd then rallied in front of the intendant's building, only a few minutes away, and demanded justice for the victim. Bravo told the workers that he would "maintain public order"; he managed to escape the building as the demonstrators began throwing rocks.[91] Some of the strikers started looting the downtown. Others attacked the merchant newspaper, *El Mercurio*; journalists and editors shot several of them and drove them off. Finally, the laborers looted the South American Steamship Company, and while marines either looked on or joined in the looting, they burned the company's building to the ground. They knew exactly who they were attacking: *El Mercurio* and the steamship line were owned by the Edwards clan, the English merchant family whose descendants now dominated the Conservative Party. The workers had control of the streets until the evening when troops arrived by train from Santiago and, after a series of battles that lasted until 2:00 in the morning, established government control.[92]

The most important difference between the events of 1903 and those in 1890 was the aftermath of the riot. In 1890, the government had suppressed the strike and not encountered serious political opposition to its actions. In 1903, Democrats and socially minded Radicals denounced the government's conduct. One of the Radicals, Fidel Muñoz, argued in Congress that the government had known the basic issues of the strike for some time before the riot and had done nothing until it was too late.[93]   The Democratic paper in Valparaiso, *La Voz del Pueblo*, denied Bravo's allegation that "agents from Buenos Aires" were behind the riot.   The majority of Valparaiso's municipal council were Democrats and Radicals, who voted to provide financial relief to the families of the 100 killed by the government. Labor societies and the Democratic Party also took up private collections for these families and those of the wounded. The council's generosity provoked the city's mayor, Gustavo Ross, to denounce the strikers as "bandits" and lament that another fifty had not been killed; he favored aid for the South American Steamship Company.[94]   Ross notwithstanding, the labor movement now had some political support and public sympathy, and the government decided to settle the strike through binding arbitration.[95]

At the same time, the authorities took steps to prevent any further labor mobilization. In Valparaiso, they created a special unit within the secret police to deal with organizers; and they began requiring permits to hold public meetings. Laborers now found it impossible to assemble. For example, Silva Fernandez, Secretary-General of the General Confederation of Workers, decided to call a meeting in Valparaiso for December 6, 1903, but Fernandez Blanco, who had replaced Bravo as intendant, banned the assembly, saying he had to preserve "public order," that such a meeting was necessary, and that workers could petition officials for public redress of any wrong.[96]   The government's apprehension extended to the nitrate zone. When thirty workers at an *oficina* in Taltal requested a raise of twenty-five cents per cart of ore, the company administrator had troops put them on a ship headed south, without their goods or back pay.[97] Early the following year, officials in Tocopilla began their persecution of Recabarren. The persistent repression helps explain why the next revolt took place in Santiago rather than in a port.

In the winter of 1905, Democrats and labor leaders in Santiago began a campaign against the tariff on imported meat. In his analysis of their efforts, Thomas Wright found that the anti-tariff forces had greatly simplified the issue. Chile relied on Argentina to supply a major part of her beef, but she protected domestic cattlemen with a high duty established in 1897. Meat prices rose each winter as bad weather reduced the flow of cattle over the Andean passes, and in 1905, all food prices were increasing as a result of government monetary policies. The Democrats, however, tried to present the issue as simple cause and effect, arguing that if the tariff were ended, meat prices would fall. They gained some support from meat retailers in the capital who feared that the high prices and the fall in demand would put them out of business. Opponents of the meat tariff organized committees in Chile's principal cities.[98]

These committees scheduled simultaneous protests for Sunday, October 22. In Santiago, they drew a crowd that my sources estimated at 12,000 to 25,000. Wright gives a higher estimate of 30,000 to 50,000.[99] The rally against the duty led to a riot in the capital, and on October 22 and 23, looters sacked shops along the central Alameda and in the business district. The army was out on maneuvers. The elite gathered at the Union Club on October 23 and organized 300 upper-class youths into a militia. They, along with the city's police and firemen, repressed the workers through indiscriminate terror, killing at least 300 and wounding 1,000.[100]

Wright provides an excellent description of the repression, but his discussion of the causes and consequences of the uprising is inadequate. An analysis of the politics of the meat tariff is an insufficient basis for understanding why the riot took place, and for comprehending the "politics of inflation." There were demonstrations at other cities and they ended without violence. The campaign against the tariff began in September and coincided with a long strike by streetcar employees. When the riot began on October 22, workers directed most of their energy to burning streetcars and tearing down utility lines; they destroyed thirty cars and wrecked the lines for the entire length of the Alameda. It was on the second day of rioting that workers turned on the business district. In other words, the riot resulted as much from the strike as from the consumer protest.[101]

The more serious shortcoming in Wright's work is his discussion of the consequences of the uprising. He points out that the peso's declining value set the stage for events in 1905 and then abandons any analysis of the exchange rate to explain what happened after that year. By 1909, in his view, the Democrats and northern Radicals had become less concerned with the meat issue, and "this reflected disillusion after years of campaigning over the inconclusive results of the duty's suspension."[102] However, his own tables show that meat and other food prices in 1909 were very close to their 1907 level; the rate of inflation had slowed dramatically. Prices stopped rising because increasing nitrate exports had increased the peso's value and stabilized the cost of consumer imports. At the same time, Montt's construction program increased employment and wages in the central valley.

Wright's work aside, the controversy over the tariff on meat illustrates the Democrats' politics of distribution. Malaquías Concha played a major role in the antitariff campaign; although, once workers took matters into their own hands, he tried to dissuade them from violence.[103] Recabarren also opposed the tariff and argued Chile could not produce beef as cheaply as Argentina, and therefore "we should desist from trying to develop the industry in this country."[104] Like the elite, those who represented organized labor wanted the government to reduce their cost of living at the expense of other domestic groups. The Democrats believed a lower tariff would reduce the cost of meat at the expense of the cattlemen. This was far from a certainty. Distributors did not have to pass savings on their costs along to consumers. Higher consumption of imported meat would have been a drain on the

balance of trade; and a negative trade balance reduces the value
of domestic currency and tends to raise prices. There were more
rural laborers than workers in the cities; and higher rural unemployment as a result of imported food might depress wages everywhere. But those who argued against the tariff appealed to the
organized minority of the urban workforce. Its members did not
raise cattle or imagine that they would ever find such employment; rural workers did not vote Democrat.

The pattern of social conflict and elite concession was clear
by 1905. The elite would resist making any concession until
popular violence forced it to do so, and then it would give in on
an immediate labor objective. It retained political control and
an ability to reverse or modify its concessions. In 1903 the
dockworkers of Valparaiso won arbitration of their dispute, and
in 1905 the government suspended the meat duty. These were relatively poor gains to show for 400 or more dead. The elite had
not conceded either the rights of workers to organize or broader
political participation. The pattern was repeated in the important railroad strikes that followed the Santiago meat riot and
preceded the revolt in Iquique.

On February 6, 1906, dockworkers and railroad men in the
port of Antofagasta struck over their lunch hour. They wanted it
extended from an hour to an hour and a half. The regional nitrate
boom and the sharp increase in rents it generated forced workers
away from the inner city; they wanted more time to go home to eat.
The merchants gave in, but the Antofagasta Nitrate and Railway
Company refused. It could run its trains because the engineers
and firemen had remained at work.[105] On Tuesday, February 7, the
strikers marched through the center calling on workers to join
their movement. They now wanted a longer lunch and a 20 percent
wage increase. The intendant Carlos Merino Caballo organized his
marines to put down the strike and armed the members, most of
whom were Balmacedists, of the local Union Club. That evening,
the marines and militia fired on laborers during a rally. The
government estimated thirty dead; laborers thought 120 were
killed. The crowd retaliated by setting fire to the central district. Results of the strike were mixed: the railroad men
failed in their objectives but wages throughout the city subsequently rose 20 to 30 percent.[106]

The next railroad strike was more successful. On May 27 and
28, 2,500 shopworkers on the central line of the state railway
walked out in Valparaiso, Talca, Concepción, Calera, and San
Rosendo. They demanded to be paid in "gold pesos" of eighteen
British pence, worth twice the exchange value of the paper peso.
They also wanted a ten-hour day. By the first week of June, the
strike spread to engineers and firemen and the line was paralyzed.
Then streetcar workers in Santiago and Valparaiso struck and tied
up both cities; they demanded better pay, shorter hours, and an
end to immigration. A frightened administration agreed to pay
the railroad men in pesos worth seventeen pence, to establish the
ten-hour day, and to forgo reprisals.[107] The settlement did not
stop the strike movement. On June 15, sailors in Valparaiso and

—an astonishing event—washerwomen in Santiago demanded better wages. Authorities broke the sailors by declaring a state of siege in the port. The railroad men kept their wage increase, but management fired the strike leaders.[108]

All of this was prologue to the uprising in Iquique. On the one hand, the government had consented to the railroad workers' demands. The *mancomunal* in Iquique admired their victory and their idea of demanding pay in pesos worth eighteen pence.[109] On the other hand, the government was more apprehensive than ever. In addition to the strikes, laborers demonstrated at Iquique in May against immigration. The government promised to reduce the rate of new arrivals. But labor leaders were slow to draw the obvious conclusion that the success of the railroad strike and the increasing militance of laborers in all major cities had raised the stakes in any future confrontation.

Many of the northern organizers believed that, because they had helped elect him, President Montt was on their side. In November, 1906, the Iquique *mancomunal* greeted the arrival of Carlos Eastman, Montt's choice as intendant, with unrestrained optimism: "We believe this is the beginning of a new era in the welfare of the people of Tarapacá." In early December, 1907, it blamed "the Parliament of the Republic" for "all the evils that have befallen us. The villainous representatives of this country have obstructed the progressive efforts of President Montt. The parliamentary orators, Jews, and businessmen are the only ones responsible for the crisis the nation is now enduring."[110]

Tarapacá was certainly in crisis. At the beginning of December, the exchange value of the peso fell to a new low. Nitrate speculators were abandoning the province for Antofagasta. Banks refused to quote the value of notes covered by nitrate stockpiles; no one, therefore, could get loans. To protect their investment in consumer goods, nitrate companies and merchants raised their prices from 20 to 50 percent.[111] These price increases triggered the uprising.

On December 7 the cargo handlers on the docks struck, demanding wages in pesos worth sixteen pence. Day laborers at the merchant firm of Gildemeister and Company joined the strike two days later; they insisted on pesos of eighteen pence. The next day, the miners at the *oficina* "San Lorenzo" walked out with the same demand. José Briggs, a miner and the son of a North American artisan, became the nitrate workers' spokesman. Briggs headed a committee which recruited strikers at other *oficinas*. His objective was to rally in Iquique for a general strike. On the weekend of December 14-15, 5,000 strikers and their families entered the city.[112]

On Sunday, December 15, the Briggs committee joined the various strike groups and the *mancomunal* within the port and formed the Central Committee of the Pampa and Iquique. Briggs became its president; Nicanor Rodriguez was its secretary; other members were Carlos Jimenez, Luis Olea, Oscar Sepulveda, and Miguel Zenteno. They held a rally at midday and drew up their demands to the government and employers: end the *ficha-salario* and establish the eighteen-pence peso, safety measures at the *oficinas*, more public schools, honesty among foremen and labor contractors, and amnesty for all strike leaders. A crowd of 6,000 then went to the intendant's building, presented their list, and thanked the intendant's secretary for not having had the police attack their demonstration.[113]

The secretary, Julio Guzman García, was in charge while Carlos Eastman visited Santiago. Santiago officials, when they heard of the strike, demanded that he suppress it; businessmen and the diplomatic corps also wanted the strike stopped.[114] Guzman could do little more than try to contain it. By the 16th, the strikers controlled the city center and had attacked the gas and electric plants. Guzman attempted mediation and, at one point, almost succeeded in persuading the miners to leave Iquique while he negotiated their demands with the nitrate company managers. When the strikers went to the railroad station, they discovered they were to travel in cattle cars and refused to leave.[115]

The Central Committee turned the schoolhouse named after President Santa Maria into its headquarters. It continued recruiting support, and by the 18th, railroad workers, bakers, plumbers, carpenters, masons, and cart drivers joined the strike. Fifteen thousand strikers—10,000 from the *oficinas*—held the city. Luis Olea, appointed the committee's director, maintained order in the ranks. Olea, a painter, began his organizing career as a leader of the anarchist resistance societies in Valparaiso. After their suppression, he went north and joined the *mancomunal* in Iquique. He coordinated the strike force that policed the workers and enforced his prohibition of alcohol. White flags flew from the strike centers to emphasize the movement's peaceful intentions. He also helped organize housing; labor families bedded down at the Santa Maria school, the hippodrome, and in bars, shacks, and tents.[116]

The city had closed when Carlos Eastman returned from Santiago on the 18th: retailers had locked up in anticipation of looting; merchants and nitrate company officials had retreated to their immigrant clubs.[117] Eastman came on the battleship *Esmeralda*, with General Silva Renard and several hundred marines and soldiers. He met the Central Committee on the morning of the 19th, congratulated its members on their success, and told them he had instructions from President Montt to settle their grievances. But first the miners would have to return to the pampa. The Committee told him about the blunder of the cattle cars and that no one would leave without a settlement. Eastman then discussed the situation with bankers, merchants, and nitrate company officials; they refused any attempt at arbitration.[118]

The final confrontation began on December 20. The government had increased its military force with the arrival of more ships from the south. It also sent agents provocateurs among the laborers, creating a justification for military reprisal.[119] The Central Committee demanded that Eastman explain his conduct, and he told them that either the miners would return to the pampa on Saturday, December 21, or he would settle the matter by force.

General Silva Renard, who was at the meeting, expressed his sympathy for the nitrate companies, which he viewed as the victims of their previously generous treatment of ungrateful employees.[120]

While this conversation took place, soldiers on the pampa began shooting strikers. At the *oficina* "Buenaventura," several hundred workers attempted to rehook a train that soldiers had uncoupled, in order to take it to Iquique. The troops opened fire, killing twenty and wounding others. That night, workers from the "Buenaventura" arrived in Iquique carrying their dead. Briggs and Olea prevented a demonstration for fear of a riot; but they could have had few illusions about the government's intentions.[121]

On the morning of the 21st, Eastman used Abdon Díaz as an inmediary, who delivered the intendant's ultimatum to board the trains and his promise that he would try to negotiate their grievances once they left. In the meantime, he declared a state of siege, censored the telegraph, and closed the *mancomunal* newspaper. The strikers concluded, as one witness put it, that Eastman "had gone over to the English." Briggs, Olea, and Morales approached the U.S. consul and asked for asylum, convinced, as they told him, that by 4:00 "they would be assassinated like dogs." He turned them down.[122] They left and led a procession to bury the martyrs of "Buenaventura," then rallied at the Santa Maria school. From there, at 1:00, they told Eastman that they were not returning to the pampa and would not give in to the use of force.[123]

Eastman turned matters over to General Silva Renard. The general assembled his forces, marched on the school and surrounded it. Some 4,500 workers and their families filled the school, and another 1,500 were massed in front of it. Laborers greeted the soldiers' arrival with hoots; some ripped open their shifts and dared the troops to fire. At the last moment, consuls of Argentina, Peru, and Bolivia begged their nationals to leave the school. All the immigrants remained—the Bolivians told their consul that they had more in common with the Chilean miners than with him. Troops handling machine guns began the massacre, firing on the strike leaders who had gathered on the school balcony. Infantry and *carabineros* fired into the crowd, and their volleys were followed by a cavalry charge. The troops arrested the survivors and marched them to the hippodrome. Along the way, many were lanced and shot by cavalry and *carabineros*. That evening, the government collected the dead and buried them in a secret, mass grave. Officials admitted 130 to 140 dead. Other, more credible, observers placed the total at 500.[124]

Those who survived the ordeal and many others on the pampa left Tarapacá. Immigrant laborers returned to Peru and Bolivia; thousands of *rotos* went south. The Nitrate Association tried to replace them by running a massive *enganche* in central Chile; it brought 5,000 recruits into the pampa in 1908. *Oficinas* tried to maintain profits by discounting *fichas* 20 instead of 10 percent. But the emigration hurt. In order to keep the new workers, the nitrate companies raised wages.[125]

For several years after Iquique workers did not resort to militant mass protest. As nitrate exports rose after 1909, however, they began to strike more often. According to the Labor Office, most of these industrial strikes were over wages. Among the most significant were those at "El Teniente," in 1911, where miners shot a manager and threatened to destroy the smelter before they were suppressed, and at Puntas Arenas, in 1912, where ranch hands and dockworkers carried out a successful general strike.[126]

"Iquique" and the "Santa Maria school" became politically synonymous among laborers with the social morality of the government. In 1910, Congress granted amnesty to Briggs and Olea, who somehow survived the carnage. The gesture made little difference to the Left: Olea died the next year of tuberculosis and Briggs never led another major strike.[127] But every year, on December 21, labor leaders gathered in Iquique. As late as 1914, their assembly drew 3,000.[128] When the Parliamentary Commission of 1913 asked workers about the causes of political radicalism, the Workers' Committee at the *oficina* "Porvenir" answered, in a letter, that

> The authorities' bloody suffocation of the peaceful
> strike on the 21st of December, 1907, completed the pat-
> tern of the crisis of patriotism throughout the nitrate
> region. A half century of systematic propagandizing,
> which might have generated a thousand anarchists opposed
> to patriotic sentiments, would never had produced the
> great moral destruction in laborers' sentiments that the
> authorities accomplished in only five minutes of shooting
> and death.[129]

Chile's social problems were the result of a class structure maintained by an elite whose economic function was to provide raw materials for the industrial nations in the Atlantic economy. The elite found it almost impossible to accept the organized efforts of workers to improve their wages. It lamented the breakdown of the social hierarchy but refused to recognize that economic growth and Chile's commercial links to Great Britain had begun the erosion of the old order. It objected to the mobilization of workers into political parties, an outcome of its own reforms. And finally, it reacted with brutal force to laborers who collectively defied authority.

A part of its contempt for the workers lay in the color distinction, inherited from the colony, between the white elite and the swarthy *rotos*; but elite attitudes toward labor derived from economic necessity. The government already found it difficult to accommodate all the interest groups who claimed a large portion of the national income; how could organized labor be incorporated into the political system? Chile would attract fewer foreign investors once real wages began to rise sharply in her export sectors. Worse, if the government made concessions to organized labor, how could it keep other workers from making similar claims?

Workers resented the narrow distribution of benefits from the export economy and government expenditures. They fought for better wages and working conditions within a dependent economy even as they raised the elite's alliance with foreign capital as a political issue. Their movement was divided into competing parties and labor associations, and it was hurt by the absence of a leader capable of combining a political with a union movement. As a result, the great labor uprisings were limited to immediate economic objectives—violent petitions to government—and labor had to improvise its tactics in each confrontation.

This is not to sell their efforts short. A few organizations won at least temporary concessions. More important, workers began, at great cost, to forge a new self-perception and to enter history as actors rather than as victims. At Iquique, they transcended their many differences in favor of collective action; that alone was extraordinary.

5. The United States Takes Over

> Prominent Chileans have called a meeting in
> Santiago today, for the purpose of discussing draw-
> ing closer to the United States.
>> R. H. Patcham, Manager of W. R. Grace
>> and Company, to Gordon Auchincloss,
>> September 28, 1918

> First Russia,
> Then Hungary,
> Germany, after that,
> And, little by little, everywhere,
> the indestructible foundations are laid for a
> New Life, dreamt by us—the so-called "deluded
> criminals."
>> *El Socialista* (Antofagasta)
>> February 17, 1920

The outbreak of the world war caused a crisis in Chile. From a
period of relative prosperity, the nitrate industry sank in three
short months into its worst depression. A financial panic and
high unemployment followed. Then, late in 1915, the Allies' need
for raw materials revived Chile's export of nitrates and copper;
the nation began to enjoy an unparalleled boom. Imports rose,
industry expanded, and the government increased the size of its
administration. At the height of the boom, however, it became
clear that economic growth would not diminish economic dependence.
British supremacy within Chile had ended, but that of the United
States had just begun.

Officials of the United States' State and Commerce Departments had long hoped their country would displace Great Britain
in Chile. In 1906, Lincoln Hutchinson, an agent for the Department of Commerce and Labor, surveyed trade opportunities in South
America and remarked that U.S. manufacturers, by imitating their
successes in Central America, Colombia, and Ecuador, could extend
their predominance to "more remote" countries. The United States

was then a distant fourth in Chile's trade, behind Great Britain,
Germany, and France. Hutchinson wrote, "The share of the United
States in the total trade is therefore comparatively small, but
it is increasing far more rapidly than that of any other country,
with the exception of Italy." The only field of imports the
United States dominated was firearms, but sales of "cars and car-
riages, medicines and drugs, colored cotton goods, canned salmon,
glassware (cheaper grades), scientific instruments and apparatus,
naval stores, mineral oils, paper, lumber and various other articles" had recently increased.[1]

In addition to overcoming obstacles to increased trade, U.S.
businessmen had to deal with the reluctance of Chileans to draw
closer to the northern power. During the War of the Pacific and
the civil war of 1891, U.S. diplomats had acted clumsily, first
trying to dissuade Chile from invading Peru and then apparently
siding with Balmaceda.[2] Chileans never accepted the Monroe Doctrine and, at the turn of the century, were made apprehensive by
the bellicosity of U.S. actions in Latin America. What is more,
important ties now existed between the Chilean elite and English
and French merchant families. No such ties existed with the
United States. The Chilean elite admired the economic growth of
the United States but found European culture, with its aristocratic traditions, much more attractive. It continued to buy its
favorite imports from Europe.

On the eve of the World War, Chile seemed in an excellent
position vis-à-vis her trading partners. Her balance of trade
was favorable. She still relied on British shipping and capital;
but the sustained period of nitrate prosperity attracted foreign
investors from other countries and gave Chile an opportunity to
bargain for better terms of investment. New foreign capital and
domestic reinvestment of export income diversified the economy.
The Guggenheim brothers, with the help of J. P. Morgan, began
their development of the "El Teniente" copper mine in 1911, and,
in 1912, purchased the site of Chuquicamata,[3] Germans invested
heavily in hydroelectric power plants and supplied an ever larger
proportion of Chile's imports. The French began development of
an iron mine and steel mill at "El Tofo," near Coquimbo. The
British continued to buy Chilean government bonds that financed
the construction of railways, irrigation systems, highways, and
even workers' housing.[4] In the southern provinces, landowners
continued development of agriculture.

But international competition to invest in Chile declined
when the war began. The British Navy forced Germany out of Chile's
trade. In this setting, the Allied nations, first Great Britain
and, once she entered the war, the United States, could dictate
the terms of trade. They did so, using the war as their justification. They used *salitre* in munitions as well as to increase
food production. In their dealings with either the government or
native businessmen, they demonstrated little regard for the for-
malities of Chilean neutrality.

Chile's dependence on the United States began during the war
because she needed new sources of capital. The loss of trade

with Germany and the nitrate depression that followed forced the
government to borrow heavily to rescue the nitrate companies and
banks. Money was tight in England; and, in desperation, Chile
turned to U.S. bankers for credit. In addition to becoming
Chile's primary creditor, the United States dramatically increased the volume of her trade with Chile: the U.S. purchased
more *salitre* and copper in exchange for consumer goods, light
machinery, and fuel. Then when the United States became a
belligerent, Washington and London reorganized the nitrate trade
to suit Allied interests. That reorganization, involving the
creation of a "Nitrate Executive," demonstrated the extent of
Chile's subordination to foreign capital.

   Throughout the war, the Chilean government reacted to altera-
tions in the domestic economy caused by changes in the Allied need
for raw materials. These included changes in the volume and
profitability of Chile's exports, the value of her peso, the availability of credit, and her supply of imports—in a word, everything. When demand for exports fell, the government cut domestic
services and increased the money supply in order to prevent financial collapse. During the war boom, it resumed spending on traditional Liberal interests. The postwar slump caused another
bout of monetary expansion. More than any other factor, the war
set the seal on the Parliamentary Regime as inflation and official corruption increased the public's cynical view of government.

   But the problems of the regime outside the formal political
system were as important as those within it. Trade depressions
and inflation revived the labor movement during the war, and it
now had a larger audience. Socialists, Wobblies, Democrats, and
leftist Radicals helped teachers and farm hands to strike, and organized the copper miners. The Bolshevik Revolution inspired
Socialists to hope that a great general strike might bring down
the government. They captured control of the Chilean Workers
Federation (FOCh) and claimed to lead 150,000 members against the
establishment.

   The first beneficiary of the regime's difficulties was
Arturo Alessandri, a leader of the Radical Party. He won a seat
in the Chamber of Deputies in 1893, served in the cabinet at various times after 1898, and in 1915 became senator for Tarapacá."
In 1920, he ran for President on a platform committed to extensive
reform of the political economy; and despite his long service in
the regime, the elite considered him a social radical.[5]

   In fact, he was exactly what he claimed to be, a reformer.
Once he gained office, he had to find some political means to resolve the crisis which he had exploited in his campaign. He proposed changing the tax system, reforming administration, and in-
corporating workers into legal unions. In his liberal view,
these reforms would improve the effectiveness of government as
arbiter of a market economy. At the same time, he openly looked
to an improvement in the volume of exports as the economic basis
of his administration. But the economy did not improve before
1922 and the reforms were not passed. The elite had lost the

presidency, but it retained sufficient power to snare the lion in
a populist dilemma. He could not court the working class without
losing the support of capitalists, both foreign and domestic, who
controlled a large number of Congressmen; but he could not satisfy
the demands of the capitalists without hurting the working class.

THE WAR AND THE NITRATE TRADE

Chile's dependence on the United States began because of the
structure of her economy. Nitrate income kept the society working. Germany was the major consumer of nitrates; and the loss of
her trade quickly depressed the nitrate provinces, then the rest
of the nation. Before the war, nitrate production was running
from 2.25 to 2.40 million tons a month. Exports were high although profits had recently fallen. But the producers were carrying little debt; and the slight downturn had not hurt either production or sales.[6] The larger companies were enjoying record
earnings. Paccha and Jazpampa Nitrate Company planned to issue a
35 percent dividend in 1914. When the war broke out, prices fell
20 percent, production fell to 1.4 million tons, and most of the
oficinas closed.[7] In December, 1914, the U.S. consul in Iquique
described the "paralyzation of everything":

> Commerce is at a standstill and financial conditions
> are getting rapidly worse. According to the local papers
> the Government is doing little to relieve the immediate
> needs of the situation, the banks can do nothing, not even
> to quote exchange, and the merchants are ordering abso-
> lutely nothing nor are they likely to give any orders
> soon.[8]

In every nitrate crisis, the government faced the same dilemma. Its revenues, which depended so heavily on nitrate income,
fell just at the moment when demand for government action increased. The bankers and nitrate producers wanted the government
to act without increasing taxes. Within these constraints the
government did what it could. In March, 1915, it cut all public
salaries from 5 to 15 percent, and laid off large numbers of employees.[9] It also provided ships to take the unemployed back to
the central ports, encouraged Peruvians and Bolivians to return
home, and set up soup kitchens in the major nitrate ports.[10]
The principal concern of the Barros Luco administration was
to prevent a complete financial collapse, and to that end, in
September, 1914, it passed legislation that helped nitrate producers, bankers, and merchants. Under the law, the government
would purchase *salitre,* paying 90 percent to the producers at the
time of the sale and the remainder when it was exported. To participate in the plan, producers had to cut production at least 20
percent. The government's purchases were paid in treasury notes
(*vales*) that then became legal tender. Under the same law, banks
could obtain treasury notes for up to 50 percent of their capital

by depositing their bonds with the government as collateral.[11] As
the government printed notes and as nitrate sales continued to decline, the value of the peso fell from 9.6 pence in July, 1914, to
seven pence by December.[12]

The government obviously could not continue this policy indefinitely. It needed foreign income in order to shore up the
peso and buy imports. It also needed to increase its own income
if it was to meet its debt obligations. European nations other
than Germany increased their nitrate purchases substantially in
1915, but the increase was not enough. The United States eventually became the major nitrate buyer, but that did not occur until 1916 (see table 5.1). In the meantime, Chile searched fran-
tically for some short-term credit to tide the country over.

TABLE 5.1 CHILE'S NITRATE SALES, 1911-20

| | Total Nitrate Sales (thousands of tons) | Distribution of Sales by Country (percentage of total sales) | | | | |
		Great Britain	Germany	Other European Nations	United States	Chile and Egypt
1911	2,591	5.6	31.4	39.7	22.2	1.1
1912	2,638	5.7	37.9	31.6	23.6	1.2
1913	2,780	4.9	32.9	43.6	17.4	1.2
1914	2,811	13.9	23.0	37.5	23.0	2.6
1915	2,701	15.0	0.0	60.4	22.4	2.2
1916	1,896	23.7	0.0	34.3	40.4	1.6
1917	2,912	9.3	0.0	42.7	46.7	1.3
1918	3,018	19.4	0.0	23.3	57.1	0.2
1919	3,018	0.9	0.0	36.1	60.9	2.1
1920	1,210	6.4	5.8	47.1	33.5	7.2

SOURCE: Hacienda, *Antecedentes*, pp. 39-41.

On October 1, 1913, Agustín Edwards, Chile's minister to
London, approached the Rothschilds for a loan. He was initially
confident of success: he considered himself a close friend of the
financial family; Chile had not floated an international loan
since 1911; and she had several million pounds of a gold conversion fund on deposit with the Rothschilds. But Albert Rothschild,
who had only recently come to head the family, was in no hurry to
back a nation whose bonds were sinking on the market. He put
Edwards off until the following July, when the minister pressed
for a decision and reminded the financier of the value of Chile's
conversion fund deposit. They met on July 14, and Albert dismissed Edwards with words the latter found "offensive" to his
country and himself. He walked out in a huff, but soon learned
the Rothschilds' real game. Leopold Rothschild met him immediately

after the incident, apologized for his brother's behavior, and
graciously offered to grant 75 percent of Chile's request on condition she back the entire loan with her conversion fund deposit.
Edwards refused—Chilean law prohibited the use of the fund in
this way—and negotiations ended.[13]

Edwards then turned to the London representative of Morgan,
Grenfell and Company of New York. The Morgan firm checked with
the Rothschilds in order to avoid offending the latter by poach-
ing on its financial territory. The Rothschilds did not object
and Morgan then agreed, on July 21, to loan Chile two million
pounds at 5 percent until December 31, 1916. Chile, in turn,
transferred eight million pounds of its conversion fund from the
Rothschilds to Morgan and promised to transfer another 1.2 million
pounds by October, 1915. The deposits would earn 3 percent interest, and Chile insisted they were not a "guarantee for any
loan." The government had to have the money by August 4, in order
to roll over its debts. Edwards promised Morgan that his government would make every effort to pay the loan ahead of schedule.
In justifying his promise, he told Santiago: "I must remind you
that, in reality, Mssr. Morgan had saved the country from a very
grave situation of insolvency which would have been ruinous for
our credit and would have seriously disturbed our finances, that
are already in difficulty because of the war and the complications it has caused."[14]

This was the first step in the new dependence. Chile needed
capital and could not raise it in London, where her bonds remained
well below their prewar value until 1917.[15] The other steps soon
followed. Chile needed to sell her minerals at a time when U.S.
farmers needed more nitrate and U.S. manufacturers more copper to
meet the demand generated by the war. And she needed to buy what
had become scarce raw materials—fuel, steel, and cement—as well
as to satisfy the home market for consumer goods.

A major problem in the development of trade between the
United States and Chile was that of exchange. Chilean producers
and merchants frequently refused to deal in dollars. An executive of the American Smelting and Refining Company complained to
Federal Reserve officials that because the dollar was not quoted
on the market in Valparaiso, in "the last six months our company
has sold in the neighborhood of U.S. $2,000,000 ninety days'
sight bills and sight drafts on New York." The bills were drawn
in British pounds and payable "at the rate for sterling on London
ruling on the day of maturity."[16] These notes were then used to
buy Chilean minerals. The problem extended to repatriating profits. Wessel, Duval, and Company, because of the difficulties of
getting exchange, resorted in 1915 to buying hides in Chile and
selling them in the United States.[17] These companies and W. R.
Grace created a lobby in Santiago to gain a license for a U.S.
bank. In January, 1916, they succeeded; the New York National
City Bank gained permission to open a branch office in
Valparaiso.[18]

In general, however, U.S. businessmen were not particularly
interested in Chile, because of more profitable opportunities

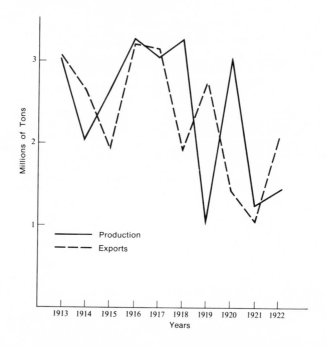

Figure 5.1   Chilean Nitrate Production and Exports,
1913-22. Source: Hacienda,
Antecedentes, pp. 21, 57.

elsewhere. U.S. officials, anxious to improve the importance of
their posts, frequently complained of commercial short-sightedness:
U.S. companies overcharged; they failed to ship goods promptly or
sent goods different from those ordered; shipments were poorly
packed and arrived in poor or useless condition.[19] Worst of all,
businessmen refused to extend credit. Europeans had always given
Chilean importers generous terms, but, as one official explained:

> American houses are well-nigh unanimous in demanding
> cash against documents, sight draft against bill of lading,
> cash with order, or other short credit terms, which in the
> majority of the cases means that the merchant is required
> to pay for the goods before they are received or, at the
> most, long before he has had an opportunity to realize on
> any portion of them.[20]

Nonetheless, trade increased. Chilean importers even trav-
eled to the United States, purchased goods, returned home, and
sold their entire stock—by showing samples—while it was still in
the customs house. Profits were high enough to cover such

piecemeal trading. In 1916, the United States sold Chile 49
percent of her imports and bought 44 percent of her exports.
(See table 5.2.)

TABLE 5.2 CHILE'S TRADE WITH GREAT BRITAIN, GERMANY,
AND THE UNITED STATES, 1911-20

	Percentage of Total Imports			Percentage of Total Exports		
	Great Britain	Germany	United States	Great Britain	Germany	United States
1911	34	26	13	44	21	15
1912	37	27	14	43	20	17
1913	35	25	17	38	21	21
1914	31	26	26	38	26	16
1915	31	6	33	37	0	43
1916	30	0	44	31	0	49
1917	22	0	50	21	0	59
1918	24	0	46	24	0	64
1919	26	0	48	24	0	42
1920	31	5	31	21	10	44

SOURCE: Great Britain, Department of Overseas Trade, *Report on
the Industrial and Economic Situation in Chile, December,
1921,* appendix iv, p. 82.

The elite attitude began to change in 1915. Juan Luis
Sanfuentes, the Balmacedist, became President and brought the
senior figures of his faction into the cabinet. Many had served
with President Balamceda in the civil war and remembered the
United States as a nation that had favored their cause.[21] Economic necessity forced other political figures to forget the past.
In September, the U.S. minister in Santiago related that old animosities, stemming from the War of the Pacific and the civil war,
had "almost entirely disappeared. All parties are now, I am happy
to state, equally friendly to the United States."[22]
     Some strains remained. The most important was Chilean appre-
hension over the Pan American Treaty, sponsored by the U.S. Under it, countries of the Western Hemisphere pledged themselves to
preserve republican forms of government. A Radical deputy, Victor V. Robles, spoke for many when he argued that the treaty was
a pretext for justifying increased U.S. intervention in Latin
America. He cited Pershing's invasion of Mexico in pursuit of
Pancho Villa as proof. Chileans also disliked the clause which
imposed compulsory arbitration of boundary disputes: Peru was
still pressing her for the return of Tacna and Arica, the northern cities taken in the War of the Pacific; and periodically

the Bolivians revived their demand for a port on the Pacific.[23]

Another difficulty involved the incorporation of the new U.S. entrepreneurs into elite society. Americans maintained their own institutions. They had established their own school, Santiago College, in 1880; and their businessmen gathered at the American Society—Spruille Braden, director of "El Teniente," was its president for a time.[24] Chileans had gradually absorbed successful European merchants through intermarriage and joint enterprises; but they could not wait the generation or two that acculturation of the Americans would require. They instead encouraged prominent U.S. citizens to enter society as soon as possible; and their sensibilities were often offended by the brash and sometimes vulgar Yankee behavior. One incident led to a major public scandal. The Naval Club at Viña del Mar, the upper-class suburb of Valparaiso, invited officers from the U.S.S. Tennessee to a ball. The ship's junior officers arrived late, became drunk, and began manhandling young girls of Chile's first families. Before they left, they broke most of the club's furniture and one officer ran around the ballroom pushing a lawn mower. What would have been treated in the United States as boyish pranks and horseplay struck the Chileans as a gross insult. The entire senior command of the Chilean Navy led the delegation demanding an apology, which it received, from the State Department.[25]

The expansion of trade, led by rising nitrate sales, overcame all difficulties. From a low of 1.8 million tons in 1914, *salitre* exports increased to 2.9 million tons in 1918; the product's average price climbed 80 percent. The total value of the trade in 1918 was 532.2 million pesos. The Guggenheim investment in copper also paid handsomely as exports of that mineral soared from 46,200 tons in 1913 to 116,600 tons in 1918; its price on the world market jumped 180 percent. At the height of the war, the United States bought 57 percent of Chile's exported *salitre* and 75 percent of her exported copper.[26]

Trade did not expand evenly, since the supply of resources needed to produce and transport Chile's exports remained in foreign hands. The British, specifically the Pacific Steam Navigation Company, dominated shipping; and it became fantastically expensive. In 1913, it cost thirty to forty shillings to ship a ton of *salitre* to Europe. Just before the war, the cost had fallen to twenty to thirty shillings, depending on whether the vessel was sail or steam. In 1916, it cost 140 shillings by sail, 160 shillings by steamship.[27] The firm of Williamson, Balfour and Company controlled the flow of English and Australian coal to the nitrate provinces; but imported coal became expensive and scarce because of the inadequate supply of shipping. From 1.2 million tons in 1914, the amount fell to 320,000 tons in 1918. Domestic production could not make up the difference; it rose only 390,000 tons during the war. Nitrate producers switched from coal to oil, buying their supply from the Union Oil Company of California and the International Petroleum Company of Toronto, both subsidiaries of Standard Oil of California.[28] Oil imports rose from 509,000 tons in 1914 to 780,000 in 1918. Before the war began, coal and oil had cost thirteen to fourteen pesos a ton; in 1917, the price rose to twenty-four and twenty-six pesos a ton; the price of oil in February, 1918, was fifty-two pesos a ton.[29] In short, much of the price increase in *salitre* went not to the producers but to Allied firms controlling ships and petroleum.

Despite these problems, nitrate companies reaped enormous profits. Dividends in 1916 were two and three times what they had been the previous year. Alianza Nitrate Company paid 15 percent; Anglo-Chilean, 32 percent; San Lorenzo, 25 percent; and Liverpool Nitrate, one of John T. North's old companies, 120 percent. Nitrate stocks on the London market rose accordingly.[30] Observers noted that the nitrate companies were actually benefiting from the high cost and difficulties of obtaining ships and fuel since the resulting shortages increased the price of their stocks in Europe and also increased speculation on future deliveries.[31] American officials in 1917 denounced the price increases as "pure speculation." One claimed, "Nitrate sometimes goes through the hands of three or four speculators before it reaches one of the Allied Governments. It has been said that even different Departments of the United States Government compete against one another."[32]

The Chilean Government was slow to think out its options in the war. Part of its problems stemmed from the need to maintain formal neutrality while nonetheless trading exclusively with the Allies. The Allies did all they could to pressure Santiago into becoming a belligerent. But Chile refused, claiming she could not afford the 100 million pesos it would cost to mobilize.[33] The real considerations were political. She had no quarrel with Germany. Her merchants leaned toward the Allies, but the army was pro-German. In the south, descendants of German colonists were now important provincial figures. They owned large estates, flour mills, and breweries. They held local government posts. And many of them identified strongly with their ancestral homeland, even speaking German in the home.[34]

The government's major concern was to increase its revenues. In January, 1917, it began demanding that producers pay the nitrate duty in gold coin. This meant that instead of paying in pesos worth eighteen pence, producers would have to pay in coins worth 24.5 pence. The producers protested and the tax increase was rescinded.[35] The government's next measure was to sell public lands which held nitrate deposits. In February and April, 1917, it auctioned lots, which had an estimated content of 6.4 million tons of *salitre*, for 20.4 million pesos. The money was spent on the longitudinal railway and on the liquidation of the short-term loans acquired during the 1914-15 slump.[36]

Some Chileans understood that the sale of nitrate lands during the boom might later prove disastrous. The postwar market looked uncertain. As early as 1915, Miguel Cruchaga, Chile's minister in Berlin, told Santiago that Germany, by improving the Haber process, had radically increased production of ammonium sulphate. She would not be a major *salitre* consumer after the war.[37] Chile's representatives in London also warned that the

British, using the cyanamide process, had improved their output of
ammonium nitrate and nitric acid, substitutes for *salitre*. But
they thought the answer to any problem of postwar demand lay in
developing new markets in Russia, India, and China.[38] Chileans
consoled themselves with two observations: *salitre*, compared to
ammonium sulphate, was a superior fertilizer; and even in wartime,
it was considerably cheaper than ammonium nitrate.[39]

While the Chilean government increased its revenues, control
of the nitrate trade passed to the Allied governments. Although
their interests were not always compatible, the Allies demonstrated a remarkable ability to cooperate in opposition to the
Chilean government. They also drew upon the aid of their nationals, who completely overshadowed the investments and influence of
Germans in Chile (table 5.3). They wanted to prevent competition
for raw materials and to protect the profits of Allied companies,
and to those ends, decided on a division of labor: trade in each
key commodity would be farmed out to one or two major companies
which would set prices and allocate supplies in accordance with
the decisions of Allied boards of trade. Company officials as
well as government figures sat on these boards. As part of this
general strategy, the Allies created the Nitrate Executive Committee in February, 1918. It met in London and coordinated the
private purchase and distribution of nitrates among member nations. The U.S. members of the Executive, as it was called, func-
tioned as subordinates of the State Department and the War Trade
Board.

The Allies began discussing the formation of the Executive
in November, 1917, when their representatives to a general con-
ference of the Maritime Transport Council met in Paris to discuss
the problems of trade and shortages of raw materials. The Council proposed at the end of its deliberations that no nation be
recognized as an economic neutral. In a memorandum sent to the
U.S. State Department, it argued that "it appears essential that
neutral countries should obtain their supplies of the controlled
specifics on the same system as the Allies, i.e., private citizens
must be prohibited from buying abroad, and the Governments must
themselves buy through the Allied organization, the amounts,
sources of origins, etc., being determined by that organization."[40]
The British proposed, and the other Allies promptly accepted the
suggestion, that one of these organizations be formed to pool the
purchase of nitrates and control their flow in the Atlantic
economy.[41]

The Allies had to decide on the private companies that would
act as its purchasing agents. The British wanted Antony Gibbs
and Sons to handle the entire trade; the United States opposed
such a monopoly. Chandler P. Anderson, Counsel on International
Affairs for the U.S. War Industries Board, wired Robert P.
Skinner, the U.S. consul-general in London, "The U.S. government
disposed to insist upon utilization of existing American importing
houses as purchasing agencies because otherwise their legitimate
business advantages during the war will be wasted, and their
position afterwards prejudiced, and also because they can

TABLE 5.3   INVESTMENTS OF GREAT BRITAIN, THE UNITED STATES, AND GERMANY IN CHILE, 1917
(In millions of U.S. dollars)

Great Britain		United States		Germany	
Chilean bonds	137.4	Chile Copper Co.	110	Insurance, business houses, and small manufactures	50.0
Insurance, business houses, and small manufactures	70.0	Andes Mining Co.	50		
		Braden Copper Co.	14	Nitrate companies	25.0
Nitrate companies	60.0	Insurance, business houses, and small manufactures	10	Chilean bonds	19.3
Chilean railroads	59.0				
Chilean Electric Light and Tramway Company	5.7	Bethlehem Steel	4	Valparaiso Light and Tramway Co.	6.0
		Chile Exploration Co.	2	Banco Alemán	2.2
Anglo-South American Bank	1.3	Du Pont Nitrate Co.	1	Banco Germánico de América del Sur	1.2
		National City Bank	1		
		Oil tanks	1		
TOTAL	333.4	TOTAL	193	TOTAL	103.7

SOURCE: Keena to Shea, Nov. 26, 1917, U.S. *Diplomatic, Correspondence*, class 8, pt. 7.

conveniently be utilized for financing purchases."[42] On December
7, 1917, the Allies agreed on a division of business: Gibbs
would be the "sole purchasing agent" for all of Europe, while
DuPont, W. R. Grace, and Wessel, Duval would share the U.S. market. The agents would buy the nitrate on the basis of prices approved by the Executive in London. Purchases could be traded
back and forth among companies according to need. The Executive
would keep track of these exchanges in order to insure supplies
to all the Allies. It would also coordinate the flow of shipping
and fuel to Chile.[43]

Chileans recognized the importance of the Executive as soon
as it was created. But neither the producers nor the government
initially believed they could prevent its control of the market.
Elite opinion accepted this outcome. *La Nación* reported that the
Executive would buy 90 percent of all nitrate exports and could
now set the price as it liked.[44] *El Diario Ilustrado* blamed the
government's passivity on the upcoming Congressional election,
and hoped the Executive might actually help the trade because the
Allies had promised "their action is taken with a view of wiping
out the middleman and competition among the purchasers and not in
order to prejudice the position of the nitrate producers." It
concluded, "This must be accepted as the way of doing business in
wartime, as the recent purchase of the Uruguayan crops has demonstrated."[45] *El Mercurio* commented that politics had left the
country with "no Cabinet, an inactive Congress and a semi-
paralyzed Government." It reported the producers had debated
forming an export trust but gave up the idea. Most of them had
received the news about the Executive "with complacency as they
feel the proposals were inspired by the best of motives." Many
of the producers and the company managers were English and
thought the Executive would protect their interests:

> The President of the Nitrate Producers Association
> has stated on a former occasion in this regard that the
> fixing of a price which is fair and in harmony with the
> high cost of production by such a committee could not but
> help the industry as it would mean the disposal of the en-
> tire supply, the regulation of the prices of petroleum,
> coal, and sacks, and above all, the certainty that the
> countries in need of nitrate for their munition factories
> would provide ships and provisions.[46]

The initial dissent from this halcyon view came from Chileans
with strong ties to Germany. Adolfo Artuzar, Chile's consul in
Hamburg, recommended his government create a producers' "syndicate"
to counter the Executive. *El Mercurio* thought his advice unrealis-
tic. "After many years in a country [Germany] where government
organization and control is probably carried to excess, he forgets
that perhaps the Chilean government is not capable of taking
charge of such a vast undertaking. His plan presupposes the existence of a government, which is exactly what this country has
lacked for years."[47] Eventually, the government and the producers

realized they could not leave control of the trade completely in
Allied hands. In May, 1918, the government moved to form a producers' cartel.[48] But its efforts were limited by Allied influence within Chile, an influence illustrated by the fate of German
nitrate companies.

The Allies boycotted all firms owned or operated by Germans
doing business with German companies. The British had first
adopted this policy when they passed the Trading with the Enemy
Act. By 1917, the Enemy list included 101 firms in Chile. In
Valparaiso, Antofagasta, and Iquique, British consuls cut off the
flow of ships and jute bags to German nitrate companies and to
Chilean companies controlled by German capital. In addition, the
British consul-general in Valparaiso drew up a list of 160 individuals in Chile, Germans or of German descent, who were to be boycotted. The U.S. consul in Valparaiso guessed, "In Chile and Peru
more than 800 of the principal firms are more or less thoroughly
controlled in the operation of their general internal as well as
import and export business."[49] Once the United States entered
the war, it adopted the same policies. American companies fired
all employees who were German or of German descent; and they
joined the Allied Committee in Valparaiso, a collection of the
local British, French, and Italian Chambers of Commerce. The
U.S. representatives on the Committee were Thomas N. Molanphy of
U.S. Steel and G. N. Blanton of the National City Bank. The U.S.
consul-general, L. J. Keena, explained that the Committee was

> to furnish a clearing house for all information which
> might be of assistance to the Allies in preventing both
> direct and indirect enemy trading. The "UNDESIRABLE"
> list which will be made up by the Allied Committee from
> information from all available sources is taken by me as a
> list which should be representative of the commercial senti-
> ment of the Allied Business Interests in general and will
> include individuals and firms against whom not sufficient
> evidence has been collected to justify their inclusion in
> the Enemy Trading Lists or because inclusion in such a list
> would give them a false importance.[50]

The war had given Allied businessmen in the port a chance
to eliminate competitors, and they made the most of it. On
February 18, 1918, Keena proclaimed that anyone trading between
Chile and the United States would have to have a license from his
office. The order took effect the following day.[51]

Finally, these discriminatory policies forced the Germans
in Chile to resist. In late 1917, as part of the boycott policy,
Union Oil and International Petroleum stopped supplying oil to
German nitrate companies, although the oil had been purchased
before the United States entered the war. The German companies,
Sloman and Gildemeister, sued in Chilean courts, demanding
that either the petroleum companies deliver the promised oil
or the courts place an embargo on any oil they imported.[52]
After several months of litigation, the Germans succeeded in

gaining an embargo against the International Petroleum Company.
In retaliation, the U.S. War Trade Board refused to issue
any license for the export of oil to Chile. U.S. officials at
first worried that the stand-off would disrupt Allied supplies of
nitrate. But the producers in northern Chile could not hold out
for long: they were caught on a credit treadmill in which they
used nitrate stockpiles as collateral to cover the rising costs
of shipping and fuel.[53] By July, the producers in Tarapacá were
desperate; the province's principal railroad had stopped running
because of the fuel shortage. Chile quickly retreated from its
position. The Sanfuentes administration dismissed the court's
ruling against International Petroleum, and its minister in Washington assured the State Department that all other difficulties
involving the case had been resolved; "the Government guarantees
they will not occur again, and nothing hereafter will disturb the
free production of nitrate."[54] The State Department's legal
counsel, Paul Fuller, urged a quick reply that would accept the
Chilean decision but blame the Chilean courts for the confrontation. He insisted the Department should also press the Chileans
to drop all litigation that was still pending against the Union
Oil Company. Fuller advised Secretary of State Frank Polk to insist on the hard line because the Enemy Trading List was so con-
troversial in Latin America. The Department's victory would be
seen as "the greatest vindication of the Allied enemy trading
policy which has occurred to date." Polk did as Fuller suggested.[55]

This was the setting in which the Chilean government created
a producer's cartel. The government's negotiating strategy was
never clear because it could not count on the undivided support
of the producers and because it and they feared retaliation by
the Allies. Negotiating tactics varied from month to month as
the Sanfuentes administration tried to guess whether the Allies
were willing to risk nitrate shortages in order to reduce nitrate
prices. Now the government had a new concern. While it wanted
to sell as much nitrate at as high a price as possible, it also
wanted a high volume of trade and an assured market in the postwar
world.

The Allied advantage in the negotiations with the Chilean
government was the level of cooperation among the Allied governments and among the companies commissioned by the Executive to
act as nitrate buyers. In March, 1918, Bernard Baruch, commissioner of the Raw Materials Division of the War Industries Board,
laid down the ground rules to the purchasing companies, insisting
they work with one another "as a war measure for controlling the
purchase and distribution of Chilean Nitrate for use in this
country this year."[56] F. G. Tollman, vice-president of DuPont and
in charge of its nitrate trade, wrote back, "We have refrained,
since October 23rd last, from all purchases of nitrate for shipment from Chile except under your specific authorization."[57]
Herbert Gibbs, head of Antony Gibbs and Sons, used his close ties
with the nitrate producers to gauge the strength of their position. For example, he told the Allies in May, 1918, that the

producers were pushing for a 16 percent price increase. He
suggested the Allies could drive the producers down by simply
shifting stocks among the Allied companies and postponing any new
purchases from Chile because the producers were not willing or
able to hold out for very long. The suggestion was put into effect. To cover Allied needs in Europe in the short term, Wessel,
Duval sold Gibbs *salitre* that was not immediately needed in the
United States. On July 9, Ambassador Joseph Shea wired Washington that the Allied tactic would soon force the producers to
terms. "The Minister [of Interior] has just fallen and expect
big producers to come out any moment as all beginning to feel
their bluff is called; if we hold firm at prices in force believe
practically all will come out, as almost nothing sold for the
last six months."[58] Shea compared the role of the Minister of
the Interior to that of a prime minister. (The analogy was in-
accurate. The President was the dominant executive official; but
the resignation or dismissal of the Minister required reshuffling
the entire cabinet and was a sign Congress had lost confidence in
the administration.) Shea estimated there were a million tons of
unsold *salitre* on the Chilean coast, enough to supply the Allies
for three to four months.[59]

However, the government's efforts to create a cartel continued after the cabinet change. By mid-June it controlled the nitrate stockpiles of the majority of the producers, and it approached the Executive with a deal: it wanted a high price for
the nitrate on hand, a rollback in the cost of imported fuels
controlled by the Executive, and a contract that would extend beyond the end of the war; in return, it offered price stability
and full cooperation on the issue of currency exchange by accepting payment from the Allies in the form of deposits in either New
York or London banks.[60] (The issue of exchange had assumed a new
importance in 1917 because by September of that year the peso's
value in dollars or pounds was double that of 1915. The Allies
worried about the drain of their gold and *salitre*'s increasing
cost. But the Chilean elite was also concerned: exporters resented the increasing real cost of labor; and the government
feared the peso's rise might discourage foreign investment. The
Chileans proposed a number of schemes to handle the problem, but
ultimately settled on the practice of not demanding shipment in
gold to cover any trade imbalance.)[61] The Allies appointed
Winston Churchill, His Majesty's Minister of Munitions, as their
representative with the Chilean government. Chile's negotiator
was Agustín Edwards. Edwards succeeded in selling the stockpiled
nitrate but not in fixing the length of the contract. Churchill
delayed settlement of the contract's length in order to avoid
buying more *salitre* than the Allies needed or buying it at a
price higher than necessary.[62]

Not everyone in the United States was happy with Churchill's
appointment and his decisions. U.S. farmers wanted an assured
supply of fertilizer and, with war-related demand at a peak,
thought it unnecessary to haggle over *salitre*'s price. They
formed a Chilean Nitrate Committee that publicly worried about

the availability of nitrate once the war was over if the Chileans were not bound to a long-term contract.[63] Ambassador Shea was more concerned that Churchill's appointment had demonstrated Britain's continued preeminence "in the shipping and commercial affairs of Chile," and that he might use his power to aid British interests in Chile over those of the United States.[64] The farmers and Shea were mistaken. The Churchill strategy worked. There was no shortage of nitrate after the war; instead a glut developed. And the British did not displace the U.S. in Chilean trade.

The war ended in November, and the European Allies cut their orders for copper and nitrates—beginning the next crisis. Chile suffered a depression that was longer and more complex than that of 1914-15. Her sales to the United States remained strong in 1919 but fell the following year: the copper market was saturated, and U.S. farmers, confronted with unsold grain and a reduction in bank loans, decreased their use of *salitre*. Western Europe began to recover in 1920, but its orders remained well below the wartime peak. Although Germany renewed her trade with Chile, she now had synthetic nitrates and was no longer a major *salitre* market.[65]

The decline in exports led to a panic that compounded Chile's miseries. Speculators in Valparaiso began hoarding ninety-day draft notes—the hard currency of the nitrate trade—and accelerated the contraction of credit that was already underway. Banks, nitrate companies, industries, and farmers faced ruin. To rescue them, the government issued more treasury notes to banks and nitrate companies: the volume of Chile's currency rose from 184.3 million pesos in 1918 to 301.1 million in 1922. In 1921 and 1922, it also issued bonds in New York worth sixty-two million dollars (roughly 452 million pesos). The peso depreciated as much as 15 percent a month during these years: in 1918 it was worth 17.1 British pence; in 1922, it fell to 5.1 pence.[66]

The strategy was a disaster for the workforce, especially that of the north, but a success for the capitalists. There were few bankruptcies. Many in the upper class even welcomed the decline of the peso. A U.S. consular official in Valparaiso observed that currency speculation was "the chief activity of the stock exchanges in the cities, and . . . is engaged to a very great extent by commercial houses, government officials, and private individuals that causes the rate of exchange to vary from day to day to an extent that is almost incredible to foreign markets."[67] An economist in Valparaiso for the National City Bank agreed that the upper class had a vested interest in inflation: they could hoard their hard currency notes and "take advantage of these conditions to sell their foreign bills when they yield the most local currency; while the wages that they pay respond but slowly to the decreased value of the local money, and the long time loans on their farms become easier to pay with each new depreciation."[68]

The export boom during the war and the subsequent depression accelerated industrial development and increased the number of large estates. The war helped native industry because it raised

the cost and reduced the availability of imports. While the total
number of industries was only slightly greater after the war than
before, the total amount of capital in manufacturing and the
volume of production were much greater. (See tables 5.4 and 5.5.)
The average rate of return on industrial investments reported to
the government was as high as 31.4 percent in 1918. The increase
in the money supply and the drop in the peso's value after the
war kept demand up and raised the price of imports. There was,
as a result, an important contrast in the fate of industry in the
two war-related crises. In the setback of 1914, several thousand
small shops failed; in 1919-22, despite a stock market crash in
1920, industrial production continued to rise.[69] According to
the source for table 5.4, the total amount of capital in industry
by 1922 was 79 percent greater than in 1916; total production was
67 percent greater, and total profits 54 percent greater.[70]

TABLE 5.4   CHILEAN INDUSTRIAL EXPANSION, 1910-22

	Number of Industrial Firms	Workers	Power Machines in Operation	Horsepower
1910	5,270	71,060	2,725	59,060
1911	5,722	74,618	2,945	61,046
1912	6,215	80,697	3,325	61,622
1913	7,841	85,008	2,930	90,522
1914	4,212	48,103	2,244	84,402
1915	6,692	61,005	2,903	115,252
1916	6,830	66,540	3,478	130,477
1917	7,982	74,943	3,478	146,943
1918	7,481	78,711	3,748	167,881
1919	7,895	79,553	3,754	169,942
1920	8,001	80,549	4,666	241,196
1921	8,148	81,991	4,953	261,454
1922	8,444	86,522	4,944	240,510

SOURCE: *Semana de la moneda celebrada en Santiago de Chile,*
         Agosto, 1924 (Santiago: Imprenta La Ilustración, 1924),
         pp. 62-63.

The government's policy also rescued farmers. The war had
provided them with an unparalleled opportunity to expand production. The number of rural properties grew by 8,000, and the
total area under cultivation increased 27 percent. The total
value of agrarian mortgages increased accordingly; and it continued to rise after the war. From 1919 to 1922, the *Caja de
Crédito Hipotecario* lent 133 million pesos to landowners; the
Chilean Mortgage Bank lent another fifty-four million.[71] The depreciation of the peso, combined with high agricultural tariffs

TABLE 5.5 CHILEAN INDUSTRIAL CAPITAL, 1915-20

| | Millions of Pesos[a] | | | | | | Origin of Capital[c] | | | |
	Industries Reporting[b]	Capital Invested	Total Costs	Value of Production	Profits	Rate of Return	Chilean	Foreign	Mixed	Corporation
1915	2,406	482.9	433.0	564.8	131.8	27.3%	27.0%	34.0%	5.1%	33.3%
1916	2,625	552.4	465.2	635.0	169.8	30.7	30.9	33.4	4.3	30.7
1917	2,738	596.2	515.9	701.3	185.4	31.1	31.2	33.7	3.3	31.5
1918	2,820	626.0	569.0	766.7	196.8	31.4	31.1	33.3	3.6	31.6
1919	2,871	702.8	708.9	905.1	196.2	27.9	28.0	32.3	4.2	35.0
1920	2,975	767.9	802.9	993.2	190.3	24.7	28.5	32.0	2.2	37.2

[a]At eighteen British pence per peso.
[b]Sources: *Anuario*, 1918, 9:1-4; *Sinopsis*, 1921, p. 98.
[c]Sources: Kirsch, "The Industrialization of Chile," p. 263; the figures of total capital invested that Kirsch uses do not completely match the amounts given above.

established in 1916, protected farms from the full consequences of the postwar depression.[72] Neither the war nor its aftermath had altered the pattern of rural development. In 1918, 65.9 percent of the farms amounted to less than 4.3 percent of the arable land, while .4 percent of them, with 5,000 hectares or more, held 13.2 percent of the land. In the early 1920s, the number of small farms remained constant; but the number of large estates increased. (See table 5.6.) Government figures also indicate that farmers increasingly overworked their soil or tried to develop less productive land. While the area under cultivation had grown, yields per hectare for most crops either declined between 1910 and 1920 or failed to increase.[73]

The balance sheet of dependent development indicates that the economy had grown but the people were still poor. Chile now had substantial industries and more farms, and was once again a major copper producer. But this growth and diversification occurred within an economic structure that continued to rely on nitrate exports to pay for the government and for imports, and on foreign capital to increase production and to cover any setback in the export sector. Growth had not led to any substantial improvement in efficiency. Most farms and industries remained small and primitive. Many manufacturers simply assembled foreign products. The country lacked the primary characteristic of all modern economies, a devotion to technological research and capital investment.

The political outcome of the period was an increase in the number of dependent interests who were organized and intent on influencing government policy. The population of intellectuals and politicians, who considered themselves economic nationalists and social reformers, had grown. They argued in favor of new taxes to reduce the government's dependence on the nitrate duty and labor legislation to help the working poor. But the direction of the economy propelled the Parliamentary Regime to draw even closer to the United States and Great Britain and to hope that recovery in the advanced countries would revive exports and its own export-based income.

THE POLITICS OF CRISIS

The Parliamentary Regime was refinanced by the export boom during the war and then began to unravel in the postwar slump. Its problems were not new but now they changed in scale. Before the war, the regime could contain political dissidents, defuse demands for reform, and repress labor. It continued in this manner after 1915, but its ability to govern became an open question. Its difficulties can be divided into related sets of problems: those involving elections and the distribution of patronge, and those dealing with social militance—the social politics of strikes and demonstrations. The two are related because politicians used social politics to influence the outcome of elections and because both turned on the distribution of benefits within the export

Map 1. Chile in the Late 1920s

Map 2. The Nitrate Provinces: Tarapacá, Antofagasta, 1900-1905

TABLE 5.6 NUMBER AND SIZE[a] OF RURAL PROPERTIES, 1915-25

	0-5 hect.	6-20	21-50	51-200	201-1,000	1,001-5,000	5,001 or more	Total	Irrigated hectares	Non-irrigated hectares	Total hectares
1915	38,759	23,101	12,495	11,122	4,501	1,083	248	91,309	862,027	12,441,679	13,303,706
1918	40,261	25,248	14,337	12,187	5,254	1,566	449	99,302	1,128,177	15 813,053	16,941,230
1925	40,624	25,529	12,861	11,786	6,773	1,895	559	100,027	1 147,065	23,834,848	24,981,913

SOURCE: *Anuario*, 1915, 7:98; 1918, 7:118; 1925, 7:5.

[a]In hectares.

economy. Arturo Alessandri, who used the threat of social violence
to assure his election, became President in 1920. To make some
sense of the crisis that preceded his victory and the political
issues that plagued his administration, it is necessary first to
discuss the evolution of the political system and of social
politics from 1915 to 1920.

The formal characteristics of the Parliamentary Regime did
not change significantly during or immediately after the war.
The Sanfuentes administration increased the bureaucracy in the
fat years and found it difficult to retain these new employees in
1919. Squabbling over patronage intensified as revenues fell;
Congress was virtually immobilized by infighting in 1919-20. But
the problem went beyond the distribution of spoils. The political system was incapable of placating the increased number of
claimants for government attention: industrialists sought protection; farmers, cheap credit; and labor, social reform. Worse,
the regime began to lose its hegemony. The public no longer believed the system worked in the national interest.

After 1915, public cynicism about government became widespread. Part of this sentiment came from Europe, where disen-
chantment with republican ideas had become intellectually fashion-
able. But part of this feeling was more specific. Even former
ministers now admitted the system was rotten.[74] Newspapers
openly discussed the extent of the corruption. During the 1915
Congressional election, journalists guessed that between 62 and
85 percent of the voters sold their ballots. One senatorial
candidate spent 50,000 pesos securing his victory.[75] A U.S. consul noted that "money was freely used" in the 1918 election. In
the provinces, candidates of the Conservative Coalition "opened
the bidding at 300 pesos and were paying 480 pesos per vote when
their funds gave out."[76]

The electorate consisted of a minority of the adult men; but
the vote totals mattered less than party control of municipal
tables and party influence in Congress. There were 244,132
registered voters in 1915 and 370,314 in 1921. Only 197,267, about
22 percent of the adult male population, voted in the Congressional election of 1921. In 1924, 260,000 voted, about 29 percent of the adult males.[77] The key to victory, however, remained
the use of patronage to retain the loyalty of local officials, who
ran the elections, and to obtain the votes in Congress if an election was disputed. Whenever the size of patronage was threatened,
politicians became desperate. Two deputies dueled over the appointment of police inspector of rural Tomé in 1915; one of them
was killed.[78] Reform parties behaved just like those of the
elite. In 1918, the Radicals in Tarapacá called out the police
to maintain control of the election tables.[79]

In order to influence the distribution of spoils, senators
and deputies continued to block appropriations and passage of the
budget. In 1915, Congress failed to pass the budget until two
months of the fiscal year had elapsed.[80] In October, 1920, it
refused to pass a bill needed to pay the salaries of public

employees; in addition, the Senate simply stopped considering any
bills already passed by the Chamber of Deputies.[81]   Partisan considerations distorted the government's accounting.   Henry Fletcher,
U.S. minister in 1915, reported:

> It is practically impossible to form a clear idea of
> the state of the Government's finances.   The Tribunal of
> Accounts in its last report, for the fiscal year 1913,
> shows that no reliance whatever can be placed on the
> Government's accounts as presented by the *Dirección de
> Contabilidad*.   Items which appear one year as paper items
> [paid with paper pesos] will appear in the following year
> as gold [paid in pesos worth 18 pence].   The value of the
> Government's property has never been accurately ascer-
> tained and is put in the accounts each year at such sums
> as suit the accounting officers.   These are but a few of
> the most glaring discrepancies.[82]

Patron-client relations still decided who received what public
office.   Tancredo Pinochet Le-Brun captured the political ethics of
the era in his memoir of the year he was Director of the School of
Arts and Crafts in Santiago.   Pinochet discovered soon after taking his post that most of his time was spent on trivia: who
should get the school's meat contract; should the director keep
two waiting rooms—one for those who were important, the "decent
people," and another for "ordinary people"?   During the slump of
1915, he cut the number of administrators and custodians.   An
oligarch called Pinochet and demanded that a gardener be rehired.
The gardener's job had been a reward for the many years he worked
for the oligarch's mother.   Pinochet explained that the man might
have been a good servant but was an incompetent gardener and the
school could not afford to continue feeding his large family.
The oligarch replied:

> I don't believe in always applying the same harsh
> rules.   Every Chilean public office is given in return
> for service of more or less importance to men of influ-
> ence.   With your system [of merit], you would destroy the
> national traditions.   You must not forget that not all
> foreign customs can be adapted for our use.   In our soil,
> one can transplant rice, perhaps even sugar cane; but you
> surely cannot grow coffee trees in Magallanes.   In our
> land, one cannot cultivate puritanism; it is an exotic
> plant, unsuitable here.[83]

The central government continued to serve as a brokerage.
Few officials held any one post for long.   Little was done in administration and nothing was initiated.   Many intendants and governors did not even bother to write the required annual report to
the Minister of the Interior.[84]   A few thoughtful men, such as
Belisario García, who was appointed governor of Osorno in 1918-
19, were bothered by this state of affairs.   García thought of

himself as a liberal and competent public servant; the local
inhabitants received him as a pariah. In his report, he tried to
empathize with the residents. Since 1891, only two or three
governors had completed their terms of office. Most of the
schools had been closed for years. The *carabineros* spent their
time hiring out to private employers rather than enforcing the
law. Judges and municipal officials were robbing the Indians of
their lands. García also found he could neither improve public
service nor eliminate the widespread dishonesty in local government.[85]

The President was the most important broker but could not
hold any agreement together for very long. Each cabinet was a
coalition of several factions; but the making and unmaking of
these coalitions took place in Congress. Every President after
1891 searched for a means to give the executive greater control.
Sanfuentes attempted to curtail Congressional influence in the
executive branch by improving his hold on patronage and using his
influence to help him elect supporters in 1918. He instead
alienated the Liberals within his cabinet. They complained of
not being appointed to judicial positions, and resigned. A long
cabinet crisis followed in which the majority of the deputies
supported the President and the majority of the senators opposed
him.[86] This was the political situation at the end of 1917, when
the Allies began forming the Nitrate Executive.

The Liberal Alliance dominated both houses of Congress
throughout the war. Despite this continuity, a significant
change was taking place in the composition of the legislature.
The rhetoric of economic nationalism was gaining at the expense
of laissez faire, and social progressives were increasing their
representation. Few political interests any longer accepted the
arguments of free trade; the role of the state in the nitrate
trade, in providing public services, and in protecting industry
was too important to be ignored. At the same time, the decline
of the Church, the creation of professional lobbies, and, most
important, the reappearance of a radical labor movement forced
politicians to at least promise social reforms. Elite factions
weakened, and in order to maintain their influence, had to re-
group. After the war, the Conservatives and Balmacedists lost so
many seats in Congress that they forged a broader alliance, one
that included older Liberals, and became the National Union.
(See table 5.7.) Senator Eliodoro Yañez, a powerful, but socially
conservative Liberal, summed up the change in attitude in 1916:
"The old maxims and ancient formulas have lost their authority as
absolute principles. The State has ceased to be the supreme regu-
lator of national laws and has become an active agent of progress,
of solutions, and of stimulation to the general interest."[87]

In the economic crisis of 1915, both the Liberal Alliance
and the Conservative Coalition wanted to increase state intervention in the economy. The Alliance, in its platform, argued for a
"true Constitutional Government," with a stronger presidency and
procedural limits on Congressional debates and budgetary delays.
It wanted honest elections, better public education, labor-

TABLE 5.7 COMPOSITION OF CONGRESS, 1912-21

	Senate				Chamber of Deputies			
	1912	1915	1918	1921[a]	1912	1915	1918	1921[a]
Coalitions								
Liberal Alliance	16	19	24	14	48	50	68	70
Conservative Coalition	18	16	13	0	69	66	46	0
National Union	0	0	0	22	0	0	0	46
Unaligned	2	2	1	1	1	2	4	2
Political Parties								
Liberals	12	13	16		21	17	26	
Conservatives	7	8	8		29	29	23	
Liberal Democrats	9	5	2		27	22	17	
Nationalists	2	3	3		13	15	9	
Radicals	3	5	6		22	28	33	
Democrats	1	1	2		5	5	6	
Independents	0	0	0		0	0	4	

SOURCES: Summerlin no. 603, Mar. 31, 1915, U.S. *Internal Affairs,*
reel 3; Billier no. 320, Mar. 9, 1918, reel 3; and Shea
report for Mar. 1921, reel 4.

[a]In 1921, the division of the Liberals, Liberal Democrats,
and Nationalists into different parties would have made party
continuity meaningless.

management regulations, and laws protecting "the position of the
small employer and the laborer."   It divided its concerns into
"social politics" and "economic politics": the first involved
such issues as health codes and measures on alcoholism, on public
charity, and for the protection of the family and "the hereditary
transmission of property"; the second required "the encouragement
of national productivity," the construction of roads, railroads,
and ports, and measures such as the protection of the merchant
marine, the reform of the banking system, and the nationalization
of insurance—all intended to prepare Chile for an "economic
battle."
    The Coalition wanted a balanced budget, the creation of a
centralized banking system, an increase in the value of the peso,
and direct state assistance to industry, the nitrate companies,
and agriculture. It favored a "discreet plan of public works"
that included irrigation projects as well as ports and railroads.
The state should help families with accident insurance and the
creation of savings institutions, pensions, and popular credit
societies. It should also build workers' housing, and subsidize
private schools. Finally, both the Alliance and the Coalition
wanted a larger military.[88]

But what would be the relation between government policies and Chile's dependence on the United States? During the war, most of the elite agreed that U.S. capital would further national progress. *El Mercurio*, which had become the principal newspaper of the capital as well as Valparaiso, worried in 1916, not that foreigners had taken over the export of copper, borax, and iron, but that there was no export tax on these commodities. Foreign mining operations, "which supply no substitute for what is taken out of the country, should offer greater compensation, a sort of rental in the form of a duty, on the deposits they exploit."[89] In every other respect, elite spokesmen saw the U.S. companies as models of virtue. *El Mercurio* described the copper companies as employers who obeyed the workers' compensation laws and "constructed large hospitals with modern operating rooms, efficient doctors, [and] nurses in clean, white linen."[90] The intendant for O'Higgins praised the Braden Copper Company's operation of "El Teniente": it paid good wages, banned liquor at the mine and in the workers' apartments, and provided the mining town of Sewall with a hospital, schools, and a cemetery.[91] Deputy Gustavo Silva Campos argued that, if Chilean employers would only emulate the management at "El Teniente," the "social questions" would disappear. He was particularly impressed by the campaign against alcoholism and the company policy of making moral conduct a consideration for promotion.[92]

Enthusiasm for the new dependence declined after the war. Elements of the Chilean elite preferred traditional ties to England and Germany. In 1920, the Edwards clan, which owned *El Mercurio*, worked closely with older merchant houses in Valparaiso trying to revive Great Britain's trade with Chile. In the south, Chileans of German descent tried to interest German firms, particularly Krupp, in investing in iron mining and agriculture.[93] Provincials, unhappy with their share of the "rent" during prosperous times, openly complained of the consequences of foreign investment during the slump. *El Sur* of Concepción argued:

> In our country, the exploitation of mineral wealth is, so far, against our interests. The great capitalists who invest here send their earnings abroad; the directing officials [of the mining companies] are foreigners that stay among us while they make their fortunes; the Chilean workmen spend most of their salaries buying necessities imported by the companies, and all this outflow goes against our commercial balance. Nothing remains in this country.[94]

But the regime remained open to foreign capital; the most important struggles over the economy took the form of social politics. The depressions and inflation of the war once again forced workers onto the defensive. Their movement remained a fragmented minority of the workforce; but they now became a formidible threat to the elite. Intellectuals, university students, and middle-class professionals as well as nitrate miners, dockworkers, and industrial laborers now expressed their dissatisfaction with the distribution of income. The regime made some adjustments to the social changes accompanying dependent development. Political parties, particularly the Radicals, increased in size by courting teachers, bureaucrats, junior army officers, and white-collar employees of the private sector. But the political order and elite society had not invested in institutions capable of eliciting sectoral rather than class interests; the government and the governed faced each other over a widening difference in income and social ideology.

The only national institution other than the government was the Church. The people no longer knelt on the street during a daily procession of the viaticum, and the majority of urban males probably did not attend Mass, but religion was still respected; so much so that, in 1915, Recabarren spent most of his campaign for a deputy seat denouncing the clergy.[95] However, the Church was unable to turn this respect into support for elite rule. It had spent the nineteenth century attacking the Liberals and trying to preserve its legal prerogatives, a struggle it had lost. By the end of the First World War, when the Church was unable to identify its political interests within the array of candidates, the Archbishop of Santiago forbade priests to endorse or denounce candidates from the pulpit.[96] But the Church had developed a social politics. Its chief concern in this sense was to retain its influence within the elite; it succeeded by creating its own university and improving its primary and secondary schools. But this commitment to the elite consumed most of its personnel and left it without the staff to reach out to other social sectors. In 1920, 2,300 priests and 3,100 nuns served a population of 3.7 million. Individual clergy became involved with labor, and laborers, particularly those in the mutual aid societies, often had their banners blessed and marched in religious processions. But paternalism was no answer to inflation and unemployment. A more subtle factor also began to weaken the Church's hold on the population. Domestic vocations did not increase fast enough to meet the Church's needs, and it resorted to importing its personnel; by 1920, 30 percent of the religious were immigrants. This reduced the ability of the Church to represent traditional and national interests in the face of foreign capital.[97]

Aside from political parties, professionals and some laborers tried to organize voluntary nonleftist associations to press for legal changes. For example, doctors and teachers created lobbies in order to reduce competition from immigrants. After 1914, the government began to impose tests and residency requirements in these fields.[98] In 1910, state railway workers created the Great Chilean Workers Federation (Gran Federación Obrera de Chile) and succeeded in reversing a pay cut by suing the state administration. After this success, the Federation tried to become an umbrella organization of mutual aid societies. It grew quickly at the war's beginning and then declined just as rapidly when it proved unable to defend its members.[99] In brief, Chile now had a variety of secular institutions, but they did not cross class

lines, nor were they vehicles for resolving such basic problems
as labor-management conflicts and unemployment. But nonelite
Chileans were learning to organize; the Labor Federation eventually became a militant Socialist organization.

The Left faced the same problems during the war as it had
before. It lacked a coherent analysis of the political economy.
It remained divided and largely reformist, reacting to each economic crisis without a larger vision of what it might become. It
included three groups: labor-oriented Democrats and Radicals,
the Socialists, and a new anarchist movement led by the Industrial
Workers of the World (IWW) or Wobblies. The Radicals had the
largest political following and were especially strong among
artisans and railroad workers; the Democrats and Socialists had
the support of the politicized elements of the nitrate and coal
miners and the dockworkers of Iquique, Antofagasta, Valparaiso,
and Concepción, and the factory workers of Santiago. The Wobblies, the last to organize, recruited Laborers who already had a
class consciousness: they were particularly successful in Valparaiso; dockworkers, boatmen, bakers, and masons in the port,
and a number of factory workers in the capital, left party-
oriented organizations to join them.[100] Workers sometimes put
ideological differences aside and cooperated in a common effort.
This was the case in Magallanes where immigrant socialists and
anarchists, most of them from Argentina, built a strong labor
front. And it occurred in the strikes of the shoe factories in
Santiago during the war.[101] Usually, labor associations remained
parochial, distrusting one another even when they were affiliates
of the same party.

Elections continued to divide the movement. In 1915, Radical
thugs broke up Socialist rallies in the nitrate provinces. Radicals and Democrats branded the Socialists as dangerous, but the
three parties shared the same general objectives: they wanted
better public schools, labor reforms, and a return to the gold
standard. The Socialists, disappointed by their showing at the
polls, often turned their editorials against the class they
claimed to represent. They ran sermons against alcoholism,
prostitution, and dancing. The latter, said one letter, seemed
harmless, but caused the seduction and social ruin of young girls
and so led them to prostitution. Recabarren frequently complained
that workers were not serious; they failed to put themselves out
on behalf of the movement.[102]

Workers were not apathetic, but most did not believe left-
wing candidates could change the social situation. In the first
war-related downturn, they could do little more than ask the government for help. In 1914, the laborers in Magallanes petitioned
Santiago for increased spending on public projects, for permission to settle on public lands, for loans to carry out that settlement, and for a ban on the export of mutton and beef because
meat prices were already too high. The mutual aid societies in
Valparaiso made similar requests, and also asked for a tax on un-
cultivated land, a new statute regulating pawnbrokers, a three-
month moratorium on the collection of rents, and the suppression

of mutual betting.[103] These requests have a common theme: the
government was being asked to pass the costs of the export crisis
to other social elements.

The government's increase of the money supply in 1915 generated an immediate response from northern laborers; then the export
boom that began in 1916 provided workers with the income and opportunities to rebuild organizations, to begin new ones, and to
strike. Most of their associations, like those of 1901-7, were
short-lived. But they demonstrated they could now organize on a
larger scale and strike for longer periods of time. The strike
movement built to a peak in 1919: Peter De Shazo estimates that
in Valparaiso and Santiago there were thirty-nine strikes in 1917,
forty-eight in 1918, and ninety-two in 1919; other estimates, that
do not seem as carefully compiled, give smaller totals for all of
Chile but indicate the same pattern of activity.[104] The movement
began among a variety of organizations, but by the end of the war,
Chile had two broad organizations devoted to sustained attacks on
the establishment: the Chilean Workers Federation (FOCh) and the
Wobblies.

The first major confrontations occurred in 1915. In June,
1915, Socialists led an unsuccessful uprising of the nitrate miners at Pozo Almonte, protesting the continued recruitment of
workers from the south.[105] Then in July they staged a defensive
strike at Chuquicamata. Luis V. Cruz, a close associate of
Recabarren, had arrived at the copper mine in February, established a newspaper, and started an industrial union. In late
July, when he had recruited 2,000 members, he was arrested by
company police on the charge of stealing dynamite from the company store. Cruz claimed that he was framed and that the police
planted the evidence at his printing shop. The union struck in
retaliation, before it was ready for such a struggle, and was
broken. From June to September, the Regional Nitrate Federation,
an association of mutual aid societies in Tarapacá, campaigned
against the libreta or work book. The government had introduced
the libreta in 1904 as a means of recording a laborer's hours and
protecting him from unscrupulous employers. Over the years, companies had turned it into a means of disciplining laborers, recording even insignificant infractions and using them as grounds
for fines. The campaign drew support from the Socialists as well
as other parties, but collapsed by October.[106]

But labor did not always lose, and as the war continued, it
began to win more often. Socialists and anarchists in Magallanes
established collective bargaining in 1915. Workers in the shoe
industry of Santiago organized their own federation in February,
1917; it began with 500 members from five factories and, after a
series of strikes and lockouts, grew to successfully represent
4,500 workers from forty-two factories by 1919. By the end of
the war, workers were winning eight strikes for every one they
lost.[107]

Workers also cooperated on a broad scale. For example, in
1917, the Socialists began joining the Great Chilean Workers
Federation (FOCh). (As the organization became more militant,

its leadership dropped the "Great" from its name.) Recabarren had always rejected the FOCh as bourgeois, and the Federation, before 1917, had banned Socialists. But that year he was out of the country, and the Federation's leaders had become less choosy. Most of its railroad workers had left it to form a new organization, and employers had begun destroying its more radical locals. Just before its convention in September in Valparaiso, Ramón Sepulveda Leal, leader of the Socialists there, urged his colleagues to enter the FOCh and turn it to the left. He argued that despite ineffective leadership in Santiago, Federation locals in the south had created combative associations. By aligning with them the Socialists would be able to break out of their traditional enclaves in Valparaiso and the north. Then, at the convention, the FOCh dropped its ban on Socialists.[108] In 1918, the Socialists worked with Democrats within FOCh locals in mounting strikes and other labor actions. In January, 1919, fresh from Argentina, Recabarren attended a regional congress of the Federation as a representative for Antofagasta.[109]

Another example, elaborated in De Shazo's study, was the development of the Wobblies. They began in 1918, reorganizing the dockworkers' movement in Valparaiso. The anarchists' leader, Juan O. Chamorro, joined the IWW after listening to sailors from the United States. The movement established industrial syndicates rather than federations and tried to foment strikes involving a variety of crafts in each sector. According to De Shazo, however, the Wobblies emerged as the most militant faction in a number of collaborative strike efforts. They were apparently unable to create a national network independent of other labor factions.[110]

At the end of the war, when labor confronted simultaneous unemployment and inflation, it was able to mount an impressive show of strength. Workers fought back with strikes and demonstrations that hit every major city. General strikes, sponsored by the FOCh in September, 1919, briefly shut down Santiago, Iquique, Antofagasta, and Chuquicamata. The FOCh also started the hunger meeting movement when it began the nucleus of what became in November, 1918, the Workers' Assembly on National Nutrition (*Asamblea Obrera de Alimentación Nacional* or AOAN). The Assembly staged rallies against the high cost of food and drew the participation of virtually all of organized labor. It demanded measures such as the abolition of the meat tariff, a ban on cereal exports, and public markets where farmers could sell directly to consumers. At its peak, in August, 1919, it atracted 100,000 demonstrators into the center of Santiago.[111]

The Sanfuentes administration stopped the labor movement with repression. It declared states of siege, arrested labor leaders, and smashed labor presses. And it mounted a campaign that characterized the movement as the result of immigrant agitators. To remedy this fictitious problem, it passed a Residence Law that permitted officials to expel any immigrant laborer on the grounds of disturbing the public order.[112] Once repression had contained the strike movement and once it was clear that the

hunger meetings had failed to generate any substantive legal
change, the government felt sufficiently secure to encourage employers and right-wing vigilantes to attack labor leaders and
student radicals.

In 1920, the government's campaign against the labor movement merged with its efforts to prevent Arturo Alessandri's election to the presidency. Social politics now overlapped with a
formal political contest. This was true despite the opposition
of many labor leaders to Alessandri's campaign. Within the organized Left, only the Democrats, as members of the Liberal Alliance, supported him. The Wobblies avoided all elections, and the
Socialists ran Recabarren for President.[113] But Alessandri
openly appealed to labor and sponsored his own rallies to demonstrate the depth of his working-class support. It was these
demonstrations rather than the number of labor votes he received
that made him appear a man of the people. His opponent heading
the new coalition of old-line Liberals and Conservatives in the
National Union ticket, was Luis Barros Borgoño—seventy years old
and president of the Union Club in Santiago. While Alessandri
toured the provinces and gave thousands of Chileans their first
glimpse of a presidential candidate, Barros Borgoño remained in
Santiago and let Nationalist newspapers carry his message. The
National Union's strength consisted of the hacendado's control of
the countryside, its superior ability to buy votes, and the control of the final count by the Sanfuentes administration.[114]

The election was held on June 25, but it was just the beginning of a series of maneuvers by both sides; the government's tactics included brutal attacks on the Left. Public rumor claimed
Alessandri had won, with 179 votes in the electoral college to
Barros' 175. The government refused to release any figures until
it checked for voting irregularities. Alessandri countered with
a rally on June 27, and when it ended in the *carabineros* shooting
some of his supporters, he hinted at the overthrow of the government.[115] While it reviewed the election, the Sanfuentes administration distracted the public with a war scare. It declared in
mid-July that changes in the governments of Bolivia and Peru
meant they would soon invade to take back territories lost in the
War of the Pacific; it immediately sent troops to the north. The
public was soon in a fit of patriotism: women joined the Red
Cross, Santiaguino youths volunteered for the army, workers at
"El Teniente" donated a day's wages to the war effort. Then the
University Student Federation, that supported Alessandri and had
often sided with workers in the struggles of 1919, published its
doubts about the government's honesty. On July 21, a mob attacked
the student headquarters in Santiago, sacked the building, and
killed four of those inside. Six days later, another mob broke
into the Numen printing firm, which published Wobbly pamphlets
and ruined its presses. In Puntas Arenas, that same day, soldiers, *carabineros*, and merchants set fire to the FOCh headquarters; four workers, trapped inside, died in the blaze.[116]

As the war scare subsided, the Sanfuentes administration was
forced to resolve the election. It became obvious, in late August,

that it had fabricated the military crisis. Worse, news returned from the north that soldiers were without food and ammunition, while in Santiago the Minister of War was accused of misappropriating supplies. Then in September, having spent twenty-eight million pesos on the mobilization, the government admitted it could not cover the salaries of public officials for the remainder of the year. Having lost all credibility, the administration accepted the idea of an electoral tribunal that would decide the outcome; on September 30, the tribunal announced Alessandri had won, with 177 votes to Barros' 176. Congress confirmed the decision on October 6.[117]

The controversies of the election obscured the disparity between taking office and achieving power. *El Mercurio*'s editor in Santiago, Carlos Silva Vildosola, was one of the few to recognize during the election how difficult it would be for either candidate to govern. In his view, the Alessandristas had tapped a "latent revolt" against the "directing class," a class that had made "the irresponsible error of ignoring discontent and attributing it to artificial agitation." Silva wanted the next administration to pass new social and economic reforms, but expected that either candidate, once in office, would fail:

> If Congress elects Señor Alessandri, he will have, on the one hand, the hostility of the directing elements, and on the other, the demands of the extremists who have placed their absurd hopes on him and who will ask him to do what no man can do at a blow, being the work of evolution. If Señor Barros Borgoño is elected, his unpopularity will be a serious drawback to the carrying out of his party's administrative program.[118]

In retrospect, Silva's remarks understated Alessandri's problems. For the editor omitted the fact that the treasury was empty. Alessandri needed to finance his many promises while not antagonizing too large a part of the elite or alienating foreign investors. He wanted to create an income tax, legalize unions, increase the budget, reduce unemployment, and limit the ability of Congressional factions to block appropriations.[119] But the elite was not about to tax itself or increase the share of government income spent on labor; and Alessandri's opposition controlled Congress.

The President hoped to reverse this situation in the elections of March, 1921. But his abrasive personality and the perennial problems of coalition government destroyed that possibility.[120] His supporters, the Liberal Alliance, split just before the election on March 5; the Radicals and Democrats ran their own candidates. The Alliance gained a majority in the Chamber of Deputies, but the National Union retained control of the Senate. Throughout the rest of his term, the Senate blocked Alessandri's social and tax reforms. By 1923, he was reduced to insulting the Senate, saying it had "bolshevized" the nation, that he would no longer submit any bills because they would "only swell the number of useless papers" and waste his ministers' time, and that, utlimately, "the people of Chile [would] neither give nor ask for quarter."[121]

Alessandri's bombast aside, his administration continued the basic policies of his predecessors. He tried to protect the domestic interests that had developed during the war, but his hopes for recovery depended on good relations with the United States; in this, he succeeded. Blair and Company, Guaranty Trust, and the National City Bank lent him the money he needed to increase railroad construction and begin a massive program of highway development. In return, he frequently complimented the United States, assuring the U.S. consul in Iquique, for example, "that American commercial enterprises would be given every facility in Chile."[122] He told a correspondent for the *New York Sun* that he admired President Harding and thought that "the great American enterprises in Chile have not only developed the natural resources of the country, but have also served as educational institutions for our people."[123] Even the Senate approved of his efforts on the financial front. His administration increased the money supply, passed new tariffs, and revived nineteenth-century restrictions of foreign vessels engaging in coastal shipping. The last measure was a blessing to the Edwards clan, which still controlled the South American Steamship Company, the largest domestic line.[124]

His administrative policies continued the centralization of power. Throughout the election and after taking office, he frequently advocated the decentralization of government. But nothing came of a proposal he submitted to Congress. It was phrased in such vague terms—omitting any mention of how provincial government should be financed—that it amounted to a political gesture. In practice, the President made executive officials more accountable to his office, and counted on the establishment of civil service examinations to reduce Congressional influence over appointments.[125]

In all, the political economy remained dependent on the United States, and Alessandri accomplished what Barros Borgoño would probably have done. The central economic question remained the distribution of export income, whether in the form of private profits or government contracts and subsidies. The President's tactics in managing the crisis meant that the workforce would continue to bear the major costs of development. Workers, however, continued their efforts to protect their income and, as they did, Alessandri emerged from behind his populist mantle. His reply to labor demands was also that of his predecessors, a few concessions accompanied by greater repression.

The great strike wave collapsed in 1920 as a result of repression. But the labor movement continued to evolve. On the one hand, the Socialist Workers Party succeeded in taking control of the executive positions and most of the newspapers of the FOCh. This raised the tactical possibility of combining a labor party's ability to bargain with the government with the labor movement's support for key strikes. There was little possibility of gaining state power, but the movement had a chance to gain greater leverage over the conduct of the government and thus improve its bargaining position in the workplace. On the other hand, the labor movement remained divided and these divisions weakened it in its crucial confrontations with the government. The success of the Socialists and their determined pursuit of party control of the FOCh, was, unfortunately, one of the major causes of division within the movement as a whole.

The Socialists' goal was to become the exclusive representative of the working class; this involved displacing the left-wing competition within the labor movement and jockeying within the political system to win seats in Congress. In their attacks on the Concha Democrats and the Wobblies, they emphasized the example of the Bolshevik Revolution and the importance of creating a tightly knit party to lead the movement.[126] But Recabarren never set his party on a revolutionary course. When Alessandri offered him the opportunity to join the Liberal Alliance ticket for the Congressional elections of 1921, he jumped at the chance.[127] Recabarren and Luis V. Cruz won seats in the Chamber of Deputies, representing Antofagasta and Tarapacá respectively, but their victory was bought at the price of further dividing the Left.

The most serious breach within the labor movement occurred after the Socialists captured control of the FOCh during the convention at Rancagua, December 25-29, 1921. Recabarren became the Federation's president; Manuel Hidalgo and Ramón Sepulveda Leal became its secretaries; Juan Pradenas Muñoz, a left-wing Democrat, won the vice-presidency. Nonsocialists such as Manuel J. Miranda and Manual Penuir, the former presidents who had opened the FOCh to everyone, lost all influence. Recabarren pushed through resolutions reorganizing the Federation along Soviet lines, demanding that locals no longer support Concha Democrats for election, and joining the Third International. As soon as the Federation convention ended, the Socialists convened in the same city, and in January, 1922, changed their name to the Communist Party.[128] All of this emphasis on ideology, especially in a movement as fluid as that in Chile, made it easy for the Alessandri administration to isolate the various workers' organizations and pick them off one by one.

Alessandri made more concessions to labor than any previous President, but then he faced a greater mobilization of workers than any besides Sanfuentes. Although the number of strikes had decreased, strike activity continued to spread to new sectors. In 1921, unemployed miners rioted against conditions in the warehouses of Santiago where they were being kept.[129] By 1922, the movement was recruiting in the countryside in order to prevent the use of rural workers as scabs in factories and the coal fields. At one strike at the estate of "San Isador" in Quillota, Luis Cruz succeeded in winning bargaining rights for the *inquilinos*.[130] At the other end of the social scale, teachers and officers of the military and the *carabineros* began to organize. That year, 1,500 white-collar employees held a convention to protest legislative delays in approving the budget; their resolution blamed Congress for the "disorderly evolution of the nation's official finances."[131]   The possibility existed, albeit a weak one, that a broad spectrum of the working and middle classes would unite against the regime or at least against the elite-controlled Senate.

But the President was unwilling to accept a labor movement he did not control or which threatened his courtship of foreign capital. The government favored compulsory arbitration where the unions were too strong, and it sided with employers when it was certain they would win. Its handling of the baker's strike in Santiago and of the nitrate miner uprising at San Gregorio illustrate its tactics. In June, 1921, Alessandri settled the bakery dispute through arbitration after the FOCh locals threatened a general strike.[132]   But that same year, the army massacred the miners at the *oficina* "San Gregorio."

The *oficinas* were once again dismissing laborers as nitrate orders fell. Companies in Antofagasta Province alone laid off 4,700 men in January. While running for deputy, Recabarren toured the nitrate region and told laborers, "The time has come for a frontal attack on Capital." On February 2, a few days after he visited "San Gregorio," the English company that owned it decided to close the operation and offered laborers a day's wages as severance. The workers rallied, recruited supporters from other *oficinas*, and demanded fifteen days' severance as well as the keys to the commissary. The English manager, Daniel Jones, waited until he had troops to back his move and then refused the demands. According to government sources, laborers opened fire, killed Jones, a lieutenant, and a sergeant, and began a battle with the outnumbered soldiers. According to the laborers, the soldiers began shooting while Jones and the lieutenant were conferring with a labor delegation; the three men were caught in the soldiers' line of fire. Both sides agree that after the initial volley, a skirmish began between the 1,300 demonstrators and the few dozen troops. Army reinforcements arrived from the port of Antofagasta and the fighting ended with thirty-five to sixty-five workers dead and another thirty to fifty wounded. Laborers who were arrested later claimed they were robbed and whipped while being sent to the port. Alessandri censored news of the massacre— the worst since Iquique—and then defended the army's conduct.[133]

The President did not order the slaughter, but had to uphold authority after the fact. The same cannot be said of the government's harassment of the dockworkers and the coal miners. The struggle on the docks resumed in January, 1921, when sailors, led by the FOCh, and dockworkers, led by the Wobblies, staged simultaneous strikes in Valparaiso. Wobblies supported the sailors' strike because the Federation had promised to include the release of Juan Chamorro, the IWW organizer who was arrested in 1920 during the war scare, in their list of demands. But once the strike began, the government convinced the Federation to break with the Wobblies because their cooperation reduced the respectability of the sailors' cause. The sailors listened and ran a separate strike effort; in the end, both they and the dockworkers were defeated.

Then in April, the merchants at Antofagasta attacked the
dockworkers over the *redondilla,* or rotation in which labor associations controlled the assignment of work and allotted jobs by
turn. Merchants claimed the practice caused "anarchy," but their
real reason was that it threatened their control of the labor
force. Contractors and merchants traditionally reduced their
labor costs by hiring only those who shopped at their company
stores; contractors also received kickbacks from those they
hired; and the *redondilla* reduced the effectiveness of both practices. The merchants staged a lockout with the cooperation of
the government, and broke the dockworkers.[134] In September, the
merchants in Valparaiso did the same thing. In December, those
in Iquique tried the same tactic, but the workers there stayed
out until April, 1922, when the government abolished the *redondilla* in all ports. Even government repression did not break the
dockworkers' spirit immediately; the Wobblies continued their
strike efforts in Valparaiso and Iquique until late 1923.[135]

The government also helped the coal companies destroy the
labor movement among the miners in Concepción Province. The major coal companies were an oligopoly, dominated by the Cousiño
and Edwards clans. But they had become uncompetitive: excavation was still done by hand; and miners had to crawl along narrow
seams that ran out from the coast under the ocean. The companies
had remained profitable only because of the high cost of imported
fuels. When fuel prices fell after the war, the largest companies decided to consolidate into one enterprise, close the older
mines, and recapitalize the best ones. Their consolidation meant
massive layoffs. Locals of the FOCh, led by two Democrats, Jaun
Pradenas Muñoz and Guillermo Vidal, began resisting the consolidation in March, 1920. President Sanfuentes tried to break the
strike, and when that failed, the companies and the Federation
settled through compulsory arbitration. Under the agreement, the
companies agreed to stop the layoffs and increase wages, but they
did not have to recognize the Federation as the miners' bargaining agent. The agreement was to last until December 31, 1921.[136]

Harassment of labor activists continued while the agreement
was in effect. Worse, Pradenas was committed to helping Alessandri win the presidency in 1920 and used scarce Federation resources during the campaign. But he lost whatever leverage he
might have gained with the new President when the Democrats
pulled out of the Liberal Alliance in 1921. On January 1, 1921,
the three major coal firms—Lota and Coronel, the Arauco Coal
Corporation, and the Rios de Curanilahue Coal Corporation—became
one, the Mining and Industrial Company of Chile; by February, the
new company was dismissing miners. The Federation struck on
March 1, and Alessandri imposed an arbitration of the strike.[137]

The Federation was gradually weakened by the length of the
conflict and by divisions within the labor movement. Throughout
1921, workers in a variety of sectors in the region were fighting
against layoffs and wage cuts: they included *inquilinos* near
Coronel, workers at the flour mills and printers in Concepción,
and dockworkers at Talcahuano. The Federation and the Wobblies

spread themselves well beyond their means. But at a time when a
united effort might have mounted a regional campaign, labor associations were at each other's throats: Democrats opposed Socialists, and the FOCh was competing with the Wobblies for followers.[138]

By late 1921, the coal companies sensed victory. The Congressional election was over; the government had sent military
reinforcements; and the firms now had large stocks with which to
meet their orders. They told the government they would not renew
their agreement with labor and intended to lay off 10 percent of
the workforce. The miners said they were also unhappy with the
agreement and wanted a better one, with more pay, better housing,
and retirement benefits. Their strike began on January 1, 1922,
when 15,000, about three-quarters of all the miners in the province, walked out. Pradenas remained their leader, but he had won
election to the Chamber of Deputies; day-to-day decisions were
made by his lieutenant, Guillermo Vidal. On January 4, Pradenas
visited the strike zone and urged the miners to establish the *redondilla* as an alternative to more layoffs. In other words, he
conceded the companies' point that the workforce was too large; he
said nothing about the repression of the *redondilla* in the northern ports.[139]

By the end of January, 1922, the miners' situation seemed
hopeless. A desperate Federation mounted a national, general
strike in order to demonstrate support for the coal miners. It
failed even in Concepción. The streetcar workers and a few railroad men walked out, but the rest of the city kept working.
Miners in the smaller towns remained on the job. Federation organizers tried to recruit laborers from the factories, but the
army was called out, arrested them, and maintained control of the
streets.[140] On February 25, the government arrested Guillermo
Vidal. Soon after, the authorities and the coal companies sponsored a rival organization, the Labor Federation (*Federación de
Trabajo*), that opposed strikes. The Mining and Industrial Company completed its program of dismissals and technical innova-
tion.[141]

The FOCh remained but its revolutionary rhetoric was now de-
void of all plausibility. By mid-1922, the government and employers had won their offensive. The nitrate miners had been
smashed. The Wobblies were in prison or in hiding. The coal
miners had lost their two-year struggle. In order to relieve
Santiago of repeated demonstrations by unemployed nitrate miners
living in hostels, and in spite of the fact the *oficinas* did not
yet require more men, Alessandri began shipping them north. In
these depressing circumstances, Recabarren left for the Soviet
Union, where he attended a Communist Congress and reported home
on the revolution's progress. At home, the new Communist Party
and the FOCh spoke optimistically of their recent "moral triumph."[142]

Chile was now on a treadmill. The growth of domestic interests within the political economy meant an increasing dependence on foreign capital with which to meet domestic demands.

Elections had become a means of obscuring the most important economic issues. While politicians, and especially Alessandri, spoke in more nationalist terms, they were more than ever hostages to fortune. If exports revived, they could make new promises; if they declined, the government had little choice but to reinflate the economy, borrow abroad, and repress the strikes and demonstrations that were certain to follow.

The new dependence on the United States, like the old on Great Britain, revolved about the sale of *salitre*. The British remained a powerful group within the nitrate industry, but they were now part of the dependent interests relying on increased nitrate sales to the United States. The established interests in the trade faced fundamental problems. Within Chile, the mobilization of the working class threatened the upper class' share of export income. Outside of Chile, Germany and England had developed synthetic substitutes for *salitre* and, although this seemed unimportant in 1923, it proved the more dangerous development to the regime.

The Sanfuentes and Alessandri administrations demonstrated that it was still possible to smash the labor movement. Unfortunately, the tactics of the labor leaders played into the government's hand. They continued to quibble with one another and use the movement as a vehicle of self-aggrandizement—electoral politics was almost the only means of mobility out of the workforce. Malaquías Concha began as a humble lawyer. When he died in 1922, he was a senator with a country estate. Juan Pradenas Muñoz, who once shoveled coal on a tramp steamer, in the years after this history became a senator for Santiago and a powerful logroller.[143] At each level of the movement, workers identified with their leaders; and the leaders' ambitions led to feuds among miners, dockworkers, sailors, and railroad men.

But the government and the nitrate producers were unable to meet the new challenge of competition from synthetic nitrates. As the supply of nitrates on the world market rose, the price fell, and the Parliamentary Regime entered a terminal crisis. Officers of the army staged a coup in 1924 that began a series of political experiments, ending in dictatorship and even greater dependence on the United States.

6. Nationalist Policies and Economic Realities

> The capitalist evolution of the upper classes
> is now intimately linked to the development of
> giant foreign firms, principally North American
> and English. The more powerful enterprises have
> dragged Chilean capital under them, providing
> them security and protection. Little by little,
> our country has been converted into a foreign fac-
> tory, and great fortunes of our land pass into the
> hands of foreigners who do not even know us. It
> is true that foreign firms help our people be-
> cause they provide a great deal of employment;
> but it is also true that the great financial oli-
> garchies that they form come to exercise a sov-
> ereignty over our country that is first economic,
> then political, and ultimately moral.
>
> Guillermo Viviani Contreras,
> *Sociología chilena,* 1926.

Exports increased and unemployment fell in 1923, but these hopeful changes were reversed by 1926. The nitrate industry suffered from declining productivity because of the exhaustion of the richest deposits and stiff competition from synthetics. Producers tried to avert ruin with a monopoly agreement to raise prices. The tactic not only reduced exports but increased the synthetics' share of the world nitrate market. Producers also pressured the government to lower their costs by reducing the nitrate tax. But no administration could afford to do that. The tax on nitrate exports provided less of the government's income than before, but it remained essential. As late as 1928, it supplied 22.8 percent of all ordinary revenues; by comparison, the income tax supplied 16.1 percent. Nitrate income was also the principal means of paying for imports; and the combined value of all customs duties was still over 50 percent of the government's ordinary income. [1]

Successive administrations in the 1920s tried to protect domestic industries in order to encourage a diversification that

would broaden their income base. They also created new taxes and
periodically attempted to reduce expenditures. But they did not
succeed in creating a fully nationalist set of policies. Foreign
entrepreneurs opposed government limitations on their activities
and increases in their costs from taxes and protectionist measures. In the face of their protests, the Chileans usually re-
lented. Domestic interests limited government initiatives at direct taxation, but continued to demand government protection and
administrative expansion. In the end, despite promises to the
contrary, each administration resorted to foreign loans to keep
itself and the economy growing.

The inability of civilian leaders to satisfy competing demands on the government led to the overthrow of the Alessandri
administration in 1924. The military had grown in size and importance throughout the Parliamentary Regime. Its seizure of
power in 1924 was the result of a reform movement among junior
officers in the army and civilian encouragement to the army to
take a more active role in politics. The reform movement began
as a reaction to the old guard of senior officers trained in the
Germanic tradition.[2] In 1919, it went beyond a desire to .change
traditions of command. Two generals, Guillermo Armstrong and
Manuel Moore, organized a dissident movement among junior officers devoted to increasing the army's role in politics and to
support of social reforms. The movement was suppressed, the
generals were forced to resign, but junior officers continued to
believe that their training and discipline made them especially
fit to rescue the country from its disorder.[3] In 1924, they
joined civilian groups to protest their low pay.[4] Alessandri ignored the danger signals and used the army as a counter to his
opponents in the Senate. The President saw the election of 1924
as his last chance to gain a Congressional majority for his reforms. He knew his opponents would use outdated election registers and control of the polls in rural areas to win. Deciding on
a tactic no President had tried since Balmaceda, he called out
the army, and had it take control of polls on election day. His
Liberal Alliance won seventy-two of 118 seats in the Chamber of
Deputies and gained control of twenty-four of the thirty-seven
Senate seats.[5]

But the new Congress was no more cooperative than the old.
It spent its sessions reviewing disputed elections. The Liberals,
instead of supporting the President, now blocked appropriations
and his bills in order to force the Alliance to pick a member of
their party as its presidential candidate for 1925.[6] Army officers became embittered because after the election, in order to
silence his critics, Alessandri forced several junior officers to
resign for having exceeded their authority. Then on September 2,
the Senate began consideration of a bill to increase its living
allowance—the Constitution still prohibited any Congressional
salary—to 2,000 pesos a month, but it had not yet approved pay
for the military. When the Senate started its deliberations,
young officers gathered in the gallery as a show of dissent.[7]

Military officials then had to choose between punishing the

officers or backing their movement. Afraid of a complete breakdown
in discipline, they did the latter. By September 5, troops were
in the streets. An intimidated Congress hurriedly passed a large
body of social legislation, including the legalization of labor
unions. Alessandri vetoed the bill increasing the Congressional
living allowance. But it was too late. On September 9, the
President, seeing he could no longer control the situation and
fearing assassination, resigned, and, with the help of the United
States ambassador, left for Argentina.[8]

Politicians who only a few days before had been arguing over
the Alliance candidate for President, accepted the coup and tried
to turn it to their advantage. Liberals and Conservatives, sen-
sitive to the issue of military discipline, kept silent. Radicals
approved the dissolution of Congress but demanded the military
convene a Constitutional convention as a first step toward returning power to civilians.[9] Democrats waited for a week before issuing a manifesto that condoned the soldiers' conduct, asked workers
not to strike, and counseled party supporters that only an increase
in labor productivity would arrest inflation.[10]

The Communists thought the coup proved the capitalist system
was in crisis; but they postponed any decision on military rule.
Recabarren was openly skeptical that the new junta would reform
anything. He doubted that soldiers who had always served "the
reigning oligarchy" and "suffocated all popular aspirations"
could now perform "the great work of the people."[11] Four days
after the coup, he told a labor convention, "The militarism in
power today is no better than a capitalist dictatorship since the
armed forces have always been the instrument and support of all
capitalist dictatorships." But he wanted to be "prudent" and
"wait a while in order to evaluate the development of the promised program"; he reminded the Left that "no bourgeois revolution
will bring happiness . . . and only the social revolution carried
out by the proletariat is and will be the means of assuring the
true social welfare."[12]

Although the reform movement consisted of junior officers,
the senior officers took command of the government and moved it
to the right. Generals Francisco Altamirano and Pablo Bennett
and Vice Admiral Francisco Nef were torn between their conservative sentiments and pressure from the younger officers to back
the new reforms. In October, they tipped their hand. The British companies objected to the Private Employees Law which established the forty-eight-hour week, time and a half for overtime,
pensions, and paid vacations for white-collar workers. The junta
stopped enforcing the law's provisions. Major Marmaduke Grove,
the most outspoken of the junior officers, protested the slow
pace of change.[13] On October 29, Roberto Salinas, Luis V. Cruz,
and Elías Lafertte, the Executive Committee of the FOCh, told
locals to prepare for a general strike to counter the government's repression of the labor movement.[14] By December, the Radical and Democratic Parties were calling for a return to civilian
rule.[15] Then the government endorsed Ladislao Errázuriz Lazcano,
a Liberal and a member of the traditional elite, for President.[16]

On January 3, 1925, the junior officers staged a *golpe* and, on January 25, took power. The new leaders, Lt. Colonel Carlos Ibañez, Lt. Colonel Mario Bravo, Major Marmaduke Grove, and General Pedro Dartnell Encina, announced their commitment to the September reforms. This change of power frightened the upper class even more than the original coup. *El Mercurio,* sensing the discord within the army before the *golpe,* worried, "Chile is a liberal country rapidly moving to the left. . . . The moral break in the military and civilian elements of the country produced by the September revolution has created a relaxation in social discipline." It urged politicians to put aside their differences and help reinstill "the impulse toward order" that had been lost.[17] The navy, the more aristocratic of the services, resisted the change in government. It seemed on January 24 that civil war might begin, repeating the division of forces in 1891. The U.S. ambassador, William Collier, was so frightened that he cabled his superiors to send warships from the U.S. Pacific fleet. However, he was assured by General Dartnell that "American interests" would be protected. Dartnell "told me he could protect everyone, even those most hated by the younger officers and by the masses."[18] Dartnell's presence on the junta notwithstanding, the upper class remained on the defensive. The junta called on Alessandri to return and help establish a new Constitution. It searched churches and elite homes for arms hidden by right-wing groups. Rumors circulated in the elite clubs of Santiago and Valparaiso that army radicals had distributed guns to the workers.[19] Alessandri agreed to return, but demanded the soldiers return to their barracks and he be allowed to resign at the end of his regular term, December 23, 1925.

The Left greeted the January *golpe* as a victory. The Executive Committees of the FOCh and the Communist Party issued a joint resolution in favor of the uprising and the call for a new Constitution. The junior officers had saved the workers the trouble of waging war on the oligarchy. They had "unfurled the banner of purification to cleanse the country of its corroding decadence." The resolution insisted the workers must now take part in the government. Every previous reform movement had betrayed the cause of social improvement once it was in power; "This is due to the working class not taking part in any of the new Governments and seeing to it that the promises are carried out. It must not recur this time."[20]

But it did. Once he returned, Alessandri supported the harsh measures of the Minister of War, Carlos Ibañez, to prevent the further mobilization of the Left. Ibañez, who supported the basic reform program of September, 1924, but opposed the Communist Party and the FOCh, maneuvered in 1925 to become the next President. He failed initially because the civilian parties united behind the candidacy of Emiliano Figueroa, but became President in 1927.

The aging Figueroa was no match for either the problems of the nitrate depression, that began in his first year in office, or the cunning of Ibañez. Ambassador Collier described him as "a

man who mingles in the life of the club and does not claim to be
better than his fellow man." Formally a Balmacedist, he had been
a rake in his youth. He spent one fortune while ambassador to
Argentina, gained appointment as Recorder of Deeds, and used the
office to build another fortune. He described himself as "belonging to the stagecoach days. In those days you got into your
coach, whipped up the horses and off we went! No complications,
no mechanics, nothing!"[21] His brother was head of the Supreme
Court; and Ibañez, who became Vice-President in 1927, forced the
President out by creating an embarrassing confrontation between
the Executive and the Judiciary. Ibañez then suppressed all opposition, banned the Communists, and had himself elected President.
Thereafter, he ruled with a puppet Congress.

The only major monograph on the period has unfortunately
concentrated on the military origins and aspects of the Ibañez
regime.[22] Ibañez was not a military solution to Chile's problems
but only another response to the deepening, systemic crisis of
economic dependence. To explain why the crisis took the form it
did, why the Left failed to gain greater influence than it did,
and how and why Ibañez managed to govern as he did requires an
examination of the political economy of the 1920s rather than of
the army. Although the form of government seemed to change, the
deeper constraints on political decisions, the more profound in-
fluences on the country's direction, did not.

REFORM AND DEPENDENCE

Despite the appearance of disorder, the 1920s were a period of
significant reform and political continuity. The governments
moved to protect and develop industry, regulate working conditions, diversify the tax structure, and arrest inflation. These
changes represented a broad consensus about the future. Chileans
now wanted greater economic autonomy. The middle class pushed
for reforms that would cement its role in government and provide
it greater economic security. Even the elite abandoned the doctrine of free trade. The questions before the society were in-
stitutional and financial. How would Chile rearrange her political system and her credit structure to carry out these changes?
The irony in this decade as in those before was that the government needed export income, especially that from nitrates, to fulfill these new public expectations; and it had to negotiate, often
on very unfavorable terms, with foreign investors to raise that
income.

The most significant innovations of the period were in the
government's tax and monetary policies. In December, 1923,
Alessandri succeeded in getting through Congress an income tax
law that took effect in January, 1924. The measure was weaker
than his original proposal; but it established new taxes on real
estate, stocks, bonds, corporate income, and salaries.[23] The following year, the junta invited W. E. Kemmerer, the "money doctor"
from Princeton University, to study the country's tax and banking

system and recommend improvements. Kemmerer's committee of U.S.
economists suggested a simplification of the income tax and tariff
schedules, the establishment of a central state bank with control
over currency, and a return to the gold standard. The Figueroa
administration instituted the committee's suggestions. The new
Central Bank used the gold conversion fund to back the peso. By
buying and selling gold and foreign bank drafts and by raising
and lowering its discount rate on its notes to other Chilean banks,
it succeeded in holding the peso to a value of six British pence.[24]
Administrations throughout the decade—until 1930—maintained a
favorable balance of trade. As a result, inflation fell appre-
ciably to about 3 percent a year between 1927 and 1930.[25]

This control over currency, however, came after a period of
intense economic turmoil. Before 1927, both the government and
the private sector were in trouble. In 1925, the junta and President Alessandri raised the salaries of public employees from 20
to 100 percent—the size of the increase depended on their positions—and created new ministries, including a Department of
Labor. They increased military pay 116 percent. By 1926, the
government faced an annual deficit of 116 million pesos. The
cost of public salaries alone amounted to 426 million pesos, 39.5
percent of all expenditures.[26] At the same time, capitalists
were demanding the government bail them out of another calamitous
bout of speculation.

Beginning in 1923, the wealthy began converting treasury
notes into gold and stocks. No one believed the government's
figures on the size of its gold conversion fund or the amount of
currency in circulation.[27] In 1924-26, the stock market passed
through a cycle reminiscent of that between 1905 and 1907. Some
of the new capital went into industry but most of it was in mining. Stocks doubled, tripled, and then plummeted to a fraction
of their high values. The shares of the Company of Llanquihue,
which was supposedly developing Bolivian tin mines, rose from
seventy-one to 168.5 pesos between January and March, 1924, then
fell to eighteen pesos by February of the following year.[28] The
decline of the market continued through 1926 as nitrate stocks
began to fall because of declining demand for *salitre*. Only industries survived the general collapse, and countered the trend
by rising in value.[29]

Public confidence fell with the state of the economy. The
most capable President would have been able to do little in 1926.
The government could not simultaneously pay higher public salaries
and give in to the producers' demand for a reduction in the nitrate tax. Nor could it arrest inflation. Previous administrations had increased the money supply by over 100 million pesos
(6 d.) in two years in order to pay for the increase in government spending. As a result, the cost of living at the end of
1925 was already 33 percent higher than in 1921; in the capital,
the cost of food was 52 percent higher.[30] Capitalists continued
to press the government for credit, and workers demanded public
employment. To meet some of these demands, the Figueroa administration borrowed in London and New York.

By February, 1927, New York bankers were placing harsh
conditions on any new credit to Chile. They demanded a moratorium
of a year on any new bond issues by the government. They permitted the government to ask for advances on future bond issues but
only up to 87 percent of their nominal value.[31] The United States
government, at the same time, pressed for a settlement of the
Tacna-Arica controversy on terms the Chileans interpreted as
favorable to Peru. The elite, trying to avoid losing face with
the public—and with the military—began blaming the United
States for all of Chile's problems. Agustín Ross recalled the era
of gunboat diplomacy and cited the conclusion of the U.S. Senate
Foreign Relations Committee that ten of the twenty-one Latin
American nations were already under the control of U.S. capital.
"Chile," he believed, "should renounce the so-called Monroe Doctrine; should cancel all pecuniary obligations with the Government
and financiers of the United States, and maintain separation from
that country in order to conserve its independence. If this is not
done, we will run the risk of grave difficulties."[32] *La Nación*
was afraid the United States would one day impose financial control on Chile as she had done in Bolivia and Nicaragua; to avoid
that, the country should cease forging "new links to the golden
chain with the North American Bankers. . . . The dollar has taken
too much copper out of our mountains and is now beginning vic-
toriously to invade our nitrate fields." It added: "Our Government officials should not forget the words of Senator Preston, approved by North American opinion, 'The Stars and Stripes will
wave over Latin America as far as Tierra del Fuego, the only
boundary the ambition of our race accepts.'"[33]

On the same issue, *El Mercurio* argued Chile had foolishly
turned its back on "its traditional bankers" and was "a victim of
a strange and unhealthy fascination with the United States."
"Great Britain," it noted, "has never mixed the commercial business of its bankers with the policy of its Government." As
proof, it mentioned George Canning's refusal to help bankers collect debts from Latin American governments in the 1830s.[34] Another paper admitted, however, that investors in the United States
now held fewer Chilean bonds than they had during the First World
War.[35] No one cared to admit the origin of the government's
problems. A beleaguered ruling group was being forced to bargain
for foreign credit but could not afford to surrender any nationalist ground.

The most important issue in Chile's dependence on foreign
capital remained the governments' policies in the nitrate sector.
If Chile could increase her nitrate income, she could reduce her
need for foreign loans and new issues of currency, Chileans now
owned more than 60 percent of the shares of nitrate companies,
although many of those companies still had British managers. Nitrate income could increase by raising output and reducing costs
or by retarding production and raising the price. Alessandri,
the interim juntas, and Figueroa let the Nitrate Producers Association try to fix a high price by controlling the expansion of
exports.

The policy the four administrations followed seemed the only plausible one. It was the simplest alternative to reducing the nitrate tax. Any other effort to reduce producers' costs would inevitably pit some of the producers against the government because the industry as a whole had no uniform costs or methods of accounting. Some of the *oficinas* operated as they had in the 1880s, with ancient boiling tanks and dozens of mules. Others used new steam equipment, trucks, and air hammers. The Guggenheims were experimenting with capital-intensive refining methods developed at the copper mines. Although Chile established the metric system in 1848, systems of measurement reflected the industry's long association with foreign capital. The dimensions of the nitrate tanks were kept in feet, the amount of liquid in them was stated in cubic meters, and the amount of *salitre* produced was calculated in Spanish *quintals*. Accounts were equally confusing. Current operating expenses of machinery were increasingly maintained in U.S. dollars; the sale price of *salitre* was stated in shillings per quintal; and labor costs were given in pesos.[36] Rather than try to standardize practices in the trade, the governments allowed the producers to fight one another within the Association over quotas and the final price. The policy not only reduced the competitiveness of *salitre* on the world market but led to direct conflicts with powerful consumer interests, principally those in the United States.

The first conflict occurred in the latter part of 1923. Existing stocks of *salitre* were being liquidated and *oficinas* were resuming production. "While none of the mines are working at full capacity," the U.S. consul in Iquique reported, "more than 50 percent of the total of this district are working part time, and others are expected to start soon."[37] The United States Congress was less concerned with the industry's recovery than with *salitre*'s price. Farmers were complaining that before the World War *salitre* sold in the United States for about $45.00 to $55.00 a ton. After the war and despite the depression, it was selling for $75.00 a ton. Farmers growing cotton, who were its major consumers, were spending $18.00 an acre on fertilizer. They argued they were absolutely dependent on *salitre* because it made it possible to bring a crop to fruition by July, before the boll weevil matured. Representative William F. Stevenson of South Carolina became the farmer's spokesman and urged Congress to establish a revolving fund of ten million dollars to pool the purchase of *salitre* and give the farmers some leverage over its price.[38]

The Congressional committee hearing testimony on Stevenson's bill called Bernard Baruch as an expert because of his role in helping the Allies organize commodity pools during the war. Stevenson asked him why, if *salitre* cost $53.00 to $59.00 a ton to buy in Chile and transport to the United States it was selling for $75.00 a ton. Baruch answered that he was not acquainted with the details of the trade but believed the U.S. buyers were "really competitors." He advised against any government purchasing program. He told the committee that the Chilean government did not own any *oficinas* as several members apparently believed, but that the government was nonetheless to blame for the product's high price. He compared the situation to that of the war and claimed the Chilean government was using the Nitrate Producers Association to advance its own interests:

> It is not so much a question of what the different nitrate importers do, although I think it is important to see that they do not get into a combination in restraint of trade or in any way make undue profits. But it seems to me the problem is to get the source of nitrates . . . the way to meet the Chileans is to try to increase the sources of supply within our country.[39]

Baruch, Henry Ford, and other major entrepreneurs were pushing for the establishment of a synthetic nitrate project, devoted to the production of cyanamide or ammonium sulphate, at Muscle Shoals, Alabama.[40] Herbert Hoover, then Secretary of Commerce, argued that creation of the plant was the only way to defeat the British-run Nitrate Producers Association. Hoover's comment on the character of the Association led to an official Chilean protest. The Chileans insisted they ran the Association, they owned most of the *oficinas,* and they were eleven of the Association's seventeen directors.[41]

The real conflict within the nitrate industry was very different from that presented by either Baruch or Hoover. The issue was not one of government control or British producers' control. The British remained an important influence within the industry because they ran many companies and because the most powerful Chileans in the nitrate sector were often of British descent and maintained contacts with London.[42] The U.S. importers and companies that produced *salitre* did not join the Association because they argued membership would violate the Sherman Antitrust Act. But in fact, the U.S. interests worked closely with the Association. Ambassador Collier was forced to admit in one report that frequently the U.S. and British enterprises had the same representatives. Frederick Wightman, for example, was general manager for W. R. Grace and Company; he was an Englishman as were most of his subordinates. As manager of W. R. Grace, Wightman was outside the Nitrate Producers Association and led the company's campaign to refuse membership. But as representative of "certain English companies, he is a Director of the Association." The American head of DuPont in Chile had kept his corporation out of the Association; but he made contributions to its fund to purchase nitrate stocks and keep them off the export market. Although they were not Association members, the law permitted U.S. importers to buy their *salitre* from the Association. It also permitted American companies to produce *salitre* and export it on their own account. It only forbade the purchase of *salitre* from one nonmember for resale to another. "It is important to bear in mind," Collier explained,

that although the American companies have stayed out of
the Association and although there is no concrete evidence
of any agreement between them and the Association, they
have apparently worked in harmony with the latter organization. There has been no price cutting by the Americans
and evidently their production has not been greatly in excess of what it would have been had they been members of
the Association.[43]

The apparent conflict between U.S. interests and the Chilean
government or British companies obscured the real conflict between
the U.S. companies involved in the nitrate trade and the Chilean
government. The American companies wanted the benefits of an international cartel in setting prices. But they wanted to avoid
any formal restriction on their own production. In May, 1924,
Alessandri bowed to increasing pressure from Chilean producers
and demanded the American companies join the Association or lose
all opportunity to bid at future public auctions of nitrate lands.
Collier sent a private note to the government objecting to the
decision, saying American public opinion would insist the companies be prosecuted as a trust if they joined the Association.
He threatened retaliation if the government prevented DuPont and
Grace from buying more nitrate lands. "Candor compels me to say
that this, in effect, would be confiscation of the capital already
invested by American firms. Unless they can secure supplies of
raw material, the capital invested will eventually prove a loss."
They had not only invested in plants but in advertising the product in the United States:

> I am sure that not only the government of the United
> States but that its bankers and business men, would con-
> sider the refusal to accept bids by Americans except upon
> condition of their joining the Association, in violation
> of the laws of their country as interpreted by able law-
> yers, as an unwarranted interference with the rights of
> the established American firms engaged in the nitrate
> business, and as a notice that American capital was not
> desired in Chile, and as an act peculiarly discriminatory
> against the citizens of that country because the contem-
> plated action affects only them.[44]

Alessandri, who was only hoping to wave the flag, was appalled
and frightened by Collier's note. He called Collier to a private
meeting on the afternoon of May 25, at La Moneda, and told the
ambassador that he had already seen to it that the ban on the
sale of nitrate lands to DuPont and Grace would last only three
years, until the end of the current Association agreement. The
government did not intend to sell any lands before then; the
market was still too weak. Collier apologized and told Alessandri
his note had been written "in ignorance of the fact the degree
had already been signed," and added it did not "contain any

challenge to the sovereignty of Chile." Alessandri was not mollified. He was still worried the note would be leaked to the public because he could not trust the clerks in the Foreign Ministry to keep it confidential. Collier finally calmed the President by telling him there was no need for a written reply.[45]

Alessandri at least preserved the outward appearance of a nationalist. The juntas were less successful. One of the first decisions of the junta after the original coup led to the purchase of nitrate lands by the Guggenheims. The government sold the lands on September 15 to raise revenues, and the Guggenheims, acting through a Chilean subsidiary, the South American Products Corporation, were the highest bidder, paying 20.1 million gold pesos, or eight million more than had been expected, for the land.[46] The junta decided to set aside the rule restricting the sale of nitrate lands to members of the Nitrate Producers Association; the Guggenheims entered the nitrate business.

But ultimately the country faced a much more serious challenge to its development than U.S. companies: the nitrate industry was becoming uncompetitive. Exports had risen from 2.2 to 2.5 million tons between 1923 and 1925; but in late 1925, they began to fall. By the last quarter of 1926, the decline had turned into a depression. Ammonium sulphate from Germany now cost less in Europe than *salitre*. The English and Germans were increasing their output of that product; and the Norwegians and Germans were turning out ever larger amounts of calcium nitrate. *Salitre* was also hurt by the depreciation of the currencies of France and Belgium relative to the British pound; this raised its price in its two most important European markets.[47] By the end of September, 1926, sales were running 56 percent of what they had been at the same time the previous year. Chile's share of the world nitrate market had fallen disastrously: in 1914, it was 55 percent; after the war it was usually about 32 percent; in late 1926, it was 16 percent.[48] By October, only forty-three of the 149 *oficinas* were in operation, and none of them was producing at full capacity. The plants laid off 25,000 men; another 70,000 lost their jobs as the depression spread. The crisis was general and reached to Puntas Arenas, where the sheep ranches counted on meat sales to the nitrate zones.[49]

The policy of supporting a fixed price for *salitre* ultimately failed to protect either the industry's profits or Chile's total nitrate income. Farmers in Europe turned from *salitre* to synthetics. Farmers in the United States demanded government action against the Association's pricing policies. The policy also failed to arrest Chile's dependence on the United States. U.S. companies gained from the Association's attempt at monopoly, and gradually expanded their interest in nitrate production. The success of DuPont and Grace must have been a major factor in attracting the Guggenheims into the trade.

The governments between 1923 and 1927 protected some native industry and reformed the tax structure and the banking system. But the fruits of these reforms came after 1926. Worse, the private sector failed to turn the brief improvement in nitrate sales

into a faster diversification of the economy. Capitalists instead
fomented another bout of stock speculation in mining companies.
As a result, despite some good initiatives which qualify the period as probably the most important reform years in the nitrate era,
each government was unable to meet its immediate obligations without expanding the money supply or borrowing from abroad. Inflation continued to cause political instability.

THE LAST MOVES OF THE LEFT

For the Left, these years were a period of substantial gains and
political frustration. The movement's problems were the same as
before; it was poorly organized, politically divided, and often
badly led. The Communist party was small. According to Ramírez
Necochea, it had only 2,000 members in the early 1920s and perhaps
4,000 or 5,000 in 1926.[50] The FOCh claimed 200,000 members,
probably an exaggeration. But its Executive Committee, dominated
by the Communists, still had little control over affiliates.
Despite these weaknesses, inflation continued to provoke labor
militancy. While Alessandri had succeeded in destroying the Wobblies and defeating the most militant elements in the FOCh, he and
the military juntas were unable to contain the entire labor movement. By 1925, the vast majority of workers who struck did not
belong to any labor organization.[51]
      The upper class never accepted the social reforms passed in
1924. Elite attitudes toward the population remained those of
the Pelucones. Chile, in the eyes of its most successful citizens, would prosper only as she increased her population with
European immigrants. In 1924, Joaquín Edwards Bello suggested
Chile bring 500,000 Germans into the country. "Chile needs to
increase its population in relation to its territory. In order
to improve the national economy, this problem must be studied:
Chile's wealth, her prosperity and civilization depend on [solv-
ing] it. We should give up our sentimentality toward the abo-
riginal race and assist German immigration, having in mind the
immensity of our resources that only await European effort."[52]
Lautaro Rosas, Minister of Hacienda in 1926, blamed the country's
economic problems on her population shortage: four million people
were not enough to sustain economic growth. He urged the govern--
ment to attract the unemployed from Germany and Great Britain and
settle them in the south.[53]
      Despite these elite attitudes, social reforms were passed,
because the workers had a new ally, the middle class of professionals and functionaries in government, commerce, and industry.
The size of this class is difficult to estimate because census
data list occupations without specifying the circumstances of employment. There were many *patrones,* or employers, who ran their
own shops, and *empleados,* white-collar workers, who earned less
than workers on the state railroads. But the census data do indicate that the sectors in which the members of the middle class
were most likely to be employed were growing: government

administration, including teachers but excluding the military, employed 31,000 in 1920 and 48,000 in 1930; the "liberal professions" included 21,000 in the earlier census and 27,000 in the later.[54] Professionals and functionaries voted, joined political parties, formed associations, were concentrated in Santiago and Valparaiso, and included the junior officers of the army. They were nationalistic in that they shared the workers' resentment of immigrants, yet they also depended on the export economy for their social position. They favored reforms that would cement their roles in the bureaucracy, education, law, and medicine, but shared many of the elite's prejudices toward the native labor force.[55]

They became a swing element in Chilean politics, anxious to prod the government for concessions but frightened of the mobilization of those below. By threatening to ally themselves with the labor movement, they succeeded in exacting attention from every administration. An example of their role was the Renters' League (*Liga de Arrendatarios*) that began in late January, 1925, among white-collar workers and mutual aid societies in Valparaiso. Anarchists as well as many nonunion workers joined; a second soon formed in Santiago; and by the second week of February, the two leagues were working together. Their leaders demanded that the junta reduce rents to 50 percent, and threatened a general strike in the two cities if their demand was not met. The junta gave in, but not before a general strike began in Valparaiso.[56] The government established a Housing Authority to reduce rents to 50 percent of their level in December, 1924, and limited rents on any new building to 10 percent of its purchase value per month. The law helped those who were already in apartments at the price of reducing the rate of new housing construction, but it said nothing about changing conditions in the tenements. The Renters' League then split between those who wanted to cooperate with the new law and the anarchists who saw housing as an issue with which to remobilize the Left; in March, the renters' movement split again when the Communists organized their own association to compete with that of the anarchists. The Housing Authority was soon dominated by middle-class bureaucrats, representing the government, and the moderate *empleados* and mutualists of the original League.[57]

Given its importance, each government tried to placate the middle class while playing on its fear of social revolution. Ultimately, Chile retained her reform legislation but enforced it selectively. Laws helping teachers and bank clerks were upheld; those helping manual laborers were periodically set aside. The Work Accident Law, for example, became a dead letter in the provinces because the Labor Department lacked the manpower to enforce it outside the capital and Valparaiso. In June, 1925, Alessandri suspended it altogether when he discovered that its provisions applied to rural labor.[58]

The eventual state solution to social militance was to employ bureaucrats as supervisors of the workforce and to improve the pay of the police and the military. This solution was not

completely clear until Ibañez gained power, but the steps taken
by his predecessors extended the authority of the state over the
individual and indirectly developed a public acceptance of the
measures he would undertake. The identity card or *carnet* first
imposed on dockworkers during the war, then on immigrants, was
by 1923 demanded of all foreign residents, including tourists.[59]
In October, 1924, the junta established the Bureau of Identifica-
tion and decreed that since several major cities already required
carnets for employment, and because "this service is indispensable in modern states for the security of the inhabitants," everyone over eighteen would now have to register with the national
agency.[60]

Inflation, however, revived the strike movement in 1925, and
the Communist Party, while it did not lead the movement, tried to
become its spokesman. The Labor Office recorded forty-one
strikes involving 12,299 workers in 1923, and 113 strikes involving 51,198 workers in 1925. Only 19,000 of the strikers in 1925
were "union members."[61] The Communists talked about the collapse
of the capitalist order, but they planned for the consolidation
of their power within the labor movement. Their newspapers
praised everything done by the Bolsheviks including the Cheka's
repression of social democrats and anarchists; in 1925, the
Chilean Party sided with Stalin against Trotsky. At home, the
party's National Executive Committee created loyalty tests and
expelled any member who failed to pass them.[62] Cruz, as president of the FOCh, then tried to turn this small nucleus into the
bargaining agent of the strike movement. The Federation shared
the opinion of many laborers that Alessandri would support strikers because of the role that popular demonstrations played in
forcing the military to relinquish office. In April, 1925, the
Federation staged a general strike in Tarapacá; it won wage increases and became the bargaining agent for the miners.[63] It
then mounted an organizing campaign at Chuquicamata in May. The
Guggenheims had sold the mine to the Anaconda Copper Mining Company in 1923, and the Federation attacked "Yankee gold" in order
to attract support. But it is clear that the strike leaders
wanted a union rather than to expel Anaconda; at one point, they
wrote Ambassador Collier stating their aims and asking him to intervene; he refused. Management responded by dismissing 1,000
miners, forcing the Federation to strike before it was fully pre-
pared. The Federation effort failed despite a sympathy strike
and the boycott of Americans by workers in the port of Antofagasta.[64]

Cruz was mistaken about Alessandri; his views on labor had
not changed. He resumed office intent on stopping the strike
movement. He told 20,000 labor supporters in Valparaiso, a month
after he regained power, that they should immediately return to
work. "In the midst of this hymn of redemption, which raises itself up to the heavens, there appears something like a cloud
which worries and grieves me. I note signs of agitation in the
country among certain classes, which I believe to be entirely un-
justified and inopportune at this time and which do not fit in

with the harmony of the moment, nor with the demands of the people." Labor should wait for its deliverance. "I say to you that you should seek the solution to your miseries and misfortunes in my love, in my loyalty, in my sympathy and in my protection, and not through the medium of upheaval."[65] In late May, the government began a crackdown in Tarapacá against the Federation. It arrested labor organizers and shut down the Left newspapers.[66] Its actions set off a general strike in Iquique. Miners on the pampa armed themselves and barricaded a few of the *oficinas*. On June 4, soldiers, *carabineros*, and marines attacked the occupied plants. At "La Coruña," the armed forces fired on the miners for a day and a half, killing at least 100.[67] The government blamed the uprising on Peruvian agitators.

After "La Coruña," Alessandri repressed the Federation everywhere. The government arrested the leaders of the organization in Antofagasta Province in mid-June. When the coal miners of Concepción struck, he wired officials to "maintain order at all cost." The strike was broken in three days.[68] In July, the President gave Carlos Ibañez command of the *carabineros*—a task formerly assigned to the Minister of the Interior. Ibañez promptly ordered the *carabineros* to "deal with professional agitators, who are corrupting the soul of the people, with an iron hand."[69] The euphoria of the second coup and Alessandri's return was over. A new Constitution, established in 1925, included the legal gains made the previous year; but labor was on the defensive. Alessandri and Ibañez opposed each other as Ibañez maneuvered for the presidency; but they agreed on destroying the Left.

Communists and other labor radicals tried to regain the initiative by forming a coalition party and running their own candidate for President. The Communist drive to participate in another electoral coalition began in late 1924 when Recabarren and Cruz lost their Congressional seats. Recabarren turned against the junta in December, 1924, and tried to create a "single front" with radical university students.[70] After his suicide—the result of a progressively debilitating disease—Manuel Hidalgo tried to organize Communists and nonparty socialists to support the junta of junior officers in early 1925. In September, 1925, Communists, socialists, and the disenchanted among the middle class met in Santiago. On October 4 they concluded their negotiations by establishing the Radical Social Union of Chilean Salaried Workers (*Union Social Radical de los Asalariados de Chile,* or URSACh). Their candidate was Dr. José Santos Salas, an army physician who had tried to enforce the new health codes during the second junta. "My candidacy," he explained, "is not of the Left, it is not extremist; it is for national salvation because it does not intend to gain privileges for any national group but to respect everyone's rights." He won 80,000 of the 260,000 votes.[71] The Left did better in the Congressional elections of 1926; the Communists won two seats in the Senate and seven in the Chamber of Deputies; the *Asalariados* won two other deputy seats.[72]

This electoral success obscured a profound failure to organize the working class. The party demanded government action to end the nitrate depression of 1926: they wanted an end to agreements with the Nitrate Producers Association, saying the "trust in England" and its high prices had created the success of synthetics; they opposed any reduction in the nitrate tax; and they wanted the government to take out more loans and increase spending on public works.[73] But the Communists had little influence on the Figueroa administration. Congress had become a study in disorder, squabbling over the remnants of patronage. Figueroa told the Communists at one meeting that he was not President of the Republic, "but Receiver of a rigged bankruptcy."[74] More important, personal quarrels and ideological infighting, together with government repression, had left the FOCh fragmented and demoralized. The effort made in elections meant that little was done about organizing workers until the year was half over. The Federation then started a drive to recruit rural workers, but the government responded by shooting *inquilinos*. The best the party could do was stage unemployment rallies and try to reconstruct coalitions with students and reformers. At one point, it was forced to admit it was without significant labor support.[75]

But the party and the Federation made one last effort to turn labor anger into a broad front against the government. On January 1, 1927, the state railway workers struck the lines leading to Santiago, and soon convinced the Santiago streetcar workers and bus drivers to join their effort. The FOCh supported them and, at a special meeting on January 14, called for a twenty-four-hour general strike to begin on January 16 at 6 a.m. Federation organizers began mobilizing 18,000 unemployed workers from the north who had been transported to the capital and were maintained by the government in warehouses. But the strike never materialized. On January 16, the streetcar workers, frightened by the government's use of strikebreakers and of being portrayed as Communists, went back to work. The Minister of the Interior, Manuel Rivas Vicuña, settled the railroad strike on January 24, promising an investigation of workers' grievances.[76]

The Communists now watched helplessly as Ibañez took over. Their newspapers, particularly *Justicia* in Santiago, repeatedly reminded readers of his admiration for Mussolini and Spain's Primo de Rivera.[77] But aside from these warnings, there was little the party could do. "Anarchists," Ibañez announced in early February, 1927, had "organized with petty political ends and some with criminal intent" and were attacking the "armed forces." "The anarchists establish newspapers, preach social revolution and are counting upon the collective cowardice of the country. They do not respect the liberty to work and in fact are the worst tyrants over the working classes. The moment has arrived to definitely break with the red ties that bind us to Moscow." Any measure was justified:

> My purpose is firm, my will resolute; today they
> will criticize, tomorrow they will applaud. I have no
> ambition but desire the greatness and happiness of the
> country. As a consequence . . . I have set forth with

absolute firmness. I will not hesitate if the situation
requires it to assume the maximum of responsibility and
powers which I may consider necessary to avoid chaos and
assure the welfare and progress of Chile.[78]

In late February, Ibañez launched an attack on the labor
Left. He closed the twenty-two Communist newspapers and had the
party's leaders and editors arrested. Later 120 Communists and
their families were deported to Juan Fernandez Island where, according to the government, "they might work out their socialistic
ideas without outside interference."[79] When teachers meeting at
a convention in Talca passed a number of socially progressive
resolutions, including social recognition of the unmarried mother
and support for those who avoided conscription, Ibañez demanded
an investigation. The Minister of Education had some of the delegates arrested, dismissed others, and suppressed the teachers'
organization. In March, the administration reduced the salaries
of state railroad workers from 5 to 15 percent.[80]

The government attempted to go beyond repression and organize
the workers into state-managed unions. On April 1, it announced
the formation of the National Vanguard of Workers and Employees
of Chile (*Vanguardia Nacionalista de Obreros y Empleados de Chile*).
In its charter the organization supported land reform, that is,
the breakup of large estates into small farms, and it favored
protection of industry. In fact, no land reform occurred under
Ibañez. The organization's purpose was obviously to steal the
issues of the Left, defusing the labor movement's potential. The
government subsequently established a new labor day in January,
and used the occasion to emphasize that workers could achieve a
better life without joining the Communists or resorting to sabotage and strikes.[81]

The rule of Ibañez set back labor and the Left. He smashed
the Chilean Workers Federation and all efforts to organize *inquilinos*. After February, 1927, he was free of any labor opposition. Once the initial wave of repression ended, a number of Communists and socialists, including Manuel Hidalgo and Ramón Sepulveda Leal, compromised themselves by trying to develop a modus
vivendi with the regime.[82] After the dictator was deposed, the
Communists reorganized, but an attempt to revive FOCh failed.

NATIONALISM AND DEPENDENCE UNDER IBAÑEZ

Throughout 1927, Ibañez consolidated his political base. He
combined promises of further social reform with calls for national
discipline. He coopted important figures in all political parties
and exiled those he could not win over or intimidate. The latter
included Conservatives such as Agustín Ross and Agustín Edwards.
Arturo Alessandri, who in 1926 had served as the first president
of the Central Bank of Chile, was also forced to leave the country. By the end of the year, the former colonel seemed omnipo-
tent. He had the support of such symbolically important figures

as Enrique Balmaceda, son of the martyred President, who served
as Minister of the Interior. Large numbers of Democrats and
Radicals accepted the new order and served in the inconsequential
Congress.[83]
   The President also had the support of the middle class and
foreign capitalists, who were happy he had silenced the labor
movement. Those who did not support him dared not say so. Soon
after his election in April, 1927, he incorporated all local police into the *carabineros,* creating a force of 11,000 men, administered by Santiago. As additional insurance, he established
an elaborate secret police.[84] Collier summed up the attitudes of
the comfortable in Santiago when he noted widespread resentment
of the government but a general acceptance of its effects. "All
classes prefer the maintenance of the regime now in power believ-
ing that [the] alternatives are civil war or an era of assassination and frightful retaliations, a communistic state or an absolute arbitrary military government."[85]
   As a counter to the nitrate depression, the new regime increased spending on public projects and the military. Ordinary
government expenditures rose only five million pesos (6d.) a year
between 1926 and 1930; but public works programs and military ac-
quisitions were carried as a series of "extraordinary expenditures." The three extraordinary budgets from 1928 to 1930 amounted
to 1,442 million pesos—54 percent of which was for public works
first proposed by Alessandri. In 1923, for example, Chile had
invested 8.4 million pesos in highways; in 1927, it spent 22.8
million.[86]
   The administration appealed to nationalist sentiment, but
rested on the export economy and heavy foreign borrowing. Domestic pressures, from industrialists and financiers, forced Ibañez
to try to protect native interests against foreign capital. But
ordinary income barely paid for ordinary expenditures. To cover
his extraordinary budgets, Ibañez increased the external debt from
1,596 million pesos in 1926 to 2,482 million in 1930. In all, his
administration spent 23 percent of ordinary revenues servicing
foreign obligations.[87] Despite efforts to protect native industry, his rule consolidated rather than arrested the influence of
the United States within Chile.
   He began by changing the nitrate policies of previous administrations. First, he created two new agencies, the Superintendency of Nitrates and the Nitrate Development Council, both
under the Minister of Hacienda. The Superintendency carried out
all functions of government supervision; it surveyed public lands,
sold them at auction, researched techniques of production and the
economics of the industry, and adjudicated disputes among producers and between producers and the government. The Council
served as a group of advisors to the President on all policies relating to the industry. Second, Ibañez decided not to renew the
price agreement of the Nitrate Producers Association after it
lapsed on July 1, 1927. A free market soon ruined a number of
small producers and forced the consolidation of those that remained; but it increased the volume of exports.[88]

He tried to reduce the industry's costs but insisted on tying the benefits of those reductions to increases in production and exports. Producers claimed their secondary costs, that is, the cost of everything but mining and refining, amounted to 76 percent of the European price of ammonium sulphate. The export duty alone was 26.3 percent of the price. But before the depression hit and while they enjoyed the revival from 1912 until 1925, even the older companies paid dividends of 12 percent and the newer, more efficient plants paid 80 percent in a year. One observer thought that because most of the companies watered their stock, real earnings before the depression amounted to 300 percent.[89] In any event, Ibañez was willing to accept the argument that the government should help producers but unwilling to go so far as to reduce the export tax. He instead tried to lower other costs. New labor regulations gave the Producers Association complete control over efforts to recruit workers to the north. And the government established its right to appropriate water rights, pipe lines, railroads, and docks in order to reduce the costs of supplies and transportation to the industry. The same measure that established the government's right of appropriation created a new tax on nitrate lands and permitted confiscation of property to collect it.[90] It would no longer pay a company simply to close its oficinas until it disposed of existing nitrate. The bill also increased the government's income by establishing a government monopoly of iodine, a by-product of the industry.

The "reforms" aroused the opposition of all nitrate producers, particularly the large companies from the United States that had invested in docks and railroads and feared expropriation. When Secretary of State Frank B. Kellogg learned of the July law, he wired Collier to protest the measure. In his view, it violated a precedent the State Department had established in Latin America by its policies in Mexico. There, the United States had insisted the Mexicans could not expropriate U.S. property under powers granted by a new constitution if the property had been purchased before the new constitution went into effect. Kellogg told Collier this seemed to be the case with the nitrate bill, which invoked the Constitution of 1925. "The Department is seriously disturbed at such a possibility and sincerely hopes that the Chilean Government does not contemplate the enactment of any legislation impairing rights which have become vested by virtue of the laws and constitution of Chile existing at the time of acquisition."[91]

But Collier did not press the matter. The lawyers for W. R. Grace and the Guggenheims, the two firms which had the most at stake, asked him not to interfere and instead began lobbying the government. Their efforts were apparently successful, for the laws were amended: the government relinquished any right to expropriate oficinas or nitrate lands and it created a special judicial branch to determine compensation for any "things of public use" it appropriated.[92] Ibañez retained the right to revise railroad rates. He succeeded in persuading the U.S. companies, Collier, and the State Department that he would use his powers to end what one U.S. official called "private monopoly and improper

speculation."[93] The United States officials interpreted his
assurances to mean he would work to reduce *salitre*'s price and
would not use the law to harm U.S. investors.

The controversy over the nitrate bills was no sooner ended
than another began over protection of shipping and coal companies.
In late August, 1927, the government began to help the native
merchant marine with public subsidies to cover tolls at the Panama
Canal; a new law also subsidized all nitrate producers who shipped
on Chilean vessels, reduced tariffs 10 percent for goods imported
on Chilean ships, and provided credits to domestic lines with
which to buy new vessels.[94] The same month, the President
launched a campaign to help the Chilean coal companies. His intent was not only to help the beleaguered companies overcome foreign competition but to reduce the country's imports of coal and
oil. He blamed backwardness of coal production on foreign nitrate
and copper companies, "[who] have never shown any strong intention
to cooperate in the harmonious development of all the nation's productive activities."[95]

Foreign firms and U.S. officials mounted an immediate campaign against the shipping law. James Heavey, the manager of
the Grace Line, complained that the tariff reductions might ruin
his company in Chile. British importers objected that since
Chilean lines only ran between South America and the United
States, U.S. exporters would gain a major advantage over them.[96]
Within a week after the law passed, the U.S. Embassy told the
Chilean Foreign Minister, "While this Government does not question the legal right of governments to subsidize shipping, [the
subsidy to cover tolls at the Panama Canal] modifies the present
status whereby the Canal is used by ships of all nations on equal
footing."[97] Kellogg instructed the Embassy to make "every effort
. . . to dissuade the Chilean Government from applying discriminatory import duties in favor of Chilean vessels." Such "discriminatory treatment" was not applied to Chilean ships in the U.S.,
and the U.S. would insist on a quid pro quo.[98]

Chilean officials tried to convince the United States representative that the subsidies, particularly those for tolls on the
canal and on nitrate cargos, were really intended to help nitrate
producers, not ruin foreign shipping lines.[99] Kellogg, however,
was adamant. Ibañez withdrew the bill and abandoned any prefer-
ential tariffs and subsidies for Chilean vessels. The only measure the government maintained was a 10 percent increase in consular fees on foreign ships. Collier considered the policy reversal
a major victory.[100]

The conflict over the coal bill pitted U.S. copper companies
against Chilean Conservatives. The Guggenheims and the Anaconda
Copper Company, which besides owning Chuquicamata had developed
the Andes Copper Company mine at Potrerillos, saw the measure as
part of a broad nationalist attack against them. After Chile had
established the income tax, subsequent revisions raised the rate
on copper companies from 5 to 15 percent. The companies were not
allowed any deduction for the depletion of ore reserves and were
allowed only 6 percent on the depreciation of equipment. The

United States, by comparison, collected only 13.5 percent on income
after generous allowances for depletion of ore and depreciation of
machinery. The companies had watched their Chilean taxes increase
from 800,000 U.S. dollars in 1924 to over 2.2 million in 1927. Of
the two major American interests, Anaconda felt the most threatened.
In November, 1927, its managers wrote Stokely Morgan, State Department chief of the Latin American Division, that the coal bill
might force Anaconda out of Chile. The bill included a tax on all
imported coal and oil. The managers felt that the Anaconda subsidiaries could neither afford to pay the tax—the additional cost
of 1.25 million dollars a year would make Chilean copper uncompetitive on the world market—nor rely on Chilean coal to meet
their needs. At the height of the First World War, Chile had
produced only 1.4 million tons a year. Andes Copper alone consumed 250,000 tons of coal each year. In order to replace all
imported coal and oil, Chile would have to raise its output by
3.3 million tons. Worse, conversion to coal would cost the companies the 5.9 million dollars they had invested in railroad
tank cars and oil-burning equipment. Of three major consumers of
fuel in Chile, the copper officials thought that only their industry would suffer: railroads could pass on the cost in higher
rates; and the government had promised the nitrate companies a 20
percent rebate on the price of domestic coal.[101]

There is no doubt the upper class had turned anti-American
in late 1927. They resented the way Chile had been treated by
New York banks; and they needed a scapegoat for the depression.
Deputy Ismael Edwards Matte argued Chile should not only protect
her domestic coal but embark on a "virile policy" against the
"American Jews, the Guggenheims and others," who controlled her
copper. Senator Luis Enrique Concha worried that the copper companies were avoiding Chile's income taxes and did not intend to
"leave us anything but the holes of the mines."[102] A columnist
in El Sur of Concepción compared the Chileans, who were "extra-
ordinarily attracted to anything novel," unfavorably to the Chinese, who were "the wisest of men" for closing their territory to
foreigners. The Chileans had foolishly invited the yanquis to
practice a "silent invasion" on the country.[103]

The government's position was more protectionist than anti-
American. The Minister of Hacienda blamed the poor state of the
coal industry on the coal companies, which had paid out unwar-
ranted dividends instead of reinvesting profits, and on British
as well as U.S. interests. He cited the fact that British shippers, anxious to have a cargo going to Chile, charged almost
nothing to carry British coal. Coal in England cost sixteen to
eighteen shillings a ton; and British coal in Iquique cost twenty-
six to twenty-seven shillings a ton, less than domestic shippers
charged to haul coal from Concepción to the north. The ordinary
freight charges on almost any other commodity were fifty to sixty
shillings a ton between Britain and northern Chile. He also
thought the Standard Oil Company, through its subsidiaries, had
carried out unfair competition against Chilean coal in the 1920s,
using its oil from Peru to undercut the price.[104]

Despite nationalist sentiment, the copper companies soon forced Ibañez to abandon the coal measure. In November, 1927, the Guggenheims sent William Braden to Santiago. Braden, accompanied by Collier, called on the President and asked him to lift the tax on "El Teniente." Collier suggested the President not impose the tax on any company until an economic study could be made of its effects on the copper sector. Ibañez agreed. The revised bill delayed the tax until the study was completed. Collier reported the copper companies were "satisfied with this amendment . . . [T]hese representatives believe that the new provision will give them an opportunity to satisfy the Chilean Government that even if the progressive tax on crude oil might be borne by the Companies, yet if they must pay this in addition to the social taxes and the present exorbitant income taxes, the stocks and bonds of American copper companies in Chile will no longer be attractive to the investing public." When the study was completed, Ibañez delayed enforcing the tax until December 31, 1931.[105]

The government not only failed to use its nitrate policies to help other domestic sectors, it also failed to help nitrate producers. Nitrate exports rose, but free trade depressed prices further. The government, searching for some solution, tried to increase exports to Germany, and was stymied by protests from the U.S. and British governments. It then permitted the Nitrate Producers Association once again to fix the price of *salitre*, a policy that soon reduced exports. In January, 1928, Congress passed a secret bill reducing the export tax on *salitre* sent to Germany by one British pound per ton. The London *Financial Times* found out about the measure, and protests followed from the American and British governments. The bill violated existing tariff agreements between Chile and each country. The Chileans argued that this was their only means to break into the German market, and that *salitre* would cost as much in Germany as it did in the United States because of higher transportation costs.[106]

Talk of another price agreement began in May, 1928. Ibañez proposed to fix a floor under *salitre* at seventeen shillings per metric quintal, i.e. about 7.7 British pounds per ton. Whenever a producer sold for less than that amount, he would receive a subsidy from the government to make up the difference. In this way, exports would increase; and while the government's share of the nitrate income would decline, it could hope its overall revenues from the tax would rise.[107]

The Guggenheims led the protests against the price agreement. They now operated the most efficient nitrate plant. In 1927, they had completed construction of the *oficina* "Maria Elena," on the Coya Norte site in Antofagasta. While the traditional Shanks system recovered only 55 to 75 percent of the *salitre* in the ore, the Guggenheim operation recovered 90 percent. Although other *oficinas* had begun investing in new technology, such as new bagging machinery they could not hope to compete with the "Maria Elena." It had the capacity to turn out 500,000 tons of *salitre* —25 to 35 percent of all exports—each year.[108]

But U.S. officials, after considering another confrontation
with Ibañez, decided it would seriously strain diplomatic relations with Chile and that the issues were not that important.
Most of the *oficinas* were still closed in mid-1928, and neither
increased sales to Germany nor a new price agreement seemed likely
to rescue the industry.[109]   The U.S. decided to let the market decide both issues.   The nitrate producers met in August, 1928, and
fixed the price at seventeen shillings a ton.   The Guggenheims
refused to sign the agreement and were forced to leave the Association meeting.   W. S. Culbertson, the new U.S. ambassador,
thought the traditional producers rather than the Guggenheims
were in trouble.   The "Maria Elena" was turning a profit at the
current price of sixteen shillings six pence a ton.   But exports
might not reach the government's target of three million metric
tons, and in that case, "the government will lack a surplus [in
revenues] out of which to pay the difference between the prices
received by producers and its guaranteed price of 17 [shillings]."
Events proved him right.   Nitrate exports leveled in early 1929
and then began to fall.   The British stopped investing in nitrate
stocks.   Ibañez tried Japanese investment but failed.[110]   The
possibilities of refinancing the sector narrowed to one, the
Guggenheims.   In 1929, they expanded their share of production by
buying the Lautaro Nitrate Company.   They were the only capitalists willing and able to take major risks to save the industry.[111]

In his visit to Chile as President-elect in January, 1929,
Herbert Hoover had recommended that the Chileans enter into a
joint program with the Guggenheims to consolidate production and
take advantage of the Guggenheims' new refining process.   In
early 1930, the Guggenheims, and the British nitrate producers
who remained, revived the suggestion.   Ibañez seized it as his
salvation.[112]   The government was near financial collapse and
his opponents were now organizing against him.   The chief negotiator for the Guggenheims was E. A. Cappelen Smith, who had pio-
neered several chemical breakthroughs in both copper and nitrate
refining for the family and was in charge of its nitrate operations.   As Harvey O'Connor explains in his biography of the
family, their nitrate operations were also in difficulty because
of *salitre*'s falling price.   To bail themselves out of an impossible situation, Smith and Ibañez agreed to pool resources and
costs in the *Compañia de Salitre de Chile* (COSACH).   The corporation would begin with three billion pesos (375 million dollars)
in capital stock, and 200 million dollars in bonds.   In exchange
for giving up the export tax, the government would receive half
the thirty million shares, four of the twelve seats on the board
of directors, a guaranteed income of 22.5 million dollars over
the next two years, half the dividends, and a 6 percent tax on
all dividends.   The other half of the shares would be divided
among the nitrate producers, with the Guggenheims acquiring the
largest portion and formal direction of the operation.   COSACH,
when it was formed in 1931, immediately became the largest corporation in South America and the Guggenheims' largest venture.[113]

Most of the nitrate interests supported COSACH.   As early as

April, 1930, when discussion about the corporation began, Jorge
Nef, former Admiral and now advisor to Lautaro Nitrate Company,
thought it the only solution to the problem of the nitrate tax:
"The success of the law depends on the qualifications of the Government representatives in the 'Cosach,' which will save the nitrate industry from a failure that has confronted us on account
of a policy of traditional ignorance."[114]   Jorge H. Jones, president of the Nitrate Producers Association, a position he had
occupied for the last thirteen years, said in July, 1930 that the
corporation should be organized as soon as possible.   "During the
many years I have been in the Nitrate Association and notwithstanding the changes that have been made in its organization I
have been able to see the impossibility of obtaining the coordi-
nation of action among its members in order to present a united
front, and to proceed with the reorganization of the industry on
a national basis.   I therefore firmly believe that the present
step is indispensable and cannot be postponed."[115]   Carlos Dávila,
Chile's ambassador to Washington, called the corporation "the only
possible solution of the problem confronting the nitrate industry."   Alberto Edwards, the former Minister of Hacienda and still
a major figure in the country, thought, "It must serve the country's interests.   Aren't the Government and the nitrate producers
precisely interested in it?   Aren't both of them satisfied with
it? . . . In the history of the nitrate industry we find nothing
but disagreement between the producers and the Government.   But
today happily both are in accord and seek the same end.   What
then could be the objection?"[116]   And finally, Emiliano Figueroa,
the former President and now the head of the Central Bank, agreed
that the corporation would be the industry's salvation.   "We have
to thank the Americans who have taken a hand in the matter and
have come to our assistance when the rope was about our necks.
We have to be grateful to them because they have gone beyond our
expectations; and they will furnish us not only with capital, but
also a modern industrial technique, perfect organization, advertising on a large scale, and the commercial experience which we
have never had."[117]
   The only opposition to the project came from those already
opposed to Ibañez for other reasons.   It was led by Agustín Edwards and Arturo Alessandri, who were still in exile.   In late
1929 they attacked the President for denationalizing the economy.
In response to their call, the major parties opposed to Ibañez
met in December, 1929, to discuss the next year's Congressional
election.   But they were unable to agree on a common program.[118]
(Ibañez avoided the election by simply suspending it in April,
1930, on the grounds the country could not afford the expense.
He instead assigned each party a quota of seats in Congress: the
parties submitted names of their candidates to the Minister of
the Interior, who chose the Congressmen from the party lists.)[119]
The President's enemies, although still disorganized and demoralized, seized on the formation of COSACH as an illustration
of their view that he no longer served the national interests.
Francisco Huneeus, writing in *Las Ultimas Noticias,* thought the

real purpose of COSACH "is to relieve a certain American firm from
its debts at the cost of the nation." He estimated the Guggenheims' debts at 1.1 billion pesos, debts which could be easily
absorbed in three billion pesos worth of stock.[120]   Ambassador
Culbertson in December, 1930, reported that the Ibañez regime now
depended on the success of COSACH:

> A list of the enemies of Cosach parallels to a large
> extent the list of Ibañez' enemies. I need hardly say
> that I hold no brief for the Ibañez regime, but he is at
> present time a stable and constructive force. He and his
> advisers are doing as well as any other group could do
> and in any case this is no time in Chile for the luxuries
> of South American politics. American interests are gener-
> ally satisfied with Ibañez and would regard any change at
> the present time as dangerous and even ruinous. Ibañez'
> enemies, however, realize that Cosach is a weak point and
> every opportunity is availed to criticize it and to abuse
> the Government for its close association with American
> interests.[121]

The corporation was a disaster. In the very first stages of
its formation, after laws were passed creating it, 10,000 miners
lost their jobs. It began operation on March 20, 1931, with
thirty-eight *oficinas* and 48,478 laborers, and by June 30, 1931,
only six *oficinas,* employing 17,000 workers, were in operation.
Production fell from 205,000 tons to 85,000 tons a month, and
Chile's total share of the world nitrate market declined from
22.9 percent in 1929 to 4.2 percent in 1932.[122]   By June, 1932,
COSACH had lost thirteen million dollars, defaulted on its bonds,
and reduced the nitrate labor force to 10,000 men. When the political situation settled in early 1933, the Chilean Senate in-
vestigated the corporation and found that its debts exceeded the
total foreign debt of the republic before 1927. The Guggenheims
escaped with a small profit. They had charged the corporation 3.5
million dollars in organizing expenses and another million in
fees, and had successfully floated their previous debts into its
stock. They also tried to collect ninety-nine million dollars
from the Chilean government for their share of COSACH bonds.[123]
The government liquidated the corporation on February 2, 1933, by
borrowing an additional 140 million pesos from the Central Bank
to cover some of its losses. The settling of accounts included a
partial payment to the Guggenheims for their bonds.[124]
  Of course, the Ibañez government did not survive the debacle.
In early 1931, it was without income from COSACH, without foreign
currency reserves, and unable to secure another foreign loan.
The President had spent the last of his foreign credit the previous year. On April 24, 1931, the government announced a massive reduction in public employment and salaries. The following
day, the stock market crashed. The regime survived by spending
its advances from COSACH and reserves in the Central Bank; after
May 31, payments on the income tax kept it going until July.[125]

Then nothing could save it. The treasury was empty, gold was
flowing out of the country, industries and merchants were going
bankrupt. Public employees, university students, physicians,
lawyers, and other professionals staged strikes and massive demonstrations. In one rally, on July 24, a physician was killed.
Ibañez declared martial law. On July 25, a teacher died in another demonstration. The next day the President resigned and
left by train for Argentina. He eventually settled in Paris.[126]

The attempt to reform the society and its politics through
strong executive government accelerated Chile's dependence on the
United States. For all his rhetoric and serious attempts at new
economic policies, Ibañez used U.S. capital to prime his nation's
recovery from the nitrate depression of 1926. By 1929, the
United States had invested 422.6 million dollars in Chile, 340
million in government bonds.[127] The nationalists who began the
military movement in 1924 lost the last of their influence in
November, 1928, when Ibañez removed the Minister of Hacienda for
objecting to further increases in the foreign debt.[128] Reviewing
the dominant position which the United States had acquired in
this former outpost of British capital, the British Commercial
Secretary in Santiago observed, "The old saying that 'trade follows the flag' may to-day well be changed to 'commerce follows
finance.'"[129] Chileans now relied on U.S. engineers to redesign
their railroads and build their highways. Anaconda and the Guggenheims monopolized copper production; DuPont was developing the
nation's borax deposits; Bethlehem Steel ran the country's only
steel mills; and International Telephone and Telegraph owned the
Chile Telephone Company, having purchased it from its British
shareholders in 1927. Chileans bought Ford automobiles, went to
Hollywood movies, and were just beginning to discover home appliances from the United States. At its fifth annual meeting in
1928, a growing Santiago chapter of the Rotary Club recognized
the dictator's role in developing U.S. investment in Chile by
making him an honorary member.[130]

What then is one to make of all the reforms and anti-American
sentiment? The reforms meant different things to different social
groups. To the elite, they represented a means to further cen-
tralize political power. To the middle class, they meant employment. To the workers, they meant the promise of a better future.
The same was true of "nationalism." For the elite, the development of protective tariffs provided a means to recapture the control of Chilean markets that regional isolation once provided.
The upper class was quite cynical in its political use of nationalist feeling. Agustín Edwards bitterly attacked Ibañez for having sold out the country, but was himself on the board of directors of the Guggenheims' Anglo-Chilean Nitrate Company.[131]
Whenever the export economy slumped, the establishment papers renewed their attacks against "imperialism." Such attacks disappeared during the brief revival of exports in 1928. For the middle class and the labor movement, nationalist rhetoric was a
means of preventing competition from immigrants.

No political group, however, developed a strategy for reducing the country's dependence on mineral exports, for diversifying the country's exports and increasing national control of them, or for diminishing the country's need for foreign capital. Alessandri and Ibañez consistently tried to diversify the government's sources of income and reduce her need for manufactured imports. They succeeded. The government did not rely as much on the nitrate export tax in 1930 as she had in 1920; and the country developed her industries. But improving the government's position within the economy was not the same as reducing economic dependence. The growth of government, and its further concentration in Santiago, increased the number of political entrepreneurs who demanded a share of export-derived income. Industrialization had a more positive effect; and until the crash, Chile had a good balance of trade. But industries relied on imported machinery and imported fuel; and the government did not require that protected industries be owned by Chileans.

Governments reformed the banking system but they did not effectively regulate the flow of capital. They could not do so. A government in debt to foreign banks and presiding over a nation that relied on fresh infusions of foreign capital could not impose conditions on investors. Nor did it have the technicians required for a more regulated economy. In 1929, a U.S. official surveyed Chile's banking laws and their enforcement, and reported that "public officials charged with the administration of the various laws were unable to furnish authoritative, detailed lists of the laws administered under their respective jurisdictions.[132] In any panic or depression, the government had only two choices: it could borrow from abroad or borrow internally. Chile was able for a few years to sustain the gold standard with foreign loans. The administrations that followed Ibañez left the gold standard and imposed exchange controls to prevent the conversion of peso profits into other currencies and the transfer of profits to other countries.[133]

Chile's political leaders, like their colleagues in the rest of the Atlantic economy, did not foresee the Great Depression. The crisis they perceived and tried to remedy was the decline of the nitrate sector in the postwar world. They generally believed *salitre*'s problems were temporary, and failed to gauge, until it was too late, the new importance of the synthetic nitrates. Writing in the midst of the nitrate depression of 1926, Harry Campbell, the U.S. consul in Iquique, noted, "neither the [Nitrate Producers] Association nor the Government has yet come to the realization that Chilean nitrate producers no longer control a world monopoly such as they have been accustomed to enjoy during the past 40 years, and all the action—or lack of action—in meeting the present situation seems to be due to their failure to grasp this essential and fundamental factor."[134]

The nitrate depression was as much a political as an economic or technical problem. There had always been a conflict between the government and the producers over the nitrate income; but the results of that conflict had never favored the more

efficient producers. The producers had learned to count on their
control of the market and their influence over the Chilean government to rescue them from periodic slumps. They had become to
mining what hacendados were to farming. In 1926, they demanded
the government reduce the nitrate tax. But it did not dare to
cut its own revenues at a time when public employment and salaries
had increased. The reform in the banking system meant the government could not resort to an older, more expedient solution:
printing money and giving it to the producers. Ibañez finally
attempted to reduce the nitrate tax. Ideally, this meant the government would exchange a lower tax rate in favor of higher exports and perhaps even increase its income. But he undercut this
initiative by permitting the producers to reduce exports in order
to raise the price. The outcome was the worst of both worlds:
exports fell and so did government income. The declining profitability of *salitre*, in turn, left the government with few options
in raising capital for the industry's rescue.

Ibañez, for all his admiration of Mussolini and Primo de
Rivera, was more an autocratic liberal than a fascist. He professed belief in the corporate state, but his heart was never in
it. He had no black shirts, and more important, no party. He
was a military man. Outside the army, his support came from the
old-line Liberals who served as his ministers and ad hoc advisors.
In many respects, he resembled the *Presidente martir* he so admired. Like Balmaceda, he disliked the pettiness of legislative
politics and wanted to replace Congressional bargaining with a
centralized, executive state. In his view, the state was a
creative force, advancing those interests which furthered economic progress. The number of competing interests meant that the
state must become stronger in order to impose the right choices.
One of his ministers, Guillermo Edwards Matte, described the purpose of government as the creation of "new institutions . . .
which do not actually represent the capitalist or working classes
but can guarantee authority and be arbiters between both of them
in order to harmonize the nationalistic ideal of production."[135]

Unlike Balmaceda, Ibañez knew that finally he was not an arbiter but a servant. Balmaceda, who lacked the centralized,
state institutions that existed in the 1920s, was willing to risk
a confrontation with powerful foreign investors and their domestic allies in pursuit of his dream of a great Chile. Ibañez,
free of any illusion that Chile would become a major power on the
continent, cooperated with "imperialists" when they provided him
the income he needed for the further centralization of authority.
COSACH was a major step not only in trying to save the nitrate
sector but in the economic evolution of the state: it was the
progenitor of many later arrangements between Chilean governments
and foreign capitalists. Ibañez lived in exile for many years,
eventually returned, and in 1952, in a genuinely free contest
was reelected President. During the campaign, he presented himself as a strong father figure, who would restore order and revive an economy in recession. The history of that sad administration belongs in another work.

7. Conclusion: The Pattern of Dependent Development

The Chilean elite accepted economic dependence as a reasonable price to pay for the construction of a centralized state. It is expensive to create and sustain political power; moreover, the requirements and cost of state authority increased over time. The elite in Chile responded to these simple facts. If the creation of a strong government in the nineteenth century required doing business with Great Britain on terms dictated by British entrepreneurs, or if the maintenance of government, in the twentieth century, meant succumbing to the demands of U.S. corporations and of the State Department, each seemed preferable to the alternative, the collapse of state power.

Chile's development in the nineteenth century was not very different from what took place in early modern Europe. Gabriel Ardant, in an essay on the creation of the modern European state, notes the crucial relation between the growth of tax power and the development of an exchange economy. So long as the population of Europe remained small, agricultural, and poor, and the various markets of the continent distant from one another, monarchs resorted to fiscal measures that frequently retarded economic growth and whose effects subsequently limited the expansion of state power. But as Ardant explains, the growth of economic activity and particularly of trade increased knowledge of economic relations and the ability of the state to increase its income from direct taxation. By the late eighteenth century, the Physiocrats of France understood that taxes should bear only on the net product of a farm or industry and not on its capital. Turning this understanding into state policy was a formidable task, accomplished only after the economic system itself became more uniform and monetized. Men in government had to learn not only how the system worked but how to develop the technical capacity and political loyalty required to tax it without causing violent rebellion.[1] The problems of the Chilean state were similar. The difference is that, while the monarchies of Europe had several centuries to form centralized governments, the Chileans lacked a monarchy as a source of public loyalty and had only decades to achieve their ends.

The Chileans did not begin without some basis for a state. The elite shared a common language and religion and a dynastic ideal of authority; its principal families were linked through marriage. Many of its members had acquired political experience in the colony or during the War of Independence. These factors remedied, to some extent, the absence of a king and the prestige nobility can bestow on a traditional government. Pelucon rule consisted of colonial practices and "republican" improvisations. The cement of the political system, aside from the coherence of the ruling class, was the militia. The state administration was yet too small to exact obedience. Rulers of Santiago apparently used offices in the militia much as the monarchies once used titles. With the title of officer, provincial landowners and merchants gained the right to use force over the immediate inhabitants. They were expected, in return, to demonstrate their loyalty to their superiors through the device of elections. This primitive state was extremely vulnerable, and the Pelucones knew from the beginning that they would not remain in power unless they increased its income. They linked Chile's economy to dynastic developments in Great Britain.

Foreign trade became the means to raise new revenues and to free the state from dependence on other, elite elements. The state was gradually able to separate its goals from the desires of some of the most powerful segments of the late colonial society: the provincial landowners and miners and the Church. It monopolized the key resources for the expansion of exports—the public lands, the minerals on them, and the legal authority to exploit both. And only the state could raise the capital for the most expensive upper-class projects: the construction of a railway system, the creation of a professional military, the creation of public schools, and the beautification of Santiago. Exports and the concentration of political power complemented one another. However, dependence was not a "stage" in Chile's development; it became a central characteristic of growth and diversification.

Government policies did not reduce Chile's need for foreign capital or her vulnerability to export slumps. This failure persisted into and through the nitrate era. Those in power never set themselves the objective of using *salitre* to reduce dependence because they preferred to maximize the immediate return from the export. Liberals needed government income, first to pay for the War of the Pacific, then to expand their patronage. All elite parties expected the nitrate fortune to lead to a rapid recovery from the downturn of the late 1870s. This desire for an immediate and high profit should not be confused with laissez faire. There were many who professed a belief in free trade; but the elite never hesitated to use government to protect its interests. The failure to break the pattern of economic dependence, even to set the goal of doing so, is best explained in terms of the relation of the political system to dependent growth.

While the elite concentrated political power in Santiago, economic growth fragmented it into competing units of dependent interests. Economic expansion also created new interest groups;

and they joined already existing elite factions or formed new ones. Politics evolved as a series of struggles over the distribution of export-derived income. The central government distributed that income indirectly through tariff laws, monetary policies, and laws governing the sale of public resources, and directly through its expenditures. As economic dependence continued, the cost of government, that is, the cost of placating a sufficient number of interests to remain in power, constantly increased. During economic booms, political leaders would try to build a ruling coalition by expanding the bureaucracy and the number of public projects. Periodic export declines would then force the government to expand the money supply, borrow from abroad, or do both in order to rescue itself and the interests it served. As public and private debts increased, the elite became dependent not only on the state of the export economy but on the availability of foreign credit.

All of this was evident before the nitrate boom; but the boom changed the political system because it accelerated the process of dependent development. Balmaceda was the first executive to recognize the pitfalls of dependence. He had expected the nitrate riches to refinance presidential rule; however, British capitalists had gained the ability to threaten his economic programs by reducing exports, and domestic opponents had acquired the means and developed the determination to restructure power within the national government. He was also the first executive to encounter a more contemporary dilemma: he had the opportunity to organize new social groups into his political base, but doing so might reduce the government's income from exports. He decided instead to repress the working class and take his chances within the existing political framework, confident he could bargain with his opponents or use his larger military to destroy them. His opponents, with the tacit cooperation of the British government, seized the economic base of the government, the nitrate zone of Tarapacá, and won the civil war.

Their victory did not resolve the underlying tensions of the political economy. Politically, the system continued to require an inflationary monetary policy and rising government expenditures as the dependent interests continued to proliferate and, in fact, became adept at pressing the government to rescue them from poor investment decisions. Economically, Chileans gradually acquired a controlling interest of the nitrate production, hacendados and small farmers increased agricultural output, and other capitalists, including many immigrants, created important industries. The government promoted higher nitrate sales and the development of other exports. Economic growth continued to rely on foreign capital—in the forms of new investments and of loans to the government—and on foreign entrepreneurs who provided credit, transportation, and technical skills in Chile's foreign trade.

The elite became concerned with the implications of dependence when it could no longer pass off the costs of its mistakes to the working class. Workers organized to demand a larger share of the export income when they recognized that, because of the way the economy had been centralized, their strikes could disrupt its operation. They fought to gain leverage in the workplace, a recognition of their unions, shorter working hours, and better pay; and their struggle entailed, as it always does, a political effort to alter government policies. While the nascent Left spoke of revolution, its basic arguments were couched in nationalistic terms, that the elite had betrayed its role in development. In the first major confrontations, the elite succeeded in containing a small and divided labor movement.

But the elite could not control events abroad which eventually reshaped the nitrate economy and the pattern of Chile's dependence. Rivalry among the major powers intensified international competition in South America, and the government took advantage of this situation to reduce its dependence on Great Britain. But Allied behavior during the First World War left the Chileans with few choices. They became indebted to the United States during the 1914-15 slump; and then the Nitrate Executive reduced the profits they might have derived from the conflict. The economic crisis of the postwar world involved not only the declining position of *salitre* as a source of nitrogen for western Europe, but the relation of government to capital in the international economy.

In Europe and the United States, governments became much more protective of their industrial base and trade interests; within Chile, the units of foreign capital became larger and politically more sophisticated. A comparison of John T. North to the Guggenheims reveals the importance of these changes. North was only one of a large number of nitrate producers. He controlled the railroad in Tarapacá, a vital element to the entire trade, and was a successful promoter in London of nitrate stocks. But he never controlled a monopoly, and exercised authority only by forming coalitions of producers and speculators. He had little direct influence with the British government. To the rulers of Great Britain, Chile was a minor outpost for economic expansion, and North little more than a hustler. The Guggenheims, however, were powerful in New York and Washington; and U.S. officials looked upon their venture in Chile as the first and most important effort to turn the country into a staging area for the penetration of the continent. Until they sold Chuquicamata to Anaconda, the Guggenheims had a monopoly position in Chilean copper production. With their enormous resources, they became the dominant investor in *salitre* within eight years after they entered the trade. The Chilean elite was correct in its impression that British enterpreneurs had behaved with greater circumspection than U.S. businessmen. But they were slower to see that this change came from the increasing concentration of capital throughout the industrialized world and that the United States was prommoting that concentration as a means of maintaining its position in international trade.

Chile's rulers also misunderstood the importance of research and technology. Chilean technicians began discussing the possibilities of competition from synthetic nitrates as early as the 1890s. The greater fear of the elite was that someday the

deposits of nitrate ore would be exhausted. Such fears notwithstanding, the government had never reviewed its policies toward
the nitrate sector. Producers and government maneuvered against
each other by forming producer "combinations" or trusts and
through the sale of public lands. But such maneuvers assumed the
predominance of *salitre* in the world market. Once German and
English technology began to erode that position, the government
and the producers were left without a frame of reference. The
Nitrate Producers Association continued to try to raise the price
by reducing exports, the government to make a quick return on
land sales, and the results of their efforts were disastrous for
both.

Finally, events after 1919 overwhelmed the oligarchy. Government policies and the postwar slump led to a political mobilization that it could not control or repress. It no longer had the
means within the state to coopt enough interests and remain in
power. Working-class militance steadily spread to new occupations, even into the countryside. The middle class used the
cause of reform to demand expensive concessions. At this point,
progressive elements might have wrested more than reform from the
government. The organized working class was small but it was far
larger than the government; it and the new organizations among
middle-class renters and professionals could have constituted a
radical realignment in politics. But neither the workers nor the
middle class possessed the class consciousness and strategic
imagination to carry out such a task. Labor leaders and political
dissidents instead saw each other as competitors for the same
audience. Workers preferred, in the end, to seek more within the
given economic framework than to entertain the possibility of
seizing the means of production. The Right reorganized, constructing a new coalition by raising the pay of bureaucrats and
army officers. Pleased with the repression of the Left, capitalists and especially New York bankers gave the new government
generous credit. Ibañez provided order and growth until the Great
Depression destroyed his export base and the willingness of foreign bankers to extend any new loans.

Obvious similarities exist between the nitrate era and
Chile's political economy in the 1960s and 1970s. Chile's recent
experience involved the growth of an economy dependent on mineral
exports, the political mobilization of workers and peasants, a
crisis in civilian rule, and upper-class support for military
dictatorship as the solution to that crisis. The similarities
are more than coincidence, but any discussion of them must avoid
the nonsense of historicism. Chile's political culture was
shaped in many important respects in the earlier period, but a
study of that period alone cannot reveal the structural problems
of the later era. Events in the nitrate years did not condemn
Chile to permanent dependence, and the country has changed significantly since 1930. It changed to the point that it could
elect a Socialist President in 1970. Despite these changes, the
attempt of Salvador Allende and the *Unidad Popular* to create
socialism through electoral victory reveals profound continuities
in Chile's development.

The dynamics of the political economy remained unchanged.
Chile exported a wider variety of minerals in the 1930s than she
had previously, but during the Second World War, U.S. demand
turned copper into the foundation of the economy. And foreign
interests controlled copper production and trade. The Great Depression reduced the number of domestic copper producers; those
that remained found it almost impossible to obtain foreign shipping and credit and could not compete at the low import price imposed by the United States. Anaconda and Kennecott—the latter
was the Guggenheim corporation that ran "El Teniente"—had the
field to themselves.[2] Within Chile, export income turned Santiago
into the exclusive nucleus of power. It was already the nation's
financial as well as administrative center by 1930. Valparaiso,
the only city that might have rivaled it economically, declined
as British merchant houses collapsed or withdrew during the depression, as industry and banking became concentrated in the
capital, and as Santiago promoted San Antonio as an alternative
port.

Income remained unevenly distributed. In 1960, the richest
5 percent of the population received 25 percent of the total income while the bottom 50 percent received 15 percent.[3] At the
end of the decade, the upper 9 percent held 35 percent of the income, the lower 45 percent only 14 percent. Chile now had a substantial middle class: 45 percent of the population received 50
percent of the income, and the nation had an average per capita
income of 600 U.S. dollars. The middle class shaped industrial
expansion; demand for appliances and automobiles increased production of consumer durables 11 percent a year. The persistence
of poverty, however, depressed demand for food and clothing so
that production of traditional consumer goods in the 1960s did
not increase significantly.[4]

A multiparty system revolved about the politics of distribution. Many saw government as a zero-sum game: one group could
not gain except at the expense of all others. After 1945, every
chief executive, with the exception of Eduardo Frei (1964-70),
presided over a coalition government. Even Frei's Christian
Democrats included the entire spectrum of dependent interests.
Simply holding an administration together absorbed most of the
time and ingenuity of each executive. In order to stimulate
growth and retain political support, each administration tried to
increase the nation's and its own return from the copper sector.
Income from taxes on the copper corporations almost tripled between 1945 and 1965.[5] Chile prospered each time the United
States went to war and suffered with each outbreak of peace.
Whenever export income and domestic savings were inadequate to
meet the economy's needs, the government increased the money supply, the foreign debt, or both. Barbara Stallings, in her review
of Chile's contemporary history, concluded that an administration
would begin with expansionary policies as it attempted to improve
its electoral support; and it would end by reducing expenditures
in order to retard inflation and allay capitalist fears of higher
taxation. Rising unemployment and persistent inflation would
then lead to the election of a different coalition.[6] Not a

single political grouping held power through two successive administrations.

Frei's government demonstrated the shortcomings of reform within this dependent economy. He won the presidency in 1964 by defeating Salvador Allende, and had the support of everyone who feared a socialist revolution. The United States government helped him through the Central Intelligence Agency which supplied money and advice on smearing the opposition during the campaign.[7] Frei promised "a revolution in liberty: land for the rural laborer, public housing for the urban poor, and better public services for everyone. His solution to foreign control of the copper sector was its "Chileanization," a program that he completed and in which the government acquired 51 percent ownership of the mines.[8] But none of these programs fulfilled public expectations. The agrarian reform became entangled in litigation as hacendados used the courts to slow its implementation. Housing construction increased but never approached the levels required to meet the needs of the urban poor or even to prevent the shortage from worsening. Industrial output began to stagnate because Chile's plants were uncompetitive in the world market and the domestic market was no longer expanding. The linchpin of the entire strategy, the copper program, was the greatest failure: in buying shares in the copper companies, the government ended paying the costs of new investment but left foreign managers running the mines; the profits of Anaconda and Kennecott reached record levels while the government's export income steadily fell. The economy faltered in 1968-69; inflation rose to 30 percent a year; and unemployment increased as well.[9]

The price of Frei's policies was an increase in dependence. Chile maintained a favorable balance of trade, but one that included new foreign capital. Foreign corporations invaded Santiago and became the major suppliers of new capital. And the government borrowed abroad, from banks, the U.S. government, and international lending agencies, in order to maintain expansion. According to the International Monetary Fund, Chile's foreign debt was 598 million dollars in 1960 and 2,067 million in 1970. Alexis Guardia notes that the IMF's calculations are 500 million dollars less than those of Chile's Central Bank, because the bank recorded debts contracted under less stringent conditions than those monitored by the Fund. At the end of the Frei administration, foreign debt was rising at 17 percent and export income at only 7 percent a year. In many instances, particularly in the case of government obligations, payment on these loans was postponed so that their full burden appeared only after 1970. In 1971, debt service consumed 35 percent of Chile's export earnings.[10]

Allende and the left-wing coalition of the *Unidad Popular* won in 1970 because of the increasing size of the electorate, the greater participation of workers in parties and unions, and the division of the opposition. The number of voters increased—in part because of the baby boom after 1945—from 2.9 to 3.5 million during the Frei years. Membership in labor unions rose from 270,000 to 551,000; the most impressive change was the organization

of the countryside where membership increased from 1,658 to
114,112. But the union movement was divided between the Left and
the Christian Democrats, who made up 24 percent of the national
labor federation, CUT (*Central Unión de Trabajadores*).[11] Allende's
decisive advantage was that the Christian Democrats and the Nationalists each ran a candidate. A substantial number of conservative Christian Democrats must have deserted Rodomiro Tomic for
the Nationalist Jorge Alessandri. In any event, Alessandri, the
son of Arturo Alessandri and President from 1958 to 1964, out-
polled Tomic but fell short of beating Allende.

Winning the presidency under these circumstances was an
enormous gamble for the Left. The *Unidad Popular* would have to
turn a legal victory, won with only 36 percent of the vote, into
a strategic success. And it would have to fulfill its broad program of nationalization and social reform at the same time as it
addressed an already serious economic crisis. But it faced a
formidable opposition. The Christian Democrats and the Nationalists made up a majority of both houses of the legislature; they
also controlled the judiciary. Capitalists did not bother to
hide their fear and hatred of the new administration. Allende
had barely taken office when the nation was plunged into a financial panic, accompanied by a massive flight of capital. The
United States government continued diplomatic relations, but the
CIA began cooperating with Allende's opponents in trying to destroy him as soon as he won the election. Even his supporters
presented problems. The *Unidad Popular* was a multiparty coalition, within which even his own party, the Socialists, was split
between advocates of an open confrontation with the "bourgeoisie"
and supporters of his legal revolution.[12] Many members of the
Left coalition did not realize the risks until it was too late.
The details of running for office, and then of fulfilling or trying to fulfill so many important objectives, seized and kept the
attention of UP officials. Leaders of the administration were
still drawing up basic plans for the future in 1972.[13]

Critics on the Left place a major part of the blame for
Allende's defeat on the President, saying his administration
moved too slowly, that it should have armed the people for an inevitable clash with the Right.[14] In fact, the *Unidad Popular*
took over the banks, the copper mines, and almost all major industries in less than three years. In addition, it tolerated the
takeover of factories by workers and a high number of land sei-
zures by the urban poor and rural laborers. For the first time
in the history of Chile, laborers had real power. Those who believe Allende should have distributed arms have yet to explain
how he could have tried to do so without provoking the immediate
and violent retaliation of the armed forces. The military made
it clear that it would support his administration only as long as
it remained within "constitutional" limits. Allende did not have
the stomach for a civil war; but it takes a peculiar point of view
to see this as a fault in character. Logistically, he was still
building labor support and would have had to pit a divided Left
against a large, well-armed Right. There is not a single instance

since the Second World War in which the working class alone has
destroyed a capitalist regime which retained the backing of the
armed forces, and of the upper and middle classes.

Those who defeated Allende argue that he tried to do too
much and led Chile into "chaos." By 1973, the economy was in
shambles. Allende, in order to attract workers to his administration, increased salaries in 1971 and paid for government
projects by turning the printing presses. The money supply rose
from 9,192 million *escudos* in December, 1970 to 20,131 million in
December, 1971, an increase of 119 percent.[15] The shortage of
imported parts, a direct result of a U.S. effort to cut off
capitalist credit to Chile, reduced production of basic goods.
By late 1972, the official value of the *escudo* bore little relation to the availability of food and clothing. Shortages became commonplace; the public had to wait in line for hours whenever goods were distributed. The middle class became bitter at
the decline of its living standards, and the black market catered
to everyone who was willing to buy goods at several times their
official value. The victors, however, conveniently overlook the
role they played and the assistance they received from the United
States in "destabilizing" Chile. Opponents of the *Unidad Popular*
resorted to paramilitary violence, sabotage, and strikes in order
to cripple the economy.

Allende's tragedy and that of the people he served was that
the presidency was an inadequate base for a revolutionary mobilization. He was caught between the constraints of the office and
carrying out his campaign promises. If he pursued an electoral
strategy, he would need to include at least part of the Christian
Democratic Party in his administration; if he pursued a strategy
of confrontation, he would have to neutralize the armed forces
and gain control of an even greater part of the economy. The
Christian Democrats saw his dilemma and exploited it, insisting
as a condition for even a discussion of an accommodation that he
reverse many revolutionary achievements. The core of the party,
moreover, was never willing to cooperate with Allende. From the
moment he left office, Eduardo Frei worked to defeat the Left.
He toured the United States and Europe trying to raise support
against the government and warning of the dangers of socialism in
Chile. Christian Democratic workers joined the strikes that
brought the economy down. Frei hoped his party and the Nationalists would win two-thirds of the Congressional seats in the elections of March, 1973. The opposition to UP could then impeach
the President. But that approach failed when UP won 43 percent
of the vote. Frei and the Christian Democrats then joined the
Nationalists in passing a congressional resolution that declared
the administration illegitimate, an act that invited the military
to overthrow it.[16]

The presidency also lacked the economic means to sustain the
society. There is ample evidence that even had Allende seized
more of the economy, its structural problems would still have
caused massive disorder. Allende could nationalize a major part
of Chile's economy, but he needed new infusions of capital to

maintain production. What is more, he needed to reorient the
purposes of production, to steer industry in the direction of
basic goods rather than consumer durables. His monetary policy
did exactly the opposite, increasing demand along already existing lines. His basic hope lay in the nationalization of the copper sector. But the copper companies, in their rush to maximize
profits, had created serious technical problems in the plants.
The President of Chile also has little say in the world copper
market. Allende denounced the embargo of credit by the United
States, but he cannot have expected Nixon and Kissinger to have
helped finance the success of the Chilean Left.[17]

Aside from the specifics of the Allende experiment, the collapse of civilian authority raises other, broader issues about
dependent development. Given the political culture and the
structure of the economy, an intensification of class conflict
had become inevitable after 1970. Even had Allende not won the
presidency, the nation faced a serious economic contraction.
Those who think that the problems lay entirely in what Allende
did or did not do have simply to look at the rest of the continent. Peru, Argentina, and Uruguay began the 1970s with governments very different from Chile's but ended the decade with
right-wing military regimes, high inflation, and massive economic
crisis. It is clear that the dependent economic order throughout
South America is suffering its most serious reverse since the
Great Depression. Even the Brazilian "miracle," the model on
which the Pinochet regime in Chile bases many of its decisions,
has ended in massive foreign debt and 60 percent inflation.[18]
Chile is not alone in being unable to combine political freedom
with economic dependence.

The military hopes that a free-trade model of economic growth
will revive the nation. It has achieved initial success—after
three years of high unemployment, spiraling prices, and declining
real wages—by inviting foreign banks and corporations to reinvest in a secure environment. Those who once touted the success
of Brazil now see the next "miracle" in Chile. But export-
oriented growth cannot assure security unless it also addresses
the problems of dependence and social injustice. The current
success is based on ignoring such problems in favor of short-term
gains. As such, it is nothing new: Chile has seen several such
miracles—the 1850s, the 1870s, the early twentieth century, and
the late 1920s. Each led to a more severe crisis than the last.
The outcome is always the same: fabulous wealth for a few successful speculators and an uneven distribution of income that
leaves a major part of the population miserable. Inevitably, the
export boom ends or the speculators suffer reverses or both; and
another political crisis is the result. In the short term, the
junta can count on the support of conservative Christian Democrats and Nationalists who understand that a return to civilian
rule would mean a remobilization of the Left. Many Christian
Democrats who hate the dictator General Augusto Pinochet consider
him preferable to answering for their conduct in 1973.

In the long term, Chile must address the issues of dependence

and social injustice because the two are related and the problems
they cause will not disappear. The nation's debt continues to
mount. The working class remains destitute. The people's political consciousness has changed. It is impossible to imagine the
military indefinitely in power, and it is impossible to think of
a civilian regime which will not have to confront the problems of
inflation, unemployment, and the outflow of national income to
foreign corporations. To address these problems will require re-
newing and rethinking the struggle waged by the Left throughout
this century.

Reference Matter

Abbreviations

A.H.	Archivo Nacional. *Ministerio de Hacienda.* Santiago. Biblioteca Nacional.
A.I.	Chile. Archivo Nacional. *Ministerio del Interior.* Santiago. Biblioteca Nacional.
Anderson.	Chandler P. Anderson Papers. Washington: Library of Congress, Manuscript Division.
Anuario.	Chile, Oficina Central de Estadística. *Anuario estadístico de la República de Chile.*
Apuntes Estadísticas.	Chile. Oficina de Estadística Comercial. *Apuntes estadísticas sobre la República de Chile.* Valparaiso: Imprenta del Universo de G. Helfman, 1876.
Auchincloss.	Gordon B. Auchincloss Papers. New Haven: Yale University, Sterling Memorial Library Archives. Manuscript Group 580.
B.O.T.	Chile, Oficina del Trabajo, *Boletín de la Oficina del Trabajo.*
Censo.	Chile. Oficina Central de Estadistica. *Censo General de la República de Chile.*
Diputados, *B.S.E.*	Chile. Camara de Diputados. *Boletín de las sesiones estraordinarias.*
Diputados, *B.S.O.*	Chile. Camara de Diputados. *Boletín de las sesiones ordinarias.*
Discurso.	Chile, *Discurso de su excelencia el Presidente de la República en la apertura del Congreso Nacional.*
F.O. 16.	Great Britain. Public Records Office. Foreign Office 16. *General Correspondence for Chile.*
G.B.P.P.	*British Parliamentary Papers: Central and South America, 1843-1899.* Irish Press Area Studies Series. Dublin: Irish University Press Microforms, 1974.
G.B.S.P.	Great Britian. Parliament. House of Commons. *Sessional Papers.*

Hacienda, *Antecedentes.* Chile. Ministerio de Hacienda.
Antecedentes sobre la industria salitrera.
Santiago: Imprenta Universo, 1925.

Hacienda, *Memoria.* Chile. Ministerio de Hacienda. *Memoria del Ministerio de Hacienda presentado al Congreso Nacional por el Ministro del Ramo.*

Interior, *Memoria.* Chile. Ministerio del Interior. *Memoria que el Ministro del Estado en el Departamento del Interior presenta al Congreso Nacional* (1880-83, 1885-1911, 1924-29).

Polk. Frank L. Polk Papers. New Haven: Yale University, Sterling Memorial Library. Manuscript Group 656.

B.S.O. Chile. Camara de Senadores. *Boletín de sesiones ordinarias.*

Sinopsis. Chile. Oficina Central de Estadística. *Sinopsis estadística de la República de Chile.*

U.S. *Despatches.* United States. Department of State. *Despatches from U.S. Ministers to Chile, 1823-1906.* Washington: National Archives Microfilm M 10, 1962. Record Group 59.

U.S. *Diplomatic.* United States. Department of State. *Records of Diplomatic Posts: Chile, 1824-1935.* Washington: National Archives. Record Group 84.

U.S. *Internal Affairs.* United States. Department of State. *Records of the Department of State Relating to the Internal Affairs of Chile, 1910-1929.* Washington: National Archives Microfilm M 487, 1963. Record group 59.

U.S. *Numerical.* United States. Department of State. *Numerical and Minor Files of the Department of State, 1906-1910.* Washington: National Archives Microfilm M 862, 1972. Record Group 59.

U.S. *Valparaiso.* United States. Department of State. *Despatches from United States Consuls in Valparaiso, 1819-1906.* Washington: National Archives Microfilm M 146, 1949.

Notes

INTRODUCTION

1 Paul E. Sigmund, *The Overthrow of Allende and the Politics of of Chile, 1964-1976* (Pittsburgh: University of Pittsburgh Press, 1977), p. 253.

2 Jorge Nef, "The Politics of Repression: The Social Pathology of the Chilean Military," *Latin American Perspectives* 1 (Summer 1975): 71-74.

3 Frederick B. Pike, *Chile and the United States, 1880-1962* (Notre Dame, Ind.: University of Notre Dame Press, 1963); and Arnold Bauer, *Chilean Rural Society* (Cambridge: Cambridge University Press, 1975).

4 Francisco A. Encina, *Historia de Chile, desde la prehistoria hasta 1891,* 20 vols. (Santiago: Editorial Nascimento, 1950).

5 Markos J. Mamalakis, "The Role of Government in the Resource Transfer and Resource Allocation Processes: The Chilean Nitrate Sector, 1880-1930," in Gustav Ranis, ed., *Government and Economic Development* (New Haven: Yale University Press, 1971), pp. 181-210.

6 Thomas F. O'Brien, "British Investors and the Decline of Chilean Nitrate Entrepreneurs, 1870-1890" (Ph.D. diss., University of Connecticut, 1976); and his articles, "Chilean Elites and Foreign Investors: Chilean Nitrate Policy, 1880-1882," *Journal of Latin American Studies* 11 (May 1979); "The Antofagasta Company: A Case Study of Peripheral Capitalism," *Hispanic American Historical Review* 60 (February 1980). Henry W. Kirsch, *Industrial Development in a Traditional Society: The Conflict of Entrepreneurship and Modernization in Chile* (Gainesville: The University Presses of Florida, 1977); and Peter Charles De Shazo, "Urban Workers and Labor Unions in Chile, 1902-1917" (Ph.D. diss., University of Wisconsin, 1977).

7 As an example, see the exchange between D. C. M. Platt, on the one side, and Stanley and Barbara Stein, on the other: D. C. M. Platt, "Dependency in Nineteenth-Century Latin America," *Latin American Research Review* 15 (1980): 113-30; Stanley J.

Stein and Barbara H. Stein, "Comment," and Platt's "Reply," in same issue, pp. 131-50.

8 Paul Baran, *The Political Economy of Growth* (New York: Monthly Review Press, 1957); Samir Amin, *Accumulation on a World Scale, a Critique of the Theory of Underdevelopment,* trans. Brian Pearce, 2 vols. (New York: Monthly Review Press, 1974); Samir Amin, *Unequal Development: An Essay on the Social Formations of Peripheral Capitalism* (New York: Monthly Review Press, 1976); Theotonio dos Santos, *El nuevo carácter de la dependencia* (Santiago: Cuadernos de Estudios Socio-Económicos [10], Centro de Estudios Socio-Económicos, Universidad de Chile, 1968), and "La crisis de la teoría del desarrollo y las relaciones de dependencia en América Latina," in Helio Jaguaribe et al., *La dependencia político-ecónomica de América Latina* (Mexico: Siglo Veintinuno, 1970), pp. 147-88. The literature about dependence theory is vast. Three solid summaries are Ronald H. Chilcote, "Dependency: A Critical Synthesis of the Literature," *Latin American Perspectives* 1 (Spring 1974); C. Richard Bath and Dilmus D. James, "Dependency Analysis of Latin America: Some Criticism, Some Suggestions," *Latin American Research Review* 11 (1976); and James M. Cypher, "The Internationalization of Capital and the Transformation of Social Formations: A Critique of the Monthly Review School," *The Review of Radical Political Economics* 11 (Winter 1979).

9 Amin, *Accumulation on a World Scale,* 1:15-18.

10 Tony Smith, "The Underdevelopment of Development Literature: The Case of Dependency Theory," *World Politics* 31 (January 1979): 247-88.

11 The best discussion of this shortcoming is by Theda Skocpol, *States and Social Revolutions: A Comparative Analysis of France, Russia, and China* (Cambridge: Cambridge University Press, 1979), pp. 24-33.

12 See, for an exposition of the problems involved, Peter Wiles, "The Necessity and Impossibility of Political Economy," *History and Theory* 11 (1972): 3-14.

1. THE ORIGINS OF ECONOMIC DEPENDENCE

1 Darío's article is in Antonio Roca del Camp, ed., *Tradición y leyenda de Santiago* (Santiago: Ediciones Ercilla, 1941), p. 175.

2 Luis Vitale, *Interpretación marxista de la historia de Chile* (Santiago: Prensa Latinoamericana, 1967), 1:163.

3 Claudio Véliz, "La mesa de tres patas," *Desarrollo Económico* (Apr.-Sept. 1963), reprinted in Hernán Godoy Urzua, ed., *Estructura social de Chile* (Santiago: Editorial Universitaria, 1971), p. 238; Mary Lowenthal Felstiner, "Kinship Politics in the Chilean Independence Movement," *Hispanic American Historical Review* (Feb. 1976): 78-79; Jaime Eyzaguirre, *Fisonomía histórica de Chile,* 3d ed. (Santiago: Editorial Universitaria, 1973), pp. 27-32.

4 Sergio Villalobos R., *El comercio y la crisis colonial: un mito de la Independencia* (Santiago: Ediciones de la Universidad de Chile, 1968), pp. 112-13, 149; Hernán Ramírez Necochea, *Antecedentes económicos de la independencia de Chile* (Santiago: Editorial Universitaria, 1959), pp. 46-56; Chile, *Boletín de leyes y decretos del gobierno, 1810-1814* (Santiago: 1898), p. 22; and Diego Barros Arana, "La proclamación de la libertad de comercio en Chile," *Revista Económica* 2 (1887): 27-30.

5 Domingo Amunátegui Solar, "Origen del comercio inglés en Chile," *Revista Chilena de Historia y Geografía* 103 (July-December 1943): 83-90; and J. A. Gibbs, *History of Antony and Dorothea Gibbs* (London: The Saint Catherine Press, 1922), p. 383.

6 Gideon Sjoberg, *The Preindustrial City: Past and Present* (New York: Free Press, 1960), p. 136.

7 José Antonio Varas, *Colonización de Llanquihue, Valdivia i Arauco o sea colección de las leyes i decretos supremos concernientes a esta materia, desde 1827 a 1871 inclusivo* (Sangiago: Imprenta de la República, 1872), pp. 7, 12, 14; and Wladimiro Tartakowsky Henker, *El problema de la migración* (Santiago: Dirección General de Prisiones, 1941), p. 173.

8 S. S. Hill, *Travels in Peru and Mexico* (London: Longman, 1860), 1:49.

9 Chile, Dirección Jeneral de Contabilidad, *Resumen de la hacienda pública desde 1833 hasta 1900* (Santiago: 1901), 5:3.

10 Great Britain, *Reports by Her Majesties Secretaries of Embassy and Legation on the Manufactures, Commerce, etc., of the Countries in which they reside*, pt. 3: *Report by Mr. Rumbold on the Progress and General Condition of Chile* (London: Harrison and Sons, 1876), p. 366.

11 Aníbal Pinto Santa Cruz, *Chile, un caso de desarrollo frustrado* (Santiago: Editorial Universitaria, 1962), pp. 35, 39-40; and Albert Hirschman, *Journeys Toward Progress* (New York: Twentieth Century Fund, 1963), pp. 165-66.

12 Hernán Ramírez Necochea, *Balmaceda y la contrarevolución de 1891* (Santiago: Editorial Universitaria, 1969), p. 40.

13 André Gunder Frank, *Capitalism and Underdevelopment in Latin America: Historical Studies of Chile and Brazil* (New York: Monthly Review Press, 1960), p. 95.

14 Pinto Santa Cruz, *Chile;* Hirschman, *Journeys toward Progress.*

15 Frank, *Capitalism*, p. 95; and Hernán Ramírez Necochea, *Historia del imperialismo en Chile* (Santiago: Editorial Austral, 1960), pp. 64-67.

16 Alexander Caldcleugh, *Travels in South America, during the years 1819-20-21; containing an account of Brazil, Buenos Ayres, and Chile* (London: John Murray, 1825), 1:372-73.

17 Thomas Sutcliffe, *Sixteen Years in Chile and Peru from 1822 to 1839* (London: Fisher and Sons, 1841), pp. 123-15; and Gilbert Farquhar Mathison, *Narrative of a Visit to Brazil, Chile, Peru, and Sandwich Islands during the years 1821 and 1822* (London: Charles Knight, Pall Mall East, 1825), pp. 214-15.

18 Aime Pissis, *Geografía física de la República de Chile*

(Paris: Institute geográfico de Paris, 1875), p. 205; William
S. W. Ruschenberger, *Three Years in the Pacific, containing
notices of Brazil, Chile, Bolivia, Peru, etc., in 1831, 1832,
1833, 1834. By an officer of the United States Navy* . . .
(London: Richard Bentley, 1835), 1:192-96; Hobson no. 16,
Oct. 15, 1836, U.S. *Valparaiso,* reel 3; and José Joaquín
Vallejo, Diputados, *B.S.O.,* Aug. 19, 1849.

19 Caldcleugh, *Travels,* 1:355-56; Maria Graham, *Journal of a
Residence in Chile during the Year 1822, and a Voyage from
Chile to Brazil in 1823* (London: Longman, 1824), p. 125; and
Vicente Pérez Rosales, *Recuerdos del pasado (1844-1860)*
(1880; Santiago: Zig-Zag, 1958), p. 145.

20 Michael Hogan to State, May 6, 1822, U.S. *Valparaiso,* reel 1.
Also Simon Collier, *Ideas and Politics of Chilean Independence, 1808-1833* (Cambridge University Press, 1967), pp. 234-
35; unfortunately, Collier blames O'Higgins' downfall on his
unpopularity among landowners without discussing the relation
of the Supreme Director's policies to the export economy.

21 Royal Historical Society, *British Consular Reports on the
Trade and Politics of Latin America, 1824-1826,* ed. by R. A.
Humphreys (London: Royal Historical Society, 1940), vol. 8,
report by Christopher Nugent on Chile, Mar. 17, 1853, p. 99;
and Hogan to State, Dec. 26, 1929, and May 10, 1832, U.S.
Valparaiso, reel 2.

22 Hogan to State, Dec. 26, 1929, and May 10, 1832, U.S. *Val-
paraiso,* reel 2; also Alberto Edwards, *La fronda aristocrática*
(Santiago: Imprenta Nacional, 1932), pp. 62-69; Chile, *Con-
stitución política y lei de elecciones de la República de
Chile* (Santiago: Imprenta Moneda, 1903) art. 5, 59; Richard
Polland no. 17, June 13, 1836, U.S. *Despatches,* reel 4;
Hacienda, *Memoria,* 1839, p. 15; J. J. von Tschudi, *Travels in
Peru, during the Yearns 1838-1842,* trans. from the German by
Thomasina Ross (London: David Bogue, 1847), p. 25; and
(General) Tomás de Iriarte, *Panoramas chilenas del siglo XIX,*
ed. Gabriel Balbontín Guenzalida (Santiago: Editorial Arcos,
1965, based on 1841 ed.), p. 56; also Hill, *Travels,* 1:78;
Philo White, *White's Narrative of a cruise in the Pacific to
South America and California on the U.S. sloop-of-war "Dale,"
1841-1843,* ed. Charles L. Camp (Denver: Fred A. Rosenstock,
Old West Publishing Co., 1965), p. 48; and (Lt.) Henry
Augustus Wise, *Los gringos: or an Inside View of Mexico and
California with wanderings in Peru, Chile, and Polynesia* (New
York: Baker and Scribner, 1850), p. 28.

23 Derived from Chile, Dirección Jeneral de Contabilidad, *Resumen
de hacienda pública,* 2:7-8; and Julio Menénder, *Estadística
comercial comparativa de la República de Chile* (Valparaiso:
Imprenta del Mercurio, 1862), pt. 2, table 14.

24 *The Neighbor* (Valparaiso), Feb. 14, 1851; and Vice-Consul
Cunningham, Talcahuano, report of Dec. 31, 1855, *G.B.P.P.,*
vol. 4, c. 214; Menénder, *Estadística comercial,* pt. 1, tables
1, 2.

25 Claudio Véliz, *Historia de la marina mercante de Chile*

(Santiago: Universidad de Chile, 1961), pp. 66, 82.

26 Ramírez Necochea, *Historia del imperalismo*, pp. 64-67; Frank, *Capitalism*, p. 68; and Menénder, *Estadística comercial*, pt. 2, table 16.

27 A copy of the treaty is reprinted in *G.B.P.P.*, vol. 4, cs. 2015, 1854.

28 George A. Merwin no. 8, Sept. 27, 1855, U.S. *Valparaiso*, reel 5; and Hacienda, *Memoria*, 1865, pp. 38-39.

29 Augustín Edwards, *Cuatro presidentes de Chile: 1841-1876* (Valparaiso: Imprenta Universo, 1932), 1:147-48; Pierre Vayssierre, "Au Chili: De L'Economie Coloniale à L'Inflation," *Cahiers du Ameriques Latines* 5 (Jan.-June 1970): 24-25; and Theodore Schneider, *La agricultura en Chile en los últimos cincuenta años* (Santiago: Imprenta Barcelona, 1904), p. 5.

30 Frank Whitson Fetter, *Monetary Inflation in Chile* (Princeton: Princeton University Press, 1931), pp. 7-8.

31 Ramón E. Santelices, in *Los bancos chilenos* (Santiago: Imprenta Barcelona, 1893), pp. 123-25, quotes the entire banking statute.

32 James Churchman to State, May 1, 1862, U.S. *Valparaiso*, reel 8.

33 Samuel Nuñez Olaechea, *Los ferrocarriles del estado* (Santiago: Imprenta Encuadernaciones Chile, 1910), p. 320; and Henry Clay Evans, Jr., *Chile and its Relations with the United States* (Durham, N.C.: Duke University Press, 1927, p. 57.

34 John Josh Murray, Caldera, Mar. 26, 1867, *G.B.P.P.*, vol. 4, c. 3891.

35 Menénder, *Estadística comercial*, pt. 1, tables 3, 4, and pt. 3, table 25.

36 For a description of this pattern see *El Guia de Arauco* (Los Angeles), July 29, 1865; and Domingo Sarmiento, in *El Mercurio* (Valparaiso), Apr. 3, 1842.

37 Claudio Gay described the new hacendados in *Historia física y política de Chile* (Paris: Thenot y Cía., 1865), 1:103-15; and Vallejo, in *El Copiapino* (Copiapó), May 9, 1845.

38 Chile, *Constitución política y lei de elecciones de la República de Chile* (Santiago: Imprenta Moneda, 1903), arts. 57, 59, 74, 82; Iriarte, *Panoramas chilenas*, p. 89; and Ricardo Salas Edwards, *Balmaceda y el parlamentarismo en Chile; un estudio de psicología política chilena*, 2d. ed. (Santiago: Imprenta Universo, 1916), pp. 23-24.

39 Iriarte, *Panoramas chilenas*, p. 97; (Lt.) James M. Gilliss, *The U.S. Naval Astronomical Expedition* (Washington, D.C.: 1855), pp. 129, 305-6; and Sergio Villalobos R. et al., *Historia de Chile* (Santiago: Editorial Universitaria 1974-78), 3:545.

40 Alberto Edwards, *El gobierno de don Manuel Montt, 1851-1861* (Santiago: Editorial Nascimento, 1932), pp. 175-201; Frederick B. Pike, "Church and State in Peru and Chile since 1840: A Study in Contrasts," *American Historical Review* 73 (October 1967): 37-38; Fernando Campos Harriet, *Historia constitucional de Chile* (Santiago: Editorial Jurídica de Chile, p. 189; and Agustín Edwards, *Cuatro presidentes*, p. 212-26.

41 Hacienda, *Memoria,* 1865, p. 19.
42 United States, Department of State, *Report upon the Commercial Relations of the United States with Foreign Countries for the year 1875* (Washington, D.C.:   1875), Report by D. J. Williamson, p. 205.
43 Salas Edwards, *Balmaceda,* 1:35; Campos Harriet, *Historia constitucional,* pp. 342-45; and Encina, *Historia de Chile,* 15: 300-312.
44 Marcial González, *La condición de las trabajadores rurales en Chile* (pamphlet, 1876), reprinted in his *Estudios económicos* (Santiago: Imprenta Gutenberg, 1889), pp. 318-19; see also Gonzalo Izquierdo F. on the liberal attitude toward rural laborers, *Un estudio de las ideologías chilenas: la Sociedad de Agricultura en el siglo XIX* (Santiago: Centro de Estudios Socio-Económicos, Facultad de Ciencias Sociales, Universidad de Chile, 1968), p. 157.
45 Benjamín Vicuña MacKenna, *La transformación de Santiago: notas e indicaciones respetuosamente sometidas a la Ilustre Municipalidad, al Supremo Gobierno y al Congreso Nacional por el Intendente de Santiago* (Santiago: Imprenta del Mercurio, 1872); and Miguel Cruchaga, *Estudio sobre la organización económica y la hacienda pública de Chile* (1875; Madrid: Editorial Reus, 1929), 1:197.
46 Chile, Dirección Jeneral de Contabilidad, *Resumen de la hacienda pública desde 1833 hasta 1900* (Santiago: 1929), 2:49 and 3:8.
47 Interior, *Memoria,* 1875, report of Intendant for Linares, 2: 336; report of Intendant for Llanquihue, 1:43; and 2:197-98, 207, 261.
48 Hacienda, *Memoria,* 1875, pp. 60-61; *Apuntes estadísticos,* p. 15; and González, "Los negocios y la crísis," in *Estudios,* p. 211.
49 James Douglas, "Chile—Its Geography, People, and Institutions," *Bulletin of the American Geographical Society* (1881): 91.
50 Hacienda, *Memoria,* 1876, vol. 7; Contabilidad, *Resumen de la hacienda pública,* 1:18-19 and 5:2; Great Britain, *Statistical Abstract for the United Kingdom, 1865-1879,* pp. 106-7; and Consul Grierson, report for the year 1878, *G.B.P.P.,* vol. 4, c. 2134.
51 Encina, *Historia de Chile,* 15:399-417; U.S. Department of Commerce and Labor, Bureau of Foreign and Domestic Commerce, *Consular Reports,* 1896, Vol. 13, pt. 1, p. 183; and William F. Sater, "Chile and the World Depression of the 1870's," *Journal of Latin American Studies* 11 (May 1979):   88-89—Sater's article is the best review of the entire crisis.
52 Domingo Amunátegui Solar, *La democracía en Chile* (Santiago: Universidad de Chile, 1946), p. 198; and Santelices, *Los bancos chilenos,* copy of statute, pp. 198-200.
53 Christian Zegers, *Aníbal Pinto, historia política de su administración* (Santiago: Editorial Universitaria, 1969), p. 93.
54 See my "Cultural Bases of Economic Imperialism: The British

in the Atacama Desert," *Journal of Economic History* 35 (March 1975); Osborne no. 83, 1878, U.S. *Despatches,* reel 30; and Bolivia, *Documentos oficiales de Bolivia relativos a la cuestión del Pacífico* (Buenos Aires: Imprenta del Pueblo, 1879), pp. 4, 33, 75.

55 Gonzalo Bulnes, *Chile and Peru, the Causes of the War of 1879* (Santiago: Imprenta Universitaria, 1920), pp. 9-33; Clement Markham, *The War between Peru and Chile, 1879-1882* (London: Sampson, Lass, Marston, Searle, and Rivington, 1882), pp. 81-92; W. J. Dennis, *Tacna and Arica, an Account of the Chile-Peru Boundary Dispute and of the Arbitrations of the United States* (New Haven: Yale University Press, 1931), pp. 61-83.

2. THE NITRATE ECONOMY AND THE CIVIL WAR OF 1891

1 There are several works on the civil war. This chapter relies most heavily on Encina, *Historia de Chile,* vols. 19-20; Salas Edwards, *Balmaceda;* and Francisco Frías Valenzuela, *Historia de Chile,* vol. 3, *La República,* 2d ed. (Santiago: Editorial Nascimento, 1965), pp. 352-417.

2 *El Diario Oficial* (Santiago), Jan. 1, 1891.

3 Encina, *Historia de Chile,* 20:38-50.

4 Salas Edwards, *Balmaceda,* 1:131-37.

5 Ramírez Necochea, *Balmaceda y la contrarevolución de 1891,* pp. 178-195.

6 Harold Blakemore, *British Nitrates and Chilean Politics, 1886-1896: Balmaceda and North* (London: The Athlone Press of the University of London, 1974), pp. 158-91.

7 Ramírez Necochea, *Balmaceda,* pp. 192-96; Blakemore, *British Nitrates,* pp. 193-206.

8 Chile, Ministerio de Hacienda, *Antecedentes sobre la industria salitrera* (Santiago: Imprenta Universo, 1925), p. 21; and Chile, Legación en Londres, *Resumen de la hacienca pública de Chile desde 1833 hasta 1914* (London: Spottiswoode and Co., 1914), p. 62.

9 Pakenham no. 21, Apr. 27, 1881, *F.O. 16,* vol. 212, and no. 44, Aug. 7, 1883, vol. 223; Logan no. 85, Apr. 7, 1883, U.S. *Despatches,* reel T-33; and *El Mercurio* (Valparaiso), Dec. 17, 1881.

10 Foote no. 83, Dec. 9, 1881, U.S. *Valparaiso,* reel 10; *Diario Oficial* (Santiago), July 7, 1882.

11 Roberto Hernández C., *El salitre: resumen histórico desde su descubrimiento y explotación* (Valparaiso: Fisher Hermanos, 1930), p. 81.

12 *El Mercurio* (Valparaiso), May 4, 10, 11, June 7, 18, 1980, and Oct. 24, 28, 1881; *El Ferrocarril* (Santiago), Sept. 15, 1880; Logan, Dec. 26, 1882, U.S. *Despatches,* reel T-33; Álvaro Covarrubías, "Informe de la Comisión Consultiva de Salitre," Hacienda, *Memoria,* 1880; and O'Brien, "British Investors," pp. 135-40, 148-49.

13 Guillermo Billinghurst, *El abastecimiento de agua potable del*

puerto de Iquique (Iquique: Imprenta Española, 1887), pp. 58-78; J. Fred Rippy, "Economic Enterprises of the Nitrate King and His Associates in Chile," *Pacific Historical Review* 17 (Nov. 1948):   457-65; and Harold Blakemore, "John Thomas North, the Nitrate King," *History Today* 12 (July 1962).

14 Drummond Hay no. 2, Apr. 24, 1883, *F.O. 16,* vol. 224; Consul Newman, Valparaiso, June, 1889, *G.B.P.P.,* vol. 4, c. 5896; Jorge Potén, Chilean Consul in Berlin, "Industria Salitrera," in Hacienda, *Memoria,* 1889, p. 33; Romeyer no. 59, Apr. 27, 1888, U.S. *Valparaiso,* reel 11; and William Eleroy Curtis, *The Capitals of Spanish America* (New York: Harper and Brothers, 1888), p. 454.

15 Great Britain, *Statistical Abstract for the United Kingdom, 1879-1893,* pp. 68-69.

16 On the combination, see Chile, Ministerio de Hacienda, *La industria de salitre en Chile* (Santiago: Imprenta Universo, 1933-34), 1:7-8; Joseph R. Brown, "Nitrate Crises, Combinations and the Chilean Government in the Nitrate Age," *Hispanic American Historical Review* 43 (May 1963); on its impact, see *A.I.,* vol. 1245, Tarapacá (1885) Gonzalo Bulnes no. 407, Mar. 5, 1885; Vice-Consul Barnet, Antofagasta, Dec. 31, 1884, *G.B.P.P.,* vol. 4, c. 4526; Hacienda, *Antecedentes,* p. 21; and Enrique Reyes N., *El desarrollo de conciencia proletaria en Chile (el ciclo salitrero)* (Santiago: Editorial Orbe, 1973), p. 66.

17 Consul Newman, Valparaiso, June, 1889, *G.B.P.P.,* vol. 4, c. 5896; and Hacienda, *Antecedentes,* p. 21.

18 Legación en Londres, *Resumen de la hacienda,* p. 62; and Chile, Dirección Jeneral de Contabilidad, *Resumen de la hacienda pública desde 1833 hasta 1900* (Santiago: 1929), 2:50.

19 Legación en Londres, *Resumen de la hacienda,* p. 94; J. Sotomayor G., Hacienda, *Memoria,* 1889, p. cxiv; report of Francisco J. San Roman, "Esploraciones al desierto de Tarapacá," Interior, *Memoria,* 1885, 1:183; A. Martinez, Intendant of Atacama, Interior, *Memoria,* 1883, 2:11-12; and Romeyer no. 78, Dec. 15, 1888, U.S. *Valparaiso,* reel 12.

20 Consul Grierson, Feb. 15, 1890, *G.B.P.P.,* vol. 4, c. 5895-88.

21 Dunn, "Report upon the Production of Wheat in Chile," no. 50, May 17, 1886, U.S. *Valparaiso,* reel 11.

22 Contabilidad, *Resumen,* 3:41, 47; and Hacienda, *Antecedentes,* p. 21.

23 Balmaceda's address is reprinted in *The Chilean Times* (Valparaiso), Mar. 16, 1889.

24 Ramírez Necochea, *Balmaceda,* p. 93.

25 Kennedy no. 42, May 14, 1890, *F.O. 16,* vol. 259; Kennedy no. 8, Sept. 5, 1890, *F.O. 16,* vol. 262; see also Kennedy to Sanderson, Sept. 30, 1890, *F.O. 16,* vol. 259.

26 *The Chilean Times* (Valparaiso), Mar. 16, 1889; and Consul Newman, Valparaiso, June, 1889, *G.B.P.P.,* vol. 4, c. 5896.

27 Kennedy no. 48, June 21, 1890, *F.O. 16*, vol. 259.
28 Kennedy no. 63, Aug. 12, 1890, *F.O. 16*, vol. 259.
29 T. Worshington, Special Commissioner, Board of Trade, Valparaiso, Apr. 14, 1898, *G.B.P.P.*, vol. 4, c. 9100; see also Contabilidad, *Resumen*, 5:2, 4.
30 Henry W. Kirsch, "The Industrialization of Chile, 1880-1930" (Ph.D. diss., University of Florida, 1973), p. 50; *The Chilian Times* (Valparaiso), Dec. 31, 1887; Vice-Consul Thomas, Dec. 7, 1886, *G.B.P.P.*, vol. 4, c. 4924, and Consul Newman, 1888, vol. 4, c. 5252-184.
31 William Howard Russell, *A Visit to Chile and the Nitrate Fields* (London: J. S. Virtue and Co., 1890), pp. 81-83; O'Brien, "British Investors," pp. 250-54.
32 Salas Edwards, *Balmaceda*, p. 96; José Manuel Balmaceda, *Discurso pronunciado por el Ministro del Interior don José Manuel Balmaceda en el sesión de 19 de Julio de 1884 de la Camara de Diputados* (Valparaiso: La Patria, 1884), p. 5: on Church-state issue, see also Logan no. 103, June 7, 1883, U.S. *Despatches*, reel T-33; and Pakenham no. 43. Aug. 7, 1883, *F.O. 16*, vol. 223.
33 Salas Edwards, *Balmaceda*, p. 99.
34 *Censo—1885*, vol. 1, introduction.
35 *Discurso—1890*, pp. 12-13.
36 Balmaceda's address is enclosed in Roberts no. 94, Jan. 1886, U.S. *Despatches*, reel T-35.
37 Interior, *Memoria*, 1887, p. lvii, 1886, 2:325-26, 423-24; and Intendant no. 78, June 21, 1885, *A.I.*, vol. 1250, Concepción (1885).
38 Intendant no. 142, Apr. 14, 1887, *A.I.*, vol. 1210, Santiago (1887); Intendant no. 98, Apr. 6, 1887, *A.I.*, vol. 1208, Coquimbo (1877); and Intendant no. 88, Apr. 9, 1887, *A.I.*, vol. 1210, O'Higgins (1887).
39 Intendant no. 748, Apr. 18, 1885, *A.I.*, vol. 1247, Atacama (1885); Intendant no. 693, Apr. 11, 1885; *A.I.*, vol. 1247, Atacama (1885); and residents to the President, archival pagination 404, n.d., *A.I.*, vol. 1206, Tocopilla (1887).
40 Roberts no. 83, Sept. 6, 1886, U.S. *Despatches*, reel T-35; and Francisco Valdés Vergara, *Guerra civil en Chile—su apreciación histórica* (Valparaiso: G. Helfmann, 1891), pp. 35-36.
41 P. L. Cuadra, Interior, *Memoria*, 1888, p. vi.
42 Salas Edwards, *Balmaceda*, pp. 157-60; and Kennedy no. 42, May 14, 1890, *F.O. 16*, vol. 259.
43 Valenzuela, *Historia de Chile*, 3:368-87.
44 Egan no. 88, Aug. 15, 1890, U.S. *Despatches*, reel T-37, and Egan no. 100, Oct. 17, 1890, reel T-38; Interior, *Memoria*, 1892, vol. 1, p. lv; and Kennedy no. 90, Oct. 24, 1890, *F.O. 16*, vol. 259.
45 Kennedy no. 106, Dec. 16, 1890, *F.O. 16*, vol. 259; and Arturo Alessandri Palma, *Chile y su historia* (Santiago: Editorial Orbe, 1945), 2:287.
46 *Discurso*, Apr. 20, 1891; and Ramírez Necochea, *Balmaceda*, p. 198.

47 *El Progreso* (Iquique), Aug. 4, 1888; although the President stressed education, in fact most of the schools had small enrollments. Ministerio de Industria y Obras Públicas, *Memoria,* 1889, pp. 11, 14-15.

48 Valdés Vergara, *Guerra civil,* pp. 41-42; and Blakemore, *British Nitrates,* p. 89.

49 Kennedy, Oct. 23, 1893, *G.B.P.P.,* vol. 4, c. 6856-58.

50 Ramón Barros Luco, Presidente de Sociedad de Fomento Fabril, letter, Apr. 30, 1888, in Ministerio de Industria y Obras Públicas, *Memoria,* 1888, p. 49.

51 Fraser no. 8, Mar. 4, 1888, *F.O. 16,* vol. 252; Martin Drouilly, Inspector General de Colonización, report, Apr. 27, 1888, Ministerio de Industria y Obras Públicas, *Memoria,* 1888, p. 223; *The Chilean Times* (Valparaiso), Dec. 31, 1887; and Kennedy, Nov. 20, 1889, *G.B.P.P.,* vol. 4, c. 5896-16.

52 H. Pérez de Arce, Hacienda, *Memoria,* 1886, p. clxii; see also Arnold Bauer, *Chilean Rural Society* (Cambridge: Cambridge University Press, 1975), appendix vii.

53 Santa Maria no. 2345, Santiago, July 17, 1885, *A.I.,* vol. 1245, Tarapacá (1885); and Intendant's annual report, May 1, 1887, *A.I.,* vol. 1406, Tarapacá (1887).

54 Theodore Child, "Urban and Commercial Chile," *Harper's Magazine* 81 (Nov. 1890):   907.

55 Consul Newman, Valparaiso, June 19, 1888, *G.B.P.P.,* vol. 4, c. 5252-184.

56 Kennedy, Nov. 20, 1886, *G.B.P.P.,* vol. 4, c. 5896-16, Roberts no. 184, Mar. 22, 1888, *U.S. Despatches,* reel T-36; on decline of peso, Contabilidad, *Resumen,* 1:19.

57 *G.B.P.P.,* vol. 4, c. 5252-184, 5896-16.

58 H. Pérez de Arce, Hacienda, *Memoria,* 1886, p. xxx-xxxii; Hacienda, *Memoria,* 1889, p. xlix; and Romeyer no. 78, Dec. 15, 1888, *U.S. Valparaiso,* reel 12.

59 Ramón E. Santelices, *Los bancos chilenos* (Santiago: Imprenta Barcelona, 1893), pp. 422-24.

60 Hacienda, *Memoria,* 1886, p. xxx.

61 Carlos Atuñez, Interior, *Memoria,* 1887, p. lxxvii; P. O. Cuadra, Interior, *Memoria,* 1888, pp. lxxi-lxxvii; and "Memoria de la Comisión Directiva del Servicio Sanitario de Cólera," Interior, *Memoria,* 1888, 2:398.

62 Romeyer no. 56, Mar. 17, 1888, *U.S. Valparaiso,* reel 11.

63 Ibid.

64 *G.B.P.P.,* vol. 4, c. 5252-184.

65 Especially Ramírez Necochea, *Balmaceda,* p. 207; see also Julio César Jobet, *Ensayo crítico del desarrollo económico-social de Chile* (Santiago: Editorial Universitaria, 1955), p. 109.

66 Encina, *Historia de Chile,* 19:131-35.

67 Hernán Ramírez Necochea, *Origen y formación del Partido Comunista de Chile* (Santiago: Editorial Austral, 1965), pp. 30-31; and Aristodemo Escobar Zenteno, *Compendio de la legislación social y el desarrollo del movimiento obrero en Chile* (Santiago: S. Vicente, 1940), p. 187.

68 Marcelo Segall, *Biografía de la ficha-salario* (Santiago:

Editorial Universitaria, 1964), p. 20.

69 See, for example, the petition of Nitrate Producers to the Government, Mar. 12, 1885, *A.H.*, vol. 1585, Tarapacá (1886).

70 Gremio de Jornaleros, Aug. 4, 1888, and Minister of Hacienda, Dec. 31, 1888, *A.H.*, vol. 1793, Tarapacá (1888); and *El Nacional* (Iquique), Jan. 3, 14, 1890.

71 *La Unión* (Valparaiso), July 2, 10, 1890; and *La Voz del Pueblo* (Iquique), July 18, 1890.

72 *El Nacional* (Iquique), July 4, 1890; *El Mercurio* (Valparaiso), July 5, 1890; *La Unión* (Valparaiso), July 11, 1890; and *La Voz de Chile* (Valparaiso), July 18, 1890.

73 *La Unión* (Valparaiso), July 6, 11, 1890; *La Voz de Chile* (Iquique), July 18, 1890; and Marcelo Segall, *Desarrollo del capitalismo en Chile: cinco ensayos dialécticos* (Santiago: Editorial del Pacífico, 1953), p. 225.

74 *The Chilian Times* (Valparaiso), July 12, 1890; *La Unión* (Valparaiso), July 9, 1890; *El Mercurio* (Valparaiso), July 8, 23, 1890; La Voz de Chile (Iquique), July 16, 1890; and Segall, *Desarrollo*, p. 230.

75 *La Voz de Chile* (Iquique), July 16, 1890.

76 Superintendent of Aduanas no. 323, June 24, 1889; and Intendant no. 1068, May 9, 1889, *A.H.*, vol. 1953, Valparaiso (1889).

77 *El Mercurio* (Valparaiso), July 22, 23, 1890; McCreery no. 13, Aug. 8, 1890, U.S. *Valparaiso*, reel 12; report of Comandancia Jeneral de Armas de Valparaiso, July 24, 1890, and report of J. Ramón Sanchez no. 1712, July 27, 1890, *A.I.*, vol. 1637, Municipalidades (1890); *The Chilian Times* (Valparaiso), July 26, 1890; and *La Unión* (Valparaiso), July 23, 25, 1890.

78 *New York Times*, May 27, 1891; also second accusation in Congressional act of deposition, Encina, *História de Chile*, 20:63.

79 Julio Bañados Espinosa, *Balmaceda, su gobierno y la revolución de 1891* (Paris: Librería de Garnier Hermanos, 1893), 1:519.

80 *El Mercurio* (Valparaiso), Aug. 26, 1890; *La Unión* (Valparaiso), Sept. 7, 1890; and Ricardo Anguita, ed., *Leyes promulgadas en Chile: desde 1810 hasta el 1 de Junio de 1912* (Santiago: Imprenta Barcelona, 1912) 3:139, law no. 3,980, Sept. 4, 1890.

81 Wharton to Egan, Sept. 16, 1890, U.S. *Diplomatic*, A 8, 1889-93, vol. 1, no. 55.

82 Valdés Vergara, *Guerra civil*, pp. 65-66.

83 *Pall Mall Gazette* (London), Mar. 24, 1887.

84 Fraser no. 9, Sept. 24, 1886, *F.O. 16*, vol. 224.

85 Kennedy no. 41, May 12, 1890, *F.O. 16*, vol. 259.

86 Joseph R. Brown, "The Chilean Nitrate Railways Controversy," *Hispanic American Historical Review* 18 (Nov. 1958): 471-74; and Kennedy, Nov. 29, 1889, *G.B.P.P.*, vol. 4, c. 5896-16.

87 Kennedy no. 7, Jan. 24, 1891, and Kennedy no. 10, Jan. 29, 1891, *F.O. 16*, vol. 264.

88 Egan no. 122, Jan. 17, 1891, U.S. *Despatches*, reel T-38; and Augusto Matte to Marquis of Salisbury, Mar. 7, 1891, *F.O. 16*, vol. 271.

89 Kennedy telegrams no. 6, Feb. 15, 1891, no. 7, Feb. 23, 1891, and no. 27, Mar. 26, 1891, *F.O. 16*, vol. 264; and Egan no. 136, Mar. 4, 1891, U.S. *Despatches*, reel T-38.
90 Foreign Office to Kennedy, Feb. 27, 1891, U.S. *Despatches*, reel T-38.
91 Egan no. 143, Mar. 17, 1891, and no. 153, Apr. 21, 1891, and Egan cablegrams of Apr. 6 and 23, 1891, U.S. *Despatches*, reel T-38.
92 Kennedy to Ricardo Cruzar, Minister for Foreign Affairs, Apr. 12, 1891, *F.O. 16*, vol. 264; see also Kennedy to Guizat, Apr. 12 and 13, 1891, *G.B.P.P.*, vol. 4.
93 Egan cites a communication shown him by the government from Colonel Robles, its commander in Iquique, no. 143, Mar. 17, 1891, U.S. *Despatches*, reel T-38; and *La Nación* (Santiago), July 31, 1891.
94 W. H. Williams to Consul Joel, Valparaiso, June 30, 1891, *F.O. 16*, vol. 269; Kennedy no. 72, July 7, 1891, *F.O. 16*, vol. 265; and Kennedy telegrams no. 16, May 4, 1891, and no. 31, July 19, 1891, *F.O. 16*, vol. 267.
95 Queenslaw no. 38, Lord Kentsford to Sir H. Norman, Aug. 25, 1891, *F.O. 16*, vol. 273.
96 Egan no. 171, June 3, 1891, U.S. *Despatches*, reel T-38; Santelices, *Los bancos chilenos*, pp. 291-306; on sales taxes, Anguita, *Leyes promulgadas*, 3:154, laws nos. 4, 202, June 8, 1891.
97 On Körner's background, Pedro Pablo Figueroa, *Diccionario biográfico de estranjeros* (Santiago: Imprenta Moderna, 1900), pp. 118-19; on battles, Consul-General Lewis Joel no. 7, Jan. 1, 1892, *F.O. 16*, vol. 269; Egan thought the government had lost 2,000 at Placillos, the revolutionaries 600, and that it lost 4,000 at Concón, the revolutionaries 2,000. Joel, however, was closer to the battles and wrote a later, more comprehensive report: Egan no. 195, Aug. 31, 1891, U.S. *Despatches*, reel T-39.
98 Kennedy to Sanderson, Sept. 15, 1891, *F.O. 16*, vol. 226.
99 J. G. Kennedy memorandum, Sept. 24, 1892, *F.O. 16*, vol. 280.
100 C. T. Maude, Apr. 22, 1892, *F.O. 16*, vol. 278; and Blakemore, *British Nitrates*, pp. 221-22, 227-39.

3. THE ERA OF EASY MONEY

1 Frías Valenzuela, *Historia de Chile*, 4:253.
2 Jorge Barría Serón, *El movimiento obrero en Chile* (Santiago: Ediciones de la Universidad Técnicade Chile, 1971), p. 44.
3 Frederick B. Pike, *Chile and the United States, 1880-1962* (Notre Dame, Ind.: University of Notre Dame Press, 1963), p. 86.
4 *The Chilean Times* (Valparaiso), Jan. 23, 1895.
5 Kennedy no. 145, Dec. 31, 1891, *F.O. 16*, vol. 226.
6 Egan no. 231, Nov. 14, 1891, U.S. *Despatches*, reel T-39; C. T. Maude no. 22, Mar. 15, 1892, *F.O. 16*, vol. 276.

7 Maude no. 55, June 6, 1892, *F.O. 16,* vol. 276.
8 Agustín Ross, *Las malas prácticas parlamentarias* (Valparaiso: Babra y Cía, pp. 1-2; *The Chilean Times* (Valparaiso), Mar. 13, 1897, and Jan. 14, 1905.
9 Wilson no. 332, Sept. 7, 1903, U.S. *Despatches,* reel T-50.
10 Fletcher no. 237, May 9, 1913, U.S. *Internal Affairs,* reel 11.
11 Copiapó, June 5, 1897, *A.I.,* vol. 2235, Municipalidades (1897); and peticiones de Comunas, Feb., 1897, *A.I.,* vol. 2234, Municipalidades (1897).
12 Intendant Los Anjeles no. 39, Apr. 12, 1897, *A.I.,* vol. 2154, Memorias (1897).
13 Yumbel, Sept. 28, 1897, *A.I.,* vol. 2238, Municipalidades (1897); and Cauquenes no. 283, Apr. 8, 1897, *A.I.,* vol. 2154, Memorias (1897).
14 Interior, *Memoria,* 1892, 1:li.
15 *The Chilian Times* (Valparaiso), May 11, 1895; and Chillan no. 15, Feb. 16, 1897, *A.I.,* vol. 2234, Municipalidades (1897).
16 Interior, *Memoria,* 1892, 1:li.
17 Interior, *Memoria,* 1895, 1:liv-lv; and 1910, p. 284.
18 Petition of residents of Maipó to Minister of the Interior, Apr. 10, 1897, *A.I.,* vol. 2235, Municipalidades (1897).
19 Interior, *Memoria,* 1910, p. 284.
20 *The Chilian Times* (Valparaiso), Feb. 27, 1897.
21 Cauquenes no. 283, Apr. 8, 1897, *A.I.,* vol. 2154, Memorias (1897).
22 Wilson no. 311, Mar. 9, 1903, U.S. *Despatches,* reel T-49.
23 Robert E. Mansfield, *Progressive Chile* (New York: Neale Publishing Co., 1913), pp. 136-37.
24 José A. Alfonso, *El parlamentarismo i la reforma política en Chile* (Santiago: Cabeza i Cía, 1909), p. 17; *El Ferrocarril* (Santiago), Mar. 6, 1906; and Paul S. Reinsch, "Parliamentary Government in Chile," *The American Political Science Review* 3 (Nov. 1909): 515.
25 *La Voz del Pueblo* (Valparaiso), July 22, 1905; the most detailed summary of the factions in this period is Manuel Rivas Vicuña, *Historia política y parlamentaria de Chile* (Santiago: Ediciones de la Biblioteca Nacional, 1964), vol. 1, pp. 51-57.
26 Strobel, Acting Sec., no. 92, June 30, 1896, U.S. *Despatches,* reel T-45.
27 Ibid.; *El Ferrocarril* (Santiago), Mar. 6, 1897.
28 *El Ferrocarril* (Santiago), June 18, 1903.
29 Diputados, *B.S.O.,* July 20, 1896, pp. 177-78; Interior, *Memoria,* 1896, p. viii; *El Mercurio* (Valparaiso), Apr. 13, 1905; *The Chilian Times* (Valparaiso), Jan. 24, 1906.
30 Jaime Eyzaguirre, *Chile durante el gobierno de Errázuriz Echaurren, 1896-1901,* 2d ed. (Santiago: Empresa Editora Zig-Zag, 1957), p. 21.
31 John Nicks no. 71, June 27, 1906, U.S. *Despatches,* reel T-52.
32 McGarr no. 105, Mar. 17, 1894, U.S. *Despatches,* reel T-43; and Lía Cortes and Jordi Fuentes, *Diccionario político de Chile* (Santiago: Editorial Orbe, 1967), pp. 283-89.
33 *El Ferrocarril* (Santiago), Jan. 1, 1898; Rivas Vicuña,

Historia politica, 1:57-67.
34 Hacienda, *Memoria*, 1904, introduction.
35 Talca no. 111, May 13, 1896, *A.I.*, vol. 2124, Municipalidades (1896); and Villa Alegre, Aug. 1, 1897, *A.I.*, vol. 2237, Municipalidades (1897).
36 Interior, *Memoria*, 1896, vol. 1, "Proyecto de reglamento para la organización i servicio de la policía."
37 Ministro de Instrucción Pública, *Memoria*, 1910, p. 12.
38 *El Ferrocarril* (Santiago), Feb. 6, 1898; *Financier* (London), Oct. 27, 1911; and *Sinopsis*, 1912, p. 43.
39 Eyzaguirre, *Chile durante el gobierno de Errázuris*, p. 283.
40 Diputados, *B.S.O.*, Sept. 1, 1897, pp. 1069-70.
41 Interior, *Memoria*, 1895, 1:lv; see also 1893, p. 644; and 1896, vol. 1, "Proyecto"; Concepción no. 18, Jan. 22, 1896, *A.I.*, vol. 2123, Municipalidades (1896); and Intendant, Santiago no. 490, Aug. 18, 1897, *A.I.*, vol. 2237, Municipalidades (1897).
42 Interior, *Memoria*, 1903, pp. 10-13; 1906, pp. 16-17; 1907-8, p. 17; 1911, pp. 10-11; 1910, pp. 195-96; and *Anuario*, 1920, Administración, p. 49.
43 The best study of the railways is U.S. Department of Commerce, *Trade Promotion Series* no. 93, 1930 (W. Rodney Long, *Railways of South America*, pt. 3, *Chile*), pp. 46-47.
44 *Sinopsis*, 1925, p. 70.
45 Acting Consul Atlee, Valparaiso report for 1911-12, *G.B.S.P.*, 1914, 90:9.
46 Winslow to State, Dec. 2, 1910, U.S. *Internal Affairs*, reel 37; Consul-General Leay, report for 1907, *G.B.S.P.*, 110:20; and Interior, *Memoria*, 1912, p. 352.
47 Lupton, Jan. 27, 1908, U.S. *Numerical*, reel 317.
48 Interior, *Memoria*, 1896, p. xxxv; 1909, pp. 37-38; and 1911, p. 68; see also Santiago no. 71, Jan. 25, 1897, *A.I.*, vol. 2234, Municipalidades (1897); and *Board of Trade Journal* (London), 1904, 44:57.
49 *The Chilian Times* (Valparaiso), Mar. 29, 1905.
50 Alejandro Venegas Carus (pseud. Julio Valdés Canje), *Sinceridad, Chile íntimo en 1910* (Santiago: Imprenta Universitaria, 1910), p. 161; and Charlotte A. Cameron, *A Woman's Winter in South America* (London: Stanley Paul and Co., 1911), pp. 143-49.
51 Interior, *Memoria*, 1893, 2:xxxi, 198-217, 1895, 1:xxii, xxxi-xl. Odette Tacla Chamy, *Panorama demográfico de Chile y su evolución en el presente siglo*, 2d ed. (Santiago: Instituto Nacional de Estadísticos, 1975).
52 *Sinopsis*, 1916, p. 61; 1925, p. 51; and Interior, *Memoria*, 1910, pp. 112-13.
53 George J. Mills, *Chile* (New York: D. Appleton and Co., 1914), p. 75.
54 Bauer, *Chilean Rural Society*, p. 216.
55 *El Ferrocarril* (Santiago), Apr. 30, 1897; see also *The Chilian Times* (Valparaiso), Aug. 11, 1897.
56 Interior, *Memoria*, 1912, p. 720.

57 Francisco Valdés Vergara, *La situación económica y financiera de Chile* (Valparaiso: Imprenta Germania, 1894), p. 73.

58 Alejandro Venegas Carus (pseud. Julio Valdés Canje), *Cartas al Exelentísimo Señor Don Pedro Montt sobre la crisis moral de Chile en sus relaciones con el problema económico de la conversion metálica* (1909; Santiago: Editorial Universitaria, 1972), p. 41.

59 Francisco A. Encina, *Nuestra inferioridad económica* (1911; Santiago: Editorial Universitaria, 1972), p. 144.

60 Ibid., p. 115.

61 Tancredo Pinochet Le-Brun, *La conquista de Chile en el siglo XX* (Santiago: La Ilustración, 1909), p. 81.

62 Encina, *Nuestra inferioridad,* p. 85.

63 Nícolas Palacios, *Raza chilena* (Valparaiso: Gustavo Schäfer, 1904), p. 389.

64 Ibid., pp. 350-59; and Venegas, *Sinceridad,* pp. 18, 47, 161; for background on both figures see Julio César Jobet, *Los precursores del pensamiento social de Chile* (Santiago: Editorial Universitaria, 1966), 1:61-64, 2:99-105.

65 Palacios, *Raza chilena,* pp. 473-83.

66 Cortes and Fuentes, *Diccionario político,* p. 443; *The Chilian Times* (Valparaiso), Jan. 12, 1895.

67 *The Chilian Times* (Valparaiso), Aug. 18, 1897.

68 Agustín Ross, *Report on the Trade between Chile and Great Britain, Presented to the Government of Chile* (London: McCorquodale and Co. for the Chilean Legation, Apr. 1892), pp. 27, 69ff, 76-77.

69 *South American Journal* (London), Oct. 27, 1894, on protectionist sentiment; on tariffs, Diputados, *B.S.O.,* June 12, 1897, p. 133; Beeche and Co., Valparaiso, to Henry Wilson, Dec. 18, 1897, U.S. *Diplomatic,* E 2, 1897-1901; U.S. Department of Commerce, *Special Consular Reports,* 1898, 20:62-63; report supplement for 1900, *G.B.S.P.,* vol. 105, cd. 786-40.

70 Caples no. 51, Nov. 27, 1900, U.S. *Valparaiso,* reel 13.

71 Chile, Superintendencia de Aduanas, *Resumen del comercio exterior de Chile* (Valparaiso: Universo, 1908), p. 40; U.S. Department of Commerce, *Report upon the Commercial Relations of the United States with Foreign Countries,* 1912, p. 164; and Report for Valparaiso, 1911, *G.B.S.P.,* 1912-13, 94:599.

72 Based on data for each year in U.S. Department of Commerce, *Commercial Relations.*

73 Rowley's report on Valparaiso, *G.B.S.P.,* 1902, 105:580.

74 Duval to John Hicks, Aug. 21, 1908, U.S. *Diplomatic,* Correspondence, 1906-8.

75 Barry Cusack-Smith, report supplement for 1900, *G.B.S.P.,* 1900, 105:651, cd. 768-40.

76 Rea Hanna to Smith, Apr. 29, 1909, U.S. *Diplomatic,* E 9, 1908-9.

77 Lewis Joel no. 128, Dec. 29, 1892, *F.O. 16,* vol. 276.

78 *El Ferrocarril* (Santiago), Dec. 18, 1892.

79 *Discurso—1893,* p. 19.

80 *Discurso—1894,* p. 22.

81 *Discurso—1895,* p. 32.

82 *The Chilian Times* (Valparaiso), Jan. 12, 16, 26, 1895.

83 Kennedy to Earl of Rosebury, Feb. 16, 1894, *G.B.P.P.*, vol. 4, c. 7293-21; and *The Chilian Times* (Valparaiso), Jan. 12, 1895.

84 *Sinopsis*, 1916, p. 66.

85 Hacienda, *Memoria*, 1896, p. lxxxiv.

86 Rowley report for 1900, *G.B.S.P.*, 1902, 105:635.

87 Julio Zegers, *Estudios económicos* (Santiago: Imprenta Nacional, 1908), pp. 153-54; *Sinopsis*, 1921, p. 71.

88 *Sinopsis*, 1925, p. 62; and Great Britain, *Statistical Abstract for the United Kingdom*, 1892-1906, p. 204.

89 Roberto Espinosa, *La reforma bancaria i monetaria de Chile* (Santiago: Imprenta Barcelona, 1913), p. 295.

90 Strobel no. 38, Aut. 24, 1895, *U.S. Despatches*, reel T-44.

91 Hacienda, *Memoria*, 1896, p. lx.

92 *South American Journal* (London), July 17, 1897; *El Correo del Peru* (Iquique), July 12, 1896; Diputados, *B.S.E.*, Jan. 24, 1896, p. 464.

93 *South American Journal* (London), July 17, 1897.

94 *The Chilian Times* (Valparaiso), July 3, 1897.

95 *El Ferrocarril* (Santiago), July 25, 1897.

96 Wilson no. 67, 1898, *U.S. Despatches*, reel 46.

97 Ibid. On bank crisis, see also *El Mercurio* (Valparaiso), June 23, 1898; and *El Ferrocarril* (Santiago), July 7-24, 1898.

98 Agustín Ross, *Chile, 1851-1910: Sixty Years of Monetary and Financial Questions and of Banking Problems* (Valparaiso: Imprenta Inglesa Westcott and Co., 1910), p. 80.

99 Wilson no. 67, Aug. 19, 1898, *U.S. Despatches*, reel T-46.

100 Wilson no. 67, 1898, *U.S. Despatches*; Espinosa, *Reforma bancaria*, pp. 311ff.

101 Wilson no. 67, 1898, *U.S. Despatches*; see also Subercaseaux, Oct. 22, 1898, *A.H.*, vol. 2631, Legación en Berlin (1895-1908).

102 Delegación Fiscal de Salitreras no. 57, June 24, 1896, *A.H.*, vol. 2737.

103 *Asociación salitrera, Circular no. 28* (Iquique), June 24, 1902; Rowley report for 1905, *G.B.S.P.*, 1906, 122:169.

104 Diputados, *B.S.O.*, Aug. 31, 1897.

105 *Asociación salitrera, Circular Trimestral* (Iquique), vol. 15, no. 60, May 13, 1898, p. iv.

106 Croker, Aug. 9, 1897, *G.B.P.P.*, vol. 4, c. 8648-13; *The Chilian Times* (Valparaiso), July 31, 1897; *Asociación salitrera, Circular no. 18* (Iquique), May 25, 1899, p. v; Hacienda, *Memoria*, 1900, p. cxii.

107 Legación en Londres (1910) Gana no. 121, Feb. 28, 1910, *A.H.*, vol. 4199.

108 Franz to U.S. Legation in Santiago, Apr. 26, 1895, *U.S. Diplomatic*, E 1, 1894-97.

109 Ibid.; and Franz letter, same vol., Apr. 27, 1895.

110 *El Ferrocarril*, Feb. 9, 11, 1898.

111 Blakemore, *British Nitrates*, pp. 246-47.

112 On specific scandals, see Iquique no. 34, May 6, 1896, *A.H.*, vol. 2737, Delegación Fiscal de Salitreras (1896); *El*

Ferrocarril (Santiago), Dec. 29, 1905, and May 6, 1911; Presidente, Apr. 21, 1914, *A.H.*, vol. 4228, Consejo salitrero (1910-14); on the general problem, Orlando Latorre González, *La sociedad nacional de minería* (Santiago: Universidad de Chile, 1943), p. 10.

113 Presidente, Apr. 21, 1914, *A.H.*, vol. 4228, Consejo salitrero (1910-14).

114 Mining company statements, *A.H.*, vol. 3412, Tarapacá (1903).

115 Hicks no. 23, Dec. 11, 1905, U.S. *Despatches*, reel T-52.

116 *London Times*, June 16, 1911.

117 *El Trabajo* (Iquique), Dec. 7, 1904; Carlos Besa, Nov. 10, 1910, *A.H.*, vol. 4228, Consejo salitrero (1910-14); *Financier* (London), May 27, 1911.

118 Hacienda, *Antecedentes y actas de las sesiones de la comisión de salitre* (Santiago: Sociedad Imprenta y Litografía Universo, 1925, p. 30.

119 Hernández, *El salitre*, pp. 168-69.

120 Santiago Marín Vicuña, *Los ferrocarriles de Chile* (Santiago: Imprenta Cervantes, 1916), pp. 39, 41.

121 Hudson, Iquique, 1908, *G.B.S.P.*, 1908, 96:631.

122 Mansfield no. 71, Feb. 11, 1904, U.S. *Valparaiso*, reel 13.

123 Alejandro Bertrand, *La crisis salitrera, 1910* (Paris: Louis-Michaud, 1910), pp. 21, 26, 43.

124 Carlos Besa, Nov. 16, 1910, *A.H.*, vol. 4228, Consejo salitrero (1910-14).

125 Carlos Besa, June 20, 1910, ibid.

126 File 825.6374/9, Fletcher no. 272, Oct. 28, 1912, U.S. *Internal Affairs*, reel 31.

127 On this same point see Fletcher nos. 279 and 285, Dec. 3, 1912, ibid.

128 On ports and harbors, Interior, *Memoria*, 1911, pp. 34-35; Jorge Hormann, "Informe presentado en 1909 al Ministerio de Hacienda," *Boletín de la Sociedad Nacional de Agricultura*, 1910, p. 356; on agriculture, Luis Galdames, *Jeografía económica de Chile* (Santiago: Imprenta Universitaria, 1911), p. 150; Mills, *Chile*, pp. 131-32; on copper mining, Mills, *Chile*, p. 144.

129 Harvey O'Connor, *The Guggenheims: The Making of an American Dynasty* (New York: Civici, Friede, 1937), pp. 346-51; Markos Mamalakis and Clark W. Reynolds, *Essays on the Chilean Economy* (Homewood, Ill.: Richard D. Irwin, 1965), pp. 214-17; U.S. Department of Commerce, *Commercial Relations*, 1907, p. 307; Interior, *Memoria*, 1911, p. 24-25.

130 Ansted, 1901 report for Coquimbo, *G.B.S.P.*, 1903, vol. 86, cd. 1386-23, pp. 500ff.; *Anuario*, 1909, 3:491.

131 Alfred A. Winslow report, Jan. 7, 1911, U.S. *Internal Affairs*, reel 25; U.S. Department of State, *Commercial Relations*, 1906, p. 185.

132 Zegers, *Estudios*, pp. 190-91.

133 Galdames, *Jeografía económica*, p. 169; *El Ferrocarril* (Santiago), Nov. 30, 1905.

134 Zegers, *Estudios*, p. 31.

135 Luis Orrego Luco, *Casa Grande* (1908; Santiago: Nascimento, 1973), pp. 194-213; see also *The Chilian Times* (Valparaiso), Nov. 25, 1905.
136 Rowley report for 1905, *G.B.S.P.*, 1906, 122:173.
137 Augusto Matte no. 320, Dec. 6, 1907, *A.H.*, vol. 2631, Legación en Berlin (1895-1908); Leay report for 1907, *G.B.S.P.*, 1908, 110:23-24.
138 Espinosa, *Reforma bancaria*, p. 341; *Sinopsis*, 1925, p. 63.
139 *Sinopsis*, 1925, p. 73; Hacienda, *Memoria*, 1917, p. 114; Leay reports for 1907 and 1910, and Finus report for Valparaiso, 1909, *G.B.S.P.*, 1908, 110:34 and 96:739; *El Pueblo Obrero* (Iquique), Aug. 20, 1907.
140 Winslow, Nov. 15, 1910, U.S. *Internal Affairs*, reel 21.
141 Espinosa, *Reforma bancaria*, p. 381; *Sinopsis*, 1925, p. 62.
142 Domingo Gana, Nov. 30, 1904, *A.H.*, vol. 2630, Legación de Chile en Londres (1895-1905).
143 Rothschilds to Gana, Sept. 27, 1910, *A.H.*, vol. 4200, Legación en Londres (1910-13).
144 Fetter, *Monetary Inflation*, p. vii.
145 Fernando Pinto Lagarrigue, *Crónica política del siglo XX: desde Errázuriz Echaurren hasta Alessandri Palma* (Santiago: Editorial Orbe, 1970), p. 27.
146 Fletcher no. 6, Aug. 26, 1909, U.S. *Numerical*, vol. 180, file 27.
147 Hicks no. 98, Nov. 24, 1906, U.S. *Numerical*, vol. 317, file 3429.
148 Francisco Valdés Vargara, *Problemas económicos de Chile* (Valparaiso: Universo, 1913), p. 359.

4. A PORTRAIT OF THE EARLY LEFT

1 Manuel Salas Lavaqui, *Trabajos y antecedentes presentados al Supremo Gobierno de Chile por la comisión consultiva del norte* (Santiago: Imprenta Cervantes, 1908), p. 585 (hereafter *Comisión consultiva*); *El Marítimo* (Antofagasta), Jan. 23, 1904.
2 *La Reforma Social* (Serena), Oct. 12, 1902, *La Voz del Pueblo* (Valparaiso), Oct. 3, 1905.
3 *Comisión consultiva*, p. 558.
4 *El Pueblo Obrero* (Iquique), Aug. 31, 1907.
5 *La Democracia* (Iquique), May 5, 1906.
6 Hernán Ramírez Necochea, *Historia del movimiento obrero en Chile, antecedentes siglo xix* (Santiago: Austral, 1956), pp. 242-44.
7 Diputados, *B.S.O.*, Aug. 6, 1897, letter from the Sociedad de Artesanos de la Union, Chillan, July 31, 1897.
8 *El Marítimo* (Antofagasta), June 26, 1903.
9 Victor Domingo Silva, *Las provincias del norte y la visita de S.E. el Presidente de la República* (Santiago: Universo, 1909), pp. 107-8.
10 Guillermo Gibbs, *La tierra y el inquilinaje* (Santiago:

Imprenta de la Libertad, 1890), pp. 20, 22.

11 *La Reforma* (Santiago), Nov. 9, 1907.

12 Eyzaguirre, *Chile durante el gobierno de Errázuriz Echaurren,* pp. 18-21.

13 Diputados, *B.S.O.,* June 13, 1903.

14 Roberto Hernandez C., *El roto chileno* (Valparaiso: Imprenta San Rafael, 1929), p. 116.

15 Guillermo Feliu Cruz, "La evolución política, económica y social de Chile," *Anales de la Universidad de Chile* 119 (1960): 54.

16 Alejandro Fariña, *Reflexiones sobre la cuestión social y política en Chile* (Santiago: Imprenta Chile, 1904), pp. 29, 101-2.

17 *El Ferrocarril* (Santiago), Mar. 20, 1903.

18 Jorge Gustavo Silva, *Nuestra evolución político-social, 1900-1930* (Santiago: Nascimento, 1931), p. 15.

19 Cortes and Fuentes, *Diccionario político,* pp. 297-98.

20 *La Voz del Pueblo* (Valparaiso), Jan. 2, 1904.

21 *El Trabajo* (Iquique), Feb. 22, 1905.

22 *El Marítimo* (Antofagasta), June 13, 1903.

23 Marx's views and the relation of rebellion to economic improvement are developed in James C. Davies, "Toward a Theory of Revolution," *American Sociological Review* 27 (Feb. 1962): 5; my explanation of the characteristics of the Chilean uprisings does not rest on the theory of "relative deprivation" alone, but is closer to "the continuation of politics by other means" that is presented by Rod Aya, "Theories of Revolution Reconsidered," *Theory and Society* 8 (July 1979): 39-99.

24 Mario Góngora, "Vagabondage et Société Pastorale en Amérique Latine (Specialement au Chile Central)," *Annales: économies, sociétés, civilisations* 121 (Jan.-Feb. 1966); and Augusto Orrero Luco, "La cuestión social en Chile," *Anales de la Universidad de Chile* 121 (1961), pp. 43-55, reprinted from *La Patria* (Valparaiso), 1884.

25 Carlos Hurtado Ruiz-Tagle, *Concentración de población y desarrollo económico—el caso chileno* (Santiago: Universidad de Chile, Instituto de Economía, 1966), p. 84.

26 Delegación Fiscal de Salitreras, no. 170, Apr. 8, 1897, *A.I.,* vol. 2152, Tarapacá (1896).

27 Silva, *Las provincias del norte,* p. 116.

28 *Censo—1907,* pp. 1299-1300.

29 Jacinto Vaello, *Estructura y evolución de la economía colonial* (Santiago: Universidad de Chile, Instituto de Economía y Planificación, 1971), p. 33; Mario Góngora, *Studies in the Colonial History of Spanish America* (Cambridge: Cambridge University Press, 1975), p. 153; Great Britain, *Reports by Her Majesty's Secretaries,* 1876, p. 390; Gilliss, *The U.S. Naval Astronomical Expedition,* p. 145; Gonzalo Izquierdo F., *Un estudio de las ideologías chilenas: la Sociedad de Agricultura en el siglo XIX* (Santiago: Centro de Estudios Socio-Económicos, Facultad de Ciencias Económicas, Universidad de

Chile, 1968), pp. 110-11; Claudio Gay, *Agricultura chilena*
(Santiago: Instituto de capacitación e investigación en reforma agraria, 1973), 1:183-85; and Marcelo Segall R., "Las
luchas de clases en las primeras decadas de la República,
1810-1846," *Anales de la Universidad de Chile* 125 (1962):
198.

30 Frederick B. Pike, "Church and State in Peru and Chile since
1840:   A Study in Contrasts," *American Historical Review* 73
(Oct. 1967):   34, 37; Gay, *Historia*, 1:168.

31 Pedro Ruíz Aldea, *Tipos y costumbres de Chile* (Santiago:
Empresa Zig-Zag, 1947), pp. 164-65.

32 Hernandez C., *El roto chileno,* pp. 86, 102.

33 *B.O.T.,* 1911, p. 64.

34 Pike, "Church and State," pp. 37-38; J. M. Spangler, *Civilization in Chile, Past and Present* (San Francisco: H. G. Parsons,
1885), pp. 101, 104-5.

35 Interior, *Memoria,* 1872, Apéndice, Valparaiso, pp. 337-39.

36 Pedro Felipe Iñiguez Irarrázaval, *Notas sobre el desarrollo
del pensamiento social en Chile, 1901-1906* (Santiago: Editorial Juridica de Chile, 1968), p. 17.

37 Eulogia Díaz Sagredo in Diputados, *B.S.O.,* June 20, 1903, p.
338.

38 *El Ferrocarril* (Santiago), Oct. 27, 1905.

39 *La Vanguardia* (Antofagasta), Apr. 11, 1907.

40 *El Trabajo* (Iquique), Oct. 4, 1902.

41 *El Ferrocarril* (Santiago), Nov. 13, 1905.

42 *B.O.T.,* 1915, no. 10, p. 135.

43 *El Trabajo* (Iquique), Apr. 10, 1907.

44 I have written a separate article on the issue of labor recruitment and immigration, "The *Enganche* in the Chilean Nitrate Sector, 1880-1930," *Latin American Perspectives* 6 (Summer 1979); see also Carl Solberg, *Immigration and Nationalism:
Argentina and Chile, 1890-1914* (Austin: University of Texas
Press, 1970).

45 *El Trabajo* (Iquique), Nov. 28, 1906.

46 *Asociación salitrera, Circular trimestral* (Iquique), no. 29,
Oct. 27, 1902, p. iii.

47 *El Trabajo* (Iquique), Feb. 2, 1902, May 18, 1902; *El Marítimo*
(Antofagasta), Nov. 14, 1903; *El Trabajo* (Tocopilla), Dec. 6,
1903; see also Hacienda, *Memoria,* 1902, Delegación Fiscal de
Salitreras, report of J. F. Campaña C., pp. 239-41.

48 *El Mercurio* (Santiago), July 10, 1905; Interior, *Memoria,*
1911, p. 39.

49 Cited in Salvador Allende Gossens, *La realidad médico-social
chileno—sintesis* (Santiago: n.p., 1939), p. 78.

50 *B.O.T.,* 1912, no. 1, report of Manuel Rodriguez Periz, pp. 72,
173.

51 *Comisión consultiva,* p. 223.

52 Interior, *Memoria,* 1911, p. 54.

53 Guillermo Eyzaguirre Rouse and Jorge Errázuriz Tagle, *Estudio
social: monografía de una familia obrera de Santiago* (Santiago:
Imprenta Barcelona, 1903), pp. 13-14, 17.

54 *B.O.T.*, 1911, nos. 2, 11, and report of Guillermo Gana, nos. 3, 69.
55 *Comisión consultiva*, pp. 39-40; Hacienda, *Memoria*, 1904, p. cxx; Intendant no. 74, Jan. 13, 1904, *A.H.*, vol. 3537, Tarapacá (1904-6); *La Voz del Pueblo* (Valparaiso), Apr. 9, 1914.
56 *El Trabajo* (Iquique), July 12, 1905.
57 Petition from Chuquicamata workers, Feb. 6, 1913, *A. H.*, vol. 4424, Intendencias (1912-14).
58 Anguita, *Leyes promulgadas*, 4:127, laws nos. 8, 435, Feb. 30, 1906.
59 Interior, *Memoria*, 1909, pp. 63-67.
60 Interior, *Memoria*, 1911, pp. 189-90; for another example, see Interior, *Memoria*, 1912, p. 428.
61 *The Chilian Times* (Valparaiso), Apr. 5, 1905; on liquor law enforcement, Vice-Consul Berry Cusac-Smith report for 1901; *G.B.S.P.*, 1902, 105:667.
62 Anguita, *Leyes promulgadas,* 4:438-39, law no. 10,370, Sept. 4, 1912.
63 *La Mañana* (Santiago), Nov. 5, 1911.
64 *Censo—1907*, pp. 1262-66, 1272, 1282-83.
65 Hacienda, *Memoria*, 1839, p. 14; and Consul Grierson, Coquimbo, *G.B.P.P.*, vol. 4, c. 2704.
66 Oscar Bermúdez M., *Historia del salitre: desde sus orígenes hasta la Guerra del Pacífico* (Santiago: Ediciones de la Universidad de Chile, 1963), pp. 366-70.
67 Senadores, *B.S.O.*, Aug. 17, 1897, address by Nathan Miers Cox, p. 595; *El Marítimo* (Antofagasta), Feb. 7, 1903.
68 *La Reforma* (Santiago) carried out surveys in 1907, requesting information from labor societies. See issues of Apr. 2, 9, 11, 12, 1907; see also Tulio Lagos Valenzuela, *Bosquejo histórico del movimiento obrero en Chile* (Santiago: Imprenta El Esfuerzo, 1941), p. 19.
69 Chile, Cámara de Diputados, *Comisión parlamentaria encargada de estudiar las necesidades de las provincias de Tarapacá y Antofagasta* (Santiago: Zig-Zag, 1913), p. 23 (hereafter *Comisión parlamentaria).*
70 Eyzaguirre, *Chile durante el gobierno de Errázuriz Echaurren*, pp. 147, 149.
71 Francisco Huneeus Gana, *Por el orden social* (Santiago: Imprenta Barcelona, 1917), pp. 28-29.
72 *La Voz del Pueblo* (Valparaiso), Oct. 21, 1903.
73 *El Trabajo* (Iquique), June 29, 1903.
74 De Shazo, "Urban Workers and Labor Unions In Chile," pp. 200-202.
75 The basic biography of Recabarren is Julio César Jobet, *Luis Emilio Recabarren: los orígenes del movimiento obrero y del socialismo chileno* (Santiago: Prensa Latinoamericana, 1955); the above generalizations are based on *El Marítimo* (Antofagasta), *El Trabajo* (Iquique), and *Las Voz del Pueblo* (Valparaiso) for 1904, and "Por que fuí expulsado de la Camara de Diputados," *El pensamiento de Luis Emilio Recabarren* (Santiago:

Camino de Victoria, 1971), 1:280-88.

76 *La Voz del Pueblo* (Valparaiso), Oct. 25, 1905.

77 *El Despertar de los Trabajadores* (Iquique), June 8, 15, and Sept. 12, 1912.

78 "Controversía con los anarquistas," *El pensamiento,* 2:422; for the setting of this comment, see Sebastian Marotta, *Movimiento sindical Argentina, su génesis y desarrollo* (Buenos Aires: Ediciones "Lacio," 1960), 1:103-32.

79 Diputados, *B.S.E.,* Jan. 7, 1903.

80 Diputados, *B.S.E.,* Nov. 15, 1904, address by Malaquías Concha.

81 Consul Greene, Antofagasta, Oct. 27, 1904, U.S. *Despatches,* reel T-51.

82 *Boletín de el Trabajo* (Iquique), May 5, 1905.

83 Vice-Consul Berry Cusack-Smith, Report for 1901, *G.B.S.P.,* 1902, 105:663.

84 Hacienda, *Memoria,* 1902, p. xxvii; *El Trabajo* (Iquique), Feb. 2, 1902.

85 De Shazo, "Urban Workers and Labor Unions in Chile," p. 212.

86 Diputados, *B.S.E.,* Jan. 2, 1903, Malaquías Concha, p. 665.

87 *El Ferrocarril* (Santiago), Jan. 3, 1903.

88 Intendant Bravo's report no. 1622, Valparaiso, May 24, 2903, *A.I.,* vol. 1704, Intendencias (1903) (hereafter Bravo's report); Peter Charles De Shazo, "The Valparaiso Maritime Strike of 1903 and the Development of a Revolutionary Labor Movement in Chile," *Journal of Latin American Studies* 2 (June 1979): 148.

89 *La Voz del Pueblo* (Valparaiso), Apr. 25, 1903.

90 Bravo's report.

91 Bravo's report; Henry L. Wilson no. 322, June 3, 1903, U.S. *Despatches,* reel T-50; Gustavo Silva, *Nuestra evolución,* pp. 16-20.

92 Alberto Acuña, Prefect of Police to Bravo, doc. no. 8, inserted in Bravo's report; and Wilson's report no. 322, June 3, 1903, U.S. *Despatches,* reel T-50.

93 Diputados, *B.S.O.,* June 19, 1903.

94 *La Voz del Pueblo* (Valparaisó), May 23, 30, 1903.

95 Bravo's report.

96 *La Voz del Pueblo* (Valparaiso), July 18, Dec. 12, 1903; Diputados, *B.S.O.,* Aug. 19, 1904, Anjel Guarello, p. 1165.

97 *La Voz del Pueblo* (Valparaiso), Oct. 21, 1903.

98 Thomas C. Wright, "Origins of the Politics of Inflation in Chile, 1888-1918," *Hispanic American Historical Review* 53 (May 1973).

99 John Hicks no. 11, Dec. 25, 1905, and telegram, Dec. 23, 1905, U.S. *Despatches,* reel T-52; *The Chilian Times* (Valparaiso), Oct. 28, 1905.

100 Wright, "Origins," p. 253; see also Escobar Zenteno, *Compendio de la legislación social,* p. 205.

101 Hicks no. 11, Dec. 25, 1905, U.S. *Despatches,* reel T-52.

102 Wright, "Origins," p. 257.

103 Escobar Zenteno, *Compendio de la legislación social,* p. 205.

104 *La Reforma* (Santiago), July 3, 1906.
105 *El Marítimo* (Antofagasta), Feb. 17, 1906; *La Vanguardia* (Antofagasta), Feb. 13, 1906.
106 *El Trabajo* (Iquique), Feb. 14, 1906; *El Marítimo* (Antofagasta), Feb. 24, 1906; *La Reforma* (Santiago), Oct. 11, 1906.
107 *La Reforma* (Santiago), May 30 and June 5, 7, 1907; Interior, *Memoria,* 1908, Anexos, Intendant of Valparaiso's report, p. 223; and Diputados, *B.S.O.,* June 6, 1907, Bonifacio Veas, p. 33.
108 *La Reforma* (Santiago), June 15, 27, and Sept. 14, 1907.
109 *El Trabajo* (Iquique), Nov. 9, 23, 1907.
110 Ibid., Nov. 3, 1906; ibid., Dec. 4, 7, 1907.
111 Consul Rea Hanna, Iquique, Dec. 16, 1907, U.S. *Numerical,* reel 28.
112 *El Trabajo* (Iquique), Dec. 7, 1907, and Apr. 29, 1908; *El Pueblo Obrero* (Iquique), Dec. 21, 1908; and Hanna, Dec. 16, 1907, U.S. *Numerical,* reel 28.
113 *El Trabajo* (Iquique), Dec. 18, 1907; *La Reforma* (Santiago), Jan. 1, 1908.
114 Rea Hanna, Iquique, Dec. 19, 1907, U.S. *Numerical,* reel 28.
115 *El Trabajo* (Iquique), Dec. 18, 1907; and Kaempffer Villagren, *Así sucedio,* p. 150.
116 *El Trabajo* (Iquique), Apr. 29, 1908; and letter of Luís Olea to *El Pueblo Obrero* (Iquique), Mar. 31, 1908.
117 Hanna, Dec. 19, 1907, U.S. *Numerical,* reel 28.
118 Oscar Bermúdez M., "El Dr. Nicolas Palacios y la industria del salitre," *Revista chilena de historia y geografía* 136 (1968): 215.
119 Kaempffer, *Así sucedio,* p. 136.
120 Letter of Luís Olea to *El Pueblo Obrero* (Iquique), Apr. 4, 1908.
121 Ibid., Apr. 7, 1908.
122 Hanna disposition to Chilean court, Feb. 20, 1908, U.S. *Numerical,* reel 28.
123 Bermúdez M., "El Dr. Nicolas Palacios," pp. 217-19.
124 Ibid., pp. 220-22; Hanna, Iquique, Dec. 24, 1907, U.S. *Numerical,* reel 28; Kaempffer, *Así sucedio,* p. 144; *El Pueblo Obrera* (Iquique), Jan. 11, 1908. Estimates of the number dead run as high as 2,000; in addition to the sources mentioned in n. 125, below, see Consul-General Leay, report for 1907, *G.B.S.P.,* 1908, p. 63; *La Reforma* (Santiago), Jan. 29, 2908; and Diputados, *B.S.O.,* Malaquías Concha, Dec. 30, 1907.
125 *Asociación salitrera, Circular* (Iquique), Aug. 4, 1908, no. 44, p. xli; *El Pueblo Obrero* (Iquique), July 17, 1909; wages in *B.O.T.,* 1907, pp. 79-82, and *B.O.T.,* 1914, no. 9, pp. 7-10.
126 *B.O.T.,* 1911, no. 1, pp. 71-75; intendant's reports for Magallanes, nos. 104 and 167, Mar. 9 and Apr. 12, 1912, *A.H.,* vol. 4424, Intendencias (1912-14).
127 *El Pueblo Obrero* (Iquique), Aug. 13, 1910.
128 *El Despertar de los Trabajadores* (Iquique), Dec. 23, 1914.
129 *Comisión parlamentaria,* p. 137.

5. THE UNITED STATES TAKES OVER

1　U.S. Department of Commerce and Labor, Lincoln Hutchinson, *Report on Trade Conditions in Central America and on the West Coast of South America* (Washington, D.C.: 1906), pp. 7, 14, 20.

2　V. G. Kiernan, "Foreign Interests in the War of the Pacific," *Hispanic American Historical Review* 35 (Feb. 1955): 28-30.

3　U.S. Department of Commerce and Labor, Bureau of Manufactures, *Daily Consular and Trade Reports,* 1911, Consul Alfred A. Winslow, "Commerce of Chile," no. 194, Aug. 19, 1911, p. 777; ibid., 1912, Winslow, "Commercial Activities in Chile," no. 215, Sept. 12, 1912, p. 1318.

4　Ibid., Winslow, "Industrial Development in Chile," no. 23, Jan. 27, 1912, p. 440; ibid., Winslow, "Chilean Notes," no. 252, Oct. 25, 1912, p. 252.

5　Sources on Alessandri's life: Ricardo Donoso, *Alessandri, agitador y demoledor* (Mexico: Fondo de Cultura Económica, 1952), vol. 1; Arturo Alessandri Palma, *Recuerdos de gobierno* (Santiago: Editorial Nascimento, 1976), vol. 1; and Cortes and Fuentes, *Diccionario político de Chile,* pp. 24-27.

6　*Asociación salitrera, Circular* (Valparaiso), Mar. 15, 1915, no. 63, p. xv; report of W. H. Lough, Special Agent, enclosed in Summerlin no. 621, May 12, 1915, U.S. *Diplomatic,* Correspondence, class 8, pt. 5.

7　*Financial Times* (London), May 6, 1915.

8　David D. J. Myers, Iquique, Dec. 15, 1914, U.S. *Diplomatic,* Correspondence, class 8, pt. 7.

9　*Diario Oficial* (Santiago), Mar. 1, 1915.

10　Myers, Oct. 22, 1914, U.S. *Diplomatic,* Correspondence, class 8, pt. 7.

11　Orlando Latorre Gonzalez, *La sociedad nacional de minería* (Santiago: Universidad de Chile, 1943), p. 78; Consul H. W. W. Bird, Antofagasta, report for 1914, *G.B.S.P.,* 1914-16, 71:428.

12　Consul-General L. J. Keena, "Chile," U.S. Department of Commerce and Labor, Bureau of Foreign and Domestic Commerce, *Daily Consular and Trade Reports, 1914,* no. 41a, 1915, p. 5.

13　Agustín Edwards, July 31, 1915, *A.H.,* vol. 4566, Legación en Londres (1913-16).

14　Ibid.

15　*Anuario,* 1925, 6:31.

16　L. Frederick to Warburg, Federal Reserve Board, Feb. 11, 1915, U.S. *Diplomatic,* Correspondence, class 8, pt. 6.

17　Letter from William C. Redfield, Mar. 1, 1915, ibid.

18　*Las Ultimas Noticias* (Santiago), Jan. 17, 1916.

19　U.S. Department of Commerce, Special Agents Series, no. 176, Harold E. Everley, *Furniture Markets of Chile, Peru, Bolivia and Ecuador* (Washington, D.C.: 1919), pp. 44, 47; and same series, no. 153, Robert S. Barrett, *Chilean Markets for Paper, Paper Products and Printing Machinery* (Washington, D.C.: 1917), p. 22.

20 Ibid., no. 164, W. A. Tucker, *Textile Market of Chile* (Washington, D.C.: 1918), pp. 43-44.
21 Rivas Vicuña, *História política,* 2:8.
22 Fletcher no. 580, Sept. 20, 1915, U.S. *Internal Affairs,* reel 3.
23 *El Mercurio* (Santiago), June 10, 1916.
24 American Society of Chile, *Americans in Chile* (Valparaiso-Santiago: Kegan, 1931), pp. 4-5.
25 *El Diario Ilustrado* (Santiago), Apr. 12, 1916; and *La Unión* (Santiago), Apr. 21, 1916.
26 *Sinopsis,* 1925, pp. 96, 97, 115; and Hacienda, *Antecedentes,* pp. 35, 41.
27 Manuel Amunategui, Paris, no. 5, Mar. 8, 1916, *A.H.,* vol. 4868, Relaciones Exteriores (1916).
28 *Sinopsis,* 1925, p. 97; *Anuario,* 1925, 7:59; Thomas W. Voetter, Antofagasta, Aug. 22, 1917, and Anderson, Memorandum, Feb. 2, 1918, U.S. *Diplomatic,* Correspondence, class 8, pt. 4.
29 *Observor* (London), Oct. 3, 1915; Skinner's telegram to State, May 19, 1918, U.S. *Internal Affairs,* reel 32.
30 Delegación del Gobierno de Chile al Comité Salitrero de Londres, July 18, 1917, *A.H.,* vo. 4966, Legación en Londres (1917).
31 Ibid., Dec. 23, 1915, *A.H.,* vol. 4790, Legación en Londres (1915).
32 Shea no. 178, Aug. 7, 1917, U.S. *Diplomatic,* Correspondence, class 8, pt. 7.
33 Memorandum from State Department's Division of Latin American Affairs, Nov. 13, 1917, *Anderson,* box 32.
34 Percy Alvin Martin, *Latin America and the War* (Baltimore: Johns Hopkins Press, 1925), pp. 265-66.
35 *Associación Salitrera, Circular* (Valparaiso), no. 76, 1918, pp. vi-vii.
36 Hacienda, *Antecedentes,* p. 53; Enclosure, Feb. 1917, *A.H.,* vol. 4960, Legación en Londres (1917); Thomas W. Voetter, Antofagasta, Feb. 2, 1917, U.S. *Diplomatic,* Correspondence, class 8, pt. 7.
37 Report from Miguel Cruchaga, Berlin, June 5, 1915, *A.H.,* vol. 4790, Legación en Londres (1915).
38 Delegación del Gobierno de Chile al Comité Salitrero en Londres, N. Salinas report no. 78, June 15, 1916, *A.H.,* vol. 4566, Legación en Londres (1913-16).
39 Salinas and Echeverría, communiqué for Delegación al Comite Salitrero, Dec. 2, 1915, *A.H.,* vol. 4790, Legación en Londres (1915).
40 Memorandum from Maritime Transport Council, *Auchincloss,* box 9, folder 237.
41 Draft of Instructions to London Embassy, Nov. 16, 1917, *Anderson,* box 32.
42 Draft of instructions to Skinner, Nov. 22, 1917, ibid.
43 Letter to Skinner, Dec. 7, 1917, and letter to American importers, Dec. 28, 1917, ibid.
44 *La Nación* (Santiago), Jan. 12, 1918.

45 *El Diario Ilustrado* (Santiago), Jan. 12, 1918.
46 *El Mercurio* (Santiago), Jan. 13, 1918.
47 *El Mercurio* (Santiago), Mar. 6, 1918.
48 Skinner to State, May 29, 1918, U.S. *Internal Affairs,* reel 32.
49 Report by Keena, Valparaiso, Aug. 25, 1917, U.S. *Diplomatic,* Correspondence, class 8, pt. 7; see also Enclosure on Trading with the Enemy Act, *A.H.,* vol. 4956.
50 L. J. Keena, Valparaiso, to W. R. Grace, Feb. 13, 1918, and Shea's correspondence, Jan. 16, 1918, U.S. *Diplomatic,* Correspondence, class 8, pt. 11.
51 Keena to Shea, Feb. 18, 1918, ibid.
52 House to American Consul, London, Feb. 21, 1918, *Polk,* drawer 77, file 213; Skinner telegram to State, July 11, 1918, U.S. *Internal Affairs,* reel 32.
53 Diary, May 14, 1918, *Auchincloss,* box 2, folder 20; and Voetter, Iquique, July 16, 1918, U.S. *Internal Affairs,* reel 32.
54 Polk to Manizaga Varela, July 27, 1918 (mentions receiving, and quotes from, Chilean's message), U.S. *Internal Affairs,* reel 32.
55 Fuller to Auchincloss, July 26, 1918, and Polk to Manizaga Varela, July 27, 1918, ibid.
56 Baruch to State, Mar. 2, 1918, U.S. *Diplomatic,* Correspondence, class 8, pt. 12.
57 Tollman to Baruch, Mar. 9, 1918, ibid.
58 Shea telegram to State, July 9, 1918, U.S. *Internal Affairs,* reel 32.
59 Shea guessed the stocks were 21.6 million quintals: ibid.
60 Memorandum from Chilean Legation in London to American Consul-General in London, June 14, 1918, ibid.
61 Letter to Albert Strauss, Secretary of Treasury, May 4, 1918, *Anderson,* box 32; Polk telegram to Paris Embassy, Aug. 3, 1918, U.S. *Internal Affairs,* reel 32.
62 Lansing to Santiago Embassy, telegram, Oct. 23, 1918, ibid.
63 William S. Myers to Lansing, Nov. 20, 1918, ibid., reel 33.
64 Shea's telegram to State, Oct. 26 and Nov. 4, 1918, ibid.
65 Lansing to Consul in Valparaiso, Aug. 15, 1919, ibid.; Great Britain, Department of Overseas Trade, W. F. V. Scott, *Report on the Industrial and Economic Situation in Chile—December, 1921* (London: H. M. Stationary Office, 1922), p. 20.
66 Munro, Nov. 17, 1920, U.S. *Internal Affairs,* reel 23; U.S. Department of Commerce, Special Agents Series, no. 224, Charles A. McQueen, *Chilean Public Finance* (Washington, D.C.: G.P.O., 1924), p. 60; *Sinopsis,* 1925, p. 73; and Great Britain, Department of Overseas Trade, M. J. MacLeod, *Report on the Financial and Industrial Conditions in Chile—April, 1923,* p. 9.
67 Munro, Feb. 3, 1921, U.S. *Internal Affairs,* reel 25.
68 Report cited in Shea no. 595, Nov. 19, 1920, ibid., reel 4.
69 Shea no. 583, Sept. 3, 1920, U.S. *Internal Affairs,* reel 4.
70 Chile, *Semana de la moneda celebrada en Santiago de Chile, Agosto, 1924* (Santiago: Imprenta La Ilustración, 1924), p. 63.

71 U.S. Department of Commerce, McQueen, *Chilean Public Finance,* p. 45.

72 On tariff law, see "Chile—New Customs Tariffs Law," Mar. 1, 1916, *G.B.S.P.,* 1916, vol. 23; John C. Wiley, Secretary of U.S. Embassy in Santiago, to Fisher Flouring Mills, Seattle, Apr. 20, 1920, U.S. *Diplomatic,* Correspondence, class 865, pt. 20, 1920.

73 *Anuario,* 1920, 6:128-30.

74 Gustavo Silva, *Nuestra evolución,* pp. 88-89; N. Novoa Valdés, *Problemas sociales* (Santiago: Imprenta Cervantes, 1912), p. 178; Rivas Vicuña, *Historia política,* 1:203.

75 Carlos Pinto Duran, *La revolución chilena* (Santiago: Imprenta Valiente y Cia., 1925), p. 137.

76 Frederick de Billier no. 320, Mar. 9, 1918, U.S. *Internal Affairs,* reel 3.

77 *Anuario,* 1915, 3:35; and Pinto Duran, *La revolución,* p. 128.

78 For a general portrait of political life, see Horacio Aranguiz Donoso, Ricardo Coudyoudmjian Bergamali, and Juan Eduardo Vargas Cariola, "La vida política chilena, 1915-1916," *Historia* 7 (1968): 15-21; on the duel, George L. Summerlin no. 669, Aug. 27, 1915, U.S. *Internal Affairs,* reel 3.

79 *El Despertar de los Trabajadores* (Iquique), Apr. 16, 1918.

80 Fletcher no. 591, Mar. 5, 1915, U.S. *Diplomatic,* Correspondence, class 8, pt. 5.

81 Shea no. 592, Oct. 29, 1920, U.S. *Internal Affairs,* reel 4.

82 Fletcher no. 591, U.S. *Diplomatic.*

83 Tancredo Pinochet Le-Brun, *Un año empleado público en Chile* (Santiago: Imprenta Universitaria, 1915), pp. 161-63; on operation of spoils system, see also Moíses Poblete Troncoso, *Nuestro seudo régimen parlamentaria* (Santiago: Numen, 1920), p. 23.

84 Interior, *Memoria,* 1920, p. 75, and 1921, p. 6.

85 Interior, *Memoria,* 1919, Belisario García, Feb. 20, 1919, pp. 727-28.

86 Shea no. 176, July 31, 1917, U.S. *Diplomatic,* Correspondence, class 8, pt. 6; Shea no. 241, Oct. 9, 1917, U.S. *Internal Affairs,* reel 11.

87 Fernando Santivan, *Don Eliodoro Yañez: el hombre y su obra* (Santiago: Santivan, 1925), p. 6.

88 Enclosures nos. 1 and 2, Despatch no. 614, U.S. *Diplomatic,* Correspondence, class 8, pt. 5.

89 *El Mercurio* (Santiago), Sept. 9, 1916.

90 Ibid., Nov. 20, 1917.

91 Interior, *Memoria,* 19197, pp. 228-29.

92 *El Mercurio* (Santiago), Nov. 12, 1920.

93 Shea, Sept. 17, 1920, and McDonough, Concepción, Feb. 26, 1921, U.S. *Internal Affairs,* reels 4, 29; and *South American Journal* (London), Apr. 2, 1921.

94 *El Sur* (Concepción), Apr. 22, 1920.

95 *El Despertar de los Trabajadores* (Iquique), Jan. 12, 1915.

96 Collier no. 51, Jan. 3, 1922, U.S. *Internal Affairs,* reel 5.

97 *Censo*—1875, p. lvi; *Censo*—1920, pp. 405, 407. The

generalizations about religion are based on *La Voz del Pueblo* (Valparaiso), Apr. 29, 1905; *Comision consultiva—1908,* p. 866; letter from the Intendant for Tarapacá, Interior, *Memoria,* 1912, p. 1057; and Junta Executiva del Partido Conservador, *La cuestión político-religiosa y el partido conservador* (Santiago: Lourdes, 1911), p. 10.

98 Shea memorandum to Donoso Carvallo, Jan. 11, 1918, U.S. *Diplomatic,* Correspondence, class 8, pt. 12.

99 Jorge I. Barría Serón, *Los movimientos sociales de Chile desde 1910 hasta 1926* (Santiago: Editorial Universitaria, 1960), pp. 109-13.

100 De Shazo, "Urban Workers and Labor Unions in Chile," 323-24.

101 Alberto Hurtado Cruchaga, *Sindicalismo: historia, teoría, práctica* (Santiago: Editorial del Pacífico, 1950), pp. 215-16; Moíses Poblete Troncoso and Ben G. Burnett, *The Rise of the Latin American Labor Movement* (New York: Bookman Associates, 1960), pp. 61-62.

102 *El Despertar de los Trabajadores* (Iquique), various issues of Jan.-May, 1915; *El Departamento* (Pisagua), Jan. 13, 1915; *El Socialista* (Valparaiso), Dec. 11, 1915; *La Unión Obrera* (Chuquicamata), Dec. 18, 1918; and *El Socialista* (Antofagasta), June 25, 1919.

103 On the strength of the Left, see *El Socialista* (Puntas Arenas), Apr. 18, May 23, July 3, 1914; and Interior, *Memoria,* 1914, report of Fernando Edwards, Governor of Magallanes, p. 25. On labor petition, Petition from Puntas Arenas, Sept. 3, 1914; Labor Petition of Socorros Mutuas, Valparaiso, Sept. 6, 1914; and Petition of Liga de Arrendatarios, Valparaiso, Oct. 12, 1914, all in *A.H.,* vol. 4658, Interior (1914).

104 De Shazo, "Urban Workers and Labor Unions in Chile," p. 347.

105 *El Despertar de los Trabajadores* (Iquique), June 15, 1915.

106 Ibid., Feb. 19, June 17, 23, July 27, Aug. 15, Sept. 14, 1915; *La Vanguardia* (Valparaiso), June 23, 1915; and Barría Seron, *Los movimientos sociales,* p. 220.

107 Interior, *Memoria,* 1914, Fernando Edwards, Governor of Magallanes, p. 26; *B.O.T.,* 1922, no. 18, table on strikes; and De Shazo, "Urban Workers and Labor Unions in Chile," pp. 317-19.

108 Troncoso and Burnett, *The Rise of the Latin American Labor Movement,* p. 62; Barría Serón, *Los movimientos sociales,* pp. 109-13; and *El Socialista* (Valparaiso), Sept. 1, 1917.

109 *El Socialista* (Antofagasta), Aug. 17, 1918, and Jan. 16, 1919.

110 De Shazo, "Urban Workers and Labor Unions in Chile," pp. 323-24, 329.

111 Ibid., pp. 338-42; Barría Serón, *Los movimientos sociales,* p. 263; *El.Socialista* (Antofagasta), various issues, Sept.-Dec., 1919.

112 *B.O.T.,* 1922, nos. 19, 24.

113 Barría Serón, *Los movimientos sociales,* p. 122.

114 Shea no. 534, Mar. 4, 1920, U.S. *Internal Affairs,* reel 3.

115 Shea no. 566, July 9, 1920, U.S. *Internal Affairs,* reel 3.

116 Shea no. 570, July 23, 1920, *U.S. Internal Affairs,* reel 3;

and Austin C. Brady, Puntas Arenas, July 31, 1920, ibid.;
Mario Barros, *Historia diplomática,* pp. 651-53; Frederick M.
Nunn, *Chilean Politics, 1920-1931. The Honorable Mission of
the Armed Forces* (Albuquerque: University of New Mexico
Press, 1970), p. 23; Frank Bonilla and Myron Glaser, *Student
Politics in Chile* (New York: Basic Books, 1970), p. 40.

117 Munro, Dec. 9, 1920, reel 23, Shea no. 583, Sept. 8, 1920,
and no. 584, Sept. 17, 1920, reel 4, U.S. *Internal Affairs.*

118 Shea no. 584, ibid.

119 Alessandri Palma, *Recuerdos,* vol. 1, appendix.

120 Donoso, *Alessandri,* 1:277.

121 Shea no. 614, Mar. 4, 1921, U.S. *Internal Affairs,* reel 4;
Shea no. 301, Feb. 1923, U.S. *Internal Affairs,* reel 5.

122 Brown, Iquique, Nov. 16, 1920, U.S. *Internal Affairs,* reel 10.

123 *New York Sun,* Apr. 19, 1922.

124 Mackinson, Valparaiso, Aug. 17, 1922, U.S. *Internal Affairs,*
reel 39.

125 Interior, *Memoria,* 1920, p. 7; *Discurso*—1921, pp. 17-18.

126 *El Despertar de los Trabajadores* (Iquique), Feb. 24, June 18,
1921, and Sept. 14, 1922.

127 *El Socialista* (Antofagasta), Aug. 26, Nov. 2, 20, 1920.

128 *El Despertar de los Trabajadores* (Iquique), Dec. 24-31, 1921;
La Federación Obrera (Santiago), Dec. 29-31, 1921, and Jan.
18, 1922.

129 Martin no. 670, May 13, 1921, U.S. *Internal Affairs,* reel 4;
see also Martin no. 538A, June 10, 1921, reel 4, and Collier
no. 32, Nov. 22, 1921, reel 5.

130 Dayle C. McDonough to Shea, Mar. 2, 1921, U.S. *Diplomatic,*
Correspondence, class 800, pt. 12; *La Federación Obrera*
(Santiago), Feb. 15, 1922.

131 *La Federación Obrera* (Santiago), June 18, 1922.

132 Martin no. 690, June 28, 1921, U.S. *Internal Affairs,* reel 4.

133 *Sucesos* (Santiago), Feb. 10, 1921; Barría Seron, *Los movimientos sociales,* pp. 303-5; Shea no. 613, Feb. 18, 1921, U.S.
Internal Affairs, reel 4; Vicuña, *La tiranía en Chile,* 1:113-
15; *El Despertar de los Trabajadores* (Iquique), Feb. 6, 10,
Apr. 7, 1921.

134 Dana G. Munro, Consul at Valparaiso, Jan. 21, Feb. 1, 1921,
U.S. *Internal Affairs,* reel 21.

135 Homer Brett, Consul for Iquique, Oct. 31, 1921, and Jan. 4,
1922, reel 5; Martin no. 716, Sept. 20, 1921, reel 5; Shea no.
559, June 24, 1920, reel 3, and no. 647, reel 4, all in U.S.
Internal Affairs, Carlos Soubletter, Dec. 7, 1921, in *Asociación Salitrera, Circular* (Valparaiso), no. xi, *El Diario
Ilustrado* (Iquique), Dec. 2, 1922; *La Federación Obrera*
(Santiago), June 7, 1922, and Oct. 11, 1923; and *El Despertar
de los Trabajadores* (Iquique), Sept. 26, 1923.

136 Dayle C. McDonough, Concepción, Feb. 3, 1922, reel 22; and
Shea no. 527, Apr. 6, 1920, reel 3, U.S. *Internal Affairs.*
La Nación (Santiago), Mar. 15, 1920; Great Britain, *Report on
Overseas Trade,* 1921, p. 57; *El Mercurio* (Santiago), May 15,
1920.

137 Shea no. 599, June 24, 1920, reel 3; Shea no. 599, December 10, 1920, reel 4; and McDonough, Feb. 11, 1922, reel 21, all in U.S. *Internal Affairs;* also McDonough, Oct. 6, 1920, U.S. *Diplomatic,* Correspondence, class 800, pt. 13 (1920); and *El Sur* (Concepción), Oct. 2, 1920.
138 McDonough, Apr. 15, 1921, May 2, 1921, and Oct. 4, 1921, U.S. *Diplomatic,* Correspondence, class 800, pt. 12.
139 McDonough, Feb. 14, 1922, ibid.; McDonough, Feb. 3, 11, 24, 1922, reels 21 and 22, and Collier no. 83, Feb. 14, 1922, U.S. *Internal Affairs,* reel 5.
140 *El Mercurio* (Santiago), Jan. 25, 1922; *La Región Minera* (Coronel), Jan. 29, 1922; *El Sur* (Concepción), Jan. 4, 5, 1922; *South Pacific Mail* (Valparaiso), Jan. 19, 1922; *El Despertar de los Trabajadores* (Iquique), Jan. 8, 1922.
141 McDonough, Feb. 24, 1922, reel 22, and Collier no. 85, Mar. 7, 1922, U.S. *Internal Affairs,* reel 5; also *El Sur* (Concepción), Mar. 21, 1922.
142 *La Federación Obrera* (Santiago), Feb. 12, 1922.
143 On Concha, see *Avancemos* (Santiago), Nov. 20, 1920, and Godoy M., *Don Malaquías Concha,* p. 76; on Pradenas, see Cortes and Fuentes, *Diccionario político,* p. 391.

6. NATIONALIST POLICIES AND ECONOMIC REALITIES

1 *Anuario,* 1930, 8:54.
2 Robbins no. 425, May 22, 1919, U.S. *Diplomatic,* Correspondence, class 800, pt. 7.
3 Robbins no. 422, Mar. 13, 1919, ibid.
4 Pinto Duran, *La revolución,* p. 10.
5 Collier no. 379, Mar. 4, 1924, U.S. *Internal Affairs,* reel 5.
6 Collier no. 455, Aug. 5, 1924, ibid., reel 6.
7 Collier telegrams, Sept. 6, 8, 1924, Collier no. 471, Sept. 15, 1924, ibid.
8 Collier no. 478, Sept. 24, 1924, ibid.; Pinto Duran, *La revolución,* p. 23.
9 Nunn, *Chilean Politics,* pp. 69-70.
10 Collier telegram, Sept. 19, 1924, U.S. *Internal Affairs,* reel 6.
11 *Justicia* (Santiago), Sept. 16, 1924.
12 Ibid., Oct. 1, 1924.
13 George A. Makinson, Valparaiso, Nov. 30, 1924, U.S. *Internal Affairs,* reel 6.
14 *Justicia* (Santiago), Oct. 29, 1924.
15 Winslow no. 525, Dec. 1, 1924, and Winslow no. 535, Dec. 6, 1924, U.S. *Internal Affairs,* reel 6.
16 Nunn, *Chilean Politics,* pp. 77-78.
17 *El Mercurio* (Santiago), Jan. 14, 1925.
18 Collier no. 562, Feb. 2, 1925, U.S. *Internal Affairs,* reel 6; see also Mackinson, Valparaiso, Feb. 1, 1925, ibid.
19 Collier no. 564, Feb. 5, 1925, ibid.; Mackinson to Collier, Feb. 8, 1925, U.S. *Diplomatic,* Correspondence, class 800,

pt. 10.
20 Text of declaration cited in report by Mackinson, Feb. 1, 1925, U.S. *Internal Affairs,* reel 6.
21 Collier no. 733, Oct. 12, 1925, U.S. *Diplomatic,* Correspondence, class 800, pt. 10 (1925).
22 Nunn, *Chilean Politics.*
23 Mackinson report, Jan. 16, 1924, U.S. *Internal Affairs,* reel 26.
24 Stinson report on currency and banking, Sept. 4, 1929, U.S. *Internal Affairs,* reel 24.
25 *Anuario,* 1929-30, 8:32.
26 Clarence G. Brooks, Acting Commercial Attaché, Oct. 28, 1926, U.S. *Diplomatic,* Correspondence, class 851, pt. 13 (1926).
27 Mackinson, Dec. 20, 1923, U.S. *Internal Affairs,* reel 25.
28 Stewart E. McMillan, Consul for Antofagasta, Feb. 12, 1925, U.S. *Internal Affairs,* reel 21.
29 *Banco Central de Chile* (Santiago), May, 1928, no. 5, stock index.
30 Winslow report, Oct. 7, 1924, U.S. *Internal Affairs,* reel 23; Stenson report, Sept. 4, 1929, U.S. *Internal Affairs,* reel 24; and Collier no. 843, May 7, 1926, U.S. *Diplomatic,* Correspondence, class 824, pt. 12 (1926); *Chile* (New York), 1927, 3:3; *B.O.T.,* 1926, no. 24, anexos xiii-xvii.
31 U.S. Bureau of Foreign and Domestic Commerce, *Commerce Reports,* Mar. 15, 1926, 1:669-70; Oct. 25, 1926, 4:212-15; Nov. 15, 1926, 4:452-53; *Las Ultimas Noticias* (Santiago), Feb. 3, 1927.
32 *La Unión* (Valparaiso), Sept. 17.1926.
33 *La Nación* (Santiago), Sept. 22, 1926.
34 *El Mercurio* (Santiago), Sept. 25, 1926.
35 *La Unión* (Valparaiso), Sept. 24, 1926.
36 Jacques Bancelín, *Algunas observaciones sobre la industria salitrera* (Santiago: Imprenta R. Harris A., 1929), pp. 5-9.
37 Ben C. Matthews, Nov. 22, 1923, U.S. *Internal Affairs,* reel 34.
38 U.S. Congress, House of Representatives, *Hearings before the Committee on Agriculture,* 67th Cong., 4th sess., Jan. 16, 25, 26, 29, and February 1, 2, 1923 (Washington: Government Printing Office, 1923), pp. 1-2.
39 Ibid., p. 13.
40 Preston J. Hubbard, *Origins of the T.V.A.: The Muscle Shoals Controversy, 1920-1932* (Nashville, Tenn.: Vanderbilt University, 1961), p. 16.
41 Collier no. 240, Mar. 6, 1923, U.S. *Diplomatic,* Correspondence, class 863, pt. 11 (1923).
42 Collier no. 399, Apr. 5, 1924, U.S. *Internal Affairs,* reel 34.
43 Collier no. 418, May 26, 1924, U.S. *Diplomatic,* Correspondence, class 863, pt. 12 (1924).
44 Collier to Chile's Minister of Foreign Affairs, Galvarino Gallermo Nieto, May 7, 1924, ibid.
45 Collier no. 418, May 26, 1924, ibid.

46 George A. Mackinson report, Sept. 22, 1924, ibid.

47 Report from Alfred Nutting, Clerk in the American Consulate General, London, to State Department, Apr. 29, 1926, U.S. *Internal Affairs*, reel 34.

48 Chile, Ministerio de Hacienda, *La industria de salitre en Chile* (Santiago: 1933-34), 1:6.

49 Collier no. 884, Aug. 2, 1926; Collier no. 903G, Sept. 4, 1926; and Engert no. 930G, Oct. 6, 1926, all in U.S. *Internal Affairs*, reel 7.

50 Ramírez Necochea, *Partido Comunista*, pp. 264-65.

51 *B.O.T.*, 1923, nos. 21, 17.

52 *El Diario Ilustrado* (Santiago), May 2, 1924.

53 Cited in report of Federick F. A. Pearson on immigration for 1926, U.S. *Internal Affairs*, reel 23.

54 *Censo*—1930, 2:xviii.

55 Guillermo Viviani Contreras, *Sociología chilena* (Santiago: Editorial Nascimento, 1926) 1:58, 60-61; and Carlos Vicuña, *La crisis moral de Chile. Conferencia dada en Buenos Aires en la Casa del Pueblo el 27 de Diciembre de 1928* (Mar de Plata: La Capital, 1929), p. 15.

56 George A. Mackinson, Feb. 13, 1925, U.S. *Diplomatic*, Correspondence, class 850, pt. 13 (1925); also De Shazo, "Urban Workers and Labor Unions in Chile," pp. 470-75.

57 De Shazo, "Urban Workers and Labor Unions in Chile," pp. 470-75; and Collier no. 569, Feb. 16, 1925, U.S. *Internal Affairs*, reel 6.

58 *B.O.T.*, 1926, nos. 24, 146; and *El Mercurio* (Santiago), June 10, 1925.

59 C. F. Deichman, Valparaiso, to John F. Martin, Santiago Charge d'Affairs, Sept. 11, 1923, U.S. *Diplomatic*, Correspondence, class 811, pt. 10 (1923); and John F. Martin, Feb. 11, 1924, pt. 9 (1924).

60 L. Lanier Winslow, Charge d'Affairs ad interim, no. 495, Oct. 23, 1924, U.S. *Diplomatic*, Correspondence, class 800, pt. 7 (1924).

61 *B.O.T.*, 1924, nos. 22, 222, and 1926, no. 24, anexos lxxii, lxxxvi.

62 *El Despertar de los Trabajadores* (Iquique), Aug. 26, 1924, and Mar. 8, 1925; *La Federación Obrera* (Santiago), June 11 and Oct. 17, 1924.

63 *El Despertar de los Trabajadores* (Iquique), Apr. 10, 12, 19, and 24, 1925.

64 O'Connor, *The Guggenheims*, p. 414; B. C. Matthews, Antofagasta, May 5, 27, 1925, and enclosed telegrams, Mar.-May, 1925, U.S. *Diplomatic*, Correspondence, class 850, pt. 13 (1925); *El Comunista* (Antofagasta), Apr. 2, 1925; *El Mercurio* (Santiago), May 1, 1925.

65 Quoted in Mackinson report, Apr. 11, 1925, U.S. *Diplomatic*, Correspondence, class 850, pt. 13 (1925).

66 Collier no. 627, May 11, 1925, U.S. *Internal Affairs*, reel 12.

67 Harry Campbell, Iquique, June 10, 1925, U.S, *Internal Affairs*, reel 21; Campbell report, June 10, 1925, U.S. *Diplomatic*,

Correspondence, class 850, pt. 13 (1925)——see also in the same source C. F. Deichman, Valparaiso, June 23, 1925, who put the number of dead and wounded as over 1,000; and Collier no. 651, June, 1925, U.S. *Internal Affairs,* reel 6.

68 Deichman to Collier, June 16, 1925, U.S. *Diplomatic,* Correspondence, class 850, pt. 13 (1925); and Collier, no. 651, June 22, 1925, U.S. *Internal Affairs,* reel 6.

69 Collier no. 668, July 7, 1925, U.S. *Internal Affairs,* reel 6.

70 *Justicia* (Santiago), Dec. 17-18, 1924.

71 Ramírez Necochea, *Partido Comunista,* p. 149.

72 *El Despertar de los Trabajadores* (Iquique), Feb. 19, 1926; *Justicia* (Santiago), Nov. 12, 1926.

73 *El Despertar de los Trabajadores* (Iquique), July 16, Aug. 3, and Nov. 10, 1926.

74 *Justicia* (Santiago), July 8, 1926.

75 *El Despertar de los Trabajadores* (Iquique), May 26, 1926; *Justicia* (Santiago), July 28, 1926; Collier no. 884G, Aug. 2, 1926, U.S. *Diplomatic,* Correspondence, class 800, pt. 10 (1926); and Engert no. 940G, Oct. 20, 1926, U.S. *Internal Affairs,* reel 7; De Shazo, "Urban Workers and Labor Unions in Chile," p. 491.

76 Collier, no. 988G, Jan. 7, 1927, U.S. *Diplomatic,* Correspondence, class 800, pt. 9 (1927); Collier no. 1016G, Feb. 22, 1927, U.S. *Internal Affairs,* reel 7; and *Justicia* (Santiago), Jan. 16, 20, 1927.

77 *Justicia* (Santiago), Feb. 11, 13, 1927.

78 Quoted in Collier telegram, Feb. 9, 1927, U.S. *Internal Affairs,* reel 7.

79 Collier telegram, Feb. 24, 1927, ibid.; and Collier no. 1179G, Sept. 19, 1927, U.S. *Internal Affairs,* reel 8.

80 Collier no. 1016G, Feb. 22, 1927, and no. 1027G, Mar. 19, 1927, U.S. *Internal Affairs,* reel 7.

81 Collier no. 1054G, Apr. 19, 1927, U.S. *Internal Affairs,* reel 19; and Collier 1289, Jan. 14, 1928, reel 7.

82 Ramírez Necochea, *Partido Comunista,* pp. 236-37.

83 Viviani Contreras, *Sociología chilena,* 1:22; Collier telegram, Nov. 19, 1927, U.S. *Internal Affairs,* reel 8.

84 Interior, *Memoria,* 1927, p. 80; Culbertson no. 89, Jan. 15, 1929, U.S. *Internal Affairs,* reel 8.

85 Collier telegram, Mar. 17, 1928, U.S. *Diplomatic,* Correspondence, class 800, pt. 10 (1928).

86 *Anuario,* 1929-30, 8:55; and Chile, Ministerio de Fomento, *Memoria,* 1927, p. 198.

87 *Anuario,* 1929-30, 8:54, 56; and Stimson report, Aug. 13, 1929, U.S. *Internal Affairs,* reel 24.

88 *Anuario,* 1929-30, 8:41.

89 George D. Hopper, Mar. 21, 1926, U.S. *Internal Affairs,* reel 21; producers' point of view in *Chile* (New York City), 1927, 3:134-35.

90 Robert R. Bradford (Iquique), Oct. 15, 1928, U.S. *Internal Affairs,* reel 20; Collier telegram, Aug. 7, 1927, U.S. *Diplomatic,* Correspondence, class 863, pt. 15 (1927).

91 Kellogg telegram to Santiago Embassy, Aug. 2, 1927, U.S. *Internal Affairs,* reel 36.
92 Collier telegram to Secretary of State, Aug. 7, 1927, ibid.
93 Francis White, Assistant Secretary of State, to Secretary of Commerce, Sept. 24, 1927, ibid.
94 Collier telegram to State, Aug. 25, 1927, U.S. *Internal Affairs,* reel 39.
95 *La Nación* (Santiago), Aug. 30, 1927.
96 Collier telegram to State, Sept. 2, 1927, U.S. *Internal Affairs,* reel 39.
97 Castle, Acting Secretary, to Santiago Embassy, Aug. 31, 1927, ibid.
98 Kellogg telegram to Santiago Embassy, Sept. 14, 1927, ibid.
99 Collier telegram to State, Sept. 17, 1927, and Collier no. 827, Oct. 30, 1927, U.S. *Diplomatic,* Correspondence, class 888, pt. 16 (1927); see also *El Mercurio* (Santiago), Oct. 26, 1927.
100 Collier no. 1253, Nov. 29, 1927, U.S. *Internal Affairs,* reel 39.
101 Letter of H. C. Bellinger, Vice-President, Chile Exploration Company, and William Wraith, Vice-President, Andes Copper Mining Company, to Stokely Morgan, Chief of the Latin American Division, State Department, Oct. 3, 1927, U.S. *Diplomatic,* Correspondence, class 863, pt. 15 (1927).
102 Cited in Culbertson no. 28, Oct. 13, 1928, U.S. *Internal Affairs,* reel 25.
103 El Rocesin, columnist, *El Sur* (Concepción), June 30, 1927.
104 *La Nación* (Santiago), Oct. 30, 1927.
105 Collier no. 1299, Jan. 19, 1928, U.S. *Internal Affairs,* reel 30; and Culbertson no. 65, Dec. 22, 1928, U.S. *Diplomatic,* Correspondence, class 863, pt. 12.
106 Olds, Acting Secretary of State, telegram to Santiago Embassy, Feb. 10, 1928, and Collier telegram to State, Feb. 13, 1928, U.S. *Internal Affairs,* reel 35.
107 Culbertson no. 5, Aug. 31, 1928, ibid.; and *Commerce Reports,* Sept. 3, 1928, Ackerman report, p. 624.
108 Collier no. 1077G, July 1, 1927, U.S. *Internal Affairs,* reel 7; and George D. Hopper, Antofagasta, to State, May 6, 1927, reel 34.
109 *Commerce Reports,* Sept. 3, 1928; Ackerman report, p. 587.
110 Culbertson no. 32, Oct. 15, 1928, and Culbertson no. 168, Aug. 30, 1929, U.S. *Internal Affairs,* reel 35.
111 Alfred Nutting, American Consulate-General, London, Mar. 27, 1929, ibid.
112 Culbertson no. 536, Jan. 12, 1931, ibid.
113 O'Connor, *The Guggenheims,* pp. 418-21, 452-57.
114 *La Nación* (Santiago), Apr. 4, 1930.
115 Ibid., July 9, 1930.
116 Ibid., June 30, 1930.
117 Ibid., July 8, 1930.
118 Lay no. 330G, Dec. 3, 1929, U.S. *Internal Affairs,* reel 9.
119 Culbertson no. 413, Apr. 10, 1930, U.S. *Diplomatic,*

Correspondence, class 800, pt. 8.

120 Francisco Huneeus in *El Diario Ilustrado* (Santiago), Oct. 3, 1930.

121 Culbertson no. 712, Dec. 19, 1930, U.S. *Internal Affairs*, reel 35.

122 Chile, Congreso, Senado, *Presentación hecha a la comisión investigadora de los actos de dictadura por la Compañía de Salitre de Chile* (Santiago: 1931), p. 4; Julio Pérez Canto, *La industria salitrera y la intervención del estado* (Santiago: Imprenta Walter Guedt, 1933), pp. 585, 589-90.

123 Chile, Senado, *Presentación hecha a la comisión investigadora,* pp. 4ff; and U.S. Senate, *Hearings before a Subcommittee of the Committee on Banking Currency, on Stock Exchange Practices,* 72nd Cong., 2nd sess., pt. 6, pp. 2298ff.

124 Pérez Canto, *La industria salitrera,* p. 604.

125 Norweb telegram, Apr. 25, 1931, U.S. *Internal Affairs,* 1930-39, file 825.51/371.

126 Culbertson no. 919, July 31, 1931, U.S. *Internal Affairs,* 1930-39, file 825.5045/51.

127 Raymond F. Mikesell, *Foreign Investments in Latin America* (Washington, D.C.: Pan American Union, Economic Research Series, 1955), p. 17; J. Fred Rippy, *Globe and Hemisphere* (Chicago: Henry Regnery Company, 1958), p. 54.

128 Naval Attaché's report, July 12, 1927, U.S. *Internal Affairs,* reel 8; Joseph Flack report, Nov. 4, 1928, reel 24.

129 Great Britain, Department of Overseas Trade, E. Murray Harvey, *Economic Conditions in Chile* (London: His Majesty's Stationary Office, 1930), p. 34.

130 Collier no. 1371, May 8, 1938, U.S. *Internal Affairs,* reel 20.

131 O'Connor, *The Guggenheims,* p. 419.

132 Julius G. Lay no. 307, Oct. 28, 1929, U.S. *Diplomatic,* Correspondence, class 851 (1929).

133 Bowman report, Dec. 7, 1931, U.S. *Internal Affairs,* 1930-39, file 825.5151/23.

134 Campbell, Jan. 20, 1927, U.S. *Diplomatic,* Correspondence, class 863, pt. 15.

135 *La Nación* (Santiago), July 6, 1928.

7. CONCLUSION: THE PATTERN OF DEPENDENT DEVELOPMENT

1 Gabriel Ardant, "Financial Policy and Economic Infrastructure of Modern States and Nations," in Charles Tilly, ed., *The Formation of National States in Western Europe* (Princeton: Princeton University Press, 1975), pp. 186-88, 204-14.

2 Clark Winton Reynolds, "Development Problems of an Export Economy: The Case of Chile and Copper," in Markos Mamalakis and Clark Winton Reynolds, *Essays on the Chilean Economy* (Homewood, Ill.: Richard D. Irvin, 1965), pp. 236-44.

3 Richard E. Feinberg, *The Triumph of Allende: Chile's Legal Revolution* (New York: New American Library, 1972), p. 81.

4 Oficina de Planificación Nacional (ODEPLAN), *Antecedentes*

sobre el desarrollo chileno, 1960-1970, vol. 1, no. 1, *Planes semestrales, Plan de la economía nacional, 1971-1976* (Santiago: ODEPLAN, 1971), cited in Alexis Guardia, Alberto Martinez, and Sergio Ramos, "General Considerations on the Chilean Economic Structure," in S. Sideri, ed., *Chile, 1970-1973: Economic Development and Its International Setting; Self-criticism of the Unidad Popular Government's Policies* (The Hague: International Instituut voor Sociale Studien——'S Gravenhage, Series on the Development of Societies, vol. 4, Martinus Nijhoff, 1979), pp. 14, 15.

5 Theodore H. Moran, *Multinational Corporations and the Politics of Dependence: Copper in Chile* (Princeton: Princeton University Press, 1974), p. 105.

6 Barbara Stallings, *Class Conflict and Economic Development in Chile, 1958-1973* (Stanford: Stanford University Press, 1978), p. 262.

7 U.S. Senate, Select Committee on Intelligence Activities, *Covert Action in Chile, 1963-1973, Staff Report,* 94th Cong., 1st sess., 1975, pp. 15-17.

8 David J. Morris, *We Must Make Haste Slowly: The Process of Revolution in Chile* (New York: Random House, 1973), pp. 31-91; and Sigmund, *The Overthrow of Allende,* pp. 23-26.

9 Stefan de Vylder, *Allende's Chile: The Political Economy of the Rise and Fall of the Unidad Popular* (Cambridge: Cambridge University Press, 1976), p. 22.

10 Alexis Guardia, "Structural Transformations in Chile's Economy and in Its System of External Economic Relations," in Sideri, *Chile, 1970-1973,* p. 54.

11 Stallings, *Class Conflict,* p. 246.

12 De Vylder, *Allende's Chile,* pp. 29-31.

13 Gonzalo Martner G., "The Popular Unity Government's Efforts in Planning," in J. Ann Zammit, ed., *The Chilean Road to Socialism (Proceedings of an ODEPLAN——IDS Round Table, March, 1972)* (Austin: University of Texas Press, 1973), pp. 69-76.

14 See, for example, Movimiento Izquierdista Revolucionaria, *Chile, the MIR, and the Tasks of Resistance* (Oakland, Calif.: Resistance Publications, 1976), pp. 36-42; and Robinson Rojas Sanford, *The Murder of Allende and the End of the Chilean Road to Socialism* (New York: Harper and Row, 1975), pp. 107-11.

15 Sergio Ramos, "Inflation in Chile and the Political Economy of the Unidad Popular Government," in Sideri, *Chile, 1970-73,* pp. 340-41; the "chaos" thesis is summarized in Robert Moss, *Chile's Marxist Experiment* (Newton Abbot: David and Charles, 1973), pp. 52-80; an able criticism of this view is de Vylder's, in *Allende's Chile,* pp. 214-20.

16 Rene Silva Espejo, *Breve historia de la Unidad Popular, Documento de "El Mercurio"* (Santiago: El Mercurio, 1974), pp. 359-75.

17 For corroborating arguments, see Edward Boorstein, *An Inside View . . . Allende's Chile* (New York: International Publishers, 1977), pp. 237-49.

18 *Latin American Regional Report: Brazil* (London: Latin American Newsletters, May 30, 1980), pp. 1, 8.

Bibliography

PRIVATE PAPERS

Washington. Library of Congress, Manuscript Division. Boxes 32,
   33, and 34. Chandler P. Anderson Papers.
New Haven. Yale University. Sterling Memorial Library Archives.
   Manuscript Group 580. Gordon B. Auchincloss Papers.
New Haven. Yale University. Sterling Memorial Library Archives.
   Manuscript Group 656. Frank L. Polk Papers.

GOVERNMENT ARCHIVES, RECORDS, AND REPORTS

Bolivia. *Documentos oficiales de Bolivia relativos a la cuestión
   del Pacífico.* Buenos Aires: Imprenta del Pueblo, 1879.
Chile. Archivo Nacional. *Ministerio de Hacienda, 1886-1918.*
   Santiago. Biblioteca Nacional.
Chile. Archivo Nacional. *Ministerio del Interior, 1887-1907.*
   Santiago. Biblioteca Nacional.
Chile. Cámara de Diputados. *Comisión parlamentaria encargada de
   estudiar las necesidades de las provincias de Tarapacá y
   Antofagasta.* Santiago: Zig-Zag, 1913.
Chile. Cámara de Diputados. *Boletín de las sesiones estraordi-
   naires, 1895-1896, 1896-1897, 1902-1903, 1904-1905, 1905-
   1906, 1906-1907.* Santiago. Consulted in Biblioteca del
   Congreso National.
Chile. Cámara de Senadores. *Boletín de sesiones ordinarias,
   1881, 1896, 1897, 1902, 1904-1908, 1913.* Santiago. Found
   in Biblioteca del Congreso Nacional.
Chile. Comisión Central del Censo. *Resultados del X censo de la
   población efectuado el 27 de Noviembre de 1930 y estadísticas
   comparitivas con censo anteriores.* 3 vols. Santiago: Imprenta Universo, 1931-35.
Chile. Congreso, 1892-93. Senado. *Acusación a los ex-Ministros
   del Despacho: Señores Don Claudio Vicuña Domingo Godoy,
   Ismael Pérez Montt, José M. Valdés Carrera, José Francisco
   Gana, Guillermo MacKenna. Pruebas rendidas durante el juicio*

ante el Senado. Santiago: Imprenta Nacional, 1893.

Chile. Congreso Nacional. *Actas de la comisión mista de legisla-ción social*. 3 vols. Santiago: Imprenta Nacional, 1921-22.

Chile. Consejo Superior de Habitaciones para Obreros. *Asamblea de la habitación barata—celebrada en Santiago los dias 28, 29, y 30 de Septiembre de 1919*. Santiago: Imprenta La Ilustración, 1920.

Chile. Dirección General de Estadística. *Anuario estadístico de Chile, 1909-1930*. Santiago: Oficina Central de Estadística, 1909-26; later, Servicio Nacional de Estadísticos y Censos, 1926-30.

Chile. Dirección General de Estadística. *Censo de la industria manufacturera y del comercio de 1928*. Santiago: Servicio Nacional de Estadísticos y Censos, 1929.

Chile. Dirección General Estadística. *Censo de la República de Chile levantado el 15 de Diciembre de 1920*. Santiago: Sociedad Imprenta y Litografia Universo, 1925.

Chile. Dirección Jeneral de Contabilidad. *Resumen de la hacienda pública desde la independencia hasta 1900*. Santiago: Direc-ción Jeneral de Contabilidad, 1901.

Chile. Legación en Londres. *Resumen de la hacienda pública de Chile desde 1833 hasta 1914*. London: Spottiswoode and Co., 1914.

Chile. Ministerio de Bienestar Social. *Memoria al Congreso Nacional, 1924, 1925, 1926, 1927*. Santiago: Imprenta Nacional.

Chile. Ministerio de Hacienda. *Antecedentes sobre la industria salitrera*. Santiago: Imprenta Universo, 1925.

Chile. Ministerio de Hacienda. *Fomento de la industria salitrera*. Santiago: Los Debates, 1889.

Chile. Ministerio de Hacienda. *La industria de salitre en Chile*. 3 vols. Santiago: Imprenta Universo, 1933-34.

Chile. Ministerio de Hacienda. *Memoria del Ministerio de Hacienda presentado al Congreso Nacional por el Ministro del Ramo, 1864-1867*. Santiago: Ministerio de Hacienda. Con-sulted in Biblioteca Nacional.

Chile. Ministerio de Instrucción Pública. *Memoria que el Ministro de Instrucción Pública presenta al Congreso Nacional, 1907, 1908, 1909, 1910, 1919*. Santiago: Minis-terio de Instrucción Pública.

Chile. Ministerio del Interior. *Memoria que el Ministro del Estado en el Departamento del Interior presenta al Congreso Nacional, 1883*. Title changed to *Memoria del Ministerio del Interior al Congreso Nacional, 1880-1883, 1885-1911, 1924-1929*. Santiago: Ministerio del Interior. Consulted in Biblioteca Nacional.

Chile. Oficina Central de Estadística. *Quinto censo jeneral de la población de Chile levantado el 19 de Abril de 1875 i compilado por la oficina central de estadística en Santiago*. Valparaiso: Imprenta del Mercurio, 1876.

Chile. Oficina Central de Estadística. *Sesto censo jeneral de la población de Chile levantado el 26 de Noviembre de 1885 y*

compilado por la oficina central de estadística en Santiago.
2 vols. Valparaiso: Imprenta de la Patria, 1889-90.

Chile. Oficina Central de Estadística. *Sinopsis estadística y
geográfica de Chile, 1890, 1891, 1893, 1898, 1899, 1905,
1916.* Santiago: Oficina Central de Estadística. Consulted in Biblioteca Nacional.

Chile. Oficina de Estadística Comercial. *Apuntes estadísticas
sobre la República de Chile.* Valparaiso: Imprenta del
Universo de G. Helfman, 1876.

Chile. Oficina del Trabajo. *Boletín de la Oficina del Trabajo,
1911-1922.* Santiago: Oficina del Trabajo. Consulted in
Biblioteca Nacional.

Chile. Senado. *Comisión investigadora de los actos de la
dictadura, subcomisión para que estudiar la gestión de la
Companía de Salitre de Chile.* Santiago: 1931. Consulted
in Biblioteca del Congreso Nacional.

Chile. Superintendencia de Aduanas. *Resumen del comercio exterior de Chile, 1907, 1909.* Valparaiso: Universo, 1908,
1910.

Chile. *Boletín de leyes y decretos del gobierno, 1810-1814.*
Santiago: Imprenta de la Independencia, 1898.

Chile. *Comisión de reformas de las leyes sociales: la legislación social.* Santiago: La Nación, 1929.

Chile. *Constitución política de la República de Chile, 30 de
Agosto, 1925.* Santiago: Universo, 1925.

Chile. *Constitución política y lei de elecciones de la República
de Chile.* Imprenta Moneda, 1903.

Chile. *Discurso de su excelencia el Presidente de la República
en la apertura del Congreso Nacional, 1881-1911, 1915-1922.*
Santiago. Consulted in Biblioteca del Congreso Nacional.

Chile. *Informes presentados a la Oficina de Estadística del
Trabajo: El Trabajo en la industria salitrera.* By E. Frías
Collao. Santiago: Imprenta Cervantes, 1908.

Chile. *Semana de la moneda celebrada en Santiago de Chile,
Agosto, 1924.* Santiago: Imprenta La Ilustración, 1924.

Chile. *Trabajos y antecedentes presentados al Supremo Gobierno
de Chile por la comisión consultiva del norte.* By Manuel
Salas Lavaqui. Santiago: Imprenta Cervantes, 1908.

Great Britain. *British Parliamentary Papers: Central and South
America, 1834-1899.* Irish Press Area Studies Series, vol. 4.
Dublin: Irish University Press Microforms, 1974.

Great Britain. Board of Trade. *Statistical Abstract for the
United Kingdom in each of the last fifteen years, 1849-1933.*
London: H.M. Stationery Office. 1880-1934.

Great Britain. Department of Overseas Trade. *Report on the Industrial and Economic Situation in Chile, 1921-1925.* Title
changed to *Economic Conditions in Chile, 1929, 1930, 1932,
1934;* and *Report on Economic and Commercial Conditions in
Chile, 1936, 1937.* London: H.M. Stationery Office.

Great Britain. Parliament. House of Commons. *Sessional Papers,
1890-1925.* On microfiche. Consulted in Microfilm Room,
University of California, Los Angeles.

Great Britain. Public Records Office. Foreign Office 16.
    General Correspondence for Chile, 1885-1895. On microfilm.
    Consulted in Bancroft Library, University of California,
    Berkeley.
Great Britain. *Reports by Her Majesty's Secretaries of Embassy*
    and Legation on the Manufactures, Commerce, etc., of the
    Countries in which they reside, pt. 3: *Report by Mr.*
    Rumbold on the Progress and General Condition of Chile.
    London: Harrison and Sons, 1876.
Great Britain. Royal Historical Society. *British Consular Re-*
    ports on the Trade and Politics of Latin America, 1824-1826.
    Edited by R. A. Humphreys. Vol. 8. London: Royal Histori-
    cal Society, 1940.
United States. Department of Commerce. Bureau of Foreign and
    Domestic Commerce. *Commerce Yearbook, 1922-1930.* 8 vols.
    Washington, Government Printing Office.
United States. Department of Commerce. Bureau of Foreign and
    Domestic Commerce. *Special Agents Series nos. 117, 153, 164,*
    169, 176, 187, 224. Washington: Government Printing Office,
    1916-24.
United States. Department of Commerce. Bureau of Foreign and
    Domestic Commerce. *Trade Information Bulletin, nos. 170,*
    324, 440, 517, 515, 525. Washington: Government Printing
    Office, 1924, 1925-28.
United States. Department of Commerce. *Trade Promotion Series*
    nos. 18, 93. Washington: Government Printing Office, 1925,
    1930.
United States. Department of Commerce and Labor. Bureau of
    Foreign and Domestic Commerce. *Consular Reports,* 1880-
    1903. 72 vols. Department and title changed to: Statisti-
    cal Bureau. *Monthly Consular Reports,* 1903-5. 4 vols. De-
    partment and title changed to: Manufactures Bureau.
    Monthly Consular and Trade Reports, 1905-9. Nos. 298-351.
    Title changed to: *Special Consular Reports,* 1909-11. 43
    vols. Title changed to: *Daily Consular and Trade Reports,*
    1911-15. 5 vols. Department and title changed to: Bureau
    of Foreign and Domestic Commerce. *Commerce Reports,* 1915-
    21. 9 vols. Washington, Government Printing Office.
United States. Department of State. *Despatches from United*
    States Consuls in Valparaiso, 1912-1906. Washington:
    National Archives Microfilm M 146, 1949.
United States. Department of State. *Despatches from United*
    States Ministers to Chile, 1823-1906. Washington: National
    Archives Microfilm M 10, 1962. Record Group 59.
United States. Department of State. *Numerical and Minor Files*
    of the Department of State, 1906, 1910. Washington:
    National Archives Microfilm M 862, 1972. Record Group 59.
United States. Department of State. *Records of Diplomatic*
    Posts: Chile, 1824-1935. Washington: National Archives.
    Record Group 84.
United States. Department of State. *Records of Diplomatic Posts,*
    1880-1930. Washington: National Archives. Record Group 84.

United States. Department of State. *Records of the Department of State Relating to the Internal Affairs of Chile, 1910-1929.* Washington: National Archives Microfilm M 487, 1963. Record Group 59.

United States. Department of State. *Report upon the Commercial Relations with Foreign Countries for the year 1859, 1870, 1875, 1876, 1896-1897, 1889-1912.* Washington: Government Printing Office.

United States. Department of State. *Reports of the Consuls of the United States on the Commerce, Manufactures, etc., of their Consular Districts, 1880-1900.* Washington: Government Printing Office.

United States. Congress. House of Representatives. 67th Congress, 4th sess. Jan. 16, 25, 26, 29, and February 1, 2, 1923. *Hearings before the Committee on Agriculture.* Washington: Government Printing Office, 1923.

United States. Congress. Senate. 72nd Cong., 2d sess. *Hearings before a Subcommittee of the Committee on Banking Currency, on Stock Exchange Practices.* Jan. 11, 12, 1933. Washington: Government Printing Office, 1933.

United States. Congress. Senate. 94th Cong., 1st sess. *Staff Report of the Select Committee to Study Governmental Operations with Respect to Intelligence Activities. Covert Action in Chile, 1963-1973.* Washington: Government Printing Office, Dec. 18, 1975.

NEWSPAPERS AND JOURNALS

Asociación salitrera, Circular. Iquique, Valparaiso. 1895-1916.
Avancemos. Santiago. 1920.
Banco Central de Chile. Santiago. 1928.
Board of Trade Journal. London. 1896-99, 1905-8.
Boletín de el Trabajo. Iquique. 1905.
Boletín de la Sociedad Nacional de Agricultura. Santiago. 1910.
Chile. New York. 1927.
Don Lucas Gomez. Iquique. 1917.
El Aliancista. Antofagasta. 1901.
El Azote. Antofagasta. 1906.
El Carpintero. Santiago. 1904.
El Combate. Santiago. 1923.
El Comercio. Iquique. 1881.
El Comunista. Antofagasta. 1925.
El Comunista. Santiago. 1921, 1923.
El Copiapino. Copiapó. 1845.
El Correo del Peru. Iquique. 1896.
El Deber. Antofagasta. 1917.
El Defensor. Iquique. 1902-5.
El Departamento. Pisagua. 1914, 1915.
El Despertar de los Trabajadores. Iquique. 1912-18, 1921-26.
El Diario Ilustrado. Iquique. 1922.
El Diario Ilustrado. Santiago. 1916, 1924, 1930.

El Diario Oficial. Santiago. 1882, 1891.
El Eco Obrero. Concepción. 1903, 1904.
El Faro Obrero. Santiago. 1920, 1921.
El Ferrocarril. Santiago. 1880, 1891-92, 1897-99, 1903-11.
El Grito Popular. Iquique. 1911.
El Guia de Arauco. Los Angeles. 1865.
El Heraldo. Arica. 1921.
El Marítimo. Antofagasta. 1903-6.
El Mercurio. Santiago. 1905-25.
El Mercurio. Valparaiso. 1842, 1880-85, 1890, 1905.
El Nacional. Iquique. 1890.
El Progreso. Iquique. 1888.
El Proletariado. Iquique. 1913-17.
El Pueblo. Iquique. 1906.
El Pueblo Obrero. Iquique. 1906-10.
El Socialista. Antofagasta. 1916-20.
El Socialista. Chuquicamata. 1919.
El Socialista. Puntas Arenas. 1914.
El Socialista. Valparaiso. 1915, 1917.
El Sur. Concepción. 1920-22, 1927.
El Trabajo. Iquique. 1901-8.
El Trabajo. Tocopilla. 1903-5.
Financial Times. London. 1910-11.
Financier. London. 1911.
Justicia. Santiago. 1924-27.
Latin America Regional Report. London. 1980.
La Asamblea. Santiago. 1916.
La Aurora Roja. Pisagua. 1917.
La Aurora. Taltal. 1916-18.
La Democracia. Iquique. 1906.
La Democracia. Santiago. 1899-1901.
La Federación Obrera. Santiago. 1921.
La Jornada. Schwager-Coronel. 1920.
La Nación. Santiago. 1918-20.
La Patria. Valparaiso. 1890.
La Reforma Social. Serena. 1902.
La Reforma. Santiago. 1906-8.
La Región Minera. Coronel. 1922.
Las Ultimas Noticias. Santiago. 1916, 1927.
La Unión. Santiago. 1916.
La Unión. Valparaiso. 1890, 1926.
La Unión Gremial. Antofagasta. 1917.
La Unión Obrera. Chuquicamata. 1915, 1918.
La Vanguardia. Antofagasta. 1906-7.
La Vanguardia. Valparaiso. 1915.
La Voz de Chile. Valparaiso. 1890.
La Voz del Peru. Iquique. 1899.
La Voz del Pueblo. Iquique. 1890, 1917.
La Voz del Pueblo. Valparaiso. 1903-6.
Libertad Electoral. Santiago. 1888.
New York Sun. New York. 1922.
Observor. London. 1915.

Pall Mall Gazette. London. 1887.
South American Journal. London. 1894, 1921.
South Pacific Mail. Valparaiso. 1922.
Sucesos. Santiago. 1921.
The Chilian Times. Valparaiso. 1885-1906.
The Neighbor. Valparaiso. 1851.
The Times. London. 1907-11.

BOOKS, DISSERTATIONS, ARTICLES, AND PAMPHLETS

Alegría, Fernando. *Como un arbol rojo*. Santiago: Editora
    Santiago, 1968.
Alessandri Palma, Arturo. *Chile y su historia*. 2 vols. Santiago:
    Editorial Orbe, 1945.
Alessandri Palma, Arturo. *Recuerdos de gobierno*. 3 vols.
    Santiago: Editorial Nascimento, 1976.
Alfonso, José A. *El parlamentarismo i la reforma política en Chile*.
    Santiago: Cabeza i Cia., 1909.
Allende Gossens, Salvador. *La realidad médico-social chilena—*
    síntesis. Santiago: n.p., 1939.
American Society of Chile. *Americans in Chile*. Valparaiso-
    Santiago: Kegan, 1931.
Amin, Samir. *Accumulation on a World Scale, a Critique of the*
    Theory of Underdevelopment. Translated by Brian Pearce.
    2 vols. New York: Monthly Review Press, 1974.
Amin, Samir. *Unequal Development: An Essay on the Social Forma-*
    tions of Peripheral Capitalism. New York: Monthly Review
    Press, 1976.
Amunátegui Solar, Domingo. *La democracia en Chile*. Santiago:
    Universidad de Chile. 1946.
Amunátegui Solar, Domingo. "Orígen del comercio ingles en
    Chile." *Revista Chilena de Historia y Geografía* 103 (July-
    December 1943).
Anguita, Ricardo, ed. *Leyes promulgadas en Chile: desde 1810*
    hasta el 1 de Junio de 1912. 4 vols. Santiago: Imprenta
    Barcelona, 1912.
Aranguiz Donoso, Horacio, Ricardo Coudyoudmjian Bergamali, and
    Juan Eduardo Vargas Cariola. "La vida política chilena,
    1915-16." *Historia* 7 (1968).
Ardant, Gabriel. "Financial Policy and Economic Infrastructure
    of Modern States and Nations." In *The Formation of National*
    States in Western Europe, edited by Charles Tilly. Prince-
    ton: Princeton University Press, 1975.
Aya, Rod. "Theories of Revolution Reconsidered." *Theory and*
    Society 8 (July 1979).
Balmaceda, José Manuel. *Discurso pronunciado por el Ministro del*
    Interior don José Manuel Balmaceda en el sesión de 19 de
    Julio de 1884 de la Cámara de Diputados. Valparaiso: La
    Patria, 1884.
Bañados Espinosa, Julio. *Balmaceda, su gobierno y la revolución*
    de 1891. 2 vols. Paris: Librería de Garnier Hermanos, 1893.

Bancelín, Jacques. *Algunas observaciones sobre la industria salitrera*. Santiago: Imprenta R. Harris A., 1929.

Baran, Paul. *The Political Economy of Growth*. New York: Monthly Review Press, 1957.

Barría, Serón, Jorge I. *El movimiento obrero en Chile; síntesis histórico-social*. Ediciones de la Universidad Técnica del Estado, 1971.

Barría Serón, Jorge I. *Los movimientos sociales de Chile desde 1910 hasta 1926*. Santiago: Editorial Universitaria, 1960.

Barros Arana, Diego. "La proclamación de la libertad de comercio en Chile." *Revista Económica* 2 (1887).

Barros Van Buren, Mario. *Historia diplomática de Chile (1541-1938)*. Barcelona: Ediciones Ariel, 1970.

Bath, C. Richard, and Dilmus D. James. "Dependency Analysis of Latin America: Some Criticism, Some Suggestions." *Latin American Research Review* 11 (1976).

Bauer, Arnold. *Chilean Rural Society*. Cambridge: Cambridge University Press, 1975.

Bermúdez M., Oscar. "El Dr. Nicolas Palacios y la industria del salitre." *Revista chilena de historia y geografía* 136 (1968).

Bermúdez M., Oscar. *Historia del salitre: desde sus orígenes hasta la Guerra del Pacífico*. Santiago: Ediciones de la Universidad de Chile, 1963.

Bertrand, Alejandro. *La crisis salitrera, 1910*. Paris: Louis-Michaud, 1910.

Billinghurst, Guillermo. *El Abastecimiento de agua potable del puerto de Iquique*. Iquique: Imprenta Española, 1887.

Blakemore, Harold. "John Thomas North, the Nitrate King," *History Today* 12 (July 1962).

Blakemore, Harold. *British Nitrates and Chilean Politics, 1886-1896: Balmaceda and North*. London: Athlone Press of the University of London, 1974.

Bonilla, Frank, and Myron Glaser. *Student Politics in Chile*. New York: Basic Books, 1970.

Boorstein, Edward. *An Inside View . . . Allende's Chile*. New York: International Publishers, 1977.

Bottomore, T. B. *Classes in Modern Society*. New York: Pantheon Books, 1966.

Brown, Joseph R. "Nitrate Crises, Combinations and the Chilean Government in the Nitrate Age." *Hispanic American Historical Review* 43 (May 1963).

Brown, Joseph R. "The Chilean Nitrate Railways Controversy." *Hispanic American Historical Review* 38 (November 1958).

Bulnes, Gonzalo. *Chile and Peru, the Causes of the War of 1879*. Santiago: Imprenta Universitaria, 1920.

Caldcleugh, Alexander. *Travels in South America, during the Years 1819-20-21; Containing an Account of Brazil, Buenos Ayres, and Chile*. 2 vols. London: John Murray, 1825.

Cameron, Charlotte A. *A Woman's Winter in South America*. London: Stanley Paul and Company, 1911.

Campos Harriet, Fernando. *Historia constitucional de Chile*.

Santiago: Editorial Jurídica de Chile, 1969.

Cardoso, Fernando Henrique, and Enzo Faletto. *Dependencia y desarrollo en América Latina*. Mexico, Distrito Federal: Siglo Veintiuno Editores, Sociedad Anónima, 1971. (English language edition: *Dependency and Development in Latin America*. Translated by Marjory Mattingly Urquidi. Berkeley: University of California Press, 1978.)

Chilcote, Ronald H. "Dependency: A Critical Synthesis of the Literature." *Latin American Perspectives* 1 (Spring 1974).

Child, Theodore. "Urban and Commercial Chile." *Harper's Magazine* 81 (November 1890).

Collier, Simon. *Ideas and Politics of Chilean Independence, 1808-1833*. Cambridge: Cambridge University Press, 1967.

Concha, Malaquías. *El programa de la democracia*. Santiago: Imprenta El Siglo XX, 1905.

Concha, Malaquías. *La lucha económica. Estudio de economía social presentado al IV Congreso Científique Americano, reunido en Santiago de Chile en 1908*. Santiago: Imprenta Nacional, 1909.

Cortes, Lía, and Jordi Fuentes. *Diccionario político de Chile*. Santiago: Editorial Orbe, 1967.

Cruchaga, Miguel. *Estudio sobre la organización económica y la hacienda pública de Chile*. 2 vols. 1875. Madrid: Editorial Reus, 1929.

Curtis, William Eleroy. *The Capitals of Spanish America*. New York: Harper and Brothers, 1888.

Cypher, James M. "The Internationalization of Capital and the Transformation of Social Formations: A Critique of the Monthly Review School." *The Review of Radical Political Economics* 11 (Winter 1979).

Davies, James C. "Toward a Theory of Revolution." *American Sociological Review* 27 (February 1927).

Dennis, W. J. *Tacna and Arica, an Account of the Chile-Peru Boundary Dispute and of the Arbitration of the United States*. New Haven: Yale University Press, 1931.

De Shazo, Peter Charles. "Urban Workers and Labor Unions in Chile, 1902-1927." Ph.D. dissertation, University of Wisconsin, 1977.

De Shazo, Peter Charles. "The Valparaiso Maritime Strike of 1903 and the Development of a Revolutionary Labor Movement in Chile." *Journal of Latin American Studies* 2 (June 1979).

De Vylder, Stefan. *Allende's Chile: The Political Economy of the Rise and Fall of the Unidad Popular*. Cambridge: Cambridge University Press, 1976.

Donoso, Ricardo. *Alessandri, agitador y demoledor; cincuenta años de historia política de Chile*. 2 vols. Mexico: Fondo de Cultura Económica, 1952-54.

Dos Santos, Theotonio. *El nuevo carácter de la dependencia*. Santiago: Cuadernos de Estudios Socio-Económicos (10), Centro de Estudios Socio-Económicos, Universidad de Chile, 1968.

Dos Santos, Theotonio. "La crisis de la teoría del desarrollo y las relaciones de dependencia en América Latina." In *La dependencia político-económica de América Latina,* edited by Helio Jaguaribe et al. Mexico: Siglo Veintiuno, 1970.

Douglas, James. "Chile—Its Geography, People, and Institutions." *Bulletin of the American Geographical Society.* 1881.

Duran, B., Alberto. *El estado libre de el Teniente y la vida obrera de las minas.* Santiago: Imprenta Universitaria, 1919.

Edwards, Agustín. *Cuatro presidentes de Chile: 1841-1876.* Valparaiso: Imprenta Universo, 1932.

Edwards, Alberto. *La fronda aristocrática.* Santiago: Imprenta Nacional, 1932.

Edwards, Alberto. *Bosquejo histórico de los partidos políticos de Chile.* 1903. Santiago: Ediciones Ercilla, 1936.

Edwards, Alberto. *El gobierno de don Manuel Montt, 1851-1861.* Santiago: Editorial Nascimento, 1932.

Encina, Francisco A. *Historia de Chile, desde la prehistoria hasta 1891.* 20 vols. Santiago: Editorial Nascimento, 1950.

Encina, Francisco A. *Nuestra inferioridad económica.* 1911. Santiago: Editorial Universitaria, 1972.

Escobar Zenteno, Aristodemo. *Compendio de la legislación social y el desarrollo del movimiento obrero en Chile.* Santiago: S. Vicente, 1940.

Espinosa, Roberto. *La reforma bancaria i monetaria en Chile.* Santiago: Imprenta Barcelona, 1913.

Evans, Henry Clay Jr. *Chile and Its Relations with the United States.* Durham, N.C.: Duke University Press, 1927.

Eyzaguirre Rouse, Guillermo, and Jorge Errázuriz Tagle. *Estudio social: monografía de una familia obrera de Santiago.* Santiago: Imprenta Barcelona, 1903.

Eyzaguirre, Jaime. *Chile durante el gobierno de Errázuriz Echaurren, 1896-1901.* 2d ed. Santiago: Empresa Editora Zig-Zag, 1957.

Eyzaguirre, Jaime. *Fisonomía historica de Chile.* 3d ed. Santiago: Editorial Universitaria, 1973.

Fariña, Alejandro. *Reflexiones sobre la cuestión social y política en Chile.* Santiago: Imprenta Chile, 1904.

Federación Obrera de Chile. *Resoluciones del cuarto congreso provincial de la Federación Obrera de Chile. Realizada en Antofagasta, 13 de Noviembre, 1921.* Antofagasts: El Socialista, 1921.

Feinberg, Richard E. *The Triumph of Allende: Chile's Legal Revolution.* New York: New American Library, 1972.

Feliu Cruz, Guillermo. "La evolución política, económica y social de Chile." *Anales de la Universidad de Chile* 119 (1960).

Felstiner, Mary Lowenthal. "Kinship Politics in the Chilean Independence Movement." *Hispanic American Historial Review* 56 (February 1976).

Fetter, Frank Whitson. *Monetary Inflation in Chile.* Princeton: Princeton University Press, 1931.

Figueroa, Pedro Pablo. *Diccionario biográfico de estranjeros.*

Santiago: Imprenta Moderna, 1900.

Frías Valenzuela, Francisco. *Historia de Chile*. 2d ed. 3 vols. Santiago: Editorial Nascimento, 1965.

Frank, André Gunder. *Capitalism and Underdevelopment in Latin America: Historical Studies of Chile and Brazil*. New York: Monthly Review Press, 1960.

Galdames, Luis. *Jeografía economica de Chile*. Santiago: Imprenta Universitaria, 1911.

Gay, Claudio. *Historia física y política de Chile segun documentos adquiridos en esta república durante doce años de residencia en ella y publicado bajo los auspicios del supremo gobierno. Agricultura*. 2 vols. Paris: Thenot y Cia., 1865.

Gibbs, Guillermo. *La tierra y el inquilinaje*. Santiago: Imprenta de la Libertad, 1890.

Gibbs, J. A. *History of Antony and Dorothea Gibbs*. London: Saint Catherine Press, 1922.

Gilliss, (Lt.) James M. *The U.S. Naval Astronomical Expedition to the Southern Hemisphere during the years 1849-50-51-52. Chile: Its geography, climate, earthquakes, government, social conditions, mineral and agricultural resources, commerce, etc*. Washington: A. O. P. Nicholson, 1855.

Godoy, M., Oscar Alfonso. *Don Malaquías Concha, su vida, sus obras, su glorificación*. Santiago: Imprenta Bellavista, 1923.

Godoy Urzua, Hernán, ed. *Estructura social de Chile*. Santiago: Editorial Universitaria, 1971.

Góngora, Mario. *Studies in the Colonial History of Spanish America*. Cambridge: Cambridge University Press, 1975.

Góngora, Mario. "Vagabondage et Société Pastoral en Amérique Latine." *Annales: économies, sociétés, civilisations* 121 (January-February 1966).

González, Marcial. *Estudios Económicos*. Santiago: Imprenta Gutenberg, 1889.

Graham, Maria. *Journal of a Residence in Chile during the Year 1822, and a Voyage from Chile to Brazil in 1823*. London: Longman, 1824.

Gutierrez, Eulogio. *Chiquicamata, tierras rojas*. Santiago: Editorial Nascimento, 1926.

Hernández C., Roberto. *El salitre (resumen histórico desde su descubrimiento y exploitación)*. Valparaiso: Fisher Hermanos, 1930.

Hernández C., Roberto. *El roto chileno*. Valparaiso: Imprenta San Rafael, 1929.

Hill, S. S. *Travels in Peru and Mexico*. London: Longman, 1860.

Hirschman, Albert. *Journeys toward Progress*. New York: Twentieth Century Fund, 1963.

Hubbard, Preston J. *Origins of the T.V.A.: The Muscle Shoals Controversy, 1920-1932*. Nashville, Tenn.: Vanderbilt University, 1961.

Huneeus, Gana, Francisco. *Por el orden social*. Santiago: Imprenta Barcelona, 1917.

Hurtado Cruchaga, Alberto. *Sindicalismo: historia, teoría, práctica*. Santiago: Editorial del Pacífico, 1950.

Hurtado Ruiz-Tagle, Carlos. *Concentración de población y desarrollo económico—el caso chileno*. Santiago: Universidad de Chile, Instituto de Economía, 1966.

Iñiguez Irrarázaval, Pedro Felipe. *Notas sobre el desarrollo del pensamiento social en Chile, 1901-1906*. Santiago: Editorial Jurídica de Chile, 1968.

Iriarte, (General), Tomás de. *Panoramas chilenas del siglo XIX*. Edited by Gabriel Balbontín Guenzalida. Santiago: Editorial Arcos, 1965. Based on edition of 1841.

Izquierdo F., Gonzalo. *Un estudio de las ideologías chilenas: la Sociedad de Agricultura en el siglo XIX*. Santiago: Centro de Estudios Socio-Económicos, Facultad de Ciencias Económicas, Universidad de Chile, 1968.

Jobet, Julio César. *Ensayo crítico del desarrollo económico-social de Chile*. Santiago: Editorial Universitaria, 1955.

Jobet, Julio César. *Los precursores del pensamiento social de Chile*. 2 vols. Santiago: Editorial Universitaria, 1966.

Jobet, Julio César. *Luis Emilio Recabarren: los orígenes del movimiento obrero y del socialismo chileno*. Santiago: Prensa Latinoamericana, 1955.

Kaempffer Villagren, Guillermo. *Así sucedio, 1850-1925. Sangrientos episodios de la lucha obrera en Chile*. Santiago: n.p., 1962.

Kiernan, V. G. "Foreign Interests in the War of the Pacific." *Hispanic American Historial Review* 35 (February 1955).

Kirsch, Henry W. *Industrial Development in a Traditional Society: The Conflict of Entrepreneurship and Modernization in Chile*. Gainesville: The University Presses of Florida, 1977.

Kirsch, Henry W. "The Industrialization of Chile, 1880-1930." Ph.D. dissertation, University of Florida, 1973.

Lefertte, Elías. *Vida de un communista*. 2d. ed. Santiago: Empresa Editora Austral, 1971.

Lagos Valenzuela, Tulio. *Bosquejo histórico del movimiento obrero en Chile*. Santiago: Imprenta El Esfuerzo, 1941.

Latcham, Ricardo. *Chuquicamata, estado yankee*. Santiago: n.p., 1926.

Latorre González, Orlando. *La sociedad nacional de minería*. Santiago: Universidad de Chile, 1943.

Lopez Loayzo, Fernando. *La Provincia de Tarapacá, 1912-1913*. Iquique: Edward M. Muecke, 1913.

Mansfield, Robert E. *Progressive Chile*. New York: Neale Publishing Company, 1913.

Marín Vicuña, Santiago. *Los ferrocarriles de Chile*. Santiago: Imprenta Cervantes, 1916.

Markham, Clement. *The War between Peru and Chile, 1879-1882*. London: Sampson, Lass, Marston, Searle, and Rivington, 1882.

Marotta, Sebastian. *El movimiento síndical Argentina, su génesis y desarrollo*. Buenos Aires: Ediciones "Lacio," 1960.

Martin, Percy Alvin. *Latin America and the War*. Baltimore:
Johns Hopkins Press, 1925.

Martner, G., Gonzalo. "The Popular Unity Government's Efforts in
Planning." In *The Chilean Road to Socialism (Proceedings of
an ODEPLAN—IDS Round Table)*, edited by J. Ann Zammit.
Austin: University of Texas Press, 1973.

Mathison, Gilbert Farquhar. *Narrative of a Visit to Brazil,
Chile, Peru, and the Sandwich Islands during the Years 1821
and 1822*. London: Charles Knight, Pall Mall East, 1825.

Menéder, Julio. *Estadística comercial comparativa de la República de Chile*. Valparaiso: Imprenta del Mercurio, 1862.

Mikesell, Raymond F. *Foreign Investments in Latin America*.
Washington, D.C.: Pan American Union, Economic Research
Series, 1955.

Mills, George J. *Chile*. New York: D. Appleton and Company,
1914.

Monteón, Michael. "Cultural Bases of Economic Imperialism: The
British in the Atacama Desert," *Journal of Economic History*
35 (March 1975).

Monteón, Michael. "The *Enganche* in the Chilean Nitrate Sector,
1880-1930." *Latin American Perspectives* 6 (Summer 1979).

Moran, Theodore H. *Multinational Corporations and the Politics
of Dependence: Copper in Chile*. Princeton: Princeton
University Press, 1974.

Morris, David J. *We Must Make Haste Slowly: The Process of Revolution in Chile*. New York: Random House, 1973.

Moss, Robert. *Chile's Marxist Experiment*. Newton Abbot: David
and Charles, 1973.

Movimiento Izquierdista Revolucionaria. *Chile, the MIR, and the
Tasks of Resistance*. Oakland, Calif.: Resistance Publications, 1976.

Nef, Jorge. "The Politics of Repression: The Social Pathology
of the Chilean Military." *Latin American Perspectives* 1
(Summer 1975).

Novoa Valdés, N. *Problemas sociales*. Santiago: Imprenta
Cervantes, 1912.

Nunn, Frederick M. *Chilean Politics, 1920-1931. The Honorable
Mission of the Armed Forces*. Albuquerque: University of
New Mexico Press, 1970.

O'Brien, Thomas Francis, Jr. "British Investors and the Decline
of the Chilean Nitrate Entrepreneurs, 1870-1890. Ph.D.
dissertation, University of Connecticut, 1976.

O'Brien, Thomas F. "Chilean Elites and Foreign Investors:
Chilean Nitrate Policy, 1880-1882." *Journal of Latin American Studies* 11 (May 1979).

O'Brien, Thomas F. "The Antofagasta Company: A Case Study of
Peripheral Capitalism." *Hispanic American Historial Review*
60 (February 1980).

O'Connor, Harvey. *The Guggenheims: The Making of an American
Dynasty*. New York: Civici, Friede, 1937.

Olaechea, Samuel Nuñez. *Los ferrocarriles del estado*. Santiago:
Imprenta Encuadernaciones Chile, 1910.

Orrego Luco, Luis. *Casa Grande.* 1908. Nascimento, 1973.
Orrego, Luco, Augusto. "La cuestión social en Chile." *Anales de la Universidad de Chile* 121 (1961).
Palacios, Jorge. *Chile: An Attempt at "Historic Compromise," the Real Story of the Allende Years.* Chicago: Banner Press, 1979.
Palacios, Nicolas. *Raza chilena.* Valparaiso: Gustavo Schäfer, 1904.
Pérez Canto, Julio. *La industria salitrera y la intervención del estado.* Santiago: Imprenta Walter Guedt, 1933.
Pérez Rosales, Vicente. *Recuerdos del pasado (1844-1860).* 1880. Santiago: Zig-Zag, 1958.
Pike, Frederick B. *Chile and the United States, 1880-1962.* Notre Dame, Ind.: University of Notre Dame Press, 1963.
Pike, Frederick B. "Church and State in Peru and Chile since 1840: A Study in Contrasts." *American Historical Review* 73 (October 1967).
Pinochet Le-Brun, Tancredo. *La conquista de Chile en el siglo XX.* Santiago: La Ilustración, 1909.
Pinochet Le-Brun, Tancredo. *Un año empleado público en Chile.* Santiago: Imprenta Universitaria, 1915.
Pinto Duran, Carlos. *La revolución chilena.* Santiago: Imprenta Valiente y Cia., 1925.
Pinto Lagarrigue, Fernando. *Crónica política del siglo XX: desde Erráruriz Echaurren hasta Alessandri Palma.* Santiago: Editorial Orbe, 1970.
Pinto Santa Cruz, Aníbal. *Chile, un caso de desarrollo frustrado.* Santiago: Editorial Universitaria, 1962.
Pissis, Aime. *Geografía física de la República de Chile.* Paris: Instituto Geográfico de Paris, 1875.
Platt, D. C. M. "Dependency in Nineteenth-Century Latin America." *Latin American Research Review* 15 (1980):113-30.
Poblete Troncoso, Moisés. *Nuestro seudo régimen parlamentaria.* Santiago: Numen, 1920.
Poblete Troncoso, Moisés, and Ben G. Burnett. *The Rise of the Latin American Labor Movement.* New York: Bookman Associates, 1960.
Prexeworski, Joanne Fox. "Mines and Smelters: The Coal Oligopoly and the Decline of the Copper Industry in Chile." Unpublished manuscript.
Ramírez Necochea, Hernán. *Antecedentes económicos de la independencia de Chile.* Santiago: Editorial Universitaria, 1959.
Ramírez Necochea, Hernán. *Balmaceda y la contrarevolución de 1891.* Santiago: Editorial Universitaria, 1969.
Ramírez Necochea, Hernán. *Historia del imperialismo en Chile.* Santiago: Editorial Austral, 1960.
Ramírez Necochea, Hernán. *Historia del movimiento obrero en Chile; antecedentes siglo XIX.* Santiago: Austral, 1956.
Ramírez Necochea, Hernán. *Origen y formación del Partido Comunista de Chile.* Santiago: Editorial Austral, 1965.
Recabarren, Luis Emilio. *El Pensamiento de Luis Emilio Recabarren.* 2 vols. Santiago: Camino de Victoria, 1971.

Recabarren, Luis Emilio. *Obras selectas de Luis Emilio Recabarren.* Edited by Julio César Jobet, Jorge Barría, and Luis Vitale. Santiago: Quimantu, 1971.

Reinsch, Paul S. "Parliamentary Government in Chile." *The American Political Science Review* 3 (November 1909).

Reyes N., Enrique. *El desarrollo de la conciencia proletaria en Chile (el ciclo salitrero).* Santiago: Editorial Orbe, 1973.

Reynolds, Clark Winton. "Development Problems of an Export Economy: The Case of Chile and Copper. In *Essays on the Chilean Economy,* edited by Markos Mamalakis and Clark Winton Reynolds. Homewood, Ill.: Richard D. Irwin, 1965.

Rippy. J. Fred. *Globe and Hemisphere.* Chicago: Henry Regnery Company, 1958.

Rippy, J. Fred. "Economic Enterprises of the Nitrate King and His Associates in Chile." *Pacific Historical Review* 17 (November 1948).

Rivas Vicuña, Manuel. *Historia política y parlamentaria de Chile.* 3 vols. Santiago: Ediciones de la Biblioteca Nacional, 1964.

Roca del Campo, Antonio, ed. *Tradición y leyenda de Santiago.* Santiago: Ediciones Ercilla, 1941.

Rock, David. *Politics in Argentina, 1890-1930 (The Rise and Fall of Radicalism).* Cambridge: Cambridge University Press, 1975.

Rojas Sanford, Robinson. *The Murder of Allende and the End of the Chilean Road to Socialism.* New York: Harper and Row, 1975.

Ross, Agustín. *Chile, 1851-1910: Sixty Years of Monetary and Financial Questions and of Banking Problems.* Valparaiso: Imprenta Inglesa Westcott and Company, 1910.

Ross, Agustín. *Las malas prácticas parlamentarias.* Valparaiso: Babra y Cía., 1902.

Ross, Agustín. *Report on the Trade between Chile and Great Britain, Presented to the Government of Chile.* London: McCorquodale and Company for the Chilean Legation, April, 1892.

Ruschenberger, William S. W. *Three Years in the Pacific, containing notices of Brazil, Chile, Bolivia, Peru, etc., in 1831, 1832, 1833, 1834. By an officer of the United States Navy* . . . 2 vols. London: Richard Bentley, 1835.

Russell, William Howard. *A Visit to Chile and the Nitrate Fields.* London: J. S. Virtue and Company, 1890.

Salas Edwards, Ricardo. *Balmaceda y el parlamentarismo en Chile; un estudio de psicología política chilena.* 2nd ed. Santiago: Imprenta Universo, 1916.

Santelices, Ramón E. *Los bancos chilenos.* Santiago: Imprenta Barcelona, 1893.

Santivan, Fernando. *Don Eliodoro Yañez: el hombre y su obra.* Santiago: Santivan, 1925.

Sater, William F. "Chile and the World Depression of the 1870's." *Journal of Latin American Studies* 11 (May 1979).

Schneider, Theodore. *La agricultura en Chile en los últimos cincuenta años.* Santiago: Imprenta Barcelona, 1904.

Segall R., Marcelo. *Biografía de la ficha-salario.* Santiago: Editorial Universitaria, 1964.

Segall R., Marcelo. *Desarrollo del capitalismo en Chile: cinco ensayos dialécticos.* Santiago: Editorial del Pacífico, 1953.

Segall R., Marcelo. "Las luchas de clases en las primeras decadas de la República, 1810-1846." *Anales de la Universidad de Chile* 125 (1962):198.

Sideri, S., ed. *Chile, 1970-1973: Economic Development and Its International Setting; Self-Criticism of the Unidad Popular Government's Policies.* The Hague: International Instituut voor Sociale Studien—'S Gravenhage, Series on the Development of Societies, vol. 4, Martinus Nijhoff, 1979.

Sigmund, Paul E. *The Overthrow of Allende and the Politics of Chile, 1964-1976.* Pittsburgh: University of Pittsburgh Press, 1977.

Gustavo Silva, Jorge. *La legislación social y la educación cívica.* Santiago: Imprenta Nacional, 1928.

Gustavo Silva, Jorge. *Nuestra evolución político-social, 1900-1930.* Santiago: Naxcimento, 1931.

Silva, Victor Domingo. *Las provincias del norte y la visita de S.E. el Presidente de la República.* Santiago: Universo, 1909.

Silva Espejo, Rene. *Breve historia de la Unidad Popular, Documento de "El Mercurio."* Santiago: El Mercurio, 1974.

Sjoberg, Gideon. *The Preindustrial City: Past and Present.* New York: Free Press, 1960.

Skocpol, Theda. *States and Social Revolutions: A Comparative Analysis of France, Russia, and China.* Cambridge: Cambridge University Press, 1979.

Smith, Tony. "The Underdevelopment of Development Literature: The Case of Dependency Theory." *World Politics* 31 (January 1979).

Solberg, Carl. *Immigration and Nationalism: Argentina and Chile, 1890-1914.* Austin: University of Texas Press, 1970.

Stallings, Barbara. *Class Conflict and Economic Development in Chile, 1958-1973.* Stanford: Stanford University Press, 1978.

Sutcliffe, Thomas. *Sixteen Years in Chile and Peru from 1822 to 1839.* London: Fisher and Sons, 1841.

Tacla Chamy, Odette. *Panorama demográfico de Chile y su evolución en el presente siglo.* 2d ed. Santiago: Instituto Nacional de Estadísticos, 1975.

Tartakowsky Henker, Wladimiro. *El problema de la migración.* Santiago: Dirección General de Prisiones, 1941.

Turri Concha, Enrique. *Malaquías Concha.* Santiago: Editorial Universitaria, 1958.

Urzua Valenzuela, German, and Anamaría García Barzelato. *Diagnóstico de la burocracía chilena (1818-1969).* Santiago: Editorial Jurídica de Chile, 1971.

Vaello, Jacinto. *Estructura y evolución de la economía colonial.* Santiago: Universidad de Chile, Instituto de Economía y

Planificación, 1971.

Valdés Vergara, Francisco. *Guerra civil en Chile—su apreciación histórica.* Valparaiso: G. Helfmann, 1891.

Valdés Vergara, Francisco. *Problemas económicos de Chile.* Valparaiso: Universo, 1913.

Valdés Vergara, Francisco. *La situatión económica y financiera de Chile.* Valparaiso: Imprenta Germania, 1894.

Varas, José Antonio. *Colonización de Llanquihue, Valdivia i Arauco o sea colección de las leyes i decretos supremos concernientes a esta materia, desde 1827 a 1871 inclusivo.* Santiago: Imprenta de la República, 1872.

Varas, Santiago Machiavello. *El problema de la industria del cobre en Chile y sus projecciones económicas y sociales.* Santiago: Imprenta Fiscal de la Penitenciaria, 1923.

Vayssiere, Pierre. "Au Chili: De L'Economie Coloniale a L'Inflation." *Cahiers du Ameriques Latines* 5 (January–June 1970).

Véliz, Claudio. *Historia de la marina mercante de Chile.* Santiago: Universidad de Chile, 1961.

Venegas Craus, Alenjandro (pseud. Julio Valdés Canje). *Cartas al Excelentísimo Señor Don Pedro Montt sobre la crisis moral de Chile en sus relaciones con el problema económico de la conversion metálica.* 1909. Santiago: Editorial Universitaria, 1972.

Venegas Carus, Alejandro (pseud. Julio Valdés Canje). *Sinceridad, Chile íntimo en 1910.* Santiago: Imprenta Universitaria, 1910.

Vicuña, Carlos. *La crisis moral de Chile. Conferencia dada en Buenos Aires en la Casa del Pueblo el 27 de Diciembre de 1928.* Mar de Plata: La Capital, 1929.

Vicuña, Carlos. *La tiranía en Chile; libro escrito en el desierto en 1928.* 2 vols. Santiago: Sociedad Imprenta y Litografia. Universo, 1935-36.

Vicuña MacKenna. Benjamín. *Historia de los diez años de la administración de don Manuel Montt.* Santiago: Imprenta Chilena, 1862.

Vicuña MacKenna, Benjamín. *La transformación de Santiago: notas e indicaciones respetuosamente sometidas a la Ilustre Municipalidad, al Supremo Gobierno y al Congreso Nacional por el Intendente de Santiago.* Santiago: Imprenta del Mercurio, 1872.

Villalobos R., Sergio. *El comercio y la crisis colonial: un mito de la Independencia.* Santiago: Ediciones de la Universidad de Chile, 1968.

Villalobos R., Sergio, et al. *Historia de Chile.* 4 vols. Santiago: Editorial Universitaria, 1974-78.

Vitale, Luis. *Interpretación marxista de la historia de Chile.* Santiago: Prensa Latinoamericana, 1967.

Viviani Contreras, Guillermo. *Sociología chilena.* 2 vols. Santiago: Editorial Nascimento, 1926.

von Tschudi, J. J. *Travels in Peru, during the years 1838-1842.* Translated from the German by Thomasina Ross. London:

David Bogue, 1847.

White, Philo. *White's Narrative of a cruise in the Pacific to South America and California on the U.S. sloop-of-war "Dale," 1841-1843.* Edited by Charles L. Camp. Denver: Fred A. Rosenstock, Old West Publishing Company, 1965.

Wiles, Peter. "The Necessity and Impossibility of Political Economy." *History and Theory* 11 (1972).

Wise, (Lt.) Henry Augustus. *Los gringos: Or an Inside View of Mexico and California with wanderings in Peru, Chile, and Polynesia.* New York: Baker and Scribner, 1850.

Wright, Thomas C. "Origins of the Politics of Inflation in Chile, 1888-1918." *Hispanic American Historical Review* 53 (May 1973).

Zammit, J. Ann, ed. *The Chilean Road to Socialism (Proceedings of an ODEPLAN—IDS Round Table, March, 1972).* Austin: University of Texas Press, 1973.

Zegers, Christian. *Aníbal Pinto, historia política de su administración.* Santiago: Editorial Universitaria, 1969.

Zegers, Julio. *Estudios económicos.* Santiago: Imprenta Nacional, 1908.

Index

JACKET DESIGNED BY CAROLINE BECKETT
COMPOSED BY QUALITY TYPING SERVICE, MADISON, WISCONSIN
MANUFACTURED BY CUSHING MALLOY, INC., ANN ARBOR, MICHIGAN

Library of Congress Cataloging in Publication Data
Monteón, Michael, 1946-
Chile in the nitrate era.
Bibliography: pp. 227-244.
Includes index.
1. Chile—Economic conditions. 2. Chile—Economic
policy. 3. Nitrates—History. 4. Fertilizer industry—
Chile—History. 5. Chile—Commerce—History. I. Title.
HC192.M659   330.983'06   81-70009
ISBN 0-299-08820-0   AACR2